Groups

The McGraw-Hill Social Psychology Series

This popular series of paperback titles is written by authors about their particular field of expertise and is meant to complement any social psychology course. The series includes:

Groups
A User's Guide

by Carol K. Oyster, Ph.D.
University of Wisconsin at LaCrosse

Boston   Burr Ridge, IL   Dubuque, IA   Madison, WI
New York   San Francisco   St. Louis
Bangkok   Bogotá   Caracas   Lisbon   London   Madrid   Mexico City
Milan   New Delhi   Seoul   Singapore   Sydney   Taipei   Toronto

To my father, Dale Eugene Oyster
7/31/20–11/21/96
Blesséd be.

McGraw-Hill Higher Education

A Division of The **McGraw-Hill** *Companies*

GROUPS: A USER'S GUIDE

This book is printed on acid-free paper.

1 2 3 4 5 6 7 8 9 0 DOC/DOC 9 0 9 8 7 6 5 4 3 2 1 0 9

ISBN 0–07–048245–4

Editorial director: *Jane E. Vaicunas*
Senior sponsoring editor: *Rebecca H. Hope*
Senior developmental editor: *Sharon Geary*
Senior marketing manager: *Chris Hall*
Project manager: *Sheila M. Frank*
Production supervisor: *Enboge Chong*
Coordinator of freelance design: *Rick D. Noel*
Senior photo research coordinator: *Lori Hancock*
Compositor: *GAC/Indianapolis*
Typeface: *10/12 Palatino*
Printer: *R. R. Donnelley & Sons Company/Crawfordsville, IN*

Cover designer: *Sheilah Barrett*
Interior designer: *Kathy Theis*
Cover art: *Crowd VII by Diana Ong © SuperStock Inc.*
Photo research: *Mary Reeg Photo Research*

The credits section for this book begins on page 358 and is considered an extension of the copyright page.

Library of Congress Cataloging-in-Publication Data

Oyster, Carol K.
    Groups : a user's guide / Carol K. Oyster.—1st ed.
        p.   cm.
    Includes bibliographical references and index.
    ISBN 0–07–048254–4
        1. Social groups.   I. Title.

HM716 O87   2000
305—dc21
                                                99-047177
                                                CIP

www.mhhe.com

Brief Contents

Contents

Foreword

Groups is dead, long live Groups!

The central place that the group dynamics school played in earlier social psychology has been usurped by a more individualistic, cognitively flavored brand of contemporary social psychology. Indeed, many have proclaimed group dynamics and the study of groups to be dead. So why are we here to praise the study of groups, and the social psychology of group processes, in a joyful, loud chorus rather than quietly attending its sad wake?

Perhaps it is because the contemporary analysis of groups is so central to an understanding of how we, as individuals, are positioned in our lives, in our society, within a myriad of groups, and how those groups help to define who we are, and what are the tasks and challenges that can be handled and met only within the context of group functioning. There are few domains of our existence that are not influenced in some direct way by the values, beliefs, norms, and actions of groups and their members. Although those in individualistically oriented societies argue for the supremacy of the person, we too all live our lives enmeshed in overlapping and often dominating groups. Earlier social psychological analysis of groups was too heavily influenced by concern for understanding processes in work groups, in industrial settings, the application of which was to get workers to be more productive while maintaining high morale (for no greater pay). Related group dynamics research and application moved into the realm of training group leaders through encounter group strategies and tactics to be more effective, but the group under analysis was the encounter group itself and not so much the group the newly inspired manager was going out to influence. The "subjects," groups, and the researchers all narrowly represented the dominant sectors of society in the 1950s and decades following— white, American, male, middle-class researchers, and lower-class work groups. The study of group dynamics ran out of steam as the workplace was being refashioned by forces of diversity, technology, and globalization, and as psychology moved away from an interest in complex group processes, such as cohesiveness, and toward simpler ones that could be studied experimentally with

x

cognitive tasks and easy-to-administer questionnaires. It became near impossible to find psychologists willing to declare themselves as group dynamacists, as has also become true of the loss of "motivational researchers" from the psychological scene.

But in recent times the study of groups has been revived, with more exciting paths to explore, vigorous young researchers expanding its domains, and curious minds ready to integrate knowledge from psychology, social psychology, sociology, and business that relate to the role of groups in modern life. One powerful force in its resurrection has been the catholicity of psychology in opening its previously confined focus to embrace cultural psychology, gender studies, life-span research, and studies of race and ethnicity. Groups suddenly are US, and those all about us, not just alienated workers in a factory in a remote mill town. Groups are gangs, fraternities and sororities, soldiers, unions, Little League teams, fan clubs, TV talk show audiences, cults, paparazzi, "Star Trekkies," and much more that are interesting to understand, not only for research social psychologists and our students but for the general public as well.

So in comes Carol Oyster with the best book ever written about groups to give us all we want and need to know about groups in her wonderfully accessible new book, *Groups: A User's Guide*. This book will make converts of individualists, make alienated social cognitive psychologists desire at least to form dyads, and give a new generation of students and young researchers a positive view on the vitality and breadth of applicability of the psychology of groups. Why? Because the way this author introduces us to the new look in group psychology is as exciting as it is inviting, informing as it is entertaining. She gives her book "voice," the gentle, but caring personal voice of a teacher guiding her students into new realms of experience. She gives her book "authorial presence," the clear sense of an expert telling us about the way it really is. And she gives her book "vibrant immediacy," with accounts and stories and data from an incredible array of contexts that will tweak students' curiosity to go beyond the names they have heard about in the media to their substance—Hell's Angels, SWAT teams, Los Angeles gangs, Heaven's Gate cultists, the Olympic gold medal winning women's hockey team, the new militias, and more.

The scope of her inquiry explodes the traditional boundaries of group study by embracing the diversity of gender, race, ethnicity, and cultural considerations. Oyster goes from crisp definitions of all the basic concepts to lively examples of them drawn from everyday life, current events, and literature; for example, elaborating on role playing via having the reader imaging acting the role of Mercutio in *Romeo and Juliet*. Opening brief vignettes are problems that readers solve bit by bit as they accumulate sufficient knowledge in each chapter. Want relevance? Every chapter ends with detailed essays of the application of basic principles to current real-world groups, issues, and people—among them, the O.J. Simpson trial, the role conflicts of Hillary Rodham Clinton, gang initiations, the U.S. military's conflicting policies on gay soldiers, global problems of immigration, and dealing with new stresses in the workplace, to name a few. Current and classic research get equal billing but both are described in ways that use their scientifically gathered evidence to support conclusions and key points, but not in praise of research for its own sake, as in many other texts. The author knows much about groups, and knows how to communicate her knowledge and passion for understanding the dynamics of groups—a potent combination that gives this book its special appeal and this author a place apart from her peers in this field. So we are here to honor the old but dormant tradition in group dynamics, while we cheer on Carol Oyster, as the new spokesperson for the contemporary psychological study of groups.

This innovative McGraw-Hill Series in Social Psychology has been designed as a celebration of the fundamental contributions being made by researchers, theorists, and practitioners of social psychology to improving our understanding of the nature of human nature and enriching the quality of our lives. It has become a showcase for presenting new theories, original syntheses, analyses, and current methodologies by distinguished scholars and promising young writer-researchers. Common to all of our authors is the commitment to sharing their vision with an audience that starts with their colleagues but extends out to graduate students, undergraduates, and all those with an interest in social psychology. Some of our titles convey ideas that are of sufficient general interest that their message needs to be carried out into the world of practical application to those who may translate some of them into public action and public policy. Although each text in our series is created to stand alone as the best representative of its area of scholarship, taken as a whole, they represent the core of social psychology. Many teachers have elected to use them as in-depth supplements to a basic, general textbook, while others organize their course entirely around a set of these monographs. Each of our authors has been guided by the goal of conveying the essential lessons and principles of her or his area of expertise in an interesting style that informs without resorting to technical jargon, that inspires readers to share their excitement by joining in utilizing these ideas or in participating in the research endeavor to create new and better ideas.

I welcome Carol Oyster as the newest member of this special fraternity of educators. And, I welcome you, dear reader, to join the group of similarly situated students who will enjoy and benefit from her scholarship, her wonderfully lucid writing style, her sense of how to teach effectively in prose as she does so well in the classroom, and her dedication to the science of social psychology.

Philip G. Zimbardo
Series Consulting Editor

About the Author

CAROL OYSTER obtained her Ph.D. in social psychology from the University of Delaware in 1982, choosing to escape from the "real world" into academia a decade after receiving her B.A. in psychology from UCLA. She is professor of psychology at the University of Wisconsin at LaCrosse. This represents her second textbook, the first on the topic of research design. She has numerous publications in a number of facets of psychology and social psychology, having served as the statistical and design consultant on many, and changing areas of focus often due to a short attention span, but always working on topics related in some way to stereotyping and women's issues.

Preface

Before we get into the book itself, I want to prepare you for what you are going to encounter. This book is deliberately written in a different style and format from that with which you may be more familiar. This difference is based on fifteen years of teaching, and examining and using more different texts for the same classes than I care to remember.

First, since I have never once used the chapters in a textbook in the order offered by the author, I have deliberately made each chapter freestanding. There are no transitions from the previous chapter nor to the next chapter. If knowledge based on material I have discussed previously is necessary to fully understand a topic under discussion, I will refer the reader to the chapter in which the material was initially discussed. This frees the instructor from having to use the chapters in any particular order (although obviously I find this order compelling) or even from using all of the chapters if they are not all useful for a particular course.

Second, I have tried to maintain a fairly informal and low-key approach to the subject matter. I try to write the way I talk when I'm teaching. This informality by no means implies that the material is unimportant. I simply feel that students are much more likely to learn from a text they find interesting to read, one that doesn't try to bowl them over with jargon or a tone more appropriate for a journal article. Using this informal tone, I can describe research studies (which are included in abundance) and students often don't even recognize they've been reading research material.

Third, I have included three types of pedagogical tools in each chapter. In the first, at the beginning of each chapter I have a short vignette which applies to some point made in the chapter. Students are asked to predict the outcome based upon their level of knowledge at that time. Somewhere later in each chapter I refer to the vignette and explain what the "experts" would predict. I deliberately do not call attention to the "answer" as my method requires students to search for the point in the chapter where they can check their accuracy and acuity.

Second, throughout each chapter there are STOP signs which ask students to make an application of a principle to their own lives, to consider the principles in relation to other groups (gender or cultural), or to see if they can otherwise apply the information. These present occasions for the instructor to stop the class and encourage in-class discussion, or to make an assignment based on the material.

Finally, my experience with texts that start a chapter with an example then try to tie the entire contents of the chapter back to that example usually fail miserably. I find myself puzzled by what I see as the convoluted logic used to try to make the connection. Instead, as explained before, I include within the chapters multiple opportunities for students to actively involve themselves with the material through the use of short vignettes or consideration of applications to their lives.

The final extended Application at the end of the chapter is intended to try to draw on as many of the chapter topics as possible. These applications are varied across disciplines, and some of them are not "politically correct," or are the source of controversy. This is particularly true of the applications regarding role conflict in Chapter 1 and immigration in Chapter 10. I assure you that my research for these applications is based on references just as are all of the applications. These, however, make use of references on the politically unpopular side of controversial issues. That is deliberate on my part. Challenging preconceived notions and values ideally forces individuals to examine those very notions and values. To me that constitutes critical thinking and education at its best.

Finally, try to have fun with the book. Take time to discuss controversial issues. If you disagree with the text, do your own research to prove me wrong. There's no escaping the realities of group dynamics in life, so why not learn the rules so you can play to your best ability?

Acknowledgements

Writing can be one of the loneliest activities in which a human can engage. Although it's so true as to be a cliché that no one writes a book alone, when push comes to shove there's no one but you at the keyboard. However, when you're not actively writing, reading sources, or taking notes, the process of writing engulfs your entire life. You truly can't do it alone. You need friends who will listen to you endlessly prattle about the topic (and won't tell you to shut up when they're bored—though you know they are), and people who will force you out of yourself occasionally to remember what real life can be like. You need family who will put up with a mentally absent member, late meals (or none at all), a dirty house, disturbed family plans, and much less personal attention. You need an understanding editor and publisher. I've been blessed in having all these. Many thanks to:

- My student helpers: David Lee, Meghan Statz, and Rebecca Waech for all those hours in the library;
- My research apprentice, Leah Geislinger, for critiquing chapters from a student perspective;
- My colleagues Betsy Morgan, Sara Sullivan, and Mike Kuhlman for ideas and references;
- My friends Mary Zeiss Stange, Wendy Gell, Sybie Weathers, D. B. Kates, Jr., and C. B. Kates for providing laughter and other worlds;
- My editors at McGraw-Hill, Sarah Thomas, Mickey Cox, and Sheila Frank, who showed extraordinary patience as my chaotic life led me to miss deadline after deadline, yet always had something pleasant and useful to say;
- My kids: Katherine, Meighan, Missy, Simone, Clousseau, S. D. Catt, Charlotte, Jackie, and Claire.

All I can say is this: Thanks. I truly couldn't have done it without you.

CHAPTER 1

Basic Group Principles

What Would YOU Predict?

Joan is the first elected leader of the newly organized Honors Students' Association. For the first meeting she has a choice as to whether the group should organize themselves primarily as a social organization, a community service group, or a political influence group. Very few of the members know each other except by sight. What would be the most effective way to handle the first meeting?

INTRODUCTION

Have you ever stopped to count, or even think of, all the groups to which you belong? After fifteen years teaching at the college level about group dynamics, I thought I'd count mine. I stopped counting when I reached twenty current groups. These include my family of origin, five professional groups, work groups on the job, executive committees of committees, multiple friendship groups, feminists, women in general, citizens of the city, state, and the United States . . . well, you get the idea. Human beings are group animals. We are born into groups and work with various types of groups until we die. Despite the vast differences in the purposes and types of groups, all have certain basic principles in common. We refer to these as **group dynamics.** They include such things as the ways we divide up power, the ways we communicate, the roles we perform, the level of loyalty or attachment to the group, and many other principles we'll discuss in this book. Therefore, this book will not focus exclusively on one type of group, such as families or therapy groups. Why limit your effectiveness? Once you begin to recognize group dynamics in action, you can apply your knowledge to the groups to which you belong.

Does this mean that once you finish this course and this text you'll know everything there is to know about groups? Of course not. No one does. Because you are limited in the amount of time in a course and because there is a particular type of group that you will most commonly encounter in your lives, we are going to focus primarily on the dynamics of the small, task group. We will discuss more briefly other types of important groups, such as minority groups, particularly as membership in these groups has an impact on behavior in task groups. We are not going to discuss the psychology or sociology of audiences, crowds, or mobs but consider the groups you may encounter in your daily lives: relationships, families, friendship groups, work groups on the job, juries on which you might be called to serve, your residence hall council, your sports teams, and your social organizations such as sororities and fraternities. In this chapter we will discuss the basic principles that define the type of group we will be studying. And, although the information we'll cover comes from a number of disciplines (psychology, sociology, business), we will primarily focus on the psychology of the group, which means we'll focus on the people in the group and how they affect and are affected by the group.

One thing that is probably included in almost every textbook you've used has been a chapter on the methods of studying the particular subject matter at hand. Surprise! There is no methods chapter in this book. There are positive and negative aspects to that, from both our perspectives. From your point of view, you won't have to AGAIN go over means, standard deviations, correlations, t tests, etc. However, from my point of view, since all knowledge in psychology is based on empirical (research) sources, you will be expected to have a basic understanding of statistical principles. You may need to check your "old stats" book occasionally.

One difference from your basic statistics course you will find when studying group dynamics, however, is that often the unit of analysis (the subject, if you will) is the group and not the individual. We may have a sample of 100 individuals divided up into twenty groups, but when we do our analyses we will probably be most interested in the behavioral differences (e.g., the accuracy of problem solving) between the groups. This is not a trivial consideration. We really don't have 100 subjects, we have twenty. This affects our ability to make certain statistical inferences regarding **statistical significance** of a study. Also, under certain circumstances we will have to decide whether the most effective way to handle a situation is to have the individual make the decision, solve the problem, or do the task; or whether it would be more effective to use a group. In order to make reasoned and reasonable decisions we should know the circumstances that affect the quality of our decision on the level of productivity we attain.

Another goal of this text is to be as inclusive as possible. In the past, American psychology has been guilty of serious tunnel vision. We believed that if a phenomenon occurred with white, middle-class, heterosexual, American male individuals then it must be true of people in general. This was not based on some nefarious conspiracy—it merely reflects the identities of the researchers and the contents of their worlds. We have now come to realize that while past research is not in and of itself incorrect, individual characteristics such as gender, race, and culture can impact groups in very dramatic ways. The first summary of sex differences was published in 1974 (Maccoby & Jacklin) and reviewed literature starting from at least twenty years before that point. We are just beginning to see the results of research on ethnic and cultural differences within the United States and around the world on group dynamics. Whenever possible, the results of such research has been included in this text.

> *Over the centuries Western thought has been central in the experiences of a privileged few whose particular views of the world and experience within it have shaped what is known. How else can we explain the idea that democracy and egalitarianism were defined as central cultural beliefs in the nineteenth century while millions of African-Americans were enslaved? . . .*
>
> *The exclusion of women, African-Americans, Latinos, Native Americans, gays and lesbians, and other groups from formal scholarship has resulted in distortions and incomplete information not only about the experiences of the excluded groups, but also about the experience of more privileged groups.*
>
> **(Wilson, 1996, p. 1)**

Let's pause for a moment before we dive in. There have been a number of types of groups listed above. Count and make a list of how many apply to you. Start with student. Do you have a job? A family? A partner? Are you Asian-American? Do you belong to a church group or other religious organization? Do you sing in a choir? Are you a cheerleader, or a football player? Keep going. Surely you've been in groups I haven't mentioned (e.g., Boy Scouts, Girl Scouts). How does this compare with your classmates? Are there any groups to which many of you belong that haven't been included? Which groups are most important to you? Keep these groups in mind as we consider the characteristics that groups have in common.

Remember that each small group that has a task to perform (win the football game or study together for exams or raise the children) will operate under the same basic set of principles. Once you get good at spotting this in action, your interactions with others will never be quite the same again. Ready? Step up to the starting line, and let's go.

The obvious first step might be to start with exploring the definitions of groups. However, there are several important dichotomies we need to explore to provide context for the rest of our discussion on groups. In other psychology courses you may have run into some of these fundamental differences or splits on issues. For example, in many areas of psychology the question of **nature vs. nurture** is a source of discussion and/or dissension. If we see sex differences in behavior, is it because of biological differences of some kind (nature), or because boys and girls are taught to behave differently (nurture)? Although this topic is of tangential interest in the study of group dynamics (e.g., why do people form groups?), this is not one of our primary dichotomies.

PRELIMINARY ISSUES: TASK AND SOCIOEMOTIONAL ISSUES OF GROUPS, AND FORMAL VS. INFORMAL GROUPS

Our first dichotomy has to do with the two levels of issues that are constantly coexisting within task groups. Obviously one level concerns the task itself. We have a job to complete. "**Task dimension** refers to the relationship between group members and the work they are to perform—the job they have to do and how they go about doing it" (Ellis & Fisher, 1994, p. 22). But at the same time, since groups are composed of individuals, we have to consider the social dimensions of the groups. "**Social dimensions** refers to the relationships of group members with one another—how they feel toward one another and about their membership in the group" (Ellis & Fisher, 1994, p. 22). Task dimensions are related primarily to **productivity** factors in the group while social dimensions refer to the **cohesiveness** or closeness of group members. These issues are closely intertwined and inseparable. If we have a group that lacks cohesion it will be extremely difficult to get them to focus on producing a quality decision or product—the task dimension is affected. If a group is extremely successful in accomplishing their tasks, the group tends to have positive feelings toward each other and the group. The direction of causation is unclear and probably works in both directions. The U.S. women's hockey team won the gold medal in the 1998 Winter Olympic Games. Were they able to be successful because they were so cohesive as a team? Or did the cohesiveness come from the fact that they were performing so well?

The American women's hockey team demonstrates cohesiveness in celebration of their gold medal performance.

New groups tend to shy away from dealing with the social dimensions of a group and try to dive directly into the task. What should Joan do? She should force the group to get to know each other and develop relationships before they start the task or the group will not be as productive and efficient as they could be otherwise. Fortunately, there are myriad icebreakers and problem-solving tasks that can be employed in guiding the group through this uncomfortable phase. By allowing the group to interact informally in a structure that has no bearing on the formal task, the relationships that serve as the source of the social dimensions are encouraged to begin.

One of the questions we need to consider in assigning tasks is whether it is most appropriate to use an individual or a group. Often an important consideration in that decision will be the productivity and the cohesiveness of the group. Productivity may be enhanced by use of a group with its heterogeneity and thus multiplicity of resources. However, the complications of the social dimension might require the use of an individual.

There have been three types of tasks identified: (1) *production tasks*, (2) *discussion tasks*, and (3) *problem-solving tasks* (Hackman, 1968). In production tasks there is a tangible product at the end of the job. A group that works together to build a float for the homecoming parade or the Rose Bowl Parade held each New Year's Day in California must come up with a completed object before their task is complete. In discussion tasks there is not necessarily any tangible result. A task force that is called to examine issues of homophobia or racism in an organization may or may not be required to develop a report on their findings nor even necessarily come to any definitive conclusions. If they are required to write a report, they become a problem-solving group. They have come up with a product, which is the attempted solution to a problem rather than a float or a car or a Super Bowl title.

The interconnection between task and social dimensions means that we will need to consider both when we analyze any group. However, the issues are not of equal importance in every group. In a basketball team the primary issues have to do with winning the game—the task issue. Certainly a team with low cohesion will have more trouble completing the task, but league rankings are not based upon how well the team gets along. A quilting club, on the other hand, that consists of a group of people who gather weekly to work in parallel on their quilting projects and to compare them and talk is primarily focused on the social dimension. It matters less to them that they get their projects done by a deadline than that they have a chance to interact with individuals with the same interests (and maybe escape from the house one night a week). We will be constantly tripping over this dichotomy between social and task dimensions because it impacts on many of the issues we will be considering in this text: communication, leadership, coordination, influence, and power.

The second primary dichotomy we will need to keep in mind as we examine the issues of groups is the formal vs. the informal aspects of the group. All groups function at both levels and we need to keep in mind their interrelationship and the possibility that they are not in synch with each other and therefore interfering with the functioning of the group. The **formal aspects of the group** have to do with explicit rules and control. The various branches of the military are extremely formal organizations. Behavior in these organizations is governed by the Uniform Code of Military Justice (UCMJ) and behaviors that in other groups would perhaps be considered unkind, embarrassing, or immoral can constitute actionable, punishable offenses in the military. In 1997, Lt. Kelly Flinn, the first woman fighter pilot in the Air Force, a woman with a previously brilliant career in the military, was forced to resign to avoid facing a court-martial which could send her to prison for her affair with another Air Force officer. Fraternization, and especially adultery (her partner was married) are illegal in the military. President Clinton is commander in chief of the armed forces, yet he is not governed by their rules. It is clear from his admissions and the testimony of others at the impeachment hearings that Clinton committed adultery (unless you agree with his narrow definition of sexual activity, that it consists only of intercourse). However, he does not face the same potential outcomes as Lt. Flinn. Articles of impeachment voted by the House of Representatives dealt with his lying under oath while giving a court deposition about extramarital relationships, which the House defined as committing perjury, and his allegedly asking others to lie to cover up his behavior, thus suborning perjury.

Surgical or emergency room teams are also highly formal organizations. During an operation, when a surgeon gives an order or demands a particular instrument, the nurses do not feel free to question her choices or discuss alternative procedures. The surgeon gets her scalpel. SWAT teams, police officers, and fire fighters must also have a high degree of formal organization in order to effectively accomplish their jobs. What these types of teams also have in common is an uncommonly stressful environment in which their tasks must be accomplished. We will examine the effects of this additional component in Chapter 11.

Informal aspects of groups are usually far less focused on rules and control. **Cliques** that develop in school-age children are a good example. In cliques the issue is popularity, however it is defined. Because of the strong influence of peers on children, parents can only hope that their high school-age children will join cliques where good grades and achievement are the criteria for popularity, not promiscuity and antisocial behavior such as shoplifting.

But, as with the task/social dimension dichotomy, the formal/informal dichotomy exists in every group. In the most formal of groups there is the informal shadow equivalent. In organizations, there are often very formal communication networks. In the military, individuals recognize differences in formal rank by salutes or other greeting rituals (or lack thereof). One can get into just as much trouble for saluting the "wrong" people as for failing to salute the "right" ones. Orders such as transfers and postings may be communicated formally in writing. However, the informal shadow equivalent of this formal communication system is the **"grapevine."** This often lightning-fast, word-of-mouth form of communication can be quite accurate regarding task aspects of the group. It can also be quite inaccurate regarding gossip concerning the personal lives of group members. We'll discuss the grapevine more in Chapter 4 on communication in groups. On to our basic definition of the group.

STOP Without looking at the definition below and considering the groups you listed earlier, how would you define a group? Write down the aspects the groups have in common. What aspects do you consider to be the most important? How does your list match with the lists of others in your class or group? Where do you disagree? How do your lists compare with the definition provided below?

WHAT IS A GROUP?

The definitional characteristics of a group might have seemed obvious to you until you were asked to come up with a list. Probably your list didn't match exactly the list of your peers. However, unless this is your first psychology course (and I hope that's not the case), you have figured out by now that we psychologists are a contentious bunch. That's right, **we** can't even agree on the basic characteristics of what constitutes a group. For our purposes, we're going to consider the following: *size, roles, status, interpersonal relations, cohesiveness* (defined as the strength of the relationships within the group), *interaction, goals, temporal change,* and *norms*. This is a fairly standard list, which will be found in most generic group dynamics texts. It's the definitions applied to the terms themselves that sometimes cause problems.

Size

How many psychologists does it take to change a light bulb? (You'll find the answer in Chapter 11!) How many people does it take to constitute a group? The controversy is not over **size**—whether ten or eleven people are necessary. It's much more basic than that. The controversy is over whether two people or three people are required to "count" as a group. Interestingly, in counseling we sometimes find the same question asked about what constitutes a family. Is a couple a family, or must there be a child or children?

While some psychologists do not classify two people as a group, I believe that when we look at what groups do—communicate, coordinate their efforts toward some end, get along with each other (or at least decide how they will relate to each other), decide on their level of commitment to the group, allocate resources and power, work together (interact), adjust to change over time, and establish patterns of behavior in relation to each other—it becomes really difficult to distinguish these actions from those of any two people in a relationship. In fact, I believe that the application of group dynamics principles to **dyadic** (two-person) relationships such as friendships, dating couples, and life partners makes understanding those relationships somewhat easier (not "easy," just a bit less difficult). If I'm arguing with my partner over who gets to use the better car to go to work tomorrow, it might simplify things greatly if we realized we were not communicating effectively, or that what we were really trying indirectly to deal with was an issue of power and control in the relationship. When you stop to think about it, just how often do people really know what they're fighting about? (We'll consider this issue in depth in Chapter 4 on communication and Chapter 10 on conflict.)

 What do you think? Is a dyad a group? Write down three arguments on each side of the issue, and discuss them with your classmates.

Now for a little **jargon.** Jargon is the term that applies to the specialized language that is developed by groups. Terms develop specific meaning to the group that often serves to simplify communication within the group. Unfortunately, however, these terms may escape into the common vernacular with an entirely different usage. Take, for example, the term "brainstorming." It's everywhere! My daughter came home from third grade and talked about how they had brainstormed ideas in class that day. And I'm sure that's what the teacher called it. I'm equally certain that they didn't do what in group dynamics is referred to as brainstorming. Brainstorming as done "by the rules" increases both the quality and quantity of ideas in a group. Done as it usually is in groups not trained in the technique, it has been shown to actually decrease quality and quantity of ideas (again we'll discuss this further in Chapter 6). Other terms that have escaped from psychology are "ego" and "identity crisis." These terms generally mean one thing when used in general conversation and quite another within the discipline.

So jargon has another function. Besides facilitating conversation within the group, it serves as an exclusionary device to keep others from understanding what we say. Unfortunately, we are often unaware of this facet of jargon when we speak with someone from a different group and it can become the source of embarrassment or of potentially serious miscommunication.

Group dynamicists have a number of terms referring to the size of a group. Two people constitute a dyad (which, as I've already stated, we will consider a group). A **triad** is (in this context) three people in a group. Anything smaller than twenty people is usually considered a **"small group,"** although the dynamics in a group of four is certainly different than in a group of twelve.

One question often asked about group size relates to the "ideal size" of a group. Of course, there isn't a simple answer. The simplistic answer is that it depends. It depends on the task to be done, it depends on the characteristics of the individuals in the group, it depends on the structure of the situation, etc. However, since we're currently limiting our consideration to small, task-related groups, we can give an only slightly ambiguous answer. Generally, for most discussion or problem-solving tasks, a group size of between four and six is optimal. (For production tasks, often the larger the task the more people you need.) A group of four to six provides you with a variety of resources that is the advantage of working with a group without adding the complications in social dimensions and task dimensions such as scheduling of a larger group. Fortunately, when asked to form groups for tasks, individuals tend to gravitate toward groups of just this size.

Roles

Role is a term we've borrowed from sociology. It was introduced by G. H. Meade (1934) and elaborated by Goffman (1967) to refer to describe sets of expected behaviors at two levels. **Role perception** is your perception of how you are expected to behave. **Role expectation** is how others believe you should behave in certain situations. Roles are "powerful determinants of behaviors" (Schein, 1980, p. 24).

The analogy to a role in a play or movie fits almost perfectly here. If you are cast in the role of Mercutio in Shakespeare's play *Romeo and Juliet*, you can read your lines from the script and get your blocking (moves) from the director. Your role perception is your interpretation of the part. The director's role expectation is his idea of how you should play the part. Hopefully, these coincide. Sometimes they don't, and that's a problem we'll discuss below.

When you are first cast into a role in a play, or when you enter a new group, you don't know how to behave. It takes a while to learn how you fit in with the other roles in the group. Over time, and with rehearsal, each individual in the play or group learns how their roles interact, and the roles become predictable and stable. They come together in a psychological contract in the group (Baker, 1985). Thus roles are **complementary.** If I'm playing the role of teacher, you know that your role is to play the part of student. If you're playing the part of husband, you (and your wife) have perceptions and expectations of her complementary behaviors.

If, for some reason, a group member departs from their expected role, it can cause problems for the entire rest of the group. If the rest of the troupe expects to be acting *Romeo and Juliet,* and the first character on stage begins lines from another play, everyone is confused. The same is true if, in the middle of a play that has otherwise been going well, someone blows their lines. Not only are they in trouble, they've potentially thrown off the rest of the cast as well. That's why often actors learn all the lines in a scene—not just their own. That way if someone blows a line or simply loses their place, the correct behavior (in this case, the line) can be "fed" to them and the show can go on.

Another aspect of roles is their **clarity.** Acting in a play is relatively easy because someone has provided us with both our movements and words. The first day on a new job is a different matter. Of course we have some idea of what we've been hired to do, and in effective organizations we've had some training and maybe there's even some sort of manual to which we can refer if we don't know what to do next. However, even in the best of situations, there will be some *role ambiguity*. Invariably something will happen on that first day that no one explained and to which we haven't a clue as to how to respond. With luck, over time and with experience this ambiguity will diminish and we'll become clear and comfortable with our role. Often this happens because the behavior of others (complementarity) creates our niche for us. Role ambiguity is a reason why many people dislike joining new groups. No one knows what to say or do so everyone is uncomfortable. One of the major reasons for group dropouts in the early stages is the discomfort caused by role ambiguity. After a while the group sorts things out and everyone relaxes.

Different roles in a group have different levels of **complexity.** To refer again to our drama model, the role of Romeo has far more lines and action than does the role of Mercutio. When my nephew discovered that his class would be presenting a production of *Romeo and Juliet*, he asked to be cast as "the corpse on the bottom." He clearly did not want to take on a very public, complex role. The role of leader in a group is much more complex than is the role of harmonizer— the clown who can be counted on to make a wisecrack or tell a joke to break the tension when conflict arises.

Finally, in defining roles we have another dichotomy. Linton (1936) differentiated between achieved and ascribed roles. **Achieved roles** are roles over which we exert some control. We work to attain that position. We audition for the play. We run for office. We attend college to become a graduate. So there's an element of choice in achieved roles. **Ascribed roles,** on the other hand, are role expectations placed on us based on who we are, not what we do. Gender, race, and age are a few of the characteristics that constitute ascribed roles. We have no choice in where we fall on any of these, yet others expect us to perform certain—often stereotypical—behaviors based on these characteristics.

What roles do you play? List the achieved roles separately from the ascribed roles. Which roles are most central to your concept of yourself? Which roles are the most comfortable to enact? Which (if any) are uncomfortable for you?

Gender will be an issue of importance in this book. Gender and sex are not the same. Sex is based on biological characteristics from the genetic to the hormonal levels. "Gender is a social construction, not a biological inevitability" (Reskin & Padavic, 1994, p. 5). Gender works in societies to identify those activities and behaviors appropriate for each sex. These assignments influence the way the sexes are treated, the expectations for behaviors from the sexes, and the behavior of individuals in groups. In all cultures that have been contacted by anthropologists, there is differentiation in the expected behavioral roles between men and women. What is interesting is that there is not a great deal of consistency in these expectations. What is considered "masculine" in one culture may very well be considered "feminine" in another. Yet, within their own culture, individuals are expected to comply. For example, in our culture, even though some people believe that there is a relaxation of expectations based on gender, it is still true that a woman in business who behaves as aggressively as a man in a similar position will be considered either a "bitch" or "butch" while he will be applauded for his entrepreneurial spirit (Tannen, 1994).

Research on sex-role expectations has shown that individuals from other cultures have their own cultural expectations that may conflict with American stereotypes. Kulik (1995) examined the attitudes of Israeli students compared to college students who emigrated from the Soviet Union. The Israelis were much more liberal regarding gender roles than the immigrant students not only in terms of behavioral expectations but also in labeling more nontraditional and prestigious occupations as feminine rather than masculine. Crittenden (1991) found that Taiwanese women were more self-effacing in conversation than

Taiwanese men or American men or women. The model for behavior for these women is Chinese culture in which self-effacement is an expectation, an expectation not part of the American feminine stereotype.

Even in the United States, however, sex-role stereotypes are far from dead. Ivey (1995) conducted a study on family roles using practicing counselors, social workers, psychologists, and psychiatrists as participants. These clinicians saw a videotape of either a mother-led or a father-led family. Tradition in the United States, of course, as well as past research (Parsons & Bales, 1954) identifies the male as the appropriate head of the household. Participants in this study perceived the mother-led family to be less psychologically healthy, and the father in the patriarchal family was seen as healthier than the father in the matriarchal family. While there is evidence that all things being equal a child is better off in a family with two parents, the research has not identified specific problems associated with which parent is dominant. Thus this assumption that the family is by definition less healthy because it has a strong female figure could be a little disturbing when you consider that these participants are the very people to whom individuals and families turn when they feel in need of guidance. This study would suggest that perhaps therapeutic intervention might foster traditional sex roles.

Sex roles have not applied equally to all American women, however. The stereotypes have tended to focus on white, middle-class, heterosexual women.

> *White women, for example, have fought notions of "ladylike" behaviors that require feigned weakness on their part; they fight to be seen as strong and capable. In contrast, women of color struggle under assumptions that often cast them as strong physical laborers; they instead fight to be seen as capable of being "a lady," of being perceived as worthy of the cultural status that accompanies "ladies."*
>
> **(Duerst-Lahti & Kelly, 1995, p. 1)**

And even though the average age in our population is increasing as the "baby boomers" hit their fifties, there are still some pretty rigid age-associated behavioral expectations. People tend to have a very negative reaction to makeup and sexy clothing on girls they perceive as too young. And "seniors" on in-line skates or surfboards are considered objects of amusement. We are awed by people such as comedian George Burns who remain active well into their nineties.

We can determine many of the societal expectations for ascribed roles from the media. It is particularly interesting to examine several current advertising campaigns depicting grandmothers. They are usually shown as having blue hair, wearing aprons, and cooking something—or totally dismayed because a new product has displaced the need for them to cook something. Given the demographic statistics about our culture at this time, it is not at all extraordinary for a woman in her forties to be a grandmother. Most women in our culture at that time in their lives are still vital and active in their career and leisure pursuits. Yet we marvel at women such as Sophia Loren and Lena Horne and "how good they look *for their age.*" If there was truly an acceptance of aging, then we would not need to spotlight such individuals. This type of comment implies that if they really looked their age they would not be attractive.

How old is your grandmother? Does she fit the stereotypes presented in the media? Do you know any grandmothers who do? How do you think grandmothers are supposed to behave? Would you take your grandmother in-line skating?

Of course, men are not exempt from sex-role stereotyping. However, in American society, the male is considered the norm—the standard against which the "other" is to be measured (Tannen, 1994). While this makes it easier for men in some ways, it also denies them the opportunity to express their feminine, softer side lest they violate the stereotype. As is true with "masculine" women, men who are "too feminine" are often immediately assumed to be homosexual. But not allowing men these feminine behaviors forces them to constrict their emotional expression which may result in their having difficulty in emotional relationships with their partners and children. There have long been complaints that fathers do not spend enough time or play a large enough role within the family or with their children. Yet when they do, their masculinity may come into question. And given the societal expectation that they will be the strong, ambitious, successful breadwinner for the family, it's difficult to figure out when this time with the family is supposed to occur.

It's clear how ascribed roles emerge—they are culturally determined. However, the emergence of achieved roles bears consideration. Bormann (1990) presented the model shown in Figure 1.1. According to this model, **role emergence** is achieved through the method of learning known as *operant conditioning.* This is simply a fancier (or more jargon-laden) way of saying that when we perform a behavior and are rewarded for it, the behavior is likely to recur. If we are ignored, punished, or not rewarded, the behavior is less likely to recur and may eventually disappear.

In this model, a time comes in a group when a need arises for a particular behavior to be performed—perhaps the group needs to draw up a schedule of deadlines for portions of the project upon which they are working. Individual A decides to perform the behavior. According to this model, she can receive three types of response from the group which will influence her subsequent behavior in a similar situation. The group can approve (reward her), disapprove (punish her), or provide ambiguous feedback. These responses will influence her behavior when the need again arises within the group for the same behavior. If the first attempt was rewarded, she will retain the behavior as her own. If she received disapproval she will usually not persist—the behavior will be picked up by another group member. If the feedback on the first attempt was ambiguous, then she will probably keep trying until one of two things occurs: (1) she finally gets clear feedback one way or the other, or (2) the group assigns the behavior to someone else.

One area the model neglects is the situation in which A's behavior is ignored. We know from other learning situations that eventually this will lead to extinction or disappearance of the behavior. But this is usually preceded by a temporary increase. The classic example is the child throwing a temper tantrum. Child development specialists suggest the best way to handle this situation is to ignore the behavior. When the behavior doesn't work, it will go away. In the meantime, however, there is often an increase in the number and decibel level of the tantrums. But it's often difficult to ignore an irritating behavior for one reason or another. Children often save tantrums for grocery stores because they know that their parents are particularly likely to do almost anything to quiet them down so they don't look like "bad parents." It's also bad form and potentially dangerous for the child to simply turn your back and walk away from the flailing child on the floor. However, if you leave the room at

FIGURE 1.1. *Bormann chart.*
Source: "Model of Role Emergence" from Small Group Communication: Theory and Practice, *3rd Edition by Ernest G. Bormann, p. 165. Copyright © 1990. Reprinted by permission of Ernest G. Bormann.*

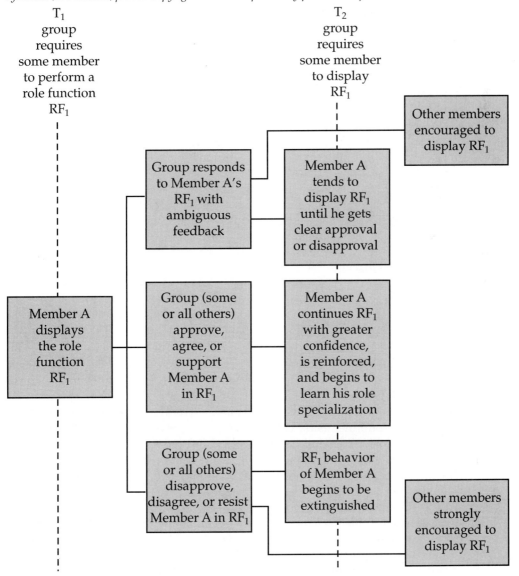

home when a child starts a tantrum, it often abruptly stops since there's no longer an audience to which to play. In a group, a member who whines to get her way can be so intensely irritating it's just easier to give in than to ignore her and have the frequency increase. But it's always important to understand that in Bormann's model, behavior that is rewarded will increase in frequency. Since the rewards or punishments for the same behavior may differ across situations, it is important to understand that roles are group-specific. The fact that an individual is a leader in one group does not tell us that he is a leader in all the groups in which he participates.

Earlier in this chapter we discussed the task/social dimension dichotomy. This applies to the roles we find in groups (Bales, 1950; Benne & Sheats, 1948; Reiken & Homans, 1954). In terms of roles, however, we add a third category—individual roles. These are roles that are either irrelevant or counterproductive to the success of the group.

Task roles are behaviors that facilitate the group's attainment of their goals. They include the initiator who pushes the group to move on the task; the information provider who seeks outside information and resources; the opinion giver who provides suggestions on the task; the elaborator who takes ideas and embroiders upon them to make them more useful to the group; the coordinator who makes sure that things stay on schedule; the critic who makes sure that the best ideas generated by the group are used in the task; and the energizer who keeps "going and going and going," and encourages everyone else to do the same. Must one person do all these tasks? Only if they're doing the task alone. In a group we may well see these roles spread out across members. The leader, however, is responsible to see that all these roles are fulfilled.

The social dimension is satisfied by group maintenance roles which involve the feelings and relationships of the group members as the task is accomplished. These include the encourager who serves as cheerleader; the supporter who provides backing for the ideas of timid members; the harmonizer who makes sure that the group climate doesn't become too tense by telling jokes or making wisecracks; and the gate keeper whose job is to make sure that everyone is included to an equal extent, which may mean drawing out some individuals and limiting domination by others. Again, a single individual need not serve all these functions, but in a successful group all will be enacted.

Individual roles can disrupt, distract, or destroy a group. These are behaviors that are focused inward for the individual's self-aggrandizement rather than the good of the group. They all have in common that they prevent work on the task by taking up group time and energy. The aggressor likes to pick fights with other group members. The blocker never agrees with anything the group tries to do, thus sabotaging group cohesion and progress on the task. The dominator wants everything done their way and won't listen to others' ideas. The final two individual roles, the recognition seeker and the self-confessor seem to have in common the need for lots of attention. The recognition seeker tries to take credit for everything anyone in the group accomplishes, and the self-confessors are so busy telling everything about themselves ("spilling their guts") that they don't get anything done themselves, prevent others from getting things done, and make many people uncomfortable at the inappropriate level of self-disclosure. A leader in a group needs to try to eliminate or prevent these behaviors. Individuals whose goals are to get attention are actually the easiest to deal with. If the group can determine a task-related method of attention-getting the need will be satisfied and the negative behavior will tend to go away.

Which types of roles are easier for a group to deal with effectively? That depends on the stage of development of the group. Very early on in a group's experience it is easier to dive straight into the task than to deal with the social dimensions. Many groups will begin the task without even introducing themselves to each other. This is not a good idea, as we will discuss in Chapter 2, because until roles and relationships get sorted out, the group will not be productive and anything produced will not be of optimal quality. So our friend Joan (remember?) should discourage the group from making any important decisions until there has been some time for the group to interact and get to know each other better.

Problems with Roles: Role Strain and Role Conflict

We all play a multiplicity of roles. You have a role to go with each group you identified at the beginning of the chapter. When the behavioral demands of the roles don't conflict, or are not too demanding or too vague, we can generally get along juggling numerous roles. Unfortunately, that best of all possible worlds is not always reality. We have already discussed *role ambiguity* as a potential problem. Now we'll consider two other possible problematic situations, **role strain** and **role conflict.**

Role strain comes when there are simply too many demands placed upon us. We cannot fulfill all of the behaviors required of all of our roles at the same time. It's not that the roles are inherently incompatible, it's just too much. Role strain can also come about when the roles we are expected to enact are too complex for us—we're in over our heads. Early in my career teaching at a small, private college I was asked at the last minute to teach an advanced algebra course. Since I was new at the job I agreed, despite my inexperience. I managed to stay about two pages ahead of the class—however, there were often questions I could not answer without going to one of my colleagues in the math department.

There were initially three kinds of role conflict identified: (1) intra-role conflict, (2) inter-role conflict, and (3) interpersonal role conflict (Baird & Weinberg, 1977). Brenner and Molander (1977) identified a fourth type of role conflict— ethical role conflict. Intra-role conflict occurs when there is confusion of the role perception of the individual and the role expectations of others. For example, it is not uncommon for a clerical employee to be expected to report to several supervisors. Everyone agrees that the individual's job involves typing, filing, and answering phones. However, if Supervisor Jones expects you to work for him 60 percent of your work hours and Supervisor Yamamoto expects you to work for her 70 percent of your hours, you have a serious problem. The expectations are incompatible—they simply cannot all be met.

Another type of intra-role conflict that is being seen more frequently of late is the intra-role conflict created by differing definitions of the roles of husband and wife. Whatever else can be said about the "old days" when father knew best and June baked cookies while Beaver was at school, the behavioral expectations for husbands and wives were very clearly delineated. Everyone knew what they were getting into when they said "I do." Now that there has been some softening of sex roles, couples who have not discussed their expectations prior to the wedding may have a nasty surprise when he discovers that while his definition of "wife" includes sharing the income production, doing all of the housework, and staying home with the kids, her definition includes sharing the income production, having a maid, and not having any children. What to do? This may be the easiest type of role conflict to solve. "All" you have to do is communicate. (There are quotation marks around the word "all" because I realize that's a tall order, which is why we'll spend all of Chapter 4 talking about communication.)

Inter-role conflict is when the behavioral demands of two or more roles are incompatible. For example, your office always has staff meetings on Wednesday afternoons at 3 o'clock and your daughter wants you to coach her soccer team, which practices at 3 o'clock on Wednesday afternoons. Since you can't be at two places at once, you have a problem. In another example, you pay your tuition by working evenings and can usually arrange your work schedule around your class schedule. One evening you go in to work and are informed that a co-worker has mononucleosis and will be out of work for a week and you're needed to stand in. You're flattered and you could certainly use the extra money, but the hours you'd need to work are full-time during the day during final exams week! Or, your son's Little League championship game falls at the same time you have been invited to speak at a charity luncheon. Or, your elderly, widowed mother wants your family to spend Christmas with her in California and your elderly, widowed mother-in-law wants your family to spend Christmas with her in Maine. I could go on, but you get the picture. Surely there must be a way out.

Inter-role conflict was recognized as a problem as early as 1958 when Gross, Mason, and McEachern presented a model for its solution. Viewed from the present, it appears astoundingly naïve, but everything must be viewed in context. In 1958 we did not have many women in the work force and many roles were more clearly defined and separated than they are now. Gross et al. suggested three alternative solutions: (1) conform to one role or the other; (2) compromise between the roles; and (3) free yourself from one role or the other. Sounds good on paper. And actually these may be plausible solutions when we talk about the conflict between two achieved roles. If you want to solve the conflict between your meetings and the soccer team and you have enough clout, change the time of one or the other and you're out from under the conflict. If, however, the conflict is between an achieved role and an ascribed role, or two ascribed roles, you're in trouble. You can't stop being what you are—so you really can't opt out of an ascribed role.

Let me give you a true example of conflict between an achieved and an ascribed role.

> *In 1993 an elevator operator at the House of Representatives repeatedly told a newly elected African-American woman that she could not use an elevator reserved for members of the House. Finally it dawned on the elevator operator that the woman was a Representative.*
>
> *(Reskin & Padavic, 1994, p. 13)*

So who cares if you make people uncomfortable? You're nice, you're personable, you have good hygiene, you're smart and good at what you do. Congratulations, but unfortunately that really seems to matter far less than it should. First impressions are frequently established very quickly and based upon obvious information such as sex or race, which may be the trigger for stereotyping (Deaux & Wrightsman, 1988).

> *It is also true, however, that when we already have a schema in our memory for a certain class of people or event, our encoding of new information will be influenced by those expectancies.*
>
> *(Deaux & Wrightsman, 1988, p. 113)*

Thus it is very possible that impressions will be formed that are quite durable and very much in line with any stereotypical thinking of the observer. But what does this role conflict mean for the group?

As early as 1978, research in organizations by Kahn, Wolfe, Quinn, Snoeck, and Rosenthal found that inter-role conflict in organizations was associated with low job satisfaction (for all concerned), lowered productivity, low self-confidence, low confidence in the group, and a sense of futility. In addition, inter-role conflict may also affect the ability to communicate effectively (Koehler, Anatol, & Applebaum, 1976; Oyster, 1982). As we shall see in Chapter 4, effective communication is difficult enough when we share the same language or code with the person with whom we are trying to communicate. The problem increases not only with role conflict, but also when we are working with someone who is very different from us.

It isn't surprising then, that as diversity in the workplace is increasing, so is the incidence of inter-role conflict. Moore and Gobi (1995) studied work-family role conflict in Jewish women employed in a traditional profession (secondary school teacher) as compared to Jewish women employed in a nontraditional profession (university professor). Women in the male occupations spent less time on domestic and family roles and more time at work, and since the home burden appears to be the primary factor in work-family role conflict, these women suffered less role conflict than the high school teachers. These women appear to actually be making a choice between roles. What we don't know is the effect on their marriages and families because of this choice. Kramer and Kipnis (1995) studied conflicts generated between employment and eldercare responsibilities for men and women. Eldercare is assuming the responsibility and caretaking tasks for an elderly relative (usually a parent). The women were more likely to perform the eldercare, to report role strain (primarily from role overload), and to feel higher levels of burden than were the men.

Koberg and Chysmir (1989) and Wiersma and Van den Berg (1991) all studied the effects of jobs on marriages, another example of inter-role conflict. Koberg and Chysmir found that when measuring reported gender-role conflict in managerial and nonmanagerial men and women, managerial women reported the highest levels of sex-role conflict of any of the other groups. This might be interpreted as an indication that they, more than any of the other groups, were violating societal expectations and feeling the results. Wiersma and Van den Berg found that work-home role conflict was negatively related to family climate for both men and women. The more that participants felt a conflict between their jobs and their families, the poorer the situation at home. This spillover effect can't be good for the relationships involved—or for the performance of these individuals on their jobs. Thus it is extremely important to remember that although role conflict may be most obvious in the reactions and behaviors of the single individual, all members of the group are involved in the problem. We will explore this complementarity of role conflict in the application at the end of this chapter when we consider Hillary Rodham Clinton, the types of role conflict she may experience, and the effects on the groups to which she belongs.

The studies cited in the previous paragraph all exemplified inter-role conflict of one type or another. A number of studies are beginning to report a number of situations where inter-role and intra-role conflict are both involved, further complicating an already complicated situation. Campbell and Snow (1992) and Cournoyer and Mahalik (1995) studied the effects of these confounded conflicts on men. Campbell and Snow found that male gender-role conflict and family involvement account for 46.8 percent of the variance in marital satisfaction. Men with lower levels of marital satisfaction were less able or willing to express emotions, had higher levels of conflict between work or school and their families, and lower levels of family cohesion. When Cournoyer and Mahalik compared college-age and middle-aged men as to their areas of conflict, they found the middle-aged men were less conflicted about success, power, and competition than were the college students. They were, however, more conflicted about how to allocate time between their work and their families. Thus their apparently more traditional sex roles allowed them to be comfortable with traditionally male characteristics, but confused about changing roles. The younger men were more comfortable about the idea of combining family and work, but more conflicted about the traditional "macho" sex-role characteristics.

Complex conflicts have also been found in studies on women. Burlow and Johnson (1992) studied African-American women with traditional or nontraditional careers. The women in traditional careers reported fewer conflicts. Since women of color have traditionally worked outside the home, choosing to work in traditional fields might constitute less of a conflict. Women in nontraditional careers such as construction or police work reported more career barriers, more career-related marital discord, less peer support, and perceived their barriers to career success as based on gender and racial discrimination, limited political clout, and colleagues' doubts about confidence. The women who would seem to "have it all" did—including increased problems apparently directly related to their success in breaking sex-role stereotypes.

A final study by Peters and Cantrell (1993) examined the sources of conflict in lesbian and heterosexual feminists. They found no gender differences based on gender-role orientation. This means neither group was more masculine or feminine than the other. Heterosexual women reported more inter-role conflict between their roles as daughters and work roles than did lesbian women. Lesbian women reported more conflict between their daughter and partner roles. They also reported less positive relationships with their co-workers and supervisors. This might have been based on disapproval of their sexual orientation on the part of their parents or colleagues, except for the fact that the amount of role conflict for lesbian women was unrelated to whether or not they had disclosed their orientation—or "were out."

Clearly the problem is not only getting more common and more complex, it is getting more serious. Despite the increase in the reported incidence of conflicts there is no corresponding increase in suggested solutions. No one seems to have any solutions other than the only slightly comforting fact that recognition of the problem and discussion may mitigate the problem somewhat. Inter-role conflict is based within the individual in that the conflicting roles are enacted by a single person; however, interpersonal role conflict is conflict between individuals rather than roles.

Interpersonal role conflict results when two or more individuals disagree over who should occupy a certain role in the group. Often the more controversial role in a group is that of leader. We more commonly think of this type of role conflict as competition. That's exactly what it is. If there's only one opportunity to lead and several individuals want the role, they will develop conflict within the group as they jostle for position. As the group matures, however, as we shall see in Chapter 3, conflict over the role of leader decreases as trust increases and the role is passed to the most capable member at any given time.

The final type of role conflict—**ethical conflict**—was studied by Brenner and Molander (1977) through a survey of readers of the *Harvard Business Review*. Simply stated, ethical conflict deals with the question of what's good for the organization vs. what constitutes ethical behavior. Fifty-seven percent of the respondents to the survey cited this as a problem in their careers. In other words, more than half the respondents felt that at times decisions they were expected to make for the good of the organization were in violation of the individuals' personal ethical standards. No gender data was reported, so it is interesting but probably not particularly useful to speculate on characteristics of the respondents.

Status

Status can be defined as the "prestige of the position" (Shaw, 1981, p. 271). It is a formal aspect of the group and implies that there are differing levels of status, thus a hierarchy. Differing roles are often associated with differences in status. And just as roles are group-specific, so is the concept of status. Status is often based on the extent of value of the individual to the achievement of group success (Baron, Kerr, & Miller, 1992). Thus one might have a high level of status in one group and not in another. *Status consensus* is the individual's level of status as agreed upon within the group (Wilson, 1996). Lack of agreement might serve as a source of conflict within the group. This could occur when an individual assigns herself a higher status within the group than do her peers.

It is important to make a distinction between status and power. Although the two are often related, they are not necessarily the same thing. Status is a formal aspect of the group—one's position on the organizational chart (e.g., one's title). *Power* is the ability to influence others' behavior. Put simply, status is the way it's supposed to be while power is the way it is. Thus, "the British monarch, for example, has exceptional status but relatively little power" (Baron, Kerr, & Miller, 1992, p. 87). Power will be discussed in Chapter 8 along with leadership.

While status often is based on ensuring success for the group (and probably should be in the best of all possible worlds), certain irrelevant personal characteristics may increase the likelihood of an individual being conferred status. The characteristics include gender, race, age, and physical attractiveness. As was true for sex-role stereotypes, white males in the United States have traditionally had more automatic status than women of any color. "In addition, sexual myths and paranoia about blacks and Latinos play an especially vicious role in undergirding white people's racial fears and stereotypes" (Blood, Tuttle, & Lakey, 1992, p. 139). They go on to state, "People are just beginning to have a glimpse of what oppression based on age involves. The fact is that our society is almost totally blind to the dignity and capacities of the very young and the very old" (pp. 139–140). In the United States, then, it could be argued that status has been positively related to the lightness of one's skin, as well as the "right" age, gender, and sexual orientation.

Violating the expectations about heterosexuality also costs in terms of status. Many homosexual men and lesbian women are not open about their orientation because of the oppression to which they may well be exposed—through legal channels, as well as the extreme fear and hatred of nonheterosexuals known as *homophobia*. Wisconsin Congressman Steve Gunderson was for six terms an extremely effective and well-respected Republican legislator in the United States House of Representatives. He was also gay, with a long-term life partner. This fact was not well known, as Senator Gunderson correctly anticipated the possible reactions to his "coming out." When he announced he would not run again, a grass roots movement was begun to encourage him to change his mind, because in his next term (which according to the polls he would probably have won) he would potentially assume the chairmanship of an agricultural committee extremely important to the Wisconsin economy. Any newly elected replacement would lack the seniority necessary to receive such a post. In the meantime, other individuals had expressed an interest in running to fill his seat. When it looked as if Gunderson might, in fact, change his mind, the Wisconsin media reported that Gunderson had been informed that his sexual orientation would become a central issue in the primary campaign in the form of a "smear campaign" should he run again. In order to spare his own and his partner's dignity, Gunderson chose not to seek to regain the office.

Individuals with those external characteristics that affect status in society often find that these external characteristics either artificially raise or lower their influence in a particular group. A student committee choosing which dance troupe to bring in for a performance on campus would probably find that the president of the student body would have undue status in the group (even if she was an engineering major and everyone else was from the dance department). Conversely, a community committee deciding whose statue to place in the new city park would probably virtually ignore the opinions of someone with a history of convictions for child molestation. But these outside influences may only be relevant if there are stratified levels of status within the group.

The need for levels of status within the group is often affected by the size of the group. The larger the organization, the more likely you will find multiple levels of status, simply to make management possible. Imagine trying to run General Motors as a democratic organization. It would simply be impossible because of the sheer numbers of people and tasks involved. One way to try to reduce the steepness (number of levels) of status in an organization is to break it up into smaller units, which might be more manageable with fewer status levels. Gore (the company that manufactures such products as Gore-tex fabrics) has dealt with this issue in the state of Delaware by having a number of small sites within mere miles of each other. By keeping the unit small, the need for many levels of status is reduced. Each unit is managed as a semiautonomous group.

Gender also has been seen to affect the preference for the number of levels of status in groups. In general (and remember, this **is** a generalization) men in groups are much more interested in increasing the number of levels of status. Tannen (1994) explains this as a by-product of men's tendency to be more comfortable communicating in ways that indicate who is "one-up" or "one-down" in terms of status in the conversation. Women, on the other hand, are more concerned with connectedness and positive relationships within the group and are less concerned with status differences (Forsyth, 1990). Thus rather than enhancing the number of status levels, all-female groups often will try to function in a "leaderless" fashion—which is often quite inefficient (as we'll discuss in more length in Chapter 8). This democratic tendency in female groups may be based on the anticipated effects of status differentiation on relationships between members in the group.

Think back again to the list of groups you made at the beginning of the chapter. Which groups have high levels of trust between members? Why do you think this is true of these particular groups? Are there any groups you listed where lack of trust is a problem? Can you identify the conditions that fostered this distrust? Is this group very effective in completing its tasks?

Interpersonal Relations: Trust and Cohesiveness

Probably the two most important aspects of the **interpersonal relations** in groups are *trust* and *cohesiveness*. "**Trust** refers to the confidence we have in other people that we believe we can predict their behavior and rely on our predictions" (Wilson, 1996). Deutsch (1960) believes that without trust a group cannot work together. Trust is partly a function of personal characteristics such as social orientation (to be discussed in Chapter 10 on social dilemmas) (Cunha, 1985), and partly upon a history of working together and having people perform in a trustworthy manner. As we will see in the next chapter, trust takes time to develop and is an aspect of the group that cannot be hurried, but must develop naturally if the group is to function well. Groups that do not develop trust between members function ineffectively in terms of production because their inability to trust each other to accomplish portions of the task may lead to great redundancy of effort or refusal to divide the group task into individual tasks for fear someone will drop the ball and hurt the group.

The strength of positive interpersonal bonds (such as trust and liking) in a group is known as **cohesiveness.** Cohesiveness is related to the productivity of the group, but not in a simple, direct fashion (Robbins, 1989). The two often appear together in a reciprocal relationship—in that high productivity is seen in groups with high cohesiveness and vice versa. The problem is that the direction of causation is not clear. Do groups succeed because they have high cohesiveness? Or does success lead to high cohesiveness?

Robbins (1989) posits a relationship between levels of cohesiveness and performance expectations. He believes that high productivity results from a combination of high cohesiveness and high-productivity expectations—everyone gets along and expects to do well. Moderate productivity is believed to result from one of two conditions: (1) low cohesiveness paired with high-productivity expectations (we're expected to do well, but we don't like each other enough to communicate or coordinate well), or (2) low cohesiveness and low-productivity expectations (we don't like each other and we expect to do poorly). Low productivity is expected to result from high levels of group cohesiveness paired with low-productivity expectations. In this situation we like each other so much and expect to accomplish so little that we can spend our time socializing rather than working.

Shaw (1992) cites a number of positive consequences for the group based on high levels of cohesiveness:

1. In highly cohesive groups there is more communication among the members.
2. In highly cohesive groups members are friendlier and more cooperative with each other.
3. Cohesive groups have a higher level of control and influence over the behavior of their members.
4. Groups with higher cohesiveness achieve their goals more effectively.
5. Cohesive groups express more satisfaction with the group experience.

Since cohesiveness is perceived as a positive characteristic, it is something that can, and should, be cultivated. Unlike trust, there are techniques that can be used to increase the cohesiveness of a group. The first involves creating a history—spending time together. Dating couples, for example, tend to draw closer when they have spent enough time together that they can say to each other, "Remember when we . . ." A history of success is even better. The Super Bowl win in 1997 by the Green Bay Packers seemingly brought all of Wisconsin together. In any public place it was probable that at least a third of the individuals would have some sort of Packer clothing on. In one extreme example, I was in a mall and a couple was wheeling their toddler in a stroller down the aisle of a store where I was browsing. The father wore a Packers turtleneck and jacket, the mother was in a Packers football jersey, jacket, and scarf, and the child was wearing a Packers jumpsuit, jacket, and hat. The child was clearly just beginning to talk and every few seconds exclaimed "Packers!!" while wildly clapping its hands. And no one in the store (except me) paid the slightest attention.

Another way to increase the cohesiveness of a group is to make admission into the group difficult. Exclusivity is attractive to many people. And we tend to value something equally to what it cost us to attain it. In dating, it has been found that women who will go out with anyone who asks are not perceived as being nearly as desirable as women who are very selective about whom they will date (Hatfield, Walster, Piliavin, & Schmidt, 1973). The reasoning is apparently, "she's very choosy and will only go out with the best and she's going out with ME! She's terrific!" Admission can also be made difficult by the severity of the initiation process that must be gone through (another form of cost). This initiation effect will be discussed as part of the process of socialization into the group in Chapter 3.

The size of a group is generally inversely related to its cohesiveness. This is at least partly based on the fact that the more people involved, the more potential relationships. Think of how much easier it is at my university to get to know everyone in the Psychology Club consisting of approximately 40 people compared to getting to know all 450 psychology majors! There is, however, an interaction between the size of the group, the gender of the individuals in the group, and cohesiveness. In a study examining the effects of gender and size on cohesiveness, groups of four or sixteen were either all male, all female, or mixed in gender. The same-sex groups were more cohesive when they were small. In the mixed group, the larger groups were more cohesive (Libo, 1953). Other aspects of same-sex groups have been found to affect cohesiveness.

Groups consisting of all same-sex members seek to forge bonds between and among themselves. They also try to force co-workers to "affirm their heterosexuality, femininity, or masculinity" (Reskin & Padavic, 1994, p. 12). This is just as true for male groups as it is for female groups. However the methods by which they go about establishing friendship, goodwill, and "normalcy" differ (Reskin & Padavic, 1994).

All-female groups often focus social interaction around personal issues. They talk about their male partners and their children and celebrate weddings and babies. Not only do these celebrations allow them to take time off work, they also help form a sense of community when there is diversity within the group. Women of whatever culture, ethnicity, or race have families and thus have these personal occasions in common with their different group members. Thus these celebrations help form bonds that strengthen cohesiveness.

Male groups, on the other hand, employ equally sex-role stereotypic methods of creating cohesiveness within the group. They engage in "gender displays" (Reskin & Padavic, 1994, p. 11) such as using sexual language and talking about sex. They will also seek to establish camaraderie and reduce status difference through rituals such as taking turns buying doughnuts or beers for the group.

When women enter all-male groups the groups often attempt to form cohesive bonds with each other that exclude the only woman. One technique is to talk incessantly about sports (which women aren't supposed to understand or like) or to discuss sex and exchange graphic sexual banter (which may be intended to embarrass the woman). Another technique is to deliberately refrain from swearing, talking about sports, or talking about sex and making it clear to the woman that she is the reason they cannot behave in their normal fashion and is, therefore, unwanted. In a bizarre sort of way, the presence of the outsider brings the others closer together and increases their cohesiveness.

Interaction

In the type of group we are examining, **interaction** is an integral part of the group process. The group meets to plan, or work on, or monitor progress on its task. There are the formal (the "meeting" part of the process) and the informal (task-irrelevant socializing) group interactions.

Wilson (1996) identifies three types of meetings/interactions of small groups. First is the **information-sharing meeting.** These meet on a regular basis, have a predictable agenda, and have established a clear set of procedures. There is, however, no expectation that any decisions will be made. An example of this type of meeting would be the City Council calling a "town hall" meeting to explain the new recycling system adopted for the city. The second type of meeting is designed to make a particular (or particular set) of decisions. **Decision-making meetings** can be exemplified by a sorority meeting to elect officers for the coming academic year, or the Supreme Court meeting to decide on cases. The final type of meeting is the *special-event meeting.*

> *The special-event experience is different from the other two kinds of meetings in some particular ways, but it is also sufficiently like the others—it may involve information sharing and/or decision making—to allow you to find some overlap. . . ."*
>
> **(Wilson, 1996, p. 10)**

An example of a special-event meeting would be the annual meeting of any large organization, such as the American Society of Criminology (ASC), where research and informational papers are presented, policy decisions are made, and professional contacts are established.

Interaction is certainly affected by the size of the group. There might be thousands of individuals at the ASC annual meeting and only five in the group assigned in your child development class to work on a project together. It's easy to guess where you'll have the most interaction with group members (think repeated, quality interaction, not just sitting in a room with 500 other people listening to a paper presentation).

Size is also going to affect the difficulty of the different types of meetings. Probably the most affected will be the decision-making meeting. As we will discuss in the chapter on decision making (Chapter 7), the more people involved in the decision, the more formal the process must become if the group is to come to a decision at all. Decisions on a bill in Congress must use far more rigid rules than a small committee. *Robert's Rules of Order* is an agonizingly detailed set of procedures written just after the Civil War (or the War Between the States, or the War of Northern Aggression, or the "recent unpleasantness" depending on where in the country you are reading this book) with which to conduct decision-making meetings (Robert, 1868). In the same way, the roles taken on by various individuals become more important to interaction as the size of the group increases. I'm much more likely to meet the president of the student body on my campus than I am the president of the United States of America.

Goals

Goals are the reason for a group's existence, the reason for existing as a group. Again, the group's goals can be formal or informal, depending upon the group. The nominating committee of the Democratic political party has the specific goal of identifying (and hopefully getting elected) a candidate from their party. A group of friends who went to college together and meet annually to keep up with each other obviously has a much more informal goal.

Formal group goals tend to be long-range (Wilson, 1996). They focus upon the attainment of some achievement or the end of some process. Goals steer group behavior in a specific direction and help to keep the group from straying off task and wasting resources. It's often difficult, however, if you start out with a long-range goal—however specific it might be (e.g., get a Democrat elected president)—to readily identify the actual behaviors necessary to attain that goal. If you are a college student, I would assume that your goal is to graduate. That's certainly an attainable goal—but not all at once. First you must go through a series of intermediate and short-term goals. In this case, an *intermediate goal* might be finishing the courses in your major. But before you can do that, you have to break it down even further into a short-term goal of deciding upon your major. Each semester (or quarter) you must attain the **short-term goals** of deciding upon, registering for, and passing certain classes.

To move back to the group level, in order to elect a president, the Democrats first must win enough electoral votes in enough states to win. But before that, they must decide who to run, which is decided at least in part by attaining enough delegates from enough states to nominate at the convention. This often involves winning primary elections or caucuses in the states. Although initially the order of determination may seem backwards, first the group should decide its ultimate goal, the intermediate goals necessary to get there, and the short-term goals necessary to reach the intermediate goals. The more behaviorally specific the goals, the easier it will be for the group to identify strategies to reach them. (This whole process, by the way, is known in business circles as *strategic planning*.)

Groups are, however, constituted of individuals. And these individuals may have their own personal agendas or *personal goals* for the group. This is not necessarily good or bad, as some personal goals support the group goals while some personal agendas subvert group goals. Take, for example, a committee that is organized to plan the Cherry Blossom Festival in Washington, D.C. each year. The formal committee goal is to arrange the events, invite the participants, etc. The **informal group goal** may be to have some fun and meet some interesting (or important) people in the process. Now let's look at the individual goals of two participants. Helga is a realtor. She has joined the committee for the same reason that she participates in a lot of committees—to make contacts. Often, when someone wants to sell or buy a house they choose their realtor either from direct experience in another real estate transaction, or through word-of-mouth recommendation. Thus it behooves her to work very hard and very efficiently to make a good impression on the other committee members so that when they need a realtor, they'll remember how capable she is and call her. Her individual goal certainly supports the group goal of planning an effective festival. Tallulah is going through a divorce. She's heard that this committee is a place to meet (and hopefully connect socially with) wealthy, important men. Instead of focusing on work, she's going to be spending her time socializing and flirting. This will probably get in the way of work being accomplished.

STOP If possible, watch the movie *The Big Chill* (1983). This movie depicts a reunion of college friends at the funeral of one from their group. In addition to the common goal which is to bury and mourn their friend, each individual has their own goals they wish to accomplish during the weekend the group spends together. Discuss these separate goals and how they contribute to the group.

Goals affect the productivity of the group. *Goal-setting theory* (Locke, 1968) states that specific, difficult goals result in higher productivity. We've already discussed why specific goals are desirable. But why difficult? Won't that discourage everyone if the goals aren't reached? Not necessarily. Think of it this way. You are a member of a group collecting for a charity. You establish a goal of $100,000. Despite all your efforts you "only" collect $90,000. Compare that to an established goal of $50,000, which you attain with ease. You've achieved your goal, but in the first instance even though the goal was missed, almost twice as much money was collected.

Who should establish the goals for the group? The leader? The group? Some outside entity? Sometimes that's not something over which the group has control. There is some evidence, however, that group participation in the setting of the goal will result in more effort to reach the goal (Latham & Yukl, 1983) and that groups will set and accept more difficult goals for themselves than they would accept from an outside source. And there is good evidence that participation in the goal-setting process does promote acceptance of the goals (Erez, Earley, & Hulin, 1985).

Temporal Change

Temporal change is simply the development of the group over time. A couple isn't the same after two years of marriage as they were on their first date. An intramural sports team is (hopefully) more effective by the end of the season than when they first formed at the beginning of the school year. Over time individuals have the opportunity to determine their roles, interact with each other, establish their status in the group, and accomplish other important tasks. We'll take the next chapter to discuss the process of group development. Fortunately for us, the process of change is so similar across different types of groups that we can look at patterns of development that are very broadly applicable.

Norms

"Norms describe how common behavioral and intellectual standards have developed in the group" (Moscovici, 1985, p. 373). Put more simply, **norms** are "the way things are done around here." All groups have norms. There is some controversy over whether norms are only implicit (unwritten) or whether they can also be explicit (written) (Andrews, 1988). I believe that only unwritten expectations qualify as norms. If they are explicit then they are not norms, they are rules. Rules are easier. You can look them up somewhere. If you are going to be attending an extremely formal dinner party and you expect to find four forks, three spoons, and five glasses, you can look in an etiquette book to find what utensil is used when, where, and how.

Norms are tougher to figure. If you take a new job that doesn't require you to wear a uniform, what are you going to wear the first day of work? How are you going to find out? How will you know whether people at this office are informal enough to discuss families and outside interests, or whether things are kept on a strictly businesslike basis? You're just going to have to fake it and hope you don't make a mistake. Generally, being as neutral yourself as possible and observing others for a bit will give you clues. However, don't worry about knowing if you break a norm. The group will let you know. In fact, often that's how we discover the existence and content of specific norms.

Most groups develop common classes of norms (Robbins, 1989). *Performance-related norms* tell members how hard to work, how to work, the appropriate level of output, and the appropriate types of communication. *Appearance norms* tell members how to dress to be identified as a member of the group. Gangs like the Los Angeles Crips or the Bloods have colors to indicate gang membership—the Crips wear blue and the Bloods wear red. Although it may sound trivial, individuals passing through "gang territory" and unaware of the gang colors have been killed for innocently wearing the "wrong" color clothing. *Informal social arrangements* norms govern behaviors such as who you routinely have coffee with on your breaks on the job. Over my years of teaching I've observed a norm that students use to govern their behavior. On the first day of class, they enter the room and choose a seat. The norm is that this becomes "their" seat for the remainder of the semester. Should someone else occupy that chair during a subsequent class, the "owner" often gets quite ruffled.

Finally, *allocation of resources norms* determine who gets the goodies. At my university, departments are given a certain number of "merit increase" dollars to distribute to faculty, but the way the money is distributed is up to the individual department. Some departments simply divide the money by the number of department members (not very good for motivational purposes, but it does tend to reduce conflict), while others create various forms of performance rankings and give differing amounts of money based on one's position in the rankings.

If all groups have norms, why do we have them? Baron et al. (1992) cite three reasons. The first reason is that controlling behavior through the use of norms may be crucial to the group's survival or success. Norms also make social life more predictable and efficient. Finally, norms reduce the uncertainty or confusion in unpredictable, unusual, or threatening environments. Norms are mechanisms of control. If you wish to belong to a group, you must follow the norms. Failure to do so jeopardizes your membership.

What if you break a norm? As mentioned above, you'll usually be quickly informed by the group that "that's not the way it's done around here." Usually an increased amount of attention is given to the norm-breaker in an attempt to bring the person back into line. If the individual still violates the norms, they may be excluded from the group.

If you think your behavior isn't controlled by norms, think again. Or try walking up the left side of a staircase. Or shaking hands with your left hand. Or walking up to someone you don't know very well and standing about six inches away while you speak with them. The word "norm" is the basis for the word "abnormal." We reserve that word for someone who won't or can't follow the norms of society. Such people frighten us. In extreme cases, we lock them up in mental institutions (Szasz, 1970).

In a course I teach on social psychology, I asked students, if they felt comfortable doing so, to identify a social norm and break it, then report the results to the class. One student, wearing a strapless, red sequined, floor-length evening dress, went to the (only) mall in town, and simply walked from one end to the other. Did I mention the student was male? And quite hirsute (hairy). He was approached by security guards five times for simply walking the length of the mall. He had broken no rules, but people stopped and stared, and some called security officers!

Summary

We've begun our journey into group dynamics by learning the very most basic principles of groups. We determined that this book will focus on small, task-oriented groups. We discovered that in all such groups there are task-related and socially oriented issues at both the formal and informal levels. We've defined groups as consisting of two or more people who assume roles in the group, who may have varying levels of status, who interact with each other, who develop different strengths of relationships (cohesiveness), who agree on goals as a group but still retain individual goals, who change over time, and whose behavior is governed by the development of norms for behavior.

Key Terms and Phrases

achieved roles
ascribed roles
clarity (of roles)
cliques
cohesiveness
complementary roles
complexity of roles
decision-making meetings
dyad (dyadic)
ethical conflict
formal aspects of groups
formal group goals
goals
grapevine
group dynamics
individual roles
informal aspects of groups
informal group goals
information-sharing meetings
interaction
interpersonal relations

jargon
nature vs. nurture
norms
productivity
roles
role conflict
role emergence
role expectation
role perception
role strain
short-term goals
size (of group)
small group
social dimensions
statistical significance
status
task dimensions
temporal change
triad
trust

APPLICATION

Hillary Rodham Clinton: A Study in Potential Role Conflicts

Hillary Rodham Clinton, wife of President Bill Clinton has lived a life full of potential role conflicts of all the types discussed above. Ms. Rodham was born in a Chicago suburb in 1947, and grew up during a time in American history when it was still unusual for women to graduate from college, much less take on serious careers. Her family was very traditional—two younger brothers, a father who owned his own business, and a mother who stayed home to care for the family. Her family was relatively well-off and lived in an upper middle-class suburb. Her family voted Republican, but was not particularly political. Although her mother had not attended college, she was determined that all of her children would receive college educations—regardless of gender. Hillary attended the very exclusive Wellesley College.

According to all accounts, Ms. Rodham took Wellesley by storm. She was extremely bright, aggressive, and popular. She majored in political science with a minor in psychology. During her senior year she was elected president of college government and her peers chose her to be a speaker at the commencement ceremonies. Her evolution into a strong, assertive, independent woman was evidenced by her speech. The invited outside speaker was Senator Edward Brooke of Massachusetts who was African-American and a liberal Republican. Ms. Rodham was so offended by his speech that she chose to rebut his remarks on the spot—a move considered radical enough in that place and time to land her a place in the pages of *Life* magazine.

During the 1960s many women attended college to "earn my Mrs." Ms. Rodham was definitely not one of them. After graduating from Wellesley, she attended Yale Law School, where during her second year she met Bill Clinton. His friend (and later cabinet member) Robert Reich told *Maclean's* magazine

Hillary Clinton smiles in spite of all of the potential sources of role conflict in her life.

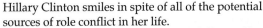

Clinton admitted that at first Hillary "scared him" (King, 1993). They dated for the next year, then after graduating in 1973, Clinton went back to Arkansas to teach law and Hillary took a job in Washington. They kept in touch through letters. In 1974, Hillary called the dean of the University of Arkansas Law School (who had previously offered her a job) and asked if there were any openings. She was hired to teach criminal law. She and Clinton resumed their relationship. They married in October of 1975; however, she did not change her name, retaining Ms. Rodham.

Clinton was elected attorney general of Arkansas in 1976. This required a move to Little Rock (the state capital) and a new job for Ms. Rodham. She was quickly scooped up by the Rose Law Firm, one of the most prestigious law firms in the city. Her primary interest carried over from her previous job with the Children's Defense Fund and she focused on laws and cases dealing with children's issues. Her success and her independence along with the philosophical support of her husband became an issue in his campaign for governor in 1978. Arkansas was not a liberal state and both Clinton and Rodham were perceived as having very liberal attitudes. However, that did not stop Clinton from being elected, at the age of thirty-two, the youngest governor in the United States. His liberal attitudes and actions (including the birth announcement for daughter Chelsea in 1980 as being born to "Governor Bill Clinton and Hillary Rodham" [King, 1993]) and his wife's continuing successful career instead of assuming traditional "First Lady" duties, proved too much for the electorate, however, and he was defeated in a reelection bid in 1980.

Clinton accepted a job at the Wright, Lindsey, and Jennings Law Firm, and rumors started to surface about extramarital affairs in which Clinton was involved. He ran for governor again in 1982, however, with a transformed wife. She had updated her appearance from her heavy glasses and "hippie" clothes and began to be known under the name of Mrs. Hillary Clinton. They won. Clinton continued to serve as governor of Arkansas with Hillary playing a large behind-the-scenes role in state education matters, continuing to practice law, and at the same time serving as "First Lady" (with all the associated ceremonial duties) and mother to Chelsea, until Clinton's election as president of the United States in 1992.

During the presidential election campaign, Hillary's feminism and independence again became an issue, as did the continued rumors of Clinton's extramarital affairs. During the campaign she made several comments in interviews that created much controversy. In order to counter the rumors of problems in the marriage, the Clintons gave a joint interview on the television show "60 Minutes" with interviewer Steve Kroft. It was scheduled to appear on January 30, 1992 immediately after the Super Bowl in order to attract the largest possible audience. When Kroft complimented them on working on their marriage and having reached an understanding, she insisted on her sincerity in supporting her husband by saying, "You know, I'm not sitting here some little woman standing by her man like Tammy Wynette" (King, 1993, p. 148). This incensed a lot of women who felt she was belittling the country singer who had "stood by her man" through a stormy marriage including drug problems. It also angered a lot of people with traditional ideas about women's roles and the role of the "First Lady" of the United States.

Later in the spring of 1992 when pressured about working as a lawyer and not staying home and being a homemaker, wife, and mother, she said, "I suppose I could have stayed home, baked cookies and had teas, but what I decided was to fulfill my profession, which I entered before my husband was in public life" (Brock, 1996, p. 265). Again the homemakers howled and many invidious comparisons were made of Hillary with then First Lady Barbara Bush—a white-haired grandmother who was extremely popular.

After the election, Hillary tried a number of ways to soften her image. She even had one of her favorite cookie recipes (that she baked with Chelsea) published in a woman's magazine. However, as evaluations of the first term were being made by a three-man committee appointed by the president to help with strategies for the campaign for a second term, the report was very negative. Part of this report, written by supporters of Clinton, is described as follows:

> *The book on Hillary Clinton was not much better. In general, the committee found that Hillary was perceived as a successful career woman who did not particularly care for her homemaking chores. She was seen as an outspoken, obstinate individual, very intelligent, very opinionated, very sure of herself. She also appeared overwhelmingly obsessed with power and career.*
>
> *She was thought to be domineering, cold, harsh, and defiant. Her attitude toward her husband was perceived as distant at best and glacial at worst. There seemed to be very little softness or femininity about her.*
>
> *. . . The good news? There wasn't any.*
>
> *(King, 1993, p. 164)*

As of 1998, Mrs. Clinton has been embroiled in a series of controversies and questioned by Independent Counsel Kenneth Starr regarding some potentially unethical and illegal financial dealings in real estate known as the "Whitewater" affair. In the meantime, alleged mistress Gennifer Flowers has become vocal again since the president has apparently admitted to a sexual relationship with her after previously denying the existence of any such relationship. White House intern Monica Lewinsky and her attorneys are dueling with Counsel Starr regarding a deposition she gave denying a sexual relationship with Clinton. Another woman, Kathleen Willey, has come forward and accused the president of assaulting her outside the Oval Office when she asked to meet with him. Yet, Hillary Rodham Clinton has been one of Clinton's staunchest and most vocal supporters throughout this whole situation.

Clearly, Mrs. Clinton has been forced to deal with a number of situations of role conflict. She is not a popular First Lady with the American people. She dared to violate many expectations. As one of her biographers stated:

> *Hillary may stand convicted of intellectual rigidity, elitism, moral vanity, and poor judgment. . . . Viewing her actions in light of the rough-and-tumble nature of American politics, one must finally ask: Has Hillary really done anything more egregious than that which most political figures do as a matter of course?*
>
> *(Brock, 1996, p. 417)*

Discussion Questions

Apply the concepts from the chapter to consider the following questions:

1. Identify at least one example of each of the types of role conflict (intra-role, inter-role, interpersonal role, and ethic role) as described above. What did Hillary do to solve the situations?
2. If the statement: " . . . was seen as an outspoken, obstinate individual, very intelligent, very opinionated, very sure . . . appeared overwhelmingly obsessed with power and career" was made about a male politician, do you think it would be so damning? Why or why not?
3. Discuss how the role of First Lady could represent an example of a compounding of intra-role, several flavors of inter-role, and interpersonal conflict. Is this situation inevitable, or did Hillary create her own problems?
4. Role conflict is complementary. What kinds of role conflicts do Bill and Chelsea Clinton suffer because of Hillary's behavior?

CHAPTER 2

Why People Form and Choose Groups

- **Introduction**
- **Why? The Functional Approach to Group Formation**
  - *Survival: Physical*
  - *Survival: Psychological*
  - *Socially-Based Needs*
- **How Do People Decide Which Groups to Join?**
  - *Social Exchange*
  - *Fairness*
    - *Equality*
    - *Equity*
- **Situations and Characteristics That Affect Attraction**
  - *Similarity*
  - *Geographical Proximity*
  - *Physical Attractiveness*

APPLICATION: The Psychological Function of Militias

What Would YOU Predict?

Robert, Louise, Meng, and David are college roommates. Although Robert and David are very good about paying their shares of the rent on time and keeping the apartment in good shape by doing their share of the housework, Louise often doesn't have the money for her share of the rent on the first of the month, and is very sloppy in her personal habits—leaving clothes laying around and dishes unwashed. Meng comes through each time and provides the money or cleans up the apartment. How do you think Louise feels? How do you think Meng feels?

INTRODUCTION

In Chapter 1 we defined groups and their characteristics. We still have not considered the reasons that people join groups or decide among the alternatives of which groups to join. In most situations people probably have multiple reasons for making specific choices. This is called **overdetermination.** So we'd be wasting our time to try to isolate the single reason. This idea of multiple causation will remain useful throughout the remainder of this text. When a group is not functioning as well as we would expect, or like, we should always consider

33

multiple causes for the dysfunction. Solving only one will generally not have much impact. In this chapter, then, we will explore the various reasons that might explain why people form groups, how they make the determination of which groups to join, and examine characteristics that affect our level of attraction to an individual or group.

WHY? THE FUNCTIONAL APPROACH TO GROUP FORMATION

So why do people form groups? There appear to be a variety of purposes for joining, but all appear to involve the satisfaction of some need by group membership, much in the same way that food satisfies the need we call hunger. This approach to explaining group formation is known as the **functional approach.** In each case we'll look for the function that the group serves for the individual. A number of different needs have been identified over the years covering a wide range of possible needs. Probably all are true to at least some extent. We'll divide the different types of **survival needs** satisfied by group membership into two categories: groups serving the function of physical and psychological function and groups that serve social needs. We'll consider each in turn.

Survival—Physical

The idea of group formation for physical survival comes to us from the discipline known as **sociobiology** introduced by E. O. Wilson. Sociobiologists believe that human social behavior is based upon some biological source—chemical (hormonal) or structural or genetic. The discipline is based upon the theory of evolution introduced by Darwin (1871). As you have probably studied in biology courses, this theory seeks to explain how various characteristics are passed down from one generation to the next. We know now that characteristics such as blue eyes are passed down in the genetic material in the sperm and ova supplied by the parents. Sociobiology takes an additional step in assuming that there are genes that also control behaviors. They identify all behaviors as having the single aim of perpetuating the species and assuring that our own genetic material will be passed along to the next generation. Thus they suggest that all behavior can be explained based upon some biological mechanism.

Based upon these assumptions, sociobiologists believe that early in the evolution of the human species, group membership was a survival-enhancing trait. Those who lived together in groups were more likely to live long enough to pass this tendency on to their offspring. Individuals who did not belong to groups were much less likely to survive to reproduce.

There is an impressive list of reasons why individuals in groups are more likely to survive: provision of food, defense, physical nurturance, and reproduction. If we go all the way back to hunting and gathering societies, it is easy to see why a group is at an advantage. The individual hunter or gatherer may or may not encounter enough food to satisfy their body's needs. The more people hunting or collecting plants and roots, the more likely it is that someone will find some—or if everyone is lucky, there will be lots of food. Groups are particularly useful in hunting. A single hunter may be forced to limit him- or herself to small game. A group can take on large game and can also increase the likelihood of a kill. Present-day hunters often engage in what they call a "drive" in which some hunters move through the territory deliberately making noise to frighten the game towards several members who stand ready to make the kill. Of course the downside to the fact that you are more likely to find food is that you have to share, but from the perspective of sociobiology, enough to sustain the group is better than a single individual having enough (and thus surviving) while the rest of the group starves.

Regardless of how skilled they are in defense of themselves, all humans suffer the defensive disadvantage of having to sleep. Sleeping individuals are vulnerable to attack. Once you have at least two people in a group, you can have constant defense by sleeping in shifts. A group is also able to take on a more substantial threat than a lone individual—in this case the old cliché, there is strength in numbers, is true.

The individual hunter or the pregnant woman who tries to go it alone can be particularly vulnerable. If the hunter breaks a leg and has no one to help, starvation becomes a grim, real probability. Or the individual's ability to protect himself may be so compromised that he falls prey to some other predator. Human women are vulnerable during the course of giving birth, and human babies are essentially helpless for an extended period of time and depend on others to keep them alive. Should a mother give birth away from others and die from complications, it is a virtual certainty that the child will also die. In a group, however, if the mother should die, others in the group can take on the task of nurturing the child and the mother's genes will have made it into the next generation.

Finally, and most obviously, natural reproduction takes two. While science marches on and in vitro fertilization and other transplant procedures are more common I suspect people will continue to prefer the old-fashioned method of reproduction.

STOP Make a list of all those people upon whom you depend for your survival. Consider your needs for shelter, food, protection, and procreation. Are there any other important survival needs that you feel should be included? Could you survive for any length of time physically without the aid of others? (There are some people who do, although I doubt college students are included in that category.)

Although I've placed these examples in the far distant past, most of these functional reasons for groups still exist. We depend on others to grow, process, and sell us our food (although rare individuals are able to take care of all of their own nutritional needs). We depend upon our military or our police to protect us. We take care of our ill and disabled. And we form bonds with partners which may lead to procreation. So it does appear that groups do serve the functional purpose of allowing us to survive. And if the sociobiologists are correct, then this tendency just keeps getting stronger and stronger as those without the genetic disposition decrease each generation.

The more we learn about child development, both physically and psychologically, the more we recognize the importance of the bonds that children form with adults. We do not have any direct experimental evidence in this area as the types of deprivation that would be necessary to expose vulnerable infants to would be cruel and unethical. Instead, we will examine animal research, personality theories, and research with slightly older children.

Early on in the exploration of this area of the **need for nurturance,** there were a number of competing theories as to why infants formed bonds with their primary caretaker. (From now on I'm going to refer to this person as mother because in our society it is still most often the mother who takes primary care of the infant. It is clear, however, that when the primary caretaker is the father the same types of bonds form with him.) What was not controversial, was the importance of bonding.

> *Attachment behaviour is regarded as a class of social behaviour of an importance equivalent to that of mating behaviour and parental behaviour. It is held to have a biological function specific to itself and one that has hitherto been little considered.*
>
> *(Bowlby, 1969, p. 179)*

Bowlby (1969) believed that "there is in infants an in-built propensity to be in touch with and to cling to a human being" (p. 178). This was one of the approaches, the others being based on the reinforcement value of receiving food from the mother or having other needs met. Bowlby was positing a need for physical cuddling and comforting and contact. He presented as proof of the bonding that formed between the mother and child the fact that the child generally begins to recognize and respond differentially toward the mother at about four months, and **proximity-maintaining behavior** is shown when the mother leaves and the child either cries, or, several months later when mobile, will follow her. Animal research on bonding produced results that indicated that the presence and comforting touch of the mother-figure provided important stability for infant monkeys (Harlow & Harlow, 1966).

Personality theorist Erik Erikson (1968) believed that personality develops through a series of steps or stages. Theories of this type are generically referred to as *successive stage* theories. The steps are believed to be the same for all entities explained by the theory, and they must be passed through in a very specific order. Erikson's theory of personality development meets these criteria. Erikson was a neo-Freudian who had adopted the idea of developmental stages from Freud. However, while Freud believed that the personality was basically completely formed by the age of six or seven years, Erikson's theory cites stages lasting through adult life. In each one of these stages Erikson believes that there is a psychological task or characteristic that must be acquired during this stage or it will not be developed unless there is later therapeutic intervention. Erikson believes that the task to be accomplished during the first year of life is the acquisition of trust. If children do not learn to trust during this time, they will be distrustful, particularly of other people, for the rest of their lives.

How did Erikson believe that children develop this ability to trust? After all, during most of the first year children are not capable of much voluntary behavior. They cannot talk in any meaningful way and until sometime close to the end of this period they are also sedentary. When an infant has any need—they're hungry, or uncomfortable, or frightened, or need a new diaper—they really only have one way of expressing themselves. They cry. Now, anyone who has been around an infant or infants for an extended period realizes that very early on children are able to vary the sound of those cries. In other words, a hungry baby does not sound like a baby in pain. Erikson believed that the responsiveness of the environment to the baby's needs was the key to forming the ability to trust. If a child's signals are met consistently with a helpful response, then they begin to learn that the world is a dependable, safe place.

There is research that would appear to support Erikson's theory. Those children who in the first year of life have a responsive environment develop a strong, **secure bond** and in Erikson's terms learn to trust. Children who are not so well treated develop **insecure bonds.** Cross-cultural research in this area has found that in North America, about two-thirds of children have secure attachments to their mothers. The types of insecure bonds develop differentially across cultures. In North America and Europe the avoidant style of insecure bond is the most prevalent of the three. In Israel and Japan, however, the resistant-insecure style is the more common (Van Ijsendoorn & Kroonenberg, 1988).

So it would appear that there is at least indirect evidence that there is an inborn human need for nurturance. Since this need must be satisfied by contact with another person and we have defined a group as potentially consisting of two people, then we can include this need as one of the reasons people form groups.

Another reason for group formation based on psychological survival is based on Freud's theory of the personality. Only one portion of the three (the **ego**) was *conscious.* The other two (the **id** and **superego** were described as *unconscious.* Freud was the first to introduce this idea that behavior could be controlled by portions of the personality over which we had no conscious control and to which we lacked access. Freud and the neo-Freudians who came after believed that the **unconscious psychological needs** controlled people's behavior so that the needs could be satisfied. Because these needs were unconscious, the person would not be aware of why they were performing certain behaviors. Measuring these needs or determining their existence is obviously problematical.

An entire classification of measuring devices, developed to measure the unconscious, are known as **projective techniques.** Projectives are based on ambiguity. The person being tested is given a stimulus or asked a question to which there is no clear correct or socially desirable response. The person thus is forced to fall back on their own personality and project (much as a movie projector throws a film on a blank screen) their personality onto the situation.

Murray developed the *Thematic Apperception Test (TAT)* to measure the unconscious needs (Murray, 1938). Among the needs Murray was interested in were the needs for affiliation and power. The test consists of black-and-white drawings of ambiguous situations and one blank card. The individual being tested is asked to tell a story about what is going on in the card. The blank card is obviously the ultimate projective tool as any story told must be coming from the individual. The individual is usually given about ten cards. Then the material given is examined for themes.

> *In assessing the importance or strength of a particular need or press for the individual, special attention is given to the intensity, duration and frequency of its occurrence in different stories, as well as to the uniqueness of its association with a given picture.*
>
> *(Anastasi, 1968, pp. 499–500)*

There have been serious questions about whether the TAT is measuring unconscious needs or the individual's imagination (Anastasi, 1968). So why are we discussing the TAT at all? Because Murray posited the unconscious needs for **affiliation** and **power** and needed a way to measure them. Affiliation is the need to be around other people. Power is the need to control others. Obviously joining a group would be a way to satisfy both of these needs. These needs are perceived as individual difference factors, which simply means that some people will have a high need for affiliation while others have a low need for affiliation. Thus joining groups would be much more important for the first individual than for the second.

"I have to take one three times a day to curb my insatiable appetite for power."

Source: © The New Yorker Collection 1977 Dana Fradon from cartoonbank.com. All rights reserved.

Since projectives have inherent problems (although they do tend to predict behavior fairly accurately), another method of measuring these needs was developed. The *Fundamental Interpersonal Relations Orientation (FIRO-B)* was developed to measure three needs: (1) inclusion, (2) control, and (3) affection (Schutz, 1966). The needs were measured along a continuum. The need for inclusion was described as, at one end, the wish to be involved, to be with others, and at the opposite end, the desire to be left alone or ignored. This sounds a great deal like Murray's need for affiliation. The need for control was described as ranging from the need to influence, lead, and be dominant and persuasive to wanting to be influenced, lead, dominated, and persuaded. This would appear to correspond to Murray's **need for power.** Finally, Schutz's third need was the need for affection—ranging from wanting to have intimacy and warmth in relationships to wanting to be distant and not closely attached to others. It would seem that the primary difference in inclusion and affection is the difference between quantity and quality of relationships.

This test would appear to deal with our problems with the TAT. It correlates with behaviors; behaviors described by Murray as indicating the existence of certain unconscious needs. Satisfaction of these needs requires other people. So again we have identified a functional reason for group formation based on the need to ensure psychological survival. We will turn now to socially-based needs that can be satisfied by group membership.

Socially-Based Needs

The first socially-based classification of needs to be satisfied by group formation and membership is the group of **informational needs.** If I want to know how warm it is outside, I can measure the temperature using a thermometer. If I want to know how tall I am, I can measure my height with a tape measure or yardstick. If, on the other hand I want to know whether the course on group dynamics is difficult, or who is the "best" dog in a dog show, I have to depend upon the information I can get from other people.

STOP Have you ever taken someone shopping with you to determine how you look in a particular garment? Have you solicited someone's opinion of a movie before spending your own money to see it? How many other ways can you think of that you acquire important information from other people? Discuss this with your class or group (another example of obtaining information from others).

When you stop to think about it, there is really very little we know that comes from an objective measure such as a thermometer or a yardstick. So our source of validation and information comes from others. Festinger (1954) referred to this process as **social comparison.** We use the process of social comparison to help us evaluate ourselves. There are three basic tenets of this theory: (1) people have the need to evaluate their own opinions and abilities accurately, (2) without having direct physical standards (like the thermometer)

Two young women demonstrate
the exchange of information as
they advise each other on their
clothing selections.

we compare ourselves to others, and (3) we want to compare with others who
are similar to ourselves. In order to see the power of these effects, we turn now
to the classic literature in the field by examining a series of research studies.

Sherif (1935) was one of the first to recognize the power of other's opinions
on our own. He based his study on an interesting physical phenomenon known
as the **autokinetic effect.** In a totally blackened room, a stationary point of light
if stared at long enough will appear to start to move around. This is part of the
wiring of the visual system. And it is important in this study to remember that
the light never moves. In the first stage of the research, Sherif brought individuals into the darkened room, asked them to stare at the light, then to estimate
the distance it moved. Then another individual was brought into the room. This
person was a confederate of Sherif's—an individual whose behavior had been
coached in advance. The confederate was to make a guess of the movement of
the light which was either much higher or lower than the guess of the research
participant. After discussion between the two, participants' guesses soon
moved closer to that of the confederate (in both situations—higher and lower
guesses). Again, the light NEVER moved. So the participant was influenced by
the information received from the confederate.

Estimating the distance a light moves is really a relatively trivial task. Suppose we have to evaluate a situation and determine whether there is an emergency to which we need to respond. What then? Latane and Darley (1970) asked
college men to fill out some questionnaires in a small room. One group of the
men were alone in the room, the others filled out the forms in the company of
two confederates of the experimenters (of course the actual research participants did not know that they were confederates). As soon as the experimenter
left the room, smoke began billowing out of a vent in the wall. Smoke is not
usually a good sign in a room without a fireplace. The experimenters had

ordered the confederates to behave as if nothing was happening. The smoke became so thick that it was difficult to breathe in the room. Participants who were alone in the room didn't have anyone from whom to gather information. Most of them got up, walked around the room, and within four minutes 75 percent had left the room to find the experimenters. When the participants were with the confederates, only 10 percent reported the smoke. They just sat there and choked! The information they were indirectly receiving from the confederates was that the situation was not an emergency, and that's the way they behaved.

Some psychologists even believe that we depend upon information from others to identify what emotions we are feeling. Schacter's (1964) theory of emotion states that emotions consist of two parts. The first is the degree of physiological arousal experienced. (The arousal he refers to is the agitated state brought on by the release of the chemical epinephrine which triggers the **fight-or-flight** response in humans.) The second component of emotions consists of the cognitive label we attach to those physical sensations. If we have a logical explanation for the feelings, we won't attach an emotional label. If my hands are shaky and sweaty and my heart's beating fast but I also remember that I've had an entire pot of coffee to drink that day, I'll write off the feelings to caffeine and go on about my business. If, however, I have no good explanation for the feelings and I'm talking to an extremely attractive man, I might interpret these feelings as indicators of attraction.

To test this theory, Schacter and Singer (1962) injected participants with epinephrine. They told half about the real symptoms and effects associated with the chemical. The other half of participants who received the injection were given a false set of symptoms—including dizziness and headache. The subjects were then placed in a room with a confederate. Half of the confederates acted very happy and euphoric. The other half acted extremely angry. So we have four groups: knowledgeable-epinephrine with a happy model; knowledgeable-epinephrine with an angry model; innocent-epinephrine with a happy model; and innocent-epinephrine with an angry model.

The theory would predict that those who could correctly identify the source of their physical state would not use an emotional label, and would not report feeling any particular emotion. It would predict that those who received the stimulant but didn't know that it was the source of their arousal would look to the emotional state of the model (angry or happy) and identify their own emotional state as matching the model. That's just what happened.

So far, then, we have evidence that—in an ambiguous opinion situation, a potentially dangerous ambiguous situation, and in a situation where we are required to identify something as basic as how we are feeling—we depend upon others for information. Now we're going to take a little digression. I promise, however, we're coming back to this same discussion of informational needs.

Another area that interested Schacter was the effect of anxiety on the desire to be with other people (affiliation) (Schacter, 1959). He recruited two groups of female college students to participate in an experiment on the perception of pain from electric shocks. To one group he gave instructions intended to create a high level of anxiety. He told them that they would be receiving very strong shocks that were very powerful but wouldn't do any permanent damage. The second group was intended to create low fear so the shocks were described as so weak they would feel like a "tickle." Each group was told they would have to wait ten minutes while the shock generator was calibrated. They were told they could stay in the room with the other participants, or they could go into individual cubicles. So he asked them to write down their preference and the strength of that preference. In the high-fear condition, 62.5 percent of the participants wanted to stay right where they were. If fear were not affecting the choice, it should be 50/50 as to where the women chose to wait. In the low-fear condition, 33 percent of the women wanted to stay together.

In a follow-up study, Schachter created high-fear groups and offered them a choice of waiting alone or with other study participants for one group, and for the other group their choice was waiting alone or with a group of students waiting to see their academic advisors. The preponderance of students wanted to wait with other study participants.

The question, of course, is WHY do these people want to affiliate when they're frightened? One more study and I think you'll see how this loops back into informational needs. Hospital patients waiting to receive heart bypass surgery were given a choice of roommates. They could room with someone who was also awaiting the surgery, or they could have a roommate who had already undergone the surgery (Kulik & Mahler, 1989). Patients overwhelmingly wanted to room with the patient who had already had the surgery.

The reason for this choice is the same as for the Schacter studies. Patients wanted to talk with the roommates about the surgery to gather information about what to expect. The same was true of the participants in Schacter's studies.

There are other compelling socially-based reasons to join groups. We may join groups for emotional support (as is discussed in Chapter 11), we may join study groups for tangible assistance, we join a group such as a political party because we share common goals with the group. We may also join groups because we identify with the group (Go Spurs!). Or perhaps our membership in and identification with a large group such as an ethnic group or gender-based group is essential to our self-concept and self-esteem. Clearly then, the tendency to join groups is probably overdetermined and has as much to do with our survival as our social needs. Given that we are going to join groups, the next question is how do people choose which groups to join?

HOW DO PEOPLE DECIDE WHICH GROUPS TO JOIN?

Although there has been a relatively large amount of research on what characteristics and situations attract people to each other, there are not many theories that seek to integrate the information. We will discuss several of these theories.

Social Exchange

The first theoretical approach is the social exchange perspective. Social exchange refers to an individual's analysis of the costs and rewards that will be incurred by establishing a relationship or entering a group. Because of the social norm of reciprocity, there will always be an expectation that we will return favors or in some way make up for the goods we receive from others (Gouldner, 1960).

This norm is what makes us uncomfortable when someone does something for us that we cannot for some reason repay. It is not uncommon for someone who has been rescued from a life-threatening situation to appear ungrateful when in fact they simply know of no way in which to repay or reciprocate such a profound act. Individuals in this situation feel even worse when the hero is a stranger. At least with someone we know and with whom we have an ongoing relationship, there will be future opportunities to gradually even the situation.

According to Foa and Foa (1974), there are six types of rewards we can reap by belonging to a group: (1) love, (2) money, (3) status, (4) information, (5) goods, and (6) services. These can be arrayed along two dimensions: *particularism* and *concreteness*. Particularism is the amount of the value of the reward based upon who provides the reward.

> *The value of love, or more specifically of such things as hugs and tender words, depends very much on whom they come from. Thus love is a particularistic reward. In contrast, money is useful regardless of whom it comes from, money is a nonparticularistic or universal reward.*
>
> **(Sears, Peplau, & Taylor, 1991, p. 224)**

Concreteness is the extent to which the reward is tangible as compared to symbolic in nature. Money is quite concrete; love or status are symbolic. The amount and types of rewards we receive in the social interaction will influence how desirable we find the group after we have balanced them against the costs involved. Costs include such things as time, energy, resources, and having to make choices about how to use them. A group that requires us to put in a great deal of time, energy, and creativity to the extent that we must forgo some other, more pleasant form of behavior, will need to be rewarding in some important ways or we will not consider the exchange "worth it." Let's say that you are considering joining a social fraternity. As a new member you may be required to purchase clothing (such as a jacket with the name of the fraternity), you might be expected to put in some time as a pledge helping with the upkeep of the fraternity house, you might be required to spend a certain number of evenings studying under the supervision of the "pledge master," and you certainly will be expected to attend fraternity functions. This may be balanced by the status you gain on campus for belonging to this particular fraternity, the fraternity might have access to a ski cabin and another on a beach, and your membership might help you increase your status further by helping you get elected student body president. However, those costs might not be worth it if you have just begun to date a woman from a "rival" sorority who would like to have you study and socialize with her.

Up to this point in the discussion we've talked about the balance of costs and rewards as if this balance influences both the desirability of joining and belonging to a group and whether or not we will continue to be a member of the group. Another approach to social exchange is a theory by Thibault and Kelley (1959) which considers these two dimensions—satisfaction and retention—as two separate issues. Thus it is not automatically the case in **social exchange theory** that if we are happy in a group we will stay and if we are unhappy we will leave.

I'm sure almost everyone has at one point in time or another had a job they hated. Between college and graduate school I had a secretarial job at which I was miserable. I would start watching the clock immediately after I arrived and count down to break time. Then to lunch. Then to quitting time. If I was so unhappy, why did I stay? I needed to support myself and at the time the economy was in bad shape and jobs were hard to come by. As soon as I found a better job, I did leave. This separation of the two issues is what differentiates Thibault and Kelley's theory from others we have (and will) discuss.

The amount we are attracted to a group or relationship and how satisfied we are once there is determined, according to this theory, by our **comparison level** (abbreviated **Cl**). This is the amount we believe we deserve to receive in the situation. Each person's comparison level is different because it is based upon our own idiosyncratic history. If we were treated as the little prince as a child, we may as an adult expect to continue to be treated royally. Our comparison level may also change as we have new experiences. In order for us to be satisfied in the group, the amount of rewards we are receiving must at least match our comparison level. If we're getting enough, we're satisfied. If we're getting more, we're happy.

But because comparison levels are so individual, the same number of rewards that makes me happy in a group might make you miserable, because my comparison level is so low that a relatively modest number of rewards suffices. Your comparison level, however, is much higher than mine, and is also higher than the amount of rewards we are receiving. If, over time, I come to expect more and you come to expect less, then our individual levels of satisfaction may change. But our level of satisfaction is not related to whether or not we continue with the group.

Continuation with the group is based on our **comparison level for alternatives** (abbreviated Cl_{alt}). The theory assumes that we will be aware of the environment and any alternative situations we could enter. We can leave relationships, we can change churches, we can leave jobs, or drop out of clubs. And we will if we find one that looks better to us. And that's an important point to make. It's our perception of the preferability of the other situation that makes up our minds. We may or may not be correct in our perceptions.

By separating the two dimensions of satisfaction and continuation, this theory rather neatly explains what otherwise might strike us as confusing situations. Thus happy people sometimes leave groups, and unhappy ones sometimes stay. If you have a job where you are satisfied with the work you do, like your co-workers, and are receiving an acceptable salary, you may be relatively content. But if you get a call from a "headhunter" offering you a position that pays an additional $10,000 per year, you will probably leave. (Unless you perceive that the money is being used as a lure because the job is so horrid.) Or, if you are dating a man who is good to you and you care for him, but you run into the "love of your life" at your high school reunion, find out he's recently divorced, and interested in starting to see you again, you may very well drop the first relationship.

A question that many people ask about battered spouses (male or female) is "Why do they stay? Why don't they just leave?" This theory can explain this very well. First of all, the person who is being abused may be extremely unhappy. Or they may have over time begun to believe that they deserve the mistreatment they are receiving. But most often, they feel there aren't any viable alternatives. The breakup of any marriage, whether or not both partners work, reduces the money available to each while increasing the expenses. Each must now pay for housing and food. If there are children, they will usually stay with the mother (although that depends upon which spouse is the abuser). If she takes the children, she now must alone pay for their expenses. Often she leaves with just the clothes on her back so all the clothing and household goods must be replaced. And for the biggest cost of all, a woman is much more likely to be killed by her spouse if she tries to leave. Safety becomes a huge factor so she just stays and takes the beatings. Even with all the attention being paid to the problem of spouse abuse there are not enough safe places or shelters to provide means of escape. For many abused spouses, the alternatives look like jumping from the frying pan directly into the fire.

The approaches to social exchange, then, are all based upon a cost-benefit analysis of the situation. Are we getting enough out of the group to be satisfied? Is the group costing too much compared to our rewards? Can we find another group where the balance will be more to our liking?

 Have you ever stayed with a job or in a group where you were unhappy? Why? Does the social exchange theory explain the reasons satisfactorily? Can you give other reasons why you stayed?

Fairness

The second aspect of theory regarding satisfaction in groups takes a slightly different tack. The question here is whether or not we feel we're being treated fairly. Now, "fair" is a relative word. What I consider fair, you might consider grossly unjust. The question of fairness comes into play in groups when we consider how we'll distribute rewards—the "goodies" that come from working with the group.

Equality

One system of distribution is *equality*. The rewards are simply divided by the number of people contributing. People who don't want to work very hard or contribute very much to the group tend to like this distribution system very much. People who work very hard and contribute "more than their share" tend to really dislike this system. It certainly does not help to motivate hard work. If I am guaranteed an equal share of profits, where's my motive to contribute? When motivation is not a problem, however, when all of us in the group are intensely involved in the project and know that the effort will result in a better outcome of the task leading to higher rewards, equality is an acceptable distribution scheme. Women also tend to favor distribution by equality whereas men prefer other schemes we'll discuss later. This harks back to Tannen's (1994) work on the tendency for men to identify a one-up position for themselves in the group while women favor connection. Equal outcomes tend to establish a less hierarchical system.

One aspect of human nature that both social exchange approaches and equality of distribution of rewards tend to overlook is our tendency to compare what we receive with what others receive. People don't work in a vacuum—particularly in a group. Employees in organizations compare the sizes of their raises, students in classes compare their grades on exams, and children can be exasperatingly precise about just how many pieces of candy each one receives. Let's go with the candy example for a moment. If Bobby goes to ten houses on Halloween and gets fifteen pieces of candy and his brother Bill goes to thirty houses and gets sixty pieces of candy, although Bobby might be jealous of the sheer volume of candy, odds are good that he'll recognize that Bill worked harder for his rewards. But if they go to the same number of houses and Bill comes home with more candy, Bobby is likely to feel cheated—and Bill might feel guilty because the situation is not fair.

Equity

So now we've come upon another concept of fairness—**equity.** Equity can be defined as the situation in which a person's profits are proportional to their contributions (Deutsch, 1985). So those who work harder, profit more. And despite the howls of protest I get from student groups when I force them to assign grades but preclude them from giving everyone the same grade (an equality-based distribution scheme), I firmly believe that in every group there is some differentiation in the amount of contribution across group members.

Walster, Walster, and Berscheid (1978) formalized a theory of equity. It is based upon three principles:

1. People will try to maximize their outcomes;
2. Groups can maximize collective rewards by making rules about reward distribution; and
3. When we feel the distribution of rewards has been inequitable we feel disturbed and will move to restore equity.

In other words,

1. People want to get as much as they can;
2. Groups can decide how they will share the wealth by using some scheme (equity or equality) of reward distribution;
3. If I feel the rewards were not fairly distributed, then I'm unhappy and I'll try to do something to "fix" the problem.

We can also express the principle of equity in an equation:

$$\frac{\text{My outcomes}}{\text{My contributions}} = \frac{\text{Your outcomes}}{\text{Your contributions}}$$

This equation represents a situation of equity—I won't care if you get more as long as you've "earned" it in some way. If I am hired into the same department of an organization in which you work and I handle only ten accounts and get paid $20,000 a year, I'm not going to resent your earning $45,000 a year if you handle more accounts, have more seniority, and handle more important accounts.

However, if we're hired at the same time, with the same education, handle the same level of accounts but the equation looks like this:

$$\frac{\text{My outcomes} = \$20,000}{\text{My contributions} = 20 \text{ accounts}} = \frac{\text{Your outcomes} = \$30,000}{\text{Your contributions} = 20 \text{ accounts}}$$

I will not be a "happy camper." We're making the same contributions, but you're getting more. I will perceive the situation as inequitable. (According to the theory, so will you. Remember Bill and Bobby. We'll expand on these feelings shortly.) In this situation I will feel **underbenefitted.** This is the distress Walster et al. describe in step 3 of their model. I'm unhappy and I want it fixed. I want equity restored. In this situation, you are **overbenefitted**—you are getting more than you've earned. In the final version of the Halloween example, Bill was overbenefitted while Bobby was underbenefitted. A situation of inequity existed. Inequity has been related to negative moods in married couples (Schafer & Keith, 1980) and in friendships in elderly widows (Rook, 1987).

There are two approaches to restoring equity to this situation. I could actually change one of the numbers in the equation. I could insist that my workload be reduced so that proportionally I'm making the same per account as you are. I could insist on a raise. Bobby could insist on more candy. I could also try to affect your numbers. I could ask the boss to give you more work or to reduce your salary (neither of which, I suspect, you'd perceive as a friendly move). Or Bobby could ask their mother to take away some of Bill's candy.

If I'm able to change anything at all, it will probably be my side of the equation. Another approach would be for me to simply work less hard. In any case, I'm changing the reality of the situation or restoring **actual equity.**

Or, perhaps I recognize that I really don't have much chance of changing the actual situation. In this case I may reconsider the situation. I may be able to rationalize a reason why I'm getting less. Maybe I went to a less prestigious school, or did less well in school, or came into the job with less work experience than you did. Maybe Bill feels he deserves more candy because he was required to supervise Bobby and thus the extra candy is justified because of his extra responsibility. All of these things might affect my perception of your contributions and I can rationalize why our outcomes are unequal. This is called restoring **psychological equity.**

Remember I mentioned that according to the theory you should also be distressed by the inequity of the situation (even though you are the one receiving the benefit of the inequity). You might feel guilty because the social norm of equitable fair play is being violated (Brehm, 1992). Actually, however, some research shows that overbenefitted individuals do not always feel bad or guilty (Hatfield, Greenberger, Traupmann, & Lambert, 1982; Traupmann, Hatfield, & Walster, 1983). If you are feeling bad, you could restore actual equity by going to the boss and asking for more work, asking for a decrease in salary, or just working as hard as you can to deserve the extra outcomes. You're probably more likely, however, to move to restore psychological equity.

Schemes that have actually been tried to motivate workers include overpaying them in proportion to the work they are doing. Supposedly this creates a feeling of being overbenefitted and the workers will work harder. It actually works for just about as long as it takes workers to rationalize why they really are worth so much, and the level of productivity drops right back to where it was. It appears, then, that there is a relationship between the type of inequity felt and the preferred method to solve the problem. People who are underbenefitted want things fixed—they want actual equity restored. People who are overbenefitted can figure out reasons why the situation isn't inequitable after all—they restore psychological equity.

In our roommates' situation stated at the beginning of the chapter, Louise is being overbenefitted and Meng is being underbenefitted. My guess is that Meng would be more unhappy than Louise and might restore actual equity by doing less, or restore psychological equity by convincing herself that Louise has too many classes and needs time to study so she can pull up her grade point average to graduate. Or Meng might confront Louise and ask that she carry her share of responsibilities. One factor that might affect the choice is how long they have been roommates. The level of development of a group affects the willingness to engage in conflict, as will be discussed in Chapter 3.

There is, of course, one other solution to the problem of being underbenefitted. That is leaving the situation either physically or psychologically. Walster, Trapmann, and Walster (1978) found that underbenefitted spouses were particularly likely to engage in extramarital affairs—a way of mentally leaving the inequitable situation. If Meng felt that Louise would not change, she might find another place to live.

SITUATIONS AND CHARACTERISTICS THAT AFFECT ATTRACTION

Having discussed the theories that affect attraction to a group, we shift our attention now to the situations and characteristics that increase attraction to others—to make us want to form relationships and groups. The three most important of these are *similarity*, *geographical proximity*, and *physical attractiveness*.

Similarity

We're attracted to people and groups we perceive to be similar to ourselves. These **similarities** can initially be based on extraordinarily superficial characteristics. For example in the psychology of women class I teach I find that the few men who take the course all sit together. In my group dynamics course, which is composed about equally of psychology and therapeutic recreation majors, people sort themselves out by major. Even if they don't know someone personally, if they recognize that person from another class and can thus identify some level of similarity, it's preferable to sitting next to a stranger. Two American tourists who run into each other in Paris (one from Texas and one from Maine) might well become the best of friends as long as they're in Paris. Back home, there will be many other people with whom they share more in common.

As we get to know people better, we are most attracted to those people and groups who share our beliefs, values, and attitudes. If we play chess and not soccer we join the chess club and not the soccer team. Simply put, we like to be with people whose attitudes and values agree with our own, and dislike being with those who disagree with us (Byrne, 1971).

There are a number of reasons why that might be the case. First of all, it is very supportive to have someone agree with us. It reinforces our belief that we are right. And we're attracted to those people who are clever enough to agree with us. Sharing attitudes makes us look good. And as a group sharing the same attitudes, we can reinforce each others' position. People don't randomly attend the church nearest their home. Catholic dogma preaches against birth control and abortion. By being together, Catholics reinforce these teachings. An agnostic who happens to live on the same block as the Catholic church won't attend. If they perceive themselves as spiritual they might seek out a Unitarian church to attend. Or they might choose not to join that type of group at all. People who are in favor of the death penalty do not join the American Civil Liberties Union and people who do not support the Second Amendment of the Bill of Rights of the U.S. Constitution do not join the National Rifle Association.

There are some situations in which we avoid individuals we perceive as similar. If we feel that the characteristics that we share lower our status or stigmatize us, we'll not want to join their groups (Novak & Lerner, 1968). One reason that some individuals will avoid treatment for a problem such as impotence or alcoholism or child abuse is that they do not want to be identified as or admit being someone with that problem. In the 1970s I worked with the UCLA Child Trauma Intervention Project. Our goal was to determine the most effective group therapy for adjudicated child abusers, which means they had all been convicted in court. At that time it took an overwhelming amount of evidence to convict someone so our clients were undoubtedly not innocent victims of the system. Yet when each group started that's exactly what they all insisted. They all wanted to avoid having to meet with "people like that."

Geographical Proximity

Geographical proximity is a second strong influence on attraction. It is also not unrelated to similarity. People are not randomly assigned to neighborhoods. They buy houses they can afford (financial similarity) and often specifically look for certain characteristics of the neighborhood. If people have small children, they look for an area that has kids on the block. If people are older they may look for the absence of children on the block. But even when propinquity is random, such as seating assignments in classrooms or desk placement in an office or neighbors in a college dormitory, it is more likely that these individuals will bond than they would with the student across the room, the worker on another floor of the office, or someone whose suite is in a different dorm.

Probably the primary reason for the strength of the **proximity** effect is the fact that we are repeatedly exposed to the person who lives next door, or sits next to us in class (Harrison, 1977). These people are readily accessible for interaction. After you've sat next to someone for ten weeks, three times a week, it becomes a little odd if you don't at least comment on the weather or chat about your weekend plans. If you discover some similarities, so much the better. But it has been found that mere exposure increases liking (Moreland & Zajonc, 1982).

Lots of contact gives us a sense of familiarity with the person, which can lead to a sense of comfort. If you are walking across campus at eleven o'clock at night, there's no one else around, and you suddenly hear footsteps behind you, you would probably be at least mildly concerned. If you turn and find a classmate or a neighbor you will probably be much more relieved and comfortable than if it turns out to be a stranger approaching you.

We can also look to learning theory to explain why proximity can lead to attraction. Suppose you go to a club to hear a band you really like. There you run into a colleague from work. Having pleasant interaction with this person in a situation that makes you happy is the equivalent of classical conditioning (Lott & Lott, 1974). If you have a good time in the presence of this person repeatedly, you will come to associate this person with having a good time and will seek them out (Byrne & Murnen, 1988). In addition to just the mere association with a good time, whenever we perform a behavior that results in positive outcomes for ourselves, we are likely to repeat that behavior—sort of like dog training. Instead of sitting on command and receiving a doggie treat, we repeat behavior (in this case interaction) that makes us feel good—sort of like a "people treat."

STOP What is the primary characteristic you look for in a potential romantic or dating partner? If you answered physical attractiveness, you're more honest than most. Actually, men are more likely to admit to going after looks; women are more likely to deny the fact while their behavior belies their words. Why is physical attractiveness so important? What would the sociobiologists give as a reason?

Physical Attractiveness

There is a long history of research on the effects of **physical attractiveness** on attraction in human beings. Although standards of physical attractiveness vary somewhat by culture and time, at any given time there is a culturally agreed upon standard of how people should look. And the research shows that practically from birth people conforming to the standard of attractiveness are treated more positively than those who are not as "pretty." Pretty babies get talked to more and pretty kids are treated more leniently in school (Dion et al., 1972). Teachers evaluate cute kids as smarter and more popular than other children with the same academic records (Clifford & Walster, 1973). Students rate a lecture more positively by a female professor if she is perceived as physically attractive (Chaiken et al., 1978). In mock jury studies, physically attractive defendants were given lighter sentences for most offenses (Landy & Aronson, 1969). And in mock jury studies examining the physical attractiveness of rapist and victim, it was found that physically attractive rape defendants were less likely to be convicted—especially if the alleged victim was described as not particularly attractive (Oyster-Nelson, Woods, Foney, Franklin, & Griffin, 1982).

So we want to be around attractive people. Why? There are several probable explanations. The first is based upon a social-psychological principle known as "what is beautiful is good" (Dion, Berscheid, & Walster, 1972). If a person is a "pretty package," we assume that everything about them must be positive. They must have a great sense of humor, be good to their mothers, and have a great future ahead of them. The second is that all cultures value that which is aesthetically pleasing, and an attractive person is pleasant to look at. Being in the presence of beauty is gratifying. Particularly if our association with that person is perceived by others as granting us additional attractiveness by association.

Recent cross-cultural research has found that there is evidence that there is a high level of agreement about what constitutes a "pretty" face. First, the shape of faces perceived as attractive are different than those perceived as less attractive and agreed upon by both Japanese and Caucasian research participants (Perrett, May, Yoshikawa, 1994). The face is what is referred to as **neotenous.** This face is almost childlike with large eyes, small nose, and full lips. This face is most desirable on women. Studies of female models indicate their faces are more likely to be neotenous than average women, and it has also been found that drawings of women can be made to be perceived as more or less attractive by altering the same drawing to be more or less neotenous (Jones, 1995).

In rating photographs of faces of Asian, Hispanic, African-American, and Caucasian women, by judges of the various groups, the correlations between ratings of attractiveness were astonishingly high (r = +.93). In a study involving African-American and Caucasian men rating African-American female faces and body types, the same consensus was found for ratings of facial attractiveness (r = +.94). However, the two groups of men reported different preferences for body type (Cunningham, Roberts, Barbee, Druen & Wu, 1995).

Another study of preference for body types, however, using Indonesian, African-Americans, and American Caucasians (male and female) as judges found strong agreement on the ideal woman's body shape. Three body sizes (underweight, normal weight, and overweight) and four waist-to-hip ratios (2 feminine and 2 masculine) were varied. The overweight woman was perceived as unattractive regardless of her waist-to-hip ratio (Singh & Luis, 1995).

Recent research also shows that perceived attractiveness impacts on partner selection. In a study comparing German and Dutch students, participants were asked to rate the characteristics they look for in a partner. While females reported looking for good financial prospects and high status, the males reported looking for physical attractiveness. Similar results were found in studies comparing Germans and Americans (Buss & Angleitner, 1989) and American, Russian, and Japanese participants (Hatfield & Sprecher, 1986). In all cases the men cared more about physical attractiveness than the women participants. The German men were also concerned about finding a good housekeeper. In all studies the women were looking for earning capacity and status.

So, all things being equal (although they seldom are) we will be drawn to the attractive individual(s). Whether we choose to continue to relate to this person or group will be influenced by proximity (long-distance marriages and relationships have a very low success rate) and by similarity.

Summary

In this chapter we have examined the various reasons people choose to form groups, and the characteristics that affect those choices. The tendency to form groups appears to be overdetermined by the number of different functions served or needs satisfied by group membership. Groups serve to increase our probability of both psychological and physical survival. We also obtain nurturance and information from our group.

Just as there are a number of reasons to join groups, there are multiple factors determining which groups we will join. We seek to form groups with people who will reward us. The distribution of costs and benefits in the group will impact our satisfaction with the group and whether we choose to stay. We will choose to form groups with people who are physically available to us (proximity), who are like us (similarity), and whose looks we find appealing.

Key Terms and Phrases

actual equity	overdetermination
affiliation	physical attractiveness
autokinetic effect	power
comparison level (Cl)	projective techniques
comparison level for alternatives (Cl$_{alt}$)	proximity
ego	proximity-maintaining behavior
equity	psychological equity
fight-or-flight response	secure bond
functional approach	similarity
id	social comparison
informational needs	social exchange theory
insecure bond	sociobiology
need for nurturance	superego
need for power	survival needs
neotenous	unconscious psychological needs
overbenefitted	underbenefitted

APPLICATION

The Psychological Function of Militias

During the 1990s a relatively new phenomenon began to be seen in the United States. Groups of individuals began to form groups which they called "militias." These groups were paramilitary in nature and often virulently antigovernment. When the Murrah Federal Building was bombed and destroyed on April 19, 1995, the individuals convicted as having been involved in the attack, Timothy McVeigh and Terry Nichols, were identified as having been associated with militias. By November 1995, militia leaders claimed there were well-armed groups in all fifty of the United States (Abanes, 1996). These groups included the Aryan Nations, the Idaho Organized Militia, Wisconsin's Free Militia, Militia of Montana, Michigan Militia, and Missouri's 51st Militia (Stern, 1997). Who were the people who joined these groups, and why?

We discussed in this chapter that people join groups for a number of reasons: because the group satisfies some need, because the group shares similar beliefs and characteristics, and because membership in a group can provide a feeling of security. The militias satisfy almost all of these needs for their members. To understand why, we must examine the people who joined (and continue to join) militias and the economic and social environments in which they were developed.

The 1980s and 1990s have been disastrous times for the traditional family farm. Farmers were offered loans to buy more property when interest rates were low and land was cheap—an opportunity taken by many. By the end of the seventies, however, land prices had dropped at the same time interest rates went up. At the same time, corporations were engaged in the process of vertical integration. Vertical integration is the term applied to expansion of organizations so that they become more independent. An example would be a fast-food chain that specializes in hamburgers. They are dependent upon a number of suppliers for their meat, their buns, etc. Vertical integration in this case might involve the chain acquiring the meat-processing plants, the farms that supply the cattle to these plants, and the feedlots that supply feed for the cows. They now control their own destiny to a much greater extent. Those organizations that integrated vertically thus gained almost total control of the prices that farmers could expect to receive for their products.

These financial realities, combined with crop failures associated with weather, resulted in the loss of "between 700,000 and one million small- to medium-sized family farms since 1980. . . . At the peak of the crisis in 1986 to 1987, nearly one million people were forced from their land in a single twelve-month period" (Dyer, 1997, p. 15). The drought of 1996 was expected to cause the loss of another 10,000 family farms in Oklahoma—a number that represented one-sixth of the farms in the state (Dyer, 1997). But these losses were not mourned by all:

> *As early as 1964, congressmen were being told by industry giants like Pillsbury, Swift, General Foods, and Campbell Soup that the biggest problem in agriculture was too many farmers.*
>
> *(Dyer, 1997, p. 119)*

The loss of employment creates a stress on anyone who experiences the loss of their job. However, for farmers, losing the family farm is more than simply the loss of a job. It represents a loss of a way of life that has often been passed down through the generations, and was expected to continue to be passed down through the family. Research has shown that farmers are quite different from urban individuals who shrug off job loss and look for another job (Dyer, 1997). Farmers have been seen to be proud people who experience a profound sense of failure when they lose the family farm. They are independent people who tend to be very patriotic. They are also quite devoted to family and the church. Approximately 80 percent of farmers report being affiliated with a church—mostly Protestant Christian denominations.

Jourard (1971) states that human lives are made up of a series of "projects." These projects keep us interested in life and justify our existence. People only live as long as they see their lives as meaningful. Farmers who lose their farms often have no "project" to keep them going. Militias can offer such new projects. They provide emotional support, someone to blame for the troubles (so the farmers do not have to blame themselves), and also provide the company of individuals with similar values.

One of the basic tenets of many militias is their allegiance to the "true" America (the definition of which often varies by group). There is often an oath of allegiance to the militia which includes: (1) a vow of allegiance to the Constitution of the United States, (2) a promise to protect and defend America from all enemies foreign and domestic, (3) a pledge to abide by the state constitution, and (4) an agreement to obey all "legal" laws—federal, state, and local (Abanes, 1996). The militias feed upon the patriotism of farmers and fan their fears that we as a country are heading away from independence into a "New World Order." Alliances with other nations as represented by international trade agreements such as the North American Free Trade Agreement (NAFTA) were interpreted by militia members as evidence of the weakening of American sovereignty. And President Bill Clinton frightened the farmers even more in his 1997 State of the Union address in which he talked about "one world" and how we must knock down cultural barriers in the way of free trade and global prosperity. Militia members are ready to defend the United States through the use of arms, if necessary.

The possession and use of firearms is not foreign to farmers. (In fact, it is estimated that half of ALL households in the United States possess firearms.) Most Americans believe that the Second Amendment of the Bill of Rights of the Constitution gives them the right to keep firearms. A 1995 survey by *U.S. News and World Report* found that 75 percent of Americans believe that they are given this right by the Constitution. The legal literature overwhelmingly supports this interpretation of the Constitution (e.g., see Kates, 1982; Kates & Kleck, 1997; Kleck, 1997; Kopel, 1995, among others). Government attempts at gun control are perceived by militia members as the sinister first step to confiscation of all firearms. They point out that in many cases of genocide, the first step was to disarm the population (see Cottroll, 1994). Some cities and counties have even passed legislation requiring citizens to own firearms (e.g., Catron County, New Mexico; Riverside, Washington, and Kennesaw, Georgia [Abanes, 1996; Stern, 1997]). Militia members have stated their willingness to fight to uphold their constitutional rights.

> *Militia members, like many other patriots, are being emotionally charged by an electrifying current of antigovernmentalism wrought by the crushing weight of federal regulations.*
>
> *(Abanes, 1996, p. 21)*

For farmers, then, who may already have a propensity to distrust and dislike the government, the militia position on guns increases their perceived attitudinal similarity.

Religion also plays a part in the attraction to the militia movement. The militias generally interpret the Bible as supporting rebellion. They believe that the founding fathers of the United States intended it to be a "Christian nation." This view is known as the "Dominionist" perspective—a theocratic view of government. (There is another, darker form of militia known as the Christian Identity movement, which is highly anti-Semitic.) The Bible is interpreted as stating that before the new kingdom of God there will be a "rapture" where all good Christians will be whisked away to Heaven. Before the rapture, a time of tribulation is predicted. Surely for farmers it isn't too difficult to believe that this time is close, or already here. If it is here, then there is nothing to lose in defying the government. As a new century approaches, doomsday messages increase (as they have in previous centuries). The Hale-Bopp Comet was interpreted by the Heaven's Gate group as indication that the end had come. Even Christian writers such as Pat Robertson and Hal Lindsey have contributed to the idea that the end is near (Dyer, 1997).

So, to disenfranchised farmers, there is support and similarity to the militia beliefs. Once a farmer decides to join a militia, how do these groups generally work? A meeting (held in Estes Park, Colorado in 1992) known as the Rocky Mountain Rendezvous served as a melding point for many militia groups. At this meeting an individual named Louis Beam initiated the idea of "leaderless resistance." Highly organized militias with large memberships can be infiltrated (and have often been) by government agents. Thus, as a matter of self-protection, many militias form "cells." These start with five or six people who recruit like-minded folk until the group reaches about ten in number. At that point the group splits in half with the original leader staying with the original group. After several of these divisions, individuals in a third generation group could not inform on first generation members if they wanted to. As Dyer (1997) states: "It appears that the militias are changing course, becoming more realistic and, therefore, more dangerous" (p. 208).

Are the perceptions of militia members necessarily irrational? Dyer, editor of the Boulder, Colorado, *Boulder Weekly* traveled the country and interviewed farmers and mental health professionals in the Midwest and discovered what he refers to as the "shattered heartland"—an area of the United States so disheartened that suicides, hopelessness, and militia membership abound. Each time he approached a new group with some trepidation, "but time and again I have parted from such experiences with a great appreciation for the people I've met" (Dyer, 1997, p. 201). Of course, even rational, desperate people can be dangerous:

> We should learn to view crazy antigovernment conspiracy theories as a warning rather than as joke material. If people can, in all sincerity, believe that Jewish bankers have ordered the United Nations to attack their farms in order to control the food supply of Christians and if people can believe that the government has inserted microchips in their bodies so that satellites can track their every move, then they can also believe that they are supposed to blow up a building full of kids. Timothy McVeigh believed that the government had injected a microchip into his butt to track his every move. Enough said.
>
> (Dyer, 1997, p. 213)

Discussion Questions

Apply the concepts from the chapter to consider the following questions:

1. Use Thibault and Kelley's social exchange theory to explain why militias might be particularly appealing to farmers.
2. It is probably safe to assume that farmers feel underbenefitted in their relationship to the government. How might this affect their behavior?
3. Posit a sociobiological explanation for the militia phenomenon.
4. Use the concept of overdetermination to explain the appeal of the militias for farmers.
5. If it is true that a significant segment of our society is being pushed farther and farther away from the government, can you think of any actions that might be taken by the government to reduce the appeal of the militia movement (short of making them illegal—which has already been tried and failed miserably)?

Group Development and Socialization

What Would YOU Predict?

Having just moved into a new community and being avid golfers and devout Jews, the Rosenbergs wish to find both a country club and a temple to join. Having identified their choices, they approach each group. Do you think the requirements for membership will be the same for the two groups? Which will be more difficult to join? What (if any) type of initiation will the family undergo?

INTRODUCTION: GROUP DEVELOPMENT

As we discussed in Chapter 1, groups change over time. A task force that has worked together for five years is not at all the same group they were at the start. A couple celebrating their fifth wedding anniversary is not at all like the couple on their first date. All groups and relationships change over time. In this chapter we will take two different perspectives on this change. First we will examine the group as an entity, focusing not so much on the individuals within the group, but the group as a unit. Research with such diverse groups as professional soccer players (Martin & Davids, 1995), social workers (Berman-Rossi, 1997), and psychotherapists (Unger, 1990), indicates that prior knowledge of the stages of group development can enhance group cohesion, individual self-esteem, and reduce stress within the group (Martin & Davids, 1995).

In the second part of the chapter we will narrow our focus and examine the changes that an individual moves through as they become a member of (and maybe eventually leave) the group. These two processes (**group development** and **individual socialization**) are not necessarily synchronized in any way. An individual may join a group such as a chapter of the Daughters of the American Revolution where the chapter has existed for decades with essentially the same membership. Or an individual may decide after attending one organizational meeting of the Coalition to Save the Armadillo that this just isn't their thing and never return.

MODELS OF GROUP DEVELOPMENT: STAGES OF TEMPORAL CHANGE

For task groups, developmental changes take place in fairly predictable sequence. There have been many models developed to describe these changes (e.g., Tuckman & Jensen, 1977; Cohen, Fink, Gadon, & Willits, 1980; Hare & Naveh, 1984; Wheelan, 1994). Although much alike in many ways, each of these models contributes important ideas to the understanding of the development of a group. We will focus on two of the theories and combine them into a single, integrated model of the process of group development.

In the first of the models we will examine (Tuckman & Jensen, 1977), five stages of group development are identified: (1) **forming,** (2) **storming,** (3) **norming,** (4) **performing,** and (5) **adjourning.** Apparently the names of the stages were designed to rhyme as a mnemonic device. Unfortunately, the names of several of the stages tend to conjure up inappropriate images of what goes on in the group at that stage. This model offers a consideration of the ending of groups that is lacking in the second model we will examine.

Because the Tuckman and Jensen model is so extraordinarily similar to the Cohen et al. (1980) model, we will discuss the contents of the stages together. While the Cohen et al. model lacks a consideration of the termination of groups, it divides the earliest stage of the group into two parts. It is because of significant differences between the behaviors in the group in these two stages that this model is included.

Cohen et al. also identify five stages: (1) **membership,** (2) **subgrouping,** (3) **confrontation,** (4) **individual differentiation,** and (5) **collaboration.** The models fit together as shown below:

Forming	Membership
	Subgrouping
Storming	Confrontation
Norming	Individual differentiation
Performing	Collaboration
Adjourning	

As you can see, the Cohen et al. model divides the group formation stage into two substages. This is because the qualitative changes occurring midway through the Tuckman and Jensen forming stage can be quite important in diagnosing how far a group has progressed in their development. But the Cohen et al. model never mentions the ending of a group. Groups develop to their optimum and then go on—forever. This simply isn't realistic. All groups and relationships end—even if only because of the death of the participants. Thus it's important to consider how to make the ending of a group as successful and effective for the group as the other stages.

 Think back to your first day in this class or the first day on your present job or your first date. How did you feel? Were you confident? Nervous? Anxious? Hopeful? What impression did you try to make on others? Were you "cool"? Why? Share your memories with classmates or group members.

Membership

In the **membership stage,** the group is coming together for the first times. Tension is extremely high. Most roles are ambiguous, norms are not yet developed, individuals don't know what to expect from the group. If their previous experiences have not been pleasant, they may well expect the same from this group. If, on the other hand, they have enjoyed participating in past groups, they may be eagerly anticipating the experience. But everyone is anxious. As Napier and Gershenfeld state, "Most groups are a mix of hope and trepidation" (1993, p. 482). Although perfectly normal, this trepidation is the reason for the high drop-out rate in voluntary groups at this stage. Because while everyone is nervous and anxious, everyone is pretending not to be. So no one looks tense and the individual concludes they're the only one who is! This perfectly normal sensation is called **primary tension.**

Part of this early tension is because trust is very low at this early stage. Individuals know they will be dependent upon the responsibility and competence of their fellow group members, but don't know whether the members are responsible or competent or reliable. Many individuals at this point in the group are afraid they will be "stuck" with much of the work of the group while others slack off. Individuals are often suspicious someone in the group might try to take over power in the group and behave as an autocratic leader. College-age individuals are particularly resistant to this idea of someone taking over and telling them what to do. For this particular age group, their image of leaders is often very negative. They don't think of the positive contributions of the leader, only that someone might threaten their independence. It has been suggested that perhaps this reaction is based on the fact that these individuals are not far from the home environment and are experiencing (and reveling in) relative independence for the first time.

Generally in the membership phase, conflict is nonexistent. This is because in this stage everyone is doing their best to make a good impression on all of the other group members while at the same time trying to evaluate the other group members as potential colleagues. So everyone has on their party manners. They are polite, pleasant, and absolutely superficial. Everyone is trying to be the image of the "good" group member, so they're not being themselves. Since conflict or confrontation are viewed as negative behaviors by many Americans, to exhibit this behavior at this stage of the group is to risk being ostracized or perhaps even ejected from the group.

Unfortunately, because the group members know relatively little (or nothing) about each other, many initial judgments may be based upon stereotypes. Men will be expected to be smart and leaderlike (unless they're "jocks," in which case they'll be expected to be dumb). Individuals with glasses will be expected to be intelligent. Individuals with red hair may be anticipated to have fiery tempers. And all the stereotypes based on race and age also come into play. Individuals who could make a tremendous contribution to the group may be dismissed as "just kids." Asian-Americans may be expected to be particularly diligent workers—based simply upon their race. It's not fair to allow our prejudices to color our evaluation of individuals, but that's what happens. For a group to become effective and productive, these initial impressions may need to be changed.

How many blonde jokes do you know? What image of blondes is portrayed in **STOP** these jokes? Do you think this image is accurate? Have you ever known a brunette who exhibited the behaviors expected of blondes? Were you surprised by this? Ask blondes in your class (particularly the females) if they have noticed that they are treated in ways predicted by the "dumb blonde" stereotype.

Because the group members are so caught up in this mutual evaluation, group productivity is low. Or if the group attempts any important task this early in their development, it's almost guaranteed to be a disaster in terms of quality. Why is this?

Individuals and groups only have a finite amount of energy to contribute to the group. Checking out the other members and deciding if they are trustworthy takes energy and attention. Establishing relationships is tough, so groups often dive immediately into the task of the group, trying to ignore all of the important social issues of the group. But with all of the evaluation going on there isn't really much energy available for the task.

The other important reason that the task will be a disaster is the fact that since everyone is phobic about conflict and looking like a "bad guy," the most ridiculous and idiotic ideas are greeted by the group with support and enthusiasm. Everyone knows the idea is bad, but we don't confront people we don't know for another very important reason. How will that person react if we criticize their idea? Laugh? Cry? Slap us? No, thank you. We'll wait until we have more information before we object.

Is there any way around this uncomfortable stage? No, but there are things that can be done to help the group move more smoothly through the stage. Give the group something to do, some structure, that is unimportant to the goals of the group, but requires interaction among members. Thus they can see each other in action and have a structure to hang onto (and probably complain about—which increases cohesion) while they get to know each other. These activities are usually known as "icebreakers." They can be scavenger hunts, or identifying characteristics of the other members. (Which member(s) have green eyes?) The group relaxes into the activity (often the sillier the activity the better) and begins to laugh and relate to each other more naturally. There will be time later for important task work, which will be higher quality and more efficiently performed, once the social issues are confronted and worked through.

In the first chapter we identified the characteristics of the group. How do these characteristics such as size of group, roles, status, interaction, and norms impact the group at this stage? Size of group can be dealt with easily and once and for all. Smaller groups progress through all of the stages more easily and efficiently than larger groups. This is because everything becomes more complicated as you add additional people. Communication, coordination, interaction, decision making, problem solving, identification of roles—everything takes more time and energy. That's the reason in Chapter 1 we identified an optimal size for most task groups as being between four and six members. It is also the reason that we identified a dyad as a group. Dyads have to deal with all of the issues involved in larger groups. But because there are only two people involved, sorting things out is often so simple that the individuals don't realize they're dealing with issues such as roles, communication, coordination, etc.

There is no script for an initial group meeting. People don't usually know what their roles are. And since roles are sets of behaviors, they don't know how they are "supposed" to act. And as we discussed in Chapter 1, people are extremely uncomfortable with role ambiguity. If the roles do not become clear relatively quickly, members may choose to leave the group. The one exception to this ambiguity is the already established leader. Everyone has their own ideas about how leaders behave. Thus the leader has an advantage.

This advantage is based upon the fact that in addition to knowing how leaders should behave, individuals also know what behaviors are expected on their part toward a leader, so there is some comfort there. Being a "good" group member demands following the leader. And since we're all being so agreeable and appropriate, an established leader will be followed without much question. This leader may have been appointed by some outside authority, such as when your boss makes you leader of the committee to design the new corporate logo; or the leader may be elected by the group. Whichever process is used, this leader has the advantage of legitimacy. In a group with no "legitimate" leader, the group will generally be very resistant at this stage to allowing someone to assume (stage a coup) this role and status.

Interaction in this earliest of stages is stilted, superficial, and cautious. Unfortunately, this earliest interaction is creating the norms under which the group will behave until someone objects. Every first behavior in a group establishes a precedent for subsequent behavior. If everyone shows up for the initial meeting dressed up, it will be safe to assume that they will continue to dress this way for each meeting. If the meeting was scheduled to start at 8:00 A.M. and three of five members straggle in between 8:00 and 8:10, you can probably count on never having a meeting start on time—at least until members who are bothered are comfortable enough to make an issue of the tardiness. Thus a lot of the norms that are established very early may be dysfunctional for the group. Now that you are aware of the importance of establishing positive norms for groups in which you participate, you will be self-conscious in the most appropriate ways in how you behave in the membership stage of groups, or how you lead during this important time.

Subgrouping

The second substage of the membership stage is **subgrouping.** Individuals identify others with whom they have something in common. They recognize someone from their church, or their calculus class, or they're the only two women in a room full of men. Whatever the similarity, suddenly they're not alone.

Similarity often leads to proximity in the early meetings of a group. As we enter the room, if someone looks familiar, or similar to us, we often make a point of situating ourselves near that person. Then the norm discussed above takes over and we stay near that person. And as we get to know them we begin to relax. So the tension level in the group drops during the subgrouping phase. Trust is beginning to increase—we've formed coalitions.

Open conflict is still absent during the subgrouping substage; however, coalitions may begin to maneuver themselves so that they can make a grab for power as the group develops. Very seldom does one individual start to make such moves—there is definitely strength in numbers. And because of all this relating and maneuvering, productivity is low and the quality of any product developed at this stage will probably be low in quality. Despite the surface calm, disagreement may be brewing, which will come to the surface during the next developmental stage.

Confrontation

The Tuckman and Jensen **storming stage** and the Cohen et al. **confrontation** second stage of group development are essentially identical. This is an extremely critical phase of group development. Groups that try to avoid going through this stage are probably never going to be very effective. It is possible to avoid this stage in groups that will meet for an extremely limited time, but long-term groups will almost always find themselves in this stage—and should.

This is one of the stages where I find the label "storming" used by Tuckman and Jensen sometimes puts people off. It seems to conjure up images of fistfights or shouting matches. That's not necessarily the case—unless the group tries to avoid this stage or handles it badly. In any group of people there will be some points of disagreement. These points haven't been expressed in the group in the membership stage because of the mutual attempts to impress each other. Trying to suppress disagreement is like trying to hold the lid on a pressure cooker. The more pressure that builds up, the bigger the explosion. Some groups pass through this stage without even being aware of the transition. These are usually very cohesive groups with so much trust and such good communication skills that disagreement is expressed naturally.

Rather than being a sign that the group has gone badly offtrack (an interpretation often made by those who are uncomfortable with disagreement and possible anger), the maturation into the confrontation stage is a very positive sign for the group. Granted, tension levels soar upward again as everyone wonders what will happen. But the appearance of this stage indicates that trust has been developing between group members. As I said before, we don't confront someone unless we can anticipate and trust there will be an appropriate response. So the appearance of conflict indicates that the group has been developing well. Also, groups that handle this important stage of development appropriately (again, I need to emphasize the term *appropriately*) find the group transformed on the other side. In Chapter 4 we will discuss communication skills to help get through conflict (shouting and calling names doesn't work well), and in Chapter 9 we will discuss various approaches to conflict resolution.

STOP Think back to your first argument in a group or relationship you have experienced. Wasn't there a "honeymoon" period before you actually had a squabble? For example, did you give in and watch horror movies or eat Chinese food for the first three or four dates until you finally announced to your date that you really hate horror movies and much prefer pizza? How did you feel when you finally worked things out?

What is this magic that occurs? First, as anyone who's made it through the first argument in a relationship can vouch, coming out of the disagreement with the relationship or the group still intact gives the group confidence that conflict can be handled without people being hurt. Also, there is a giant leap in the productivity of the group, both in terms of efficiency and quality. Early on in the group I can throw out almost any half-baked suggestion, one that's even clearly not good, but I trust the group won't object or criticize me, and that they'll probably accept the idea.

Once I realize my ideas will potentially be challenged, however, I'm going to be a great deal more careful in developing the ideas I present to the group. The quality of the material goes up and quality control appears for the first time in the group because they won't accept just any idea or suggestion. They will pick and choose the best of the best. So now the emphasis can be taken off the social issues of the group (because the group has confidence it can handle conflict effectively) and emphasis can be placed on the task—the reason for the group's existence in the first place—with confidence that the better ideas will be presented and prevail.

There are three types of **conflict** that appear during this stage. The first two are perfectly normal and to be expected. They appear in all groups and have a reasonable expectation of solution. The third type, which is unfortunately both the most difficult to identify and to handle, can destroy a group. The first type of conflict is known as **false** (Deutsch, 1973) or **autistic** (Holmes & Miller, 1976) **conflict.** There is apparent conflict, but upon examination, there is merely a misunderstanding. For example, Mario walks into a group meeting just as the group bursts into laughter. Mario becomes convinced that the group is laughing at him and becomes angry and confronts them. Once they explain that someone had just completed a joke and the timing was coincidental, Mario will probably want to hear the joke and will cool off. Or, as sometimes happens in a classroom or in a lecture or presentation, an individual will get up and walk out. As a teacher, I tend to immediately go back and think over what I've just said and wonder whether I might have offended the individual. Maybe I have, but maybe they simply needed to get to the day-care center before it closed, or suddenly remembered another appointment. Or maybe they needed to use the restroom. Without communication it's possible to make assumptions and attributions (explanations) that are inappropriate. In false or autistic conflict, then, there isn't an actual conflict.

In the second type of conflict, however, **contingent conflict** (Deutsch, 1973), the group does have a real conflict on its hands. Contingent conflict occurs when the behavior of an individual in the group is problematic for one or more of the other members. For example, Margaret might liberally lace her language with profanity which thoroughly offends Paul who is a born-again Christian. Or the group might have to wait to start their meetings up to half an hour because Michael is seldom on time.

There's no misunderstanding here. Behaviors will have to change to solve the conflict. Perhaps Margaret had no idea she was upsetting Paul. She apologizes and agrees to watch her language in the group out of courtesy to his beliefs. But when two people are having a problem, they are both contributing. If Paul hasn't said anything to Margaret, any conflict is as much his fault as it is hers. And if Margaret talks that way all the time, she'll probably slip occasionally in the group and Paul will have to be tolerant. Maybe group members will have to take turns calling Michael the night before the meeting (or an hour before) to remind him of the meeting. Maybe someone will need to pick him up and physically bring him to meetings.

But again, maybe there's more here than meets the eye. Perhaps the group has established a meeting time that conflicts with Michael's therapy session. He is not comfortable sharing the fact that he is in counseling, so he doesn't propose an alternative time. Or no one in the group knows that Michael's mother is terminally ill and he is under crushing stress and is trying to spend as much time as possible with her and at the same time keep up with his life. Again, if there's a legitimate reason for the behavior it should be explained. The group needs to avoid leaping to a possibly incorrect assumption about the reasons or motives behind the behavior (Margaret's just "trailer park trash" and Michael is just irresponsible) and try to find a resolution that accommodates the most people possible, in the kindest (or, at least, most civil) way possible.

STOP Have you ever been in a group where the behavior of one (or more individuals) such as being constantly late or not completing assigned work on time created real tension in the other members of the group? How long did it take for someone to bring it up in the group? Did you ever resolve the problem? Discuss the possibility that your behavior of remaining silent contributed to the problem. How could you and the group have handled the situation differently?

The final type of conflict is known both as **escalating conflict** (Forsyth, 1990) or **secondary tension** (Bormann, 1990). It is difficult to identify and potentially lethal to the group. Escalating conflict is not a single, identifiable incident. It is rather a pattern of seemingly small, unrelated contingent or false conflicts. It is the pattern that is the crucial clue. An example: At the end of the meeting of the Homecoming Committee, Carlos suggests they meet again next Wednesday. Angela says she can't make that—how about Thursday. Once the date is resolved, Angela suggests they meet at 7:00 P.M. over Thai food. Carlos says he has to work until 8:00 on Thursday and, besides, he doesn't like Thai food—how about they meet at 8:30 at a family-style restaurant.

Are these three unrelated conflicts? Not a chance. In each one we see that Carlos and Angela are going head-to-head over some seemingly trivial issue that should be readily resolved. The real issue here is who is going to have more power in the group. It is a disguised fight for control. If this is going on and the group fails to identify the pattern, they will waste huge amounts of time trying to solve each of these little spats. Their time and energy will be diverted from the task. Besides, people don't like to be around others who constantly bicker and argue. The group might just fall apart.

In escalating conflict the real source of the problem is almost always some underlying, unresolved issue. Maybe Angela and Carlos used to date each other until Carlos dumped her for Katherine. Maybe Angela just wants to make Carlos' life miserable. Although there are certainly innumerable sources for escalating conflict, the most common is a struggle for power and/or control in the group. Whatever the underlying issue, however, it must be identified, discussed, and resolved by the group. Is this easy? Of course not. Is it necessary? Only if the group wishes to continue and to be successful at their goals.

Re-norming

The next stage in the models is known as **norming** (Tuckman & Jensen) or **individual differentiation** (Cohen et al.). Here again the label used by Tuckman and Jensen is unfortunate. It would seem to imply that the group has not been developing norms throughout its development. This simply isn't true.

Norm development began during the first seconds of the group. It is true that often the trigger for the confrontation stage is one of the dysfunctional norms that was established during the membership stage and that is finally brought to the group's attention. So often the group's norms are different in the stage after the storm. But the group always had norms.

Individual differentiation is a happy and productive time for the group. Tension is at an all-time low now that the group has developed the skills to deal with conflict. Trust is also at an all-time high (assuming everyone behaved themselves in the confrontation stage). Group members have trust that they can expect they will not be hurt by group conflict.

Another phenomenon involving trust is characteristic of this stage of group development. Earlier in the group's development group members have not trusted each other to carry out their share of the work. So immature groups tend to develop arbitrary rules about "fairness" which can be quite absurd. An extreme example occurred in a course in which I routinely assign groups of students to write papers as a group—thus, their grades and success are dependent upon the responsibility of others.

For the first paper of one group in one class there were six members in the group. I had limited the length of the paper to six pages, stating I would not read past that point. The paper this particular group turned in was of substandard quality. Some of the pages were disorganized and rambling, and others were lacking sufficient detail to make their points. I confronted the group and was informed of the rule they had made to assure that each group member did exactly the same amount of work. Each person had written one page and the group had determined the number of words that should be on each page! Some were very direct in their writing, and had to "pad" their pages; others ran out of space before they ever came to the point. This was clearly not the best strategy for success. But the group members lacked sufficient trust to believe that everyone would do their part without a rule of this sort.

Once a group reaches the individual differentiation stage, however, there is sufficient trust to begin to make more intelligent decisions about the *division of labor* within the group. The most effective division of labor assigns tasks to individuals based upon their strengths and skills. If there is a financial analysis as part of the group task it only makes sense to assign it to someone with accounting or similar skills and training. People do better jobs when you play to their strengths, and people are happier doing tasks they know they can do well. So here is another reason for the increased quality of the task products of groups in this stage.

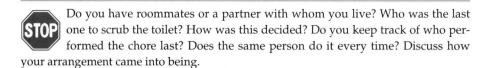

Do you have roommates or a partner with whom you live? Who was the last one to scrub the toilet? How was this decided? Do you keep track of who performed the chore last? Does the same person do it every time? Discuss how your arrangement came into being.

But wait, does a more task-based division of labor mean that everyone does the same amount of work? No, but the group doesn't feel the need to keep score. They assume that at some future point individuals who did not contribute a great deal to this task (because their skills were not needed) will make up for it on another task. In class I ask my students how many have a schedule of work posted to assign household tasks to the various roommates. Most do. Obviously they don't trust each other enough to assume the work will get done or want everyone to cycle through all the chores. But maybe one doesn't mind taking out the trash, someone else doesn't mind cleaning up the kitchen, and another loves to cook but hates to clean. I enjoy visiting my sister because I love to cook but am not tidy; she's fastidious but hates to cook. The division of labor works perfectly—we get better meals and she keeps her pristine kitchen!

At this point in their development groups usually have developed a sense of unity and purpose. They identify with the group and care a great deal that the group succeeds in its task. There is a tendency for individuals to only leave the group if they must (they graduate, they're transferred, their families move). As mentioned above, the productivity of the group has improved dramatically. Now attention and energy can be directed to success at the task—which is now a much more likely outcome. By this time the roles in the group have been sorted out along with the status of members, and the norms are clear as are the patterns and extent of interactions.

Working and Playing Well Together

The fourth stage of group development in these models is labeled **performing** (Tuckman & Jensen) or **collaboration** (Cohen et al.). This is very much like group nirvana. The group is now a mature group capable of extremely high quality work. Tension is very low. Trust is very high. Conflict is readily identified and effectively dealt with. Productivity is at its peak. The division of labor is based on skill and even the role of leader is transferred at different times to the individual in the group who can most effectively lead on a particular portion of the task. Would that this could last forever.

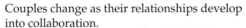

Couples change as their relationships develop into collaboration.

Termination

All groups end, even those that work very well together (despite what Cohen et al. would have us believe). It is one of the strengths of the Tuckman and Jensen model that they consider the final stage of group development to be **adjourning.** Groups spend so much time and energy working to become a group that it only makes sense to pay attention to how a group stops being a group and moves back to being individuals again. People need closure to the task and to the **termination** of or change in their relationships with each other.

Groups can end two ways—planned and unplanned. Individuals signing up for a college course or a training school or even enlisting in the military know how long their membership will last. They can prepare for the known ending of their participation in the group. For leaders of time-limited groups, it is important to occasionally refer to the ending of the group and increase the frequency of these reminders as the end comes closer. This allows people to mentally prepare themselves. Whenever possible there should be a final meeting of the group devoted to discussing the experience and the ending of the group. The group can celebrate their successes or console each other if they were not successful. The group can make decisions about where relationships will go from here. One of the task groups from one of my classes became such close friends that at the end of the semester they decided not to disband as a group but simply changed to a friendship group. Four years later they are still in touch with each other.

The worst thing that can happen to a group is to end suddenly. A company can go bankrupt. Enough individuals drop off the volleyball team that the team can't go on competing. Someone who planned to be married forever is presented with divorce papers. Individuals suddenly dumped from a group are disoriented and distressed. There is unfinished psychological business. The negativity and shock of the sudden ending often casts a shadow over the entire experience and results in a negative re-evaluation of the group experience. Try asking someone whose partner has suddenly ended the relationship how they feel about the relationship in general. Often they can't remember that there must have been some good times—through their pain all they see are the negative things. This is why a new counseling genre has developed. While marriage counseling has been around a long time, its goal was to try to save the marriage. Divorce counseling has developed to help couples learn how to adjourn their marriage in the most positive way possible.

There is a dearth of research examining whether gender affects the development of groups—although as we shall see in future chapters there is much research on differences in communication and conflict resolution styles between the genders that might affect the development of the group. There is, however, beginning to be an awareness that cultural differences can have a strong impact on the development of the group. Bantz (1993) discusses the challenges faced with the group development of a team of researchers from Israel, South Africa, the United States, and Germany. Different cultural norms in areas such as power, distance, ability to deal with ambiguity, individualism, and masculinity affected the development of the group. He found that establishing a common goal and deadline brought the group together as well as identifying and discussing the cultural differences. Parks (1987) examined the differences between Japanese and American values in the Nicheran Shoshu Academy—a branch of Japanese Sokagakkai in the United States. Conflicts rose from basic cultural differences based upon the collectivist focus of Japanese society, which values hierarchy and views the organization (group) as a means to foster individual growth, as opposed to the completely antithetical American individualistic focus, which values individual equality and lack of hierarchy as the means to personal growth within a group. Clearly much remains to be examined about the effects of cultural differences as our nation becomes increasingly diverse.

It would be naive and short-sighted not to consider the degree of cross-cultural differences within the borders of the United States. Generally, when researchers refer to "Americans" they are referring to the norms and values of the white, middle-class, androcentric culture. This point is brought home forcibly by the title of Guthrie's 1976 summary of the history of psychological research: *Even the Rat Was White.* Just as cultural differences outside the nation can disrupt our assumptions about group dynamics, there are identifiable differences in African-American, Asian-American, and Hispanic-American cultures from the model that has been taken to represent "Americans." As with gender differences, the research that has been conducted to this point has emphasized differences in culture and behavior, but not focused on how these affect group development.

There are even some groups of white citizens who are also excluded from the assumptions about American norms, values, and behaviors. They exist at both ends of the financial spectrum. Old-moneyed individuals have often been criticized for believing themselves above the rules. But groups at the other end of the financial spectrum also do not adhere to middle-class norms. Recently a comedian named Jeff Foxworthy (1996) has been building a very successful career making jokes about rednecks, a group that is often referred to by the middle class as "white trash."

But there are people who feel that this is an example of **classism** that is as corrosive as racism. During the O.J. Simpson murder trial there was a great upheaval when it was determined that one of the detectives involved was a racist. The evidence? Part of it was the fact that he had used what became known as the "n word" to describe African-Americans. Yet while racial slurs across races are taboo, it is perfectly acceptable, even considered amusing by some, to discuss and dissect poor whites. And, usually offense is not taken when the "n word" is used between African-Americans. The rules of political correctness allow for jokes about and criticism of some groups but not others.

> *It's OK to mention Caucasian inbreeding, but not African-American teen-pregnancy rates. You can rag on trailer trash, but not ghetto scum. You can make fun of truck drivers, but not lowriders. . . . So why am I perturbed by all the trash-bashing? Because they're talking about ME.*
>
> *(Goad, 1997, pp. 22 & 24)*

Jones (1979) identified five dimensions that differ between African-American and white experience, although I think these differences can also be seen between other cultural and geographic groups. These are: (1) *time*, (2) *rhythm*, (3) *improvisation*, (4) *oral expression*, and (5) *spirituality*. Attention to, and the interpretation of **time** can vary across cultures. White and Japanese cultures tend to be very attentive to time and are offended if an individual with whom they have an appointment shows up late. However, "late" is a relative term. Each year I attend a Native American pow-wow held at my university. The grand entrance is always scheduled for 1:00 P.M. For the first few years I actually showed up on time and the wait ranged from twenty to forty-five minutes. At one pow-wow the tribal chief stood up and announced to the audience that the entrance was about to start (at considerably later than 1:00). He laughed and said, "What we meant was one o'clock Indian time!"

Rhythm does not just refer to music—although a part of the traditional stereotype of American blacks was that they had great rhythm and therefore were great musicians and dancers. Rhythm also has to do with the pace of everyday life. How fast do people move? How fast do they talk? We will discuss in Chapter 4 the difficulties differences in rhythm can create in communication. Californians are often lampooned as "laid back" and languid in their rhythms and New Yorkers as driven, abrasive individuals.

I grew up in southern California and went to graduate school in the East. I was appalled by the abruptness and (what I viewed as) discourtesy of those around me. They laughed and labeled me a "typical" Californian. When I took my present teaching job in the Midwest, I was immediately labeled "one of those Eastern types." I've checked with those who've known me for years, and my rhythm hasn't changed, just the context.

Improvisation is deviating from the "rules." It can be deliberate, appropriate, and even important in situations, such as jazz music. (Really good jazz musicians don't follow the sheet music.) In other aspects of life, white American culture has tended to go "by the book." But that's only possible if the rules work for you. Excluded from many institutions and life situations, African-Americans (as well as other minorities) have had to improvise ways to get what they wanted and needed. "Faking it" can be a very useful life skill.

Oral expression differences between cultures have often been based upon access to the written exchange of a society. In the United States before the Civil War it was illegal to educate slaves. They were able to maintain much of their rich cultural heritage through the ancient tradition of storytelling. As current immigrants enter the country speaking no English, they too may maintain their cultural traditions until a subsequent generation records them for posterity. After the Vietnam War, the United States (specifically the Central Intelligence Agency) brought a tribe called the Hmong from Laos and Cambodia to the United States. The Hmong were quite helpful to the United States during the war, and abandoning them in Southeast Asia would have surely meant execution. The Hmong community in my town is among the largest in the country. The elders do not speak English, neither do most of the parents. But the children are thriving in American schools.

The Hmong are generally quite an industrious people who highly value education. School officials were quite surprised when very few parents showed up at school functions. After all, they had hired a translator to be sure that all documents sent home with the children were in Hmong. Much to the surprise and embarrassment of the school board, they were informed that the parents still couldn't read the documents. Hmong has not traditionally been a written language. A written language had been "cobbled" together after immigration to the United States. So the parents could no more read the translated documents than they could have read them in English. Why did they not immediately speak up? Because the elders recognized that the school board had tried to accommodate to their needs and did not want to embarrass or cause the school board to "lose face" (an extremely important courtesy in many Asian cultures).

Spirituality does not only refer to formal religious adherence and practice, although that is certainly one of its aspects. **Spirituality** deals with that which cannot be known or experienced directly. It involves the cosmic questions of good and evil, the origins and meaning of life, etc. For many, formal religions are a means to explore this aspect of life. For African-American slaves, a deep belief in a loving, caring God who would redeem their suffering might have been one of their only means of surviving an otherwise unsurvivable situation. Jews who escaped the Nazi death camps with their lives have often reported that their faith and trust in God was all that kept them alive.

The world is full of religions with varying beliefs and ritual practices. As the United States becomes more diverse, more of these religions become a part of the mosaic of our culture. Sadly, many religions feel they adhere to the only "correct" beliefs. These differences have often been the source of conflicts and war. As Tom Lehrer (a college professor and musical satirist/social commentator) said in 1981 in his song entitled "National Brotherhood Week": "Oh the Protestants hate the Catholics, and the Catholics hate the Protestants, and the Hindus hate the Muslims, and everybody hates the Jews." In the future we will need to overcome these cultural differences if we expect to work together in functional groups.

We have spent a great deal of this chapter discussing two of many theories. These combined theories provide us with a fairly complete picture of the process of group development. But groups are made up of individuals. What about the individual's experience of group membership? It is to this issue we now turn.

SOCIALIZATION: THE INDIVIDUAL'S JOURNEY THROUGH THE GROUP

Thus far we have focused on the group as an entity, looking at how the group members contribute to the development of the group, but we have not paid much attention to the members themselves. The process of an individual choosing, joining, belonging, and perhaps leaving a group is known as **socialization.** Again we have a situation where there is a predictable sequence of steps that individuals—and the groups they join—pass through. And as with group development we have a number of essential issues to examine at each stage of the process. These issues are: (1) **evaluation,** (2) **commitment,** and (3) **role transitions** (Moreland & Levine, 1982). Each of these processes are reciprocal between the individual and the group, so each of these issues must be examined from both the perspective of the individual, and from the group perspective.

As the individual decides which graduate school to attend, the graduate schools are evaluating the individual's credentials. The individual may decide that Yale is the place for him, only to find out that Yale doesn't want him. As we did with group development, we will combine two theories to explore group socialization.

The number of steps in the socialization model of Deaux and Wrightsman (1988) is not fixed as are the stages of group development. There are several choice points in the process of socialization that will shorten or lengthen the process. In the example just given, our poor student has been stopped at the first stage of the process. He will not be socialized at Yale. So the model looks something like this:

FIGURE 3.1. Socialization through the group process.
Figure Source TO COME

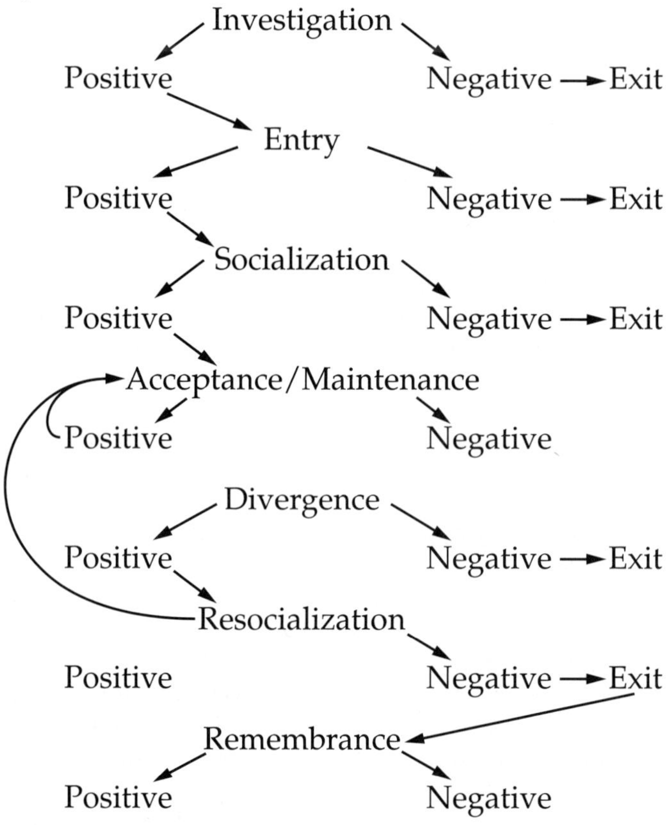

As you can see from the model in Figure 3.1, there are a number of possible paths through the process, as well as multiple exit points from the process. The only two stages that can be guaranteed for everyone are the first—entry into the process—and the last—remembering the group experience. You might also be wondering about the fact that so many paths potentially lead to negative memories of the group experience. Often a strong influence on the types of memories created after the experience is whether the decision was one-sided (the group kicks you out or you choose to leave a group that wants you to stay) or consensual. We will discuss this phenomenon at length when we reach the remembrance stage of the group.

Essential Processes in Socialization

Before we begin to examine the individual stages of the process, let's define the issues we've identified as being important at each stage. **Evaluation** is the process by which we determine whether the group has more positives than negatives to offer. Perhaps we are really interested in attending a college in New Zealand, but the tuition and the costs of travel and living simply make that choice impossible. And I can't emphasize enough that while we are evaluating a potential group or relationship, we are also being evaluated. Ideally the choices by both sides match. Often they don't. We might somehow dig up enough cash to attend the college in New Zealand only to find they have rejected our application.

Often the evaluation process is heavily influenced not by the mere qualifications and characteristics of a person, but also how well the individual and the group fit together. We do not want to invite problems with conflict in groups or with individuals unable to find a niche in the group who struggle with role ambiguity. Either situation would be upsetting and disruptive to the group. So the "best" candidate for admission to any group is the individual who appears to fit in. A study of male, female, and minority subsamples of Canadian business school graduates found that dissimilarity to the work group in terms of age, education, or lifestyle was associated with lower job challenge and poorer work group fit (Kirchmeyer, 1995). This may inevitably lead to groups searching for members who are similar to themselves. This is a problem because groups occasionally need "new blood," individuals with fresh ideas or more up-to-date skills, education, or training. It also may invite discrimination against those who aren't "like us."

In the distant past of my undergraduate years I attended a university where 95 percent of the students belonged to either a fraternity or a sorority. These groups were very selective—there was the jock fraternity, the Jewish sorority, and the African-American sorority and fraternity. There was also the blonde sorority, and, consequently, a number of instant blondes on campus.

Depending upon where in the country the Rosenbergs live (remember them from the start of the chapter?), they may find that the only country club in town does not allow admission of non-Christians. Or they may find a separate, Jewish country club. Or they may find a country club with no exclusionary rules. In their search for a temple to attend for religious services, that will depend upon whether they are Orthodox, Reformed, or Conservative. In some small communities all three groups band together because of small numbers in one temple, but the analogous situation would be Methodists, Presbyterians, and Congregationalists all attending the same church. Even though they are all Christian sects, there are differences in their rituals and beliefs.

Commitment has been defined as "enduring adherence" (Kelley, 1983, p. 313). This is the individual's willingness to invest resources such as time or money or energy in the group. It is the desire to stay with the group and ensure its success. It might be commitment to an organization through staying with them throughout your entire career, or the commitment might be to another person "until death us do part." Are evaluation and commitment related to each other? According to Thibault and Kelley's (1959) and their reformulated theory of Social Exchange (Kelley & Thibault, 1978) as discussed in Chapter 2, not necessarily. We may leave a group we like if something better comes along, or stay in a miserable situation if there is no better alternative. Both of the processes of evaluation and commitment play important roles in the process of socialization.

The final of our critical issues is role transition. As we move from stage to stage in socialization, the behaviors expected of us change and since the definition of a role is a set of expected behaviors, so do our roles. Just as we do not expect the same behaviors of an infant, a school child, a college student, and a parent in a family, movement through socialization alters expectations. Often transitions are marked with some sort of rite of passage or ceremony. The completion of high school and college are observed by graduation ceremonies. The formal commitment between partners is celebrated with a wedding. In the Jewish religion the passage into adulthood (at the age of 13) is marked by a religious ceremony known as a bar mitzvah for boys and a bat mitzvah for girls. We will identify the role transitions involved with the socialization process as we discuss the stages.

Choosing Groups

The first stage of Moreland and Levine's model (1982) is called **investigation.** At this point the individual does not belong to a group and is checking out a number of possible groups to join. We investigate before we apply to colleges, or graduate schools, or jobs. We check out potential partners before making an approach to advance the relationship. Clearly at this stage evaluation is extraordinarily important. We must find out all we can about the advantages and disadvantages of each choice. Our investigation will be very personal in that we have identified what characteristics we particularly value in the school or job or person. One person might want to go to a school with a stellar academic reputation, while another wants to find a school with a rich tradition in partying. Money might be a vital concern for one job applicant, while the opportunity to have a flexible schedule to spend time with their family might be more important to another. And certainly each of us differs to some degree as to the most important traits in a partner. Some want a pretty package, some want a sense of humor, some want to be pampered, some want a good provider. Each of these people will evaluate the same situation very differently.

 How did you decide which college to attend? What were the relevant criteria? Were you accepted to your first-choice school? If not, did your criteria change? What was the basis of your final decision?

While we are busy evaluating the school or job or person, they are also evaluating us. In the case of the school or job we must present credentials to be evaluated. A church or synagogue might also expect certain credentials—such

Before we join groups we undergo a reciprocal
process of investigation.

as a certificate of baptism or attendance at a catechism class or formal conversion to the religion. Country clubs might very well have a number of criteria. In the "exclusive" clubs, race or religion might be an exclusionary factor. Most country clubs will require a look at your financial situation. Successful groups are often quite restrictive. On the other hand, unsuccessful groups often actively seek new members and have much more lenient criteria for inclusion.

At the point when you are investigating a number of choices for groups, your commitment to any one is low. You are gathering information. But the group does not have any exclusive hold on you. If you're lucky you'll be accepted to several of the graduate schools or meet a number of potential partners. Then your only problem will be to choose. In the investigation stage, you are a nonmember. You are not bound by any of the norms or rules of the particular group. You should interview a number of places, apply to a number of schools, date a number of different people. If you want to become a member, however, it helps to "look the part." In organizations the individual who wants to be promoted to a higher level in the organization is often advised to start dressing and acting as if they were already at that level. Looking like you belong often helps you be "one of us."

Joining Groups

Congratulations! You've narrowed down your choices and made a selection. And they want you, too. The evaluation in both directions was positive. So you agree to give it a try. You become a new member and assume the behaviors of the role. Formal groups often have some sort of ceremony or initiation. If you join a church they may ask that you be baptized again. If you get engaged, an exchange of tokens may be expected. In sororities and fraternities of the past and apparently still in some colleges today (particularly the military academies and The Citadel), there is a period of hazing that serves as an initiation. Sometimes these can be incredibly brutal. Of four women (the second class of women admitted in the school's history) admitted to The Citadel which had been required by law to desegregate, forcing students to allow women, two of the women were set afire as part of their initiation. These two women dropped out.

Of the two from that class that remained, one performed so well academically that she advanced to her junior year in one year and the other was so adept at the physical tasks and fitness required that she became the head of training for the next entering class.

The more we wish to be a part of the group the more abuse we will take or the more investment we will make to the group. Country clubs (and health clubs) often ask for very large membership fees. Gangs often require the new member to undergo extreme physical abuse (the application section of this chapter will explore the various initiation practices of gangs).

Initiations

Research has found that the more difficult the **initiation** into the group, the higher the level of commitment. This is, however, only a correlation and does not imply causation. It is plausible to think that people who are practically desperate to join a group will do almost anything to be accepted. But is it possible that simply going through a painful, or costly, or embarrassing initiation will cause us to increase our commitment to the group? Actually, yes. There could be several explanations.

The first involves the theory of **cognitive dissonance** (Festinger, 1957). Human beings (at least Americans—cognitive dissonance does not work well on members of Eastern collectivist cultures) like their beliefs, attitudes, values, and behaviors to be consistent with each other. If I believe that it is important to be charitable to the poor and I donate old clothes and money to a shelter for battered spouses, my behavior is consistent with my values and I feel good about myself. If I believe in charity but use all my extra money to buy myself another fur, then my behavior is not consistent with my values and I will (according to the theory) suffer from a form of psychological discomfort known as cognitive dissonance.

Discomfort is unpleasant, and people will generally try to reduce the feeling. So something has to give. I either decide that the poor deserve it because they lack ambition and initiative (in which case my fur is no problem for me) or I take the fur back and give the money to charity. People will change whatever is easiest and least painful to change. But sometimes you can't take back the coat. You've made an irrevocable choice. What then?

So how does cognitive dissonance deal with initiations and commitment? If I pay a steep, nonrefundable membership fee to a country club, or I give away all my possessions to join a cult, or I allow myself to be set on fire and don't report it to anyone (the older brother of one of the burned cadets made the report), I look at my behavior and ask myself why I did it. An outsider might say "because you're stupid." But if I say that to myself, I've just stepped into a situation of cognitive dissonance. I'm an intelligent person with good judgment and I just made an irrevocable (and maybe not so wise) decision. I can't get my money back or it's too late to go to another school. Gosh! I must REALLY want to belong or I wouldn't have made such a sacrifice. No cognitive dissonance. The Rosenbergs found a lovely country club that charged a $10,000 membership fee. They love it. They also found a Conservative temple that was low on members and welcomed them with open arms.

Schlenker (1975) has offered another explanation for the strong connection between the severity of the initiation and high levels of commitment. This has to do less with my own internal comfort or discomfort with my behavior, and much more with what others will think of me. I could walk around telling everyone what a jerk I was, or I can develop a very strong belief that what I did was right and **save face.** I know the decision was bad, but I'm not going to let the world know.

Finding Our Niche

If the entry stage of socialization goes well, the next stage involves undergoing orientation and indoctrination to the secrets of the group. With new employment this stage is often formalized as a probationary period. You will begin to do the job to see if you can make it. The group will determine if you can be assimilated into the group without disruption, and you will work to see if you can accommodate to the group. Evaluation on both sides is again really important. They're deciding whether to keep you, and you're deciding whether to stay.

This is your first chance to see the group, or job, or person as they really are. The investigation and entry stages are a courtship of sorts. Everyone who wants you to belong is on their best manners and minimizing problems in the group. Your future mother-in-law is nice to you. You don't see your future husband or wife grubby or grumpy. The person who wants to hire you as an employee isn't going to show that wicked temper until you've been landed. It's still not too late, you can still decide that your initial evaluation was too positive and get out. Or you can get the boot. But often, possibly because of the investments you've already made (time, money, energy, emotions), your commitment to the group will be higher than theirs to you.

Home at Last

Well, you've passed muster. The probationary period is over and you are a full member of the group, or an active member of the fraternity, or a husband or wife. Evaluation never completely goes away, but it is much less a point of focus. You don't have to constantly be "on." What you must do is work with the group or your partner to identify your role. What behaviors are expected of you? This is the process of *role negotiation.* Just what does it mean to be a husband? What do members of the board of directors do—and are you expected to do the same or is there some other behavior expected of you? As you settle into your role your commitment reaches a peak and may never be higher. You may decide you love the job and stay there for your entire career. You may decide you made exactly the right choice of a partner and make a lifetime commitment. You're a full member of the group.

Disenchantment

Not every group or relationship is "happy ever after." Perhaps all the traveling that was so exciting when you started the job is now getting to be a real burden when you want to be home with your children more. Maybe you had no idea that the group you joined had such racist attitudes and evil intentions. Lots of young men are attracted to white supremacist hate groups because they are treated as adults—provided with cigarettes, alcohol, drugs, access to places to be with girls, and lots of attention that they might not get at home. As they move deeper into the movement they find out more about the group.

Religious cults are expert at attracting potential converts by a process called "love bombing" in which they shower the person with compliments and attention and all sorts of love. For someone hungry for attention, that can be a powerful lure. Later on, however, when the individuals are getting four hours of sleep a night and are expected to exist on a substandard diet and beg for money for the cult, some change their minds. (Others don't, of course, and perhaps again we're looking at the power of cognitive dissonance on Americans.) This stage was referred to in our model as **divergence.**

As commitment wavers, evaluation again becomes important. Perhaps you can't find a place for yourself in the group, or establish the types of relationships you had hoped for, or like the job as much as you expected. You step back to your role of quasi-member. Maybe you ask for a leave of absence, or a separation. As your commitment wavers, the group begins to re-evaluate you, also. If they wish to keep you, you will often be flooded with attention again. An attempt is being made at **resocialization**—bringing you back into the fold. Perhaps you all decide that you do want to stay. In that case you move back up the model into the **acceptance/maintenance stage** we referred to as "home at last." And, again, maybe you stay in this stage of low evaluation, high commitment, and full membership forever.

Disengagement

Other times, however, upon re-evaluation, you don't want to return to the group or the relationship. You leave the group, returning to your role as a nonmember. You have no commitment to the group, and you really don't care about the group. Or, you decide you want to come back and they've decided not to let you return. Or, in a best of all possible worlds the decision is mutual.

You have one last task to accomplish regarding this group, job, school, or relationship, however. That's to think back and make sense of what happened—to tie up the loose ends psychologically. Will you look back fondly, or spend your time on revenge fantasies? This is the **remembrance stage.** As we began the discussion of socialization I warned you that this stage often results in negative feelings. We'll examine some possible explanations for this unfortunate outcome, but first let's look at the circumstances under which you are likely to have fond memories of the group—and they of you.

Memory is an interesting phenomenon. Lots of people think that our memories are written on our brains like the words on this page and all we have to do is go back and find them when we want to reminisce (or do well on an exam). But memories can be changed or distorted by subsequent events. Research on memory by psychologists such as Loftus (1983) show that even the way someone is questioned about a memory can either change or create a false memory.

So the way our connection with a group ends can have a significant impact on our later memory of the entire experience.

We are most likely to have positive memories of a group experience when either the break was always part of the contract (you join the Peace Corps for two years) or when the break was brought about by an outside agent (e.g., your spouse is transferred to Seattle) and you quit your job to go along. Everyone always knew you were going—that the relationship was temporary, or they wanted to keep you and you wanted to stay, but couldn't. You can then look back fondly on your memories.

Under most other conditions, however, it is more likely that memories on both sides (yours and the group's) will be negative. The culprit? Cognitive dissonance. You leave when they want you to stay. Apparently you left for a reason. But from their perspective you're a rat and a deserter. If you were half as good as they had thought you were you would have recognized what a fabulous group they are and would have stayed. Since there can't be anything wrong with them, it must be something wrong with you. Or they fire you. Obviously they weren't happy with you and from your perspective they must be fools to let someone as wonderful as you get away.

A true example. My first full-time faculty job was with a private college that was run as a business—from the top down. This is fairly unusual in academia. Faculty usually have at least advisory powers over such matters as curriculum and admission and grading policies. Our management made all decisions by fiat. Directives were handed to our department chairs (appointed by management) who were ordered to be 100 percent supportive of the decisions. Despite wonderful colleagues, I did not want to be a part of this group. I also wanted to move to another part of the country. The year I was actively looking for other jobs (without their knowledge) was the year after I had been offered the position of chair of the department, which I declined. That same year the faculty decided to revolt. They wrote petitions and nasty letters to the administration. Although I completely agreed with their sentiments I stayed far away from any association with the rebellion because I couldn't afford to be fired (and private colleges have a frightening ability to fire at will). One of my colleagues and friends, however, chaired the meetings with the administration and signed the petitions and letters. The same week I was offered my next job, her husband was transferred to another part of the country. So we were both leaving. Although both of us still hold fond memories of the extraordinarily cohesive group of colleagues we shared, both of us were delighted to go. She kept in touch with what was happening at the school after we left. I did not.

I wasn't surprised when she called me and let me know how the administration had reacted to our leaving, which was regrets to be losing her, one of their best teachers. Wasn't it unfortunate that someone (unnamed) had misled her into becoming involved in the unpleasantness the previous year! I, on the other hand, was a demon incarnate. I had organized the faculty rebellion. How dare I leave after all they'd done and offered me? I couldn't have invented a better example of the effect of cognitive dissonance on the **remembrance stage** of socialization.

Summary

In this chapter we examined the effects of temporal change on groups. We have seen that under the best of conditions the group gels from a cluster of individuals over time into an efficient, productive entity. We discussed ways to speed up the process of developing methods of sorting out social issues before serious task work is undertaken. We talked about the need for disagreement in groups and its positive effects on the quality of the group's products. We identified types of conflicts and identified the need for good communication and conflict resolution skills, which we will explore in future chapters. We discussed the necessity of planning for the ending of the group in such a way that it will serve to have been a positive experience for the members.

In the second half of the chapter we looked at the individual's progress through the group. We looked at the progression from nonmember to quasi-member to full member, then possible withdrawal and disassociation from the group back to the status of nonmember. We discussed the role of reciprocal evaluation through the stages of socialization, as well as the changes in commitment associated with each stage. We used Moreland and Levine's (1982) basic model with the following sequence of stages:

1. Investigation
2. Entry
3. Socialization
4. Acceptance/maintenance
5. Divergence
6. Resocialization
7. Remembrance

We discussed the effects of cognitive dissonance on the valence associated with the memories of the group. And we got the Rosenbergs settled in their new community. Next we will apply these principles to the methods employed by various gangs to "jump in" or initiate new members.

Key Terms

acceptance/maintenance
adjourning
autistic conflict
classism
cognitive dissonance
collaboration
commitment
conflict
confrontation
contingent conflict
disenchantment
divergence
escalating conflict
evaluation

false conflict
forming
group development
improvisation
individual differentiation
individual socialization
initiations
interaction in groups
investigation
membership
norming
oral expression
performing
primary tension

remembrance
resocialization
rhythm
role transitions
save face
secondary tension
social exchange theory
socialization
spirituality
storming
subgrouping
termination
time

APPLICATION

"Jumped in"—Socialization into Gang Life

The term "gang" strikes terror into the hearts of many American citizens. We have images of black leather, chains, motorcycles, drugs, and perhaps death. There is no question that gangs are becoming more prevalent in American society; however, they are not a new phenomenon. Gangs are groups of individuals who follow most of the principles we have already discussed in terms of group dynamics. What we have now that is new and different is a proliferation of new gangs who do not follow the norms of the original gangs in America.

Christensen (1994) gives the following definitional characteristics of gangs. A gang is a group that:

Conspires to commit, or commits, crimes against individuals or groups, based on color, race, religion, sexual preference, national origin, or against rival gang associations.

Uses a name or common identifying sign or symbol, or has an identifiable leadership.

Has a high rate of interaction among members to the exclusion of other groups.

Claims a neighborhood and/or geographical territory.

Wears distinctive types of clothing, exhibits distinctive appearance, or communicates in a peculiar or unique style.

Probably among the earliest ethnic gangs in America was The White Hand Society which was imported from Sicily. This gang evolved into *La Cosa Nostra* (Our Thing) (Kleinknecht, 1996). This gang was essentially cloaked in secrecy until 1963 when member Joseph Valachi testified before Congress.

Gang members are willing to undergo brutal initiations to gain entrance to a valued group.

According to Valachi, in order to be a member of La Cosa Nostra, one had to be full-blood Italian. The Italian Mafia is the prototype that many Americans carry of the "gang." However, this image is dated as new gangs have joined, and in some cases superseded La Cosa Nostra in power. This may be in part because the original gang structure was divided into families with an all-powerful "godfather." This individual determined which vices were appropriate for the Mafia to engage in for profit. For many years, families were denied the permission to deal in drugs. The Mafia's original foothold in American society was supplying Americans with the liquor they desired during Prohibition. There was a huge demand that the Mafia was more than happy to supply. As new leadership took over the Mafia (often in bloody assassinations), the Mafia had to play catch-up with other gangs.

Valachi testified that the initiation ceremony in which he participated in 1930 was virtually the same as late as 1989.

In each of the cases, the inductee's fingers were pricked, a dagger and pistol were displayed on the table, a ritual paper was burned, and the new member uttered the vow of omerta, *or secrecy. More frightening still, the ritual was strikingly similar—right down to the pistol and dagger and the letting of blood—to a Camorra initiation in Naples that was recorded by a historian in 1872.*

(Kleinknecht, 1996, p. 43)

As initiations go, this may sound like a very simple ritual, but what kept Mafiosi from breaking the vow was the death penalty that would be carried out upon "snitches" or those who tried to rise above themselves in the gang's hierarchy.

The Hell's Angels gang developed as a direct by-product of World War II. In the United States 303rd Bombardier Squadron stationed in England, there was a particularly wild airplane crew. As was the fashion, each crew named their planes; this crew named theirs the Hell's Angel. When they returned to the United States after the war they organized into the "first outlaw motorcycle gang of note . . ." (Lavigne, 1996). As of 1987, there were believed to be about 1,000 members worldwide with 67 chapters in thirteen countries. The Hell's Angels fit almost perfectly Christensen's definition of a gang.

The group wars with rival gangs and believes in white supremacy. Thus, any minority is likely to be a potential target of violence. Violence is revered in the group, as indicated by the fact that one of the elite subgroups—"The Filthy Few"—must have killed for the club in order to qualify for membership in the clique.

The Hell's Angels have a number of common identifying signs as well as identifiable leadership. Members of the group ride Harley-Davidson motorcycles, wear leather clothing, and sport tattoos and gang patches. There is a very definite ritual involved with acquiring the tattoos and patches as part of the initiation process which we'll discuss later.

As far as leadership, there is a very clear hierarchical organization similar to that of an army. When the group goes on "runs," roles can be identified by the position an individual is placed in the pack. The chapter president (who is either elected by the group or self-appointed) rides at the front of the pack next to the centerline. The road captain, who is the logistician and chief of security for the group on runs and carries the club money, rides next to the president. The vice president who is the heir apparent chosen by the president rides behind the president and road captain. Behind these three ride the members with "full colors"—full members of the group. These include the secretary/treasurer who keeps a list of members, collects dues and fines, and keeps money available to pay bills and bond for members who are arrested. Behind the full color members and ahead of prospects (individuals in the stage of investigation) and honorary members rides the sergeant-at-arms who serves as the president's body guard, enforcer, and executioner.

Joining the Hell's Angels is a ritualized process. In order to become a "prospect," young men hang around the chapter's clubhouse or the bar the chapter frequents. [(Women are not allowed to join the group. They have only two roles available: "old ladies" (women who "belong" to members) or "mamas" or "sheep" (who are considered sexual community property).] The prospects run errands and do favors for the members in hopes of being noticed. If he is successful in impressing a member in good standing, he is nominated by that club member for admission. He may not wear the gang colors, but instead has an armband or vest that identifies his status. There are three votes on admission. A prospect cannot become a member unless the vote is unanimous on all three occasions. At this point, the member must commit a crime of the chapter's choosing—sometimes murder. For this he earns his club patch. Within nine days after receiving the patch, he must get the club tattoo. The patch is red printing on white cloth which reads "DEGUELO" ("no quarter" in Spanish). Members who have been to prison tattoo an asterisk between their thumb and forefinger for each detention.

While the Hell's Angels have been around for a long time, there are many newer gangs moving into or developing in American society. Often groups that feel they are underbenefitted by society and cannot gain status or stature in the community through the ordinary channels (education or a good job) will organize into gangs. There is a great deal of money to be made in the drug trade—much more than these individuals could make through the legitimate channels that are open to them.

In Los Angeles, two of the most prominent African-American gangs are the Crips and the Bloods. These are supergangs made up of hundreds of smaller groups. In a manner similar to the Hell's Angels they have also started chapters in other cities. The Crips wear blue clothing and the Bloods wear red. Being caught in the wrong neighborhood in the wrong color clothing can result in death, which unfortunately has happened to tourists who have become lost. Almost all gangs have their own colors which outsiders wear at their own risk and/or have hand signals or signs to identify their membership. The Rollin' Twenties, for example, wear exclusively gold and black clothing.

The Crips organized first in LA in the 1970s. The Bloods developed to protect themselves from the Crips and have their own language. They will not use the letter "c" (as in Crip). For example, if they want a cigarette, they will ask for a "bigarette" (Sikes, 1997, p. 8). In 1992, the Los Angeles District Attorney estimated that nearly half the young black men in LA were affiliated with a gang. Almost half (47%) of gang members were between the ages of 21 and 24.

The Lennox-13 is a Los Angeles Latino gang. Cliques of between thirty and fifty of the same-age youth belong to the larger gang. These are mostly first generation teenagers of Spanish-speaking parents who emigrated from Mexico or further south. The gang sign is an "L" formed with the thumb and forefinger.

Gang-related crime in this country has been increasing. In Los Angeles, the gangs allow girls to either join the gangs or affiliate themselves in a meaningful way, which involves participating in the crimes and carrying weapons—usually knives and guns. The crime rate for girls is lower than for boys, but rising much faster. The arrest rate for girls under 18 increased 82 percent during the period from 1989 to 1994. The rate of increase for boys was 25 percent. In the 1980s, the number of adult women in prisons jumped from 12,331 in 1980 to 43,845 at the end of the decade. Females are taking their places in the gang scene.

In San Antonio, Texas, the city is geographically divided by race. The Latinos (who represent 54% of the citizens of the city) live on the west side of town, the blacks on the east, the whites on the north, and the south side is a mixture of races. The Latino gangs jealously guard their territory. The two major gangs are the Kings and the Queens, separated by gender but affiliated with each other. The symbol of both gangs is the Disney character Mickey Mouse and the sign is the sign language "K." Initiation into both types of gangs are particularly brutal. The boys are beaten and kicked by gang members for up to ten minutes. For girls, there are more options, as identified by a Kings member:

> I'll tell you straight right now, the girls have a choice of initiations: (A) fighting one-on-one with a guy for two minutes; (B) get shot in the leg with a Glock; (C) get jumped in by chicks for a minute and a half; or (D) they can roll the dice and hope that they get two at the most.
>
> (Sikes, 1997, p. 150)

There are several references here that might need explanation. First, a Glock is a semiautomatic handgun. "Jumping in" is being beaten by the female gang members. And perhaps most disturbing of all, option D refers to the practice of "training." This involves having sexual intercourse with a number of gang members sequentially. The number thrown on the dice is the number of men with whom the girl must have sex. And these are girls as young as ten years old. After completion of her choice of options she is considered a full member of the gang.

Minority youth are not the only ones involved with gang activity. Skinheads are white youth who adhere to the principles of white superiority. This can be expressed as white separatism which calls for separate nations for the different races, or the more militant white supremacists. Thus there are racist and nonracist skinhead groups, but their actions are quite similar. The major difference is their victims. Racist skinheads hate almost everyone. They believe that the government (which they refer to as ZOG—Zionist Occupied Government) is controlled by the Jews who also control the police. The Jews are believed to have fabricated the Holocaust to create sympathy for themselves. Blacks are believed to be the "mud race"—not even really people at all. Also on the target list are Asians, mixed-race couples, and homosexuals.

*White supremacists' image of the ideal white man is . . . virile, and muscular,
standing tall and proud with his white, fertile woman at his side.*

(Christensen, 1994, p. 102)

If you happen to be white and disagree with their beliefs, or just happen to get in the way, you too can become a target.

The norms of appearance are very distinctive for skinheads. As the name implies, their heads are shaved. They sport swastikas and other tattoos and multiple piercings of their bodies. Their uniform is a flight jacket with jeans and Dr. Martens boots. Their appearance is modeled after the white working-class gangs in Britain (hence the British boots). The boots often play an integral part in the attacks on victims. In fact the stompings are sometimes referred to as "boot parties."

Socialization into the skinheads follows the type of pattern we discussed previously. First an individual who wishes to join hangs around the group as a nonmember, but a "wanna-be." Once notice is taken of the newcomer, he (or she) is known as a fence straddler. Seldom do individuals go out and don the regalia and decorations at once. The entry is more gradual and an attempt at premature full membership would not be taken well by the group members (as with any other group). The next stage is the "associate." This is the person who agrees with the ideology and participates in gang activities, but still keeps a life going outside. Most of the females fall into this category, often because they prove their fertility at a relatively young age and must take care of the children. Hardcore members devote their lives to the "cause" and are completely immersed in the lifestyle.

It has been suggested that the skinhead movement emerged as a response to the ethnic gangs and to the success of many minorities in the society. Many if not most of the skinheads are not well educated and are unlikely to be successful in traditional terms. It is very threatening, therefore, to have to compete with or watch individuals whom you consider your inferiors move ahead socially.

Most of the gangs we have examined thus far fit the patterns of group development and socialization discussed in the chapter. There is a new type of gang, however, that breaks all the "rules." And because of the new rules they have adopted, they may become particularly dangerous. Vietnamese gangs are rampant in southern California and are likely to be based just south of Los Angeles proper in Orange County in the towns of Westminster, Garden Grove, and Santa Ana. Both the Vietnamese boys and girls start to join gangs at about the age of twelve, but have often moved out by the age of twenty either into a more traditional life, or prison, or death. Some of the boys' gangs are: Cheap Boyz, Scar Boyz, Orange Boyz, Natona Boyz, Mohawk Boyz, Santa Ana Boyz, Oriental Boyz, and Lonely Boyz Only. Some of the girls' gangs are: the Dirty Punks, South Side Scissors, Banana Girlz, and IBK (Innocent but Killers) (Goad & Goad, 1994).

Vietnamese gangs are better armed than most street gangs. They tend to have high caliber weapons. Another difference is that they do not claim turf nor demand lifelong allegiance to a single gang. Members are free to move from gang to gang. The gangs cooperate with each other, but there is no overarching organization as there is for the Hell's Angels, Crips, or Bloods. They don't have "colors" or distinctive graffiti. The best way to visually identify a Vietnamese gang member is by the scars on their hands where they have extinguished cigarettes.

Even the types of crimes committed by Vietnamese gangs are different. They tend to avoid dealing drugs, preferring instead to perpetrate frauds, steal cars, steal computer chips, or commit home invasions. In this crime they take advantage of their own people's frequent distrust of banks. Thus large sums of money are often kept in the home. The gang bursts through the doors and windows and holds the family hostage until they have what they want. They will usually identify the weakest member of the family and torture that individual until they have been given all they believe to be of value in the house. If their expectations are wrong or the family refuses to cooperate, the family members are killed. They then take their booty and spend, spend, spend. Vietnamese gang members are enamored with conspicuous consumption (a way to keep valuables close and avoid banks) and are very mobile in the cars they are able to purchase.

This new type of gang is most troubling to law enforcement officers. Because the "old" gangs had developed such similar norms and patterns of behavior, the police were better able to predict crimes or incidents and to arrest perpetrators. Now they may have to learn a whole new set of rules.

Discussion Questions

Apply the concepts from the chapter to consider the following questions:

1. Given what you know about the effects of initiations on commitment to the group, which gangs described above should demonstrate the highest level of commitment to the group? Are there any extenuating circumstances that might affect your choice? What are they?
2. Girls aspiring to entry into the San Antonio Queens have a choice of initiations. What do you think of the fact that being beaten, being shot, and sexual behavior are equated with each other?
3. If you were going to try to intervene or interrupt the flow of young people into gangs, at what point in the cycle do you think the intervention would be most appropriate? Why? What sort of intervention might work? Why?
4. Why do you think the organization of the Hell's Angels is so militaristic? Do you think it has more to do with the members or the history of the group? Why?
5. Draw a comparison between the stages of socialization in the gangs discussed. Are they similar? In what ways? Different? How and why?

CHAPTER 4

Communication in Groups

What Would YOU Predict?

The staff of The Weekly Sentinel, *the newspaper of Anonymous University, is having a staff meeting. All copy must be in within the next forty-eight hours in order to make the press deadline. Because there have been some problems in the dormitories, Clarissa has been assigned to interview the chancellor on her reactions and any anticipated actions to be taken. Clarissa has not been able yet to get in to see the chancellor. She is frustrated and angry and feels she is getting the runaround so she complains to her fellow staff members. David immediately begins to suggest strategies she might use to catch the chancellor in time for the interview. Can you predict Clarissa's reaction?*

INTRODUCTION

Under the best of conditions, communication is not an easy task. Yet our ability to relate to each other and to work effectively with each other is dependent upon our communication abilities. In order for accurate communication to occur, we have to send clear messages, and learn to listen and gather sufficient information so we understand the messages of others. If that weren't complicated enough, communication between people always occurs on two levels—the verbal and the nonverbal (Reusch & Bateson, 1951). As we grow up a great deal of attention is placed on teaching us the linguistic rules of our language so we will become effective verbally. Unfortunately the same attention is not paid to helping us understand the equally important nonverbal aspects of communication. In this chapter we will discuss the many levels of communication.

MODELS OF VERBAL COMMUNICATION

We'll begin with an area where most of us feel relatively comfortable with our abilities—**verbal communication.** Unfortunately, many of us are not nearly as good at verbal communication as we believe. We may think we're surrounded by people who are not intelligent enough to understand us, or who aren't listening to us, but if we are frequently misunderstood then it is probably true that we are not sending clear messages. Don't despair. When we identify all the complexities of the various models of verbal communication it's surprising effective communication occurs as often as it does.

Each verbal message can be graphed, as shown by the model below by Fujishin (1997):

SOURCE → MESSAGE → ENCODING → CHANNELS → RECEIVER → DECODING

The **source** is the individual wishing to convey a thought to another (or others). All communication starts out as an idea in someone's head. Our ideas are influenced by: our emotions; our values, stereotypes, and prejudices; our past experience; and our level of knowledge. When we are under emotional stress or under the spell of any strong emotions we often have trouble formulating our thoughts. A mother who has just been informed of a serious injury to her child is not going to think "straight." She will be scattered and distracted— even if under other circumstances she is the model of logic and clear communication. And we've all seen depictions of the tongue-tied suitor who is so smitten that he can't stammer out a coherent sentence. Anger can also affect our ability to gather our thoughts. Often when people are angry they say inappropriate things because all they wish to do is to attack their adversary. This is an extremely dangerous situation because once you have said something hurtful you can apologize, but you can never take it back. You can't make it "unhappen." And the odds are that you may have damaged your relationship with the individual you attacked.

Our values, stereotypes, and prejudices can serve to give us tunnel vision. We simply do not have an idea occur to us because it is out of our consciousness. There was a riddle that was frequently used in research in the 1970s that I have often used in class. During the seventies only about 20 percent of students could solve the riddle. It goes like this:

A father and his son were driving along during a serious ice storm. As they rounded a bend in the road, the father lost control of the car which went off the road and hit a tree. The father was killed instantly. Fortunately, a passerby witnessed the accident and contacted emergency help. The boy was rushed to the hospital for emergency, life-saving surgery. The surgeon rushed into the room, pulling on gloves, then looked into the child's face and said, "I cannot operate on this child. He is my son." Who is the surgeon?

I'm sure that most of you immediately realized the surgeon was the child's mother. However, if in your view of the appropriate professions for men and women you think (however unconsciously) that doctors and surgeons are men, the answer will not occur to you. I was always amazed at the twisted lengths students would go through to invent a plausible answer. My favorite involved an illegitimate child who had been given up at birth and adopted by the man driving the car. The child looked just like his natural father, who was the surgeon. That's how we can be blinded to ideas because they don't fit our world view.

Our past experiences include our level of experience in learning. We need to have the vocabulary to formulate an idea. And languages accommodate to those needs. In the English language there are only a few terms for snow. The language of the Eskimos near the North Pole contained many words for various conditions of snow because it was such a salient part of their experience.

Knowledge is a funny thing. Too little will certainly make it difficult to communicate effectively, but so will too much. If you were to ask me to sing an aria from Puccini in Italian we'd both be in trouble—me, because I don't know Italian (or any arias); you, because you asked me to sing. But experts in a field are often very poor at communicating their knowledge. They know so much that they cannot imagine anyone else not having the same basis of understanding. In order to be an effective communicator you have to be able to tailor your communication to your audience. You would not explain Einstein's theory of relativity to a ten-year-old the way you would to a college physics class.

In this example, though, you would probably automatically know to simplify the vocabulary and the concepts for the child. I've sat frustrated through many a math class not having the foggiest notion what was being said. I recognized English words, but they made no sense to me. After one statistics class in graduate school I approached the professor in tears. He looked blank when I confessed I was totally clueless. Then he said, "But it all makes sense because it's based on the fact that you can describe a line by an equation. People are born knowing that!" I wasn't. He just assumed because so much of what he did was dependent upon that knowledge and since I was a graduate student he assumed I must also possess the same knowledge. Once he explained the concept to me, all the problems I had been unable to understand suddenly made sense!

STOP Can you think of any examples of situations or classes in which experts tried to explain something to you and used terminology so far above your head that you had no clue as to what they were trying to convey? What were your feelings? What did you do?

Once a person decides on an idea they wish to convey, they must create a **message.** Our message is the "idea, thought, feeling, or emotion" we wish to convey (Fujishin, 1997, p. 36). We began to touch on this issue in the previous paragraph. We must consider what our communication target is likely to understand. We create the message through the process of **encoding**—of taking ideas and translating them into some code we share with the recipient of a message. *Code* "is the set or sets of signals used in the language" (Brilhart, 1986, p. 167). If we don't share a code, we cannot communicate either verbally or nonverbally. If you speak only Urdu and I speak only Latvian, we have a problem. Of course we can use the services of a translator, but often the ideas of one language do not translate well into another. For years the Coca-Cola beverage company used an advertising slogan that when translated into Chinese said "Coke brings you back from the dead." Another recent example involved the Chinese translation of American movie titles. The film entitled "Nixon" became "The Big Liar." Neither translation conveys the original meaning at all.

Jargon is a type of code we have already discussed. Within our group jargon can facilitate communication, outside the group it can be used to confuse people or obfuscate issues. Words are after all only symbols. "There is no meaning

Jargon can become a serious barrier to accurate communication.
Source: "Doonesbury" by G.B. Trudeau. Copyright © 1983.
Reprinted by permission of Universal Press.

to a word apart from the person using and responding to it" (Brilhart, 1986, p. 169). Even when we think we recognize a word, it might be employed in entirely different ways. Americans who meet Australians or British individuals often get in trouble because the same word in the English language means very different things within the different countries' coding system. In the United States a bonnet is a form of hat worn by women. In England the word "bonnet" refers to what Americans refer to as the trunk of an automobile. In the United States the word "fag" is a derogatory reference to a homosexual individual. In England it refers to a cigarette. Could make for some interesting misunderstandings, yes?

Finally when we talk about the code of language we have to be very aware that many words (if not most) have very subjective meanings. My idea of what is fair in terms of the outcome in a lawsuit will probably differ substantially from the perception of fairness of my opponent in the suit. Another dangerous word that comes to mind is the word "elderly." We all know what constitutes elderly, right? Years ago a manager in a case I had assigned students to analyze was identified as being thirty-five years old. The group asked me to look over their rough draft and give them suggestions for improvement. I was much surprised and amused when I discovered they referred to the manager, who was also my age, as "elderly"! Ask around. Often you find that "elderly" is at least fifteen years older than the person answering the question. To a small child a college student is "old"; to a person turning fifty years old, the elderly are at least seventy-five or eighty years old.

 Can you or any of your classmates recall any situations where misunderstandings occurred because of different interpretations of a word? If someone calls someone else a "mother" what do they likely mean? Are there multiple interpretations?

Another issue in encoding the message is the level of **politeness** of the communication. In some languages (e.g., French and Spanish) a distinction is made between the formal and the familiar. We make such distinctions in English by the way we encode the message. Brown and Levinson (1987) distinguish five levels of politeness. The level of politeness used is influenced by the relationship between the speaker and target, the status of the target, and the size of the favor being requested. As the request becomes more important, we tend to be more polite. For example, if we were to have dinner with the governor, we would ask for the salt in a very different manner than we might make the same request from our younger sister at an informal dinner at home.

The first level of politeness is **bald speech.** This is a bare, unelaborated request such as, "Hand me that book." It is very direct, and the least polite of the levels. It can almost sound like a demand or order. The next level of politeness is labeled **positive politeness.** There is more influence by the closeness of the relationship between the communicator and target and a desire not to offend, so a *tag question* is added as in, "Hand me that book, will you?" This softens the impact of the request. The third level is **negative politeness.** Here the intent is to reduce the perceived imposition of the request—to make it seem as if we are asking less. Thus we would say, "Since you are standing right there, would you hand me that book?"

In the fourth level an attempt is made to mask the fact that a request is being made. In the *off-the-record* level the request would be, "Gee, I could really use that book." This can be so indirect that an insensitive or literal listener might not understand what is going on. My parents were masters of this style. Often on winter evenings one or the other would say, "Gee, don't you think it's a little cool in here?" What they were really saying, of course, was, "Would you please turn up the heater?" The indirectness of this level makes it possible for the target to ignore the request, even if it is recognized. The final level of politeness is no imposition at all. It is the *no-performance level*, where no request is made. While the theory apparently is understood by most American English speakers (Brown & Levinson, 1987), there are noticeable cultural differences we will discuss below (Holtgraves & Yang, 1992; Kroger & Wood, 1992).

The **channel** of communication refers to whether we deliver the message face-to-face, over the telephone, or in written form. Generally for Americans, the more formal the channel, the more emphasis the target places on the message. A passing comment from your employer about what a good job you are doing doesn't carry the weight of a memo on your desk containing the same information. If you really want to scare someone, put a criticism down on paper. This effect is compounded by a peculiar tendency of Americans to diminish the compliment inherent in a positive message and exaggerate the criticism in a negative message (Oyster, 1982). If you wanted to give one message of each type to the same person and wanted them to balance each other, you would need to write a glowing memo and casually make a very mild negative remark.

As we will discuss soon, the nonverbal behaviors that accompany a remark will also affect our interpretation of that remark. The channel we choose for our message affects the extent to which the listener has access to our nonverbal cues. Face-to-face, all the potential cues are available to the attentive target. The telephone eliminates our ability to "read" the face of the messenger, but we can still listen for paralinguistic cues as to the emotional content of the message. A message in written form eliminates all but the verbal content of the message. In our application at the end of this chapter on lying and the deception of deceit we will discuss the importance of nonverbal behaviors in identifying the truth.

STOP Given what you've just read about nonverbal cues, what channel would you use to tell your professor that your paper will be late because you spent the previous night at the emergency room with your roommate, when in fact you got home later than expected from a weekend ski trip? (You really want the professor to believe you.)

The use of **teleconferencing** which our new technologies have made possible also may affect the efficiency of communication. Oyster (1982) asked students in face-to-face conversation to pretend to be angry (negative emotional content) or pleased (positive emotional content) while making content-neutral statements. (A phrase such as "What time is it?" could mean that the person is being indirectly reminded they are quite late for a meeting, or that the speaker is surprised and pleased to find the person still hard at work. The meaning is taken from the nonverbal behaviors.) The target was to make a guess as to whether the message was intended to be positive or negative. These interchanges were also videotaped using a split-screen technique which allowed subsequent viewers to see both parties at the same time. In this follow-up study, these tapes were shown to subjects who were asked to make the same judgments of positively or negativity of the statements. Live dyads did significantly better at identifying the intended emotion. Apparently there are some cues that are not captured by a camera that are available to individuals in face-to-face interaction. An important area of future research would be to examine the results of these effects on the accuracy, or even the advisability, of teleconferences.

The **receiver** or target of the message uses their senses to take in the words that have been directed at them. In order for the message to have been considered successful, the receiver must also go through the process of translation (in this case **decoding**) to turn the message into an idea that is either understood or misunderstood. All of the characteristics we discussed in terms of the sender and encoding also apply here. If I try to convey a concept to you that is outside your world view, I will be unsuccessful. If you don't understand the code I use, again I will be unsuccessful. How will I know as the sender whether or not I have successfully conveyed my intended message? We will discuss that matter shortly in our discussion of feedback.

In conversations, there are attempts to verbally convey information and also to solicit information. Fujishin (1997) identified four levels of verbal communication attempting to convey information, ranging from relatively shallow conversation to messages high in importance to the source of the communication. These levels are *surface talk, reporting facts, giving opinions,* and *sharing feelings.*

Surface talk is what is commonly referred to as "small talk." It isn't meant to convey deep meanings, it is usually intended simply to acknowledge the existence of someone in our vicinity. You might remark to a person waiting on the same bench for a bus, "Nice day, isn't it?" Or you might ask about a classmate's weekend when you come to class on Monday. Actually we usually don't want an answer to a comment made at the level of surface talk. We routinely ask people who we haven't seen for a while, "How've you been?" or "How are you this morning?" The expected response is a neutral, "Fine," not a chronology or a litany of ills.

The second level of *reporting facts* is often also very impersonal. Verifiable information is being conveyed. When the treasurer of the Psychology Club informs the group of the status of the group's bank account, or the television announcer reports that there will be a free rabies vaccination clinic held at City Hall on Saturday, anyone with doubts can check to determine whether the facts are accurate. Some facts, though, are attached to emotions and opinions of the sender, in which case they can be encoded in such a way as to indicate implicit approval or disapproval. It was interesting to watch the various sources of media coverage of President Clinton's impeachment and the "spin" they put on the facts. The exact same disclosure by the independent counsel's office was reported as either devastating to or a triumph for the president. In Chapter 5 we will discuss the process of persuasion and the importance of the subjective beliefs of the individual who claims to be giving us objective facts.

When we share our evaluations of a situation in the third stage of the model (*giving opinions*), we are opening up ourselves to the target. We are disclosing something that is subjective and with which our target may not agree, making ourselves at least somewhat vulnerable. We have exposed our values and beliefs and must trust that our target is not going to take advantage of this information in a negative way.

The most personal, deepest level of verbal communication is *sharing feelings*. If I offer an opinion and you disagree with me, I might become angry or I might ask you to explain your position—then either reject it or change my own opinion. But it is unlikely I will become hurt. Men's and women's fear of closeness in relationships is based upon fear of rejection following the admission of feelings toward a partner.

> *Many difficulties experienced in the social dimension of the group could be avoided if individuals would be more willing to share their feelings before anger, resentment, or hurt got in the way of effective communication.*
>
> *(Fujishin, 1997, p. 40)*

Just as we seek to convey information, sometimes the goal of a conversation is to solicit information. The best way to do that is to ask questions. It is surprising how reluctant some individuals are to engage in this activity. Men, for example, are notorious for being unwilling to ask for directions when driving, even when it is patently clear they are lost (Tannen, 1994). I find that students are much less likely to ask questions in class than when I do consulting work with groups of police officers. Perhaps the students are concerned that "looking dumb" will affect their grades, or the fact of a large status difference with the students makes them afraid I might perceive a question as a challenge. As we'll see when we talk about feedback, one of the worst things you can do when you've tried to convey information is to ask, "Do you understand?" Most everyone will say yes, regardless.

STOP Have you and your classmates found it true that men won't ask directions, or is this just a stereotype? Are there differences in opinion in the class based on the sex of the individual expressing the opinion? If it is true, what possible explanations can you identify?

Brilhart (1986) divides the types of questions asked in group communication into two categories: those about group process and those that are task related. Here again we see the ubiquitous existence of the two levels of issues in the group. Questions regarding the social aspects of the group are: *orientation-seeking questions*, *procedure-seeking questions*, and *relational questions*.

Orientation-seeking questions involve establishing the structure of the group process. What are we doing? When are we going to do it? And so forth.

Procedure-seeking questions would include information regarding the coordination, organization, and decision making. Basically all these questions revolve around HOW the group is going to function. These first two types of questions fit into either the level of reporting facts or giving opinions. **Relational questions** involve the relationships between group members. This can involve asking someone to reveal their feelings, trying to bring out hidden agendas, resolving tensions, or preventing power struggles. This last type of question involves the level of sharing feelings—the deepest and most intimate level of communication.

Task-related questions include *information-seeking questions*, *opinion-seeking questions*, and *policy-seeking questions*. **Information-seeking questions** might involve questions of division of labor. Who is doing what? Are the graphs finished at the art department? This constitutes communication at the objective, reporting facts level. **Opinion-seeking questions** might arise after the group has generated a number of solutions to a problem and now must make a choice. Polling the opinions of the group members will provide information as to whether the group is close to a solution. Opinion seeking is at the deeper level of communication of sharing opinions and is therefore a little riskier.

The final type of task-related question is the **policy-seeking question.** Depending on whether the group has an established policy, this type of question could be considered either at the reporting facts level or the giving opinions level. It is wise to establish policy early in the group's life. This helps prevent distractions and digressions into policy making in the heat of problem solving or decision making. Trying to make policy when everyone has already determined which position they favor runs the risk of turning into a political battle rather than a procedure intended to facilitate the group.

EFFECTS OF GENDER AND CULTURE ON VERBAL COMMUNICATION

As we have already discussed, it is much easier to communicate effectively with people who share our codes. We will now examine a large body of literature that indicates that gender and cultural differences often present significant problems in verbal communication. The major issue we will see occurring repeatedly is a problem with a lack of shared codes. Fortunately, with education this problem should be relatively easy to counter.

Deborah Tannen (1990, 1994, 1995) has done extensive research in the gender differences in conversational style. She has identified two types of conversation: *report talk*, and *rapport talk*. **Report talk** is "public" talk. Its goal is to preserve independence and status by exhibiting knowledge and skill. The goal of report talk is to hold center stage in the conversation. It is most appropriate and useful in the office or when making professional presentations. **Rapport talk** is "private talk." Its goal is to make connections and to nurture relationships. Its place is in the home or in private conversations.

Neither style of conversation is "better" but each style is most appropriate for use in a particular context. The problem arises in that American men and women tend to favor one particular style in all contexts. Just as one would

If the stereotypes hold, this man is using report
talk while his audience responds with rapport talk.

expect from the sex-role stereotypes, men tend to overuse report talk and
women tend to overuse rapport talk. This is actually based upon the perceived
purpose of communication. Women use communication to hold relationships
together. Men tend to use conversation as a way to discuss activities and to
problem solve. In conversation, women want to be heard and supported. Men
will generally only discuss a problem if they are asking for ideas for solution.
Thus men tend to resent unsolicited advice. As do women.

At Anonymous University, Clarissa wasn't asking David to help her find
ways to get to the chancellor, she was merely venting her frustration. She
wanted him to sympathize with her difficulty. Her probable reaction? She will
probably feel that David is telling her she can't do her job and will react negatively to his intended help (Gray, 1994).

American women are also more likely to notice and respond to a change in
style by their conversational partner. Burgson, Olney, and Coker (1987) examined
gender reactions to the involvement of partners in communication. Males and
females were initially interviewed then were placed with confederates of the re-
searcher who had been coached in either high or low levels of involvement in
conversation. The naïve participants were looked at in terms of their reciprocity
or nonaccommodation to the style. Females were found to be more responsive
to the involvement change than were males—who tended not to accommodate.

Rapport talk is indirect (Tannen, 1994). Lakoff (1973) states that the benefits
of **indirectness** are not only building and nurturing relationships, but also defensiveness. You will recall that Brown and Levinson's (1987) off-the-record
level of politeness is intended to provide a potential mask as to the intent of the
comment. This is what Lakoff means by defensiveness. If the comment ("Gee,
I could really use that book") offends, it can be denied that any demand was being made (e.g., "I only meant that the book would be useful for my paper").
Thus indirectness may be a means used by the powerless to protect themselves.
Paradoxically, indirectness may also be used by those with power to reinforce
this power. By merely expressing a whim the powerful individual expects those
with less power to respond. In a traditionally structured family, a question by
the husband, "I wonder what time we'll eat?" is a thinly veiled command to get
the meal started.

How do you feel about indirect as opposed to direct communication? Do you believe gender, situation, or status differences are stronger determinants of which style will be used. Which style do you prefer to have people use when they communicate with you?

In some cultures, indirectness is the norm of verbal communication—regardless of gender. The Japanese, for example, tend to respond to any request affirmatively. This is because . . . "it is well known that saying 'no' is considered too face-threatening to risk . . . " (Triandis, 1994, p. 33). American women are more likely than American men to take an indirect route in conversation yet when compared with individuals from other cultures, both use a more direct style. When compared to Greek men and women, "Greek men were *as likely* as Greek women, and *more likely* than American men or women, to take an indirect interpretation" (Tannen, 1994, p. 34, emphasis added).

In other cultures, the American expectation of female indirectness and male directness is reversed. Kennan (1974) found that in a Malagasy-speaking village on Madagascar the women are seen as direct and the men indirect in conversation. Yet the men are still perceived as more powerful in the village. A comparison between verbal behaviors of third generation Japanese-American college students and college students whose families had emigrated from European Commonwealth countries (third to fifth generations) examined attitudes toward styles of conversation including indirectness, assertiveness, and egalitarian speech norms (Johnson & Marsella, 1978).

Even after three or more generations in the United States there were differences between the Japanese-Americans and the European-Americans. Japanese-Americans were more concerned with male dominance and female subordination. European-Americans endorsed more aggressiveness and assertiveness in speech and supported more egalitarian speech norms. Gender was a relatively unimportant factor (significant findings in only four of twenty factors). Thus cultural norms linger long after a change in cultures, and gender and culture can become entwined to complicate verbal communication.

The ultimate in assertiveness in communication is use of *threats*. Threats are intended to intimidate and subdue the "partner" in conversation. In American child-abusive relationships it has been found that when children show a negative reaction to adult conversation (didn't show "appropriate" submissiveness) the adult shifted to more power-assertive strategies (Bugenthal, 1993). While child abuse is clearly a negative situation, aggressiveness in verbal communication is not always viewed negatively. Eckert (as quoted in Tannen, 1994) found that American high school boys, but not the girls, reported that a number of their good friendships began with fighting.

In fact, "many cultures of the world see arguing as a pleasurable sign of intimacy" (Tannen, 1994, p. 44). Schiffrin (1984) found that lower middle-class men and women of Eastern European Jewish background found arguing as a pleasurable means of socializing. Byrnes (1986) found that Germans think that American students are uninformed and uncommitted to ideas because they are hesitant to argue about politics with individuals to whom they have just been introduced. Americans, on the other hand, often label German students belligerent because they do argue. What we are probably seeing here is the strong effect of cultural norms (especially about politeness) on verbal communication.

One drawback of much of communications research is the fact that the groups studied are artificial—arranged only for the purposes of the study, and that they only meet for a short time, a fact which they know in advance. At least one study (Wheelan & Verdi, 1992) examined American all-male, all-female, or mixed groups in terms of verbal conversational style. For the first hour they saw stereotypic sex differences and conversation patterns. However, as the groups continued to meet, the differences disappeared over time. So to further complicate the picture, the effects of group development appear to affect the verbal communication behavior of the group members.

Another dimension of verbal conversation is the use of **silence** and **interruption.** The historical pattern of research findings are not supportive of the sex-role stereotype that women talk too much (and certainly more than men) but that American men dominate conversations by interrupting more than women (e.g., Gleason & Greif, 1983; West & Zimmerman, 1983; and West & Zimmerman, 1985). This, of course, indicates that there is at least an American assumption that interruption is a sign of **dominance** and that the conversation is a fight for the floor. More recent research by James and Clark (1993) did not find the traditionally identified pattern of males interrupting females. They actually found that in same-sex groups, females interrupt each other more than do males in all-male groups. So what's going on? Does an interruption indicate a play for dominance, and if so, are we seeing a change in the American pattern?

Tannen believes that there are different types of interruptions. It is naïve to assume that just because two people are talking at the same time they are "fighting." Tannen identifies a type of interruption, used typically by American women, as an *overlap*. These **overlaps** have a very different intention than the traditionally defined interruption. Tannen views the "interruptions" of women as a question of symmetry or balance. Women tend to step on the end of others' speech in order to show their support.

> *Thus, to understand whether an overlap is an interruption, one must consider the context (for example, cooperative overlapping is more likely to occur in casual conversation among friends than in a job interview), speakers' habitual styles (for example, overlaps are more likely not to be interruptions among those with a style I call "high involvement"), and the interaction of their styles (for example, an interruption is more likely to occur between speakers whose styles differ with regard to pausing and overlap). This is not to say that one cannot use interruption to dominate a conversation or a person, but only that it is not self-evident from the observation of overlap that an interruption has occurred, was intended, or was intended to dominate.*
>
> *(Tannen, 1994, p. 36)*

Cultural differences in the speed of conversation and expectations about the length of pause between speakers can result in the occurrence of apparent interruptions. Within the continental United States there are very different speeds of conversation between New Yorkers (fast), Californians (slower), and

Midwesterners (slower still). If you are expecting a very short interval between speakers, you will begin before your partner expects. Midwesterners and Californians often identify New Yorkers as rude because of their "pushiness" in conversations. But this doesn't just hold true within the borders of the United States. Tannen (1994) found that Americans are perceived as interrupting Scandinavians, and within Scandinavians, Swedes and Norwegians are seen as interrupting Finns.

At the other end of the volubility dimension of conversation is the use of *silence*. **Silence** can be used as a sign either of power or powerlessness. Certainly not being allowed to speak ("children should be seen but not heard") indicates powerlessness. However, therapists are trained to make use of silence as a therapeutic technique. Clients will usually fill a silence rather than let it go on. Even the "powerless" party in an interaction can use silence as a power move, as in the prisoner who is being interrogated and refuses to speak. Silence and interruptions can mean power or powerlessness depending upon the context and the cultural or gender circumstances discussed before.

The final dimension we will examine in verbal conversations is the continuum from *self-effacement* to *self-aggrandizement*. American women apologize. A lot. Too much. This **self-effacement** creates a one-down position in the conversation. However, generally, American women don't mind because they are more concerned about the relationships within the group than with power (Tannen, 1990). There are actually several types of apology. One type can be taking responsibility (e.g., "I'm sorry I did not get the report to the vice president on time"). In this example the individual is admitting culpability and asking for pardon. Another type of apology is meant more to show concern or support. If a member of your group announces that they were robbed last night, a common response is, "Gee, I'm really sorry." This is not an admission of guilt. It is intended to indicate concern and sympathy. Either type of apology, however, because of the reduced power position, is inconsistent with report talk (therefore American men tend not to apologize either in public or in private).

At the other end of the continuum is **self-aggrandizement** or *boasting*. Boasting is calling attention to your own capabilities or accomplishments. In America, women and girls are not supposed to call attention to themselves, much less brag about what they've done. If they do, they are considered conceited and having made an impolite attempt to one-up some other group member. American men and boys, on the other hand, feel that by announcing their accomplishments they are showing others they merit respect and feel it is foolish to be modest and hope that others will learn of the abilities in some indirect manner. Men perceive the very real reluctance on the part of many women to boast about themselves as "foolishly self-denigrating, evidence of insecurity" (Tannen, 1990, p. 220).

American women tend to have little trouble boasting about their husbands or children, but that's not considered by women to be impolite since they are not talking about themselves. This reluctance to trumpet one's accomplishments can be very destructive to a woman's climb up the professional ladder. While women wait for someone to notice what a gem they are, the men are busy making sure their accomplishments are well known.

Women are reluctant to display their achievement in public in order to be likable, but regarded through the lens of status, they are systematically under-estimated, and thought self-deprecating and insecure.

(Tannen, 1990, p. 224)

Effective verbal communication is difficult and getting harder. As the world becomes more connected technologically, we will find that there are more and more cultural differences in patterns of which to be aware. Norms for the behaviors across genders in terms of communication further complicate the situation. Becoming open to the likelihood of our making errors and being more humble about our communicative capabilities can only serve to improve the situation.

VERBAL COMMUNICATION NETWORKS

As we have seen in a number of areas, human beings are most comfortable with the known. They establish patterns of behavior (roles), implicit rules about behavior (norms), and even prescriptive rules about the behaviors of particular groups (stereotypes). In groups, people also form patterns in the way they communicate with each other known as **networks.**

Communication networks are regular patterns of person-to-person contact that are typically characterized by the exchange of information between humans.

(Monge, 1987, p. 243)

All groups have formal and informal communication networks. The **formal network** can be thought of as what SHOULD happen. An example is an organizational chart which indicates who reports to whom. In a classroom situation the formal communication network has traditionally been between teacher and students and not between students. The **informal network** is what REALLY happens. In organizations individuals frequently "jump channels" and go over someone's head in violation of the formal network. If this is happening a great deal, there is a potentially serious problem with this group. As group dynamicists we would want to know who is being passed over and why. In classrooms, students sometimes talk to each other when they should be listening. When the informal network violates the formal network, communication efficiency can be compromised.

Networks develop over time in groups. Some connections are used frequently and some disappear from disuse. It is theoretically possible that all members of a group have strong communication links to other members in what we call an **all-channel network** as seen below in Figure 4.1. The letters indicate individuals in the group, the lines the communication links between them.

FIGURE 4.1. All-channel network.

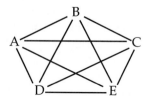

There has been a great deal of research done on all possible configurations of verbal communication networks (e.g., Tichy, 1981). The types of networks have even been named. I am deliberately not including a page of network types with their names that students might feel compelled to memorize for several reasons. First, I discourage students from memorizing anything. I want students to understand rather than parrot. Second, I have not ever encountered a situation in which these names are actually employed except in textbooks. In analyzing a group it would be much less useful to be able to "name the network" than it would be to understand the effects on the group of that particular type of network.

One aspect of the network research that is extremely important, however, is the concept of centrality. Two networks are shown in Figure 4.2. The network on the left is totally *decentralized*, the one on the right totally *centralized*.

Neither of the networks is all-channel. All-channel networks are **decentralized networks** and contain a large number of redundant links. In other words, there are too many ways a message can be passed for the group to function efficiently. The extent of centralization affects both productivity and satisfaction of the group. Generally, more **centralized networks** such as the one on the right in Figure 4.2 work best for simple problems.

Decentralized networks such as the one on the left in the figure are generally better for complex problems. Information passes more freely between group members without the filter of the individual in the center of the network and more synergy can develop. In terms of satisfaction, decentralized groups (up to and including the all-channel) foster cohesiveness within the group as people are able to establish more relationships.

And as far as I'm concerned, that's just about all you need to know about communication networks. The final point that is important is for everyone to be connected to the network. When you have an isolated member (for whatever reasons) the group is losing a proportion of their resources. Efforts should be made to identify why this person has been turned into an isolate and to remediate the situation.

We've talked a very great deal about verbal communication. However, as we discovered at the beginning of this chapter, whenever people are occupying adjacent space they are communicating, if only on the nonverbal level. Nonverbal communication can be as important or sometimes even more important than verbal communication. It is to this important subject we now turn.

FIGURE 4.2. Decentralized network (left) and centralized network (right).

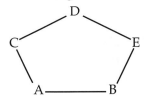 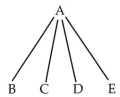

Nonverbal communication consists of all our behaviors as we deliver our verbal messages. It involves our facial expression, bodily movement, voice tone, and where we locate ourselves in proximity to the communication target. We communicate emotion and dominance through nonverbal behaviors. People are very sensitive to these cues, even though often they have not been educated in their interpretation. Nonverbal communication cues can make or break an attempted communication. When the verbal and nonverbal cues are consistent, they serve to reinforce each other and make the communication more clear. For example, when you open a gift from a friend and it is just exactly what you want, your smile and cheerful manner will reinforce your verbal expressions of pleasure. Not infrequently, though, the two levels are contradictory. If you open that same present and it is something you really dislike, you will probably still verbally express the same thanks, but nonverbally your manner may indicate disappointment. Another example of inconsistent verbal and nonverbal messages is when an individual is angry but denies the fact. No one is fooled. When nonverbal cues contradict the verbal, we believe the nonverbal message. It's very easy to lie with words, but we haven't been as carefully taught to lie with our bodies. The application section for this chapter will discuss how we can detect lying through nonverbal cues.

We will consider three categories of nonverbal behaviors that affect communication. They are *proxemic behavior, kinesic behavior,* and *paralinguistic qualities.* Proxemic behavior examines how people are affected by spatial and distance orientations. Kinesic behavior examines body motion, including gestures, body shifts, eye movements, facial expressions, and posture. It is most useful in the study of communication to examine how these behaviors are used in conjunction with the spoken word and how they modify the meaning of the verbal message. Paralinguistic qualities have to do with the physical production of speech. These include loudness, pitch, tone, and rate of speech (Ellis & Fisher, 1994).

Proxemics

Proxemic behaviors involve space, including the arrangement of people and their environment and how these arrangements affect communication. **Territory** is the space that you claim as your own. It helps groups in building unity if they can have their own identifiable space.

> *Providing a group with a specific territory is a simple and valuable technique in which nonverbal factors are used to increase group spirit so that more synergy is generated and devoted to task concerns, rather than social concerns.*
> **(Baird & Weinberg, 1981, p. 42)**

You've encountered that word *synergy* more than once so far in this book without explanation. We'll discuss it at greater length in Chapter 6 on group productivity, but for now a simple definition is the energy generated by the interaction of group members. Group territory can become an important issue in conflict resolution, as we shall see in Chapter 9. Negotiating in my territory gives me what is known in sports as the "home court (or field) advantage." I am comfortable and in charge which gives me a potentially unfair advantage in the negotiations. Sports teams prefer to play in their own familiar arena with their own fans cheering them on. And, as mentioned before, students tend to stake out their own territory in the classroom.

Just as groups have space they identify as their own, so do individuals. All cultures studied have norms about the space that an individual can claim (Hall, 1959). These norms differ greatly across cultures; however, in each culture there is a series of concentric circles with the individual at the center. It is the depth of these circles that differs. **Intimate distance** is the closest ring around the body. In America this is from our body out to about eight inches. We allow individuals with whom we are intimate to enter this distance at will. Children often enter this distance before they have learned the norms of the culture. If a nonintimate enters this space we anticipate the probability of aggression. Violation of this space is often perceived as a threat. It is uncommon in groups for this space to be used.

The next ring of personal territory is **personal distance.** In the United States this is the space approximately one and a half to four feet from our body. This area is the space in which we interact with friends and close acquaintances. Most group work is done within this space.

Intimate couples use intrusions into each others' intimate distance zones to express closeness.

Social distance is the area where we interact with casual acquaintances and business colleagues. In the United States this area is out of the range of touch, between four and twelve feet. In observing a group that is past the membership phase, if their interactions are taking place at this range there is cause for concern. This indicates that they have not yet formed a group identity.

The final ring of territory is the area in which we have our formal encounters with strangers. This **public distance** ranges outwards from the border of the social distance. The sizes of the territories that constitute individual space vary greatly among cultures as we will discuss later. The indicators of territory and their violation also differ across cultures. In individualist cultures such as the United States, one knocks on the door of someone's room or office and waits for an indication that it is appropriate to enter. Collectivist cultures such as Japan make much less notice of this barrier and will often knock as they enter the room. Such a move directed toward an individual from an individualistic country would be perceived as an invasion and a threat to the individual's authority and would probably disrupt any attempted verbal conversation (Smith & Bond, 1994).

STOP How is the space arranged in your classroom? In your office space? In your meeting rooms? Does the arrangement facilitate or inhibit interaction of individuals? In which of the above situations would you want to facilitate conversation? In which would you want to discourage interaction?

Group spatial ecology is the arrangement of the space around an individual. It includes furniture arrangement and can affect architecture by influencing the extent that interaction is required between individuals. In groups we want to encourage interaction, closeness, and face-to-face interactions so we arrange the space in a **sociopetal arrangement.** Examples would be sitting around a table, or arranging desks or chairs in a circle. We find that this nonverbal aspect of communication impacts greatly on the amount of verbal interaction we can expect within the group. The worst possible arrangement in which to try to conduct a group is the traditional rows of chairs or desks found in traditional classrooms. Almost everyone is looking at the back of someone else's head. These arrangements that discourage interaction are known as **sociofugal arrangements.** You can often tell a great deal about a teacher, trainer, or group leader by how they arrange the space they will be using for the group. A leader that wants to deliver a monologue will employ a sociofugal arrangement.

Kinesics

Kinesic behaviors are what is commonly known as **body language.** These are the physical movements we make as we communicate. The primary source of kinesic information is the face. Our faces express the emotions we are feeling at any given time. Cross-cultural research by Ekman (1992) has found that the facial expressions associated with the basic emotions are culturally universal. Americans, Japanese, Tongans can all identify that a smiling person is happy. The **display rules** for facial expression differ across cultures, however. While an angry face is an angry face worldwide, some cultures such as the Japanese discourage the expression of anger (Ekman & Friesen, 1971). Thus although the emotion is felt, it is not communicated nonverbally. Facial expressions can also be interpreted as indicating dominance or lack thereof. The smile in the United States is perceived as a gesture of submission. Unfortunately, women are trained to smile more often than are men. Dovidio, Brown, Hiltman, and Ellyson (1988) found that in arranged situations where American men and women discussed gender-linked tasks, across all conditions the women smiled more. Another aspect of the face that communicates is the use of eye contact. Americans have beliefs about the meanings of such gestures. We tend to believe that people who will not meet our gaze in conversation are not telling the truth. That may be true, but the avoidance may also indicate either shyness or adherence to the norms of another culture. Eye contact can be positive or negative in its effect. Eye contact can be interpreted as attempted connection and thus seen as positive. At the extreme we talk about lovers gazing into each others' eyes endlessly. Cladis (1985) found that trainers working with groups who made more eye contact elicited positive feedback from the audience. Eye contact can also be perceived as a challenge or a threat.

The body as well can give us good feedback about an individual's responses to our attempts to communicate with them. Students seldom have any idea how much information they convey to teachers through their facial expressions and body movements. Students restlessly shifting in their seats, refusing to meet your gaze, or staring out the window indicate that the encounter is not going well from a communication perspective. Students smiling, nodding in response to points made, and leaning forward in their seats indicate interest and involvement. Such enthusiastic reception of communication rewards the communicator and increases the likelihood of similar communication in the future. Audiences or groups indicating boredom or lack of understanding should indicate to the communicator that changes need to be made in order to be understood.

Paralinguistics

The way we use our voices in communication is known as **paralinguistics.** This includes our "oral style, articulation, intensity, phraseology, and interpretative expression" (Baird & Weinberg, 1981, p. 46). When we communicate we speak more loudly to emphasize a point or to communicate anger or dominance. When we are tense or angry, our vocal cords tighten (as do the other muscles of our bodies) and the pitch of our voice goes up slightly. Certainly varying our levels of loudness and intensity serve to make our verbal communication that much more interesting. Trainers who use contrasting volume and other vocal techniques are perceived as more credible and stimulate retention of their message to the group (Cladis, 1985).

We have been discussing several of the nonverbal behaviors that affect our ability to communicate and understand. Across cultures many of these norms differ radically. This can lead to serious miscommunication, because when there is ambiguity or disagreement between the nonverbal cues and the verbal message of the speaker, the target will focus on the nonverbal cues and lose much of the verbal message.

> *Awareness of the nonverbal cues emitted by all group members can prevent misinterpretations, halt "railroading" ventures, and add a valuable dimension of understanding to the communication process.*
>
> *(Baird & Weinberg, 1981, p. 52)*

Factors Affecting Nonverbal Communication

We have already seen in the previous discussion of proxemics, kinesics, and paralinguistic cues that there are many cultural differences, thus many opportunities for misunderstandings in the communication process.

In the area of proxemics, there are clear cultural differences in the sizes of the bands that constitute the various appropriate distances between individuals. In general, Arabs, Latin Americans, and U.S. Hispanics **(high-contact cultures)** normally interact at closer distances than do north Europeans and far Easterners **(low-contact cultures).** Cross-cultural conversations can turn into a "dance" where the individuals who are used to close proximity "invade" the space of another who responds by moving back to a more comfortable space. The pursuer may be as insulted by the standoffish behavior of the other as the pursued is by such invasive, aggressive behavior.

The area of kinesics, because it covers such a broad range of behaviors, is an area where there are many cultural differences including eye contact, body position, touching, and gestures. Eye contact has already been discussed as generally positive in American culture. Again we see differences in cultural norms. High-contact cultures such as that of Arabs, Latin Americans, and southern Europeans have a higher incidence of direct eye contact than is found in their low-contact culture counterparts, such as the Asians, Indians, Pakistanis, and northern Europeans (Triandis, 1994). Status differences can also affect the appropriate amount of eye contact during communication. Looking people directly in the eye when the speakers are of unequal status is more common in Anglo-Saxon cultures than in Latino or Native American cultures where the lower status individual is expected to lower their eyes. Individuals from high-contact cultures tend to face each other more squarely during conversation than those from low-contact cultures, who tend to angle their bodies away from each other.

Whether and where one can touch another individual also varies across cultures. Generally, the high-contact cultures include high levels of touching as well as eye contact. Other cultures such as many East and South Asians and Native Americans do not touch nonfamily members and may not even touch family members (Triandis, 1994). Handshakes are expected to be firm in some cultures (Anglo-Saxon) but soft in Latin America.

Use of the same gestures across cultures can cause serious misunderstandings. Pointing with your finger at another person is considered rude by the

Navaho (Salzman, 1991). Instead one must point with the lips. The hand signal used in America to indicate "OK" by making a circle of the thumb and forefinger can mean, "It is not good; zero" (southern France); "Give me some money" (Japan); and "Let's have sex" (Brazil) (Triandis, 1994, p. 205). Thus it's best to refrain from gestures in cross-cultural settings until you know what is considered offensive in that culture.

Finally, paralinguistic cues also differ across cultures, particularly the loudness with which it is considered polite to converse. Mediterranean cultures tend to speak more loudly than northern Europeans. Native American cultures tend to speak softly. Within Americans, social class level affects volume level. It is considered genteel in the upper classes to speak softly, while in the lower classes speech tends to be louder (Triandis, 1994).

If at this point you are despairing ever having an effective cross-cultural conversation, you're right to be pessimistic. We continue to learn more about our own and other cultures which just emphasizes the variety and number of differences between us. As Smith and Bond (1994) admit, "The prognosis for effective communication across cultural lines is not good" (p. 190).

EFFECTIVE LISTENING

So far in this chapter we've explored communication from the perspective of the individual attempting to do the communicating at both the verbal and nonverbal levels. Equally important (and maybe more so since so few of us do it well) in conversation is the art of listening. It doesn't much matter what we can or how much we try to communicate if no one listens. And most of us don't listen. We use four main ways to avoid listening: (1) *nonlistening*, (2) *listening to ignore*, (3) *listening selectively*, and (4) *listening for the ego* (Fujishin, 1997).

Nonlistening is the ultimate form of shutting off communication. We can forbid someone to talk. Obviously we can't connect with people and build relationships, much less receive ideas, if we won't allow them to speak. Not a good idea for groups.

Listening to ignore is pretending to listen when we're not. We're planning our evening or remembering we have to go to the grocery store on the way home, but we're just faking the listening part. Students have been known to use this method in class. **Listening selectively** has to do with filtering out what we don't want to hear and hearing what we want. A parent tells a teenager, "Yes, you can go to the party, but you have to be home before midnight." Odds are that only the first part of that sentence got through effectively. Two people in a group listening to the same communication may hear two very different things because we select what is salient to us. To a certain extent this is a normal process, but it is not conducive to effective communication.

Listening for the ego involves imposing our own values on whatever is said to us. We are unable to detach our own ego enough to take someone else's perspective. We won't even give ideas a chance if they clash with our beliefs—we'll dismiss and discard them without even the courtesy of consideration.

Types of Listening

So how SHOULD we listen? There have been several methods developed which are similar but are known by different labels, such as **active listening** (Fujishin, 1997) and **critical listening** (Ellis & Fisher, 1994). In either case we don't listen to communication the way we listen to music. We can listen to music without paying much attention and still enjoy it. Listening to communicate effectively involves some effort on our part. Our goal is to analyze and interpret and strive to understand. Your job is to question if you don't believe you understand what the communicator intends.

There are several strategies that can be employed in this focused listening. First, clear your mind of anything else. The communication should take place in a distraction-free environment. Thus your group should meet in a private room rather than try to meet over lunch in a restaurant or the school cafeteria. In order to listen we have to be able to literally hear what is going on. If there is too much noise or too much going on around us, we won't be able to focus. Maintain eye contact as a group and with the speaker.

When someone speaks, listen for the main points and ideas as if you were making an outline in your head. Take notes if necessary. As you make up this mental outline, is there anything that is being left out, anything that is important but is not being said? As you organize the information ask how much of it is relevant, how much you can ignore as irrelevant, and whether you need more information. If you have sufficient information to believe you understand what has been said, then evaluate the communication as objectively and nonjudgmentally as you are able.

Listening well has important effects on the group. Clinard (1985) found that in international work environments intensive listening was the best tool for understanding people. The quality of listening skills has been related to member rankings of leadership within groups (Bechler & Johnson, 1995). Better listeners are more likely to be leaders. Unfortunately, the gender of the speaker may affect how much is heard (Gruber & Gaehelein, 1979). Both male and female listeners were found to remember more of speeches by male than female speakers. Although Gruber and Gaehelein varied the topics as to whether they were identified as masculine or feminine topics, males were found to be listened to more closely regardless of the topic.

Asking Effective Questions

What if you're trying to listen and you just don't "get it"? ASK QUESTIONS. Just as we listen carefully and critically we should question critically. The point of asking questions is to gather information, not to criticize the speaker, their ideas, or values.

Ellis and Fisher (1994) offer suggestions for asking for additional information. First, don't hesitate to ask for clarification. There are lots of places where the communication could have broken down. Maybe you literally couldn't hear the speaker over side conversations. Maybe the speaker was using too much jargon or was so disorganized you couldn't follow their thoughts. Maybe you don't have sufficient background or know the underlying assumptions on which the speaker is basing their communication. Besides, in a group if you don't understand there are probably several others who don't either. Don't feel you're losing face. The only dumb question is the one you don't ask.

If the speaker needs to speak more loudly, tell them. If you can't follow their logic, ask them to lay it out for you. Ask them about the consequences of their statements. What would their conclusions suggest about the next direction for the group? Ask the difficult questions. What about the legality or ethics of the suggestions? As we will discuss in Chapter 7, groups have the obligation to make ethical decisions. Don't accuse anyone of lacking ethics or having poor values; question the possible outcomes. Anyone who feels attacked will stop listening instantly.

Finally, be tactful and kind in asking questions. Take some responsibility for the fact that you don't get it. Use good manners. Pushing people into corners (figuratively), humiliating them, or blaming them will only disrupt the group and any chances at good communication.

FEEDBACK MODELS

So now that you're deep in conversation in the group—you've just spoken and everyone seems to be listening and asking good questions—how can you be sure that they're getting the messages you intend? You can ask for feedback.

There are basically two types of feedback: *formative* and *summative feedback*. **Formative feedback** is information that is provided as the process continues. An example would be a teacher giving feedback throughout the process of a student presentation. Another is the individual grades students receive on assignments throughout the semester. They can evaluate how well they are succeeding and, if necessary, make changes to do better. Formative feedback helps us make corrections as we go.

Summative feedback is information provided after the task is completed. To follow the above examples, it would be the teacher not saying a word during the student presentation then giving a negative evaluation at the end, or a teacher who provides no grades during the semester except the final grade in the course. In each of these cases the student has had no way to check whether or not they were performing as expected. Summative feedback alone allows you to get very far offtrack without knowing. The moral? If you wonder how you're doing ask for formative feedback.

Some languages appear to have formative feedback built in. White (1989) found that Japanese born and raised in Japan used more *backchannels* than Americans. **Backchannels** are listener responses during a conversation providing evidence of understanding or asking for clarification. In cross-cultural communication with Americans, these Japanese did not alter their listening style regardless whether they were speaking with fellow Japanese or with Americans —they continued to use backchannels. Americans speaking with the Japanese took the cue and also used this formative feedback. However, they didn't use backchannels with fellow Americans.

Americans aren't hopeless cases, however. We can be taught to give effective feedback. Haslett and Ogilvie (1992) offer eight characteristics of good feedback. They are:

- *Be specific and clear.* Don't say "That's a stupid idea," say "I'm not sure that blowing up the computer is an effective idea."
- *Support your comments with evidence (e.g., "We'd all get arrested").*
- *Separate the issues from the people.* Sometimes smart people say really stupid things. Identify the idea as unworkable (stupid is a really loaded term) but do not refer to the person as stupid. As we've already seen, people become defensive (and rightfully so) after being (or feeling) attacked, and stop listening.
- *Soften negative messages.* They will be heard as much harsher than you intend (Oyster, 1982). There's no need to flatten anyone psychologically.
- *Sandwich negative messages between positive ones.* There has to have been something useful or creative about an idea. If all you ever offer is criticism, people stop listening to you. They know what you're going to say. If, however, you mix praise with negative comments, it will be seen that you have been noticing the good things and not just automatically dismissing everything that is being said. Your feedback has a far better chance of getting through.
- *Pose the situation as a mutual problem.* If I tell you that you messed something up for the group you're going to become defensive. If, however, I talk about the mess the group—as a group—is in, then we can work together to rectify the problem. We become colleagues again, not antagonists.
- *Use good timing.* If someone is already upset about anything else, that's not the best time to provide feedback unless it's really positive. Don't withhold your comments until it's too late for the group to do anything with them.
- *Use a proper manner of delivery.* Be kind. Don't blame. Be professional.

GROUP FACTORS AFFECTING COMMUNICATION

The primary group characteristic that affects the quality of communication in the group is the size. As groups become larger, the number of potential relationships and communication channels increases dramatically. In a two-person group there is one possible channel. In a six-person group there are 301 possible channels! (Kephart, 1950). In smaller groups people are more self-aware and regulate their behavior more closely than do individuals in larger groups (Mullen, Johnson & Salas, 1989). The potential for intimacy in the group goes down as the group size increases.

The size of the group affects the potential for individual contributions. As the group becomes larger, the participation of each member decreases. And, ultimately, if the group becomes too large it will split into cliques or subgroups and cease to function as a group (Napier & Gershenfeld, 1993).

Summary

We've done a lot of talking in this chapter about talking. And listening. If a group is to accomplish anything there must be effective communication both at the verbal and the nonverbal levels. Gender and cultural norms complicate the process of communication through increasing the possibilities of misinterpretations and lack of a shared code. Effective feedback is the primary mechanism through which to determine that effective communication is taking place and to correct any problems with communication.

Key Terms

active listening
all-channel networks
backchannels
bald speech
body language
centralized networks
channels
critical listening
decentralized networks
decoding
display rules
dominance
encoding
formal networks
formative feedback
group spatial ecology
high-contact cultures
indirectness
informal networks
information-seeking
  questions

interruption
intimate distance
kinesic behavior
listening for the ego
listening selectively
listening to ignore
low-contact cultures
message
negative politeness
networks
nonlistening
opinion-seeking
  questions
orientation-seeking
  questions
overlap
paralinguistics
personal distance
policy-seeking questions
politeness
positive politeness

procedure-seeking
  questions
proxemic behavior
public distance
rapport talk
receiver
relational questions
report talk
self-aggrandizement
self-effacement
silence
social distance
sociofugal arrangements
sociopetal arrangements
source (of message)
summative feedback
surface talk
teleconferencing
territory
verbal communication

APPLICATION

Liar, Liar: Lying and the Detection of Deceit

When was the last time you lied to someone? Don't pretend you've never done it. We all do. Lying is ubiquitous. We just discriminate between types and acceptability of lies. The "little white lie" is an ingrained part of our cultural norms. If your boss comes to work in one of the most unbecoming outfits you've ever seen and asks your opinion, what are you going to do? Lie. When you're just feeling terrible and a casual acquaintance asks how you are, what do you do? Lie. These are obviously qualitatively different situations than if your spouse has just been murdered and the police ask you if you did it.

Paul Ekman's research career began in looking at the nonverbal communication of emotion. As he studied the behaviors involved in communication he became interested in the behaviors that are involved in lying and in detecting lies. Ekman (1985) identifies two types of lies: concealing and falsifying. Concealing is a more passive form of lying. Concealing is when you just happen not to tell about something. Like having taken off work Friday afternoon two hours early. Is the behavior deceitful to the organization that's paying you for being there? Yes. Concealing is also when you don't mention to Aunt Melba that she's got spinach caught between her teeth. Falsifying is an active misrepresentation of the truth. If your supervisor at work asks you if you took off early on Friday and you deny it, then you're falsifying. Or if Aunt Melba asks about her teeth and you tell her they're fine. In both cases you've actively misled someone.

Is it lying if you tell a person what they want to hear, even if it isn't true? Or if you represent the truth as you know it and turn out to be wrong? Ekman would say "no." Ekman defines lying as ". . . a deliberate choice to mislead a target without giving any notification of the intent to do so" (1985, p. 41). Thus Ekman would not consider it lying to tell your mother that, no, she isn't as big as a rhinoceros. Or if you tell a friend obviously in the final stages of cancer that she's looking better. Or if you tell your boss the annual report is done not knowing that one portion has been eaten by the computer system. In the first case you have made a deliberate choice, however your mother expects your answer. The cancer patient knows she looks bad but wants to hear otherwise. You aren't lying to your boss because you have not made any choice to mislead. You gave what you believed to be correct information. But what if your spouse asks if you have been cheating and you deny your affair with a co-worker. That's a lie. Your spouse (except under very unusual conditions) would expect fidelity and truth. You've provided neither.

People lie to us all the time (and we to them). What are the clues to deceit identified by Ekman? There are two major ways to slip. The first is leakage—when you accidentally reveal a truth after having denied it. The second is a group of behaviors that indicate lying known as deception clues. Let's look at these phenomena to help you better identify when others lie—or to possibly make yourself a better liar.

Verbal lies are the easiest to handle. You can rehearse your lie in advance until it feels natural. Then when the situation comes up you know just exactly what to say. Sometimes, however, this rehearsal is what leads to detection. In police interrogations the same questions will be asked multiple times in multiple forms. If the same answer is given in the same wording to each of these queries, suspicions are raised. During the investigation of President Clinton there was one week in which three different speeches were made by three different people to the press using identical phrases. No one was fooled into thinking that these were spontaneous defenses of the president. It was patently clear that these statements had been written by one person and rehearsed by the other three. Had they not used identical phrases, no one would probably have noticed.

Another way the verbal portion of a lie can be detected is when the liar contradicts herself. The teenager tells her parents she was at the library then accidentally slips and mentions seeing someone at the coffee bar. Often given enough rope the inexperienced or guilty liar will slip.

Part of lying is faking emotions. Sometimes we try to hide an emotion, sometimes we try to pretend we're experiencing an emotion when we aren't. Having been socialized in a society that at least claims to dislike lies and liars, many of us feel uncomfortable or guilty when we lie. It is this *deception guilt* that polygraphs (the so-called "lie detectors") measure. As early as 1917 the use of physiological measure was suggested to detect deception (Marston, 1917). These measures are all indicators of an emotional reaction to the lie and include heart rate, respiration rate, galvanic skin response (GSR—or how much your palms sweat), and blood pressure (Wrightsman, Willis, & Kassin, 1987). Although this sounds good in theory, polygraphs are so very inaccurate at detecting actual lies that they are inadmissible in court proceedings as evidence in all fifty of the United States. For some reason, however, the general public just doesn't get it. The use of polygraphs as part of the selection process for job applicants was becoming so prevalent that a federal law was passed severely limiting the jobs for which such tests could be used. When accused of a crime, individuals often take a polygraph test even though it can't be admitted to the court of law because the results will have such influence on the court of public opinion.

Let's examine the accuracy of polygraphs. There are four possible outcomes of such a test. A liar can accurately be labeled as such. A truth teller also can be correctly identified. A liar can fail to be identified—a situation known as a false negative. Or a truthful person can be identified as a liar—a situation known as a false positive. If we were talking about a criminal case, in the situation of a false positive, an innocent person might be convicted. With a false negative, a liar or criminal would not be detected.

What is it the polygraph is measuring? An emotional reaction. Any emotional reaction (because at this level of measurement all emotions look the same). If an innocent person is being accused of something and placed in the position of having a polygraph test, they are usually scared. A false positive is a real possibility. If a person with a personality defect referred to as sociopathy takes a polygraph test, they will probably pass as telling the truth—no matter how much they are lying. These people have not internalized the idea that it's wrong to lie. They will register a false negative. Serial murderer Ted Bundy "passed" repeated polygraph tests. Yet before his execution in Florida he confessed to murders in the double digits.

Saxe, Dougherty, and Cross were asked by the Office of Technology Assessment based upon concern by the U.S. Congress to evaluate the accuracy of polygraphs. It was their evidence that resulted in the ban on use of polygraphs for employment purposes. They found 250 empirical studies of polygraphs. When they examined these studies, only ten of them were considered methodologically appropriate. Here's what they found:

Correct guilty decisions ...... 70.6% to 98.6%
Correct innocent decisions .... 12.5% to 94%
False negatives .... 0.0% to 29% (liars undetected)
False positives .... 0.0% to 75% (innocents called liars)
Inconclusive results .... 0.0% to 25%

Reliance upon these results could result in 29 percent of criminals going free and 75 percent of innocents being convicted. Analogue studies (using students or police candidates who were told to lie or tell the truth) showed similar findings, although there were even more false positives. As if this weren't bad enough, Lyken (1987) reports that different polygraphers reading the same record have a frighteningly low level of agreement—correlations (Kappas values) ranging from .15 to .51. In order for a correlation to be perceived as 'good' in a case of a reliability check such as this, we would want to see numbers as high as .90 or better.

So if technology won't help us detect lies, what will? There's no single place to look, but clues can be gathered from a number of behavioral sources. As we've mentioned, the verbal portion of the lie is the easiest to fake and hardest to detect. Liars are careful of their words. We can examine the face, the voice, and the body language of the individual and can often be quite accurate (certainly more so than polygraphs) when properly trained.

TABLE 4.1. The Betrayal of Concealed Information, Organized by Behavioral Clues

Clue to Deceit	Information Revealed
Slips of the tongue	May be emotion-specific; may leak information unrelated to emotion
Tirades	May be emotion-specific; may leak information unrelated to emotion
Indirect speech	Verbal line not prepared; or, negative emotions, most likely fear
Pauses and speech errors	Verbal line not prepared; or, negative emotions, most likely fear
Voice pitch raised	Negative emotion, probably anger and/or fear
Voice pitch lowered	Negative emotion, probably sadness
Louder, faster speech	Probably anger, fear, and/or excitement
Slower, softer speech	Probably sadness and/or boredom
Emblems	May be emotion-specific; may leak information unrelated to emotion
Illustrators decrease	Boredom; line not prepared; or, weighing each word
Manipulators increase	Negative emotion
Fast or shallow breathing	Emotion, not specific
Sweating	Emotion, not specific
Frequent swallowing	Emotion, not specific
Micro expressions	Any of the specific emotions
Squelched expressions	Specific emotion; or, may only show that some emotion was interrupted but not which one
Reliable facial muscles	Fear or sadness
Increased blinking	Emotion, not specific
Pupil dilation	Emotion, not specific
Tears	Sadness, distress, uncontrolled laughter
Facial reddening	Embarrassment, shame, or anger; maybe guilt
Facial blanching	Fear or anger

Let's start at the top. The face is the primary site of emotional expression. People are aware that they give away emotions with their facial expressions and will often try to control the expressions. Often people are unsuccessful because when the emotions become involved (because of guilt or because of delight at getting away with something) muscles in the face fire involuntarily because they have direct connections to the brain. The smile can be squelched, but it passes by momentarily and is known as a flicker. The smile can be faked, but it doesn't come across as a genuine smile. Ekman has identified fifty different types of smiles based on the muscles involved. False smiles are often detectable through a number of clues. Often the eyes are not involved as they are in a genuine smile. False smiles often turn on and off at inappropriate times. They occur a little too late and disappear a little too soon. They are also often asymmetrical. DePaulo (DePaulo & Kirkendol, 1989) has discovered that liars are sometimes identified because they overcontrolled the signs of emotion on their faces. She has also found that the more highly motivated the liar is to get away with the lie, the more likely it is that they will provide more nonverbal cues to their deceit (DePaulo, Stone, & Lassiter, 1985; DePaulo, LeMay, & Epstein, 1991).

The aspect of the voice most likely to give away a liar is the pitch. Tension in the vocal cords raises the pitch a bit from the normal level. Lack of emotion in a voice does not indicate truthfulness. John Dean who was involved in the Nixon administration political scandal known as Watergate was quoted as saying of his lies in court,

I took a deep breath to make it look as if I were thinking; I was fighting for control. . . . You cannot show emotion, I told myself. The press will jump all over it as a sign of unmanly weakness.

(Ekman, 1985, p. 97)

DePaulo's research (1980) indicates that individuals realize the disadvantage of lacking facial cues to deceit and feel less able to identify liars when the interaction takes place on the telephone (DePaulo, Zuckerman, & Rosenthal, 1980).

The body also leaks tensions and gives away lies. The first way is through the use of emblems. Emblems are movements whose meaning is universally understood in a cultural group such as a head nod meaning "yes" in America. These emblems are culturally specific so detection of lies through their use with someone of another culture is very difficult. Emblems can be deliberate, but they can also indicate a slip. There are two ways to identify the use of an emblem as a slip. The first is a partial action, for example, shrugging only one shoulder rather than both. The second is the appearance of an emblem out of the usual presentation position. In the United States, the meaning of the emblem of the middle finger extended toward a person while the other fingers are folded down upon the palm of the hand is well understood. In a research study, Ekman deliberately made participants angry and videotaped the exchanges between participants and a "professor." He discovered that one of the angry participants was showing this universal emblem, but with the hand held out of sight. Scratching the face with the middle finger might also be this sort of slip.

Illustrators are movements we make to illustrate our speech. Some people use their hands expressively when speaking, others use dramatic facial expressions.

In the 1930s, there was a stereotype that stated that "inferior" races such as the Jews and Gypsies used more illustrators (which were inborn) as compared to the genetically "superior" Aryans who used few illustrators. In order to use illustrators as a method of detecting deception, first you must know how many illustrators the individual usually employs. I was once told that if forced to sit on my hands I would not be able to talk. Other people do not use many illustrators when they speak. So you establish a baseline of normal behavior for a particular person, then you watch for changes. The use of illustrators generally increases with emotions such as anger, agitation, distress, or enthusiasm. When the emotion is being faked, or when an individual is carefully monitoring the words of the lie, the use of illustrators will drop in frequency.

Generally, emotional discomfort increases body movement. People scratch, play with their hair or jewelry, pick at their faces, or simply move around more in their seats. As with illustrators, the mere presence of a lot of movement doesn't indicate dishonesty per se. In both cases we should look for a change from normal behavior when a particular topic is mentioned, or questions asked.

We live in a world of truths, half-truths, and lies. Being able to sort them out from each other can certainly aid in our ability to communicate effectively with others. Unfortunately, however, it has been found that in people who are particularly physically attractive and those who are practiced in lying or have little emotional concern about lying, honesty is particularly difficult to identify by nonverbal cues (DePaulo & Kirkendol, 1989; DePaulo et al., 1991).

Discussion Questions

Apply the concepts from the chapter to consider the following questions:

1. Given the stereotypic (and actual) differences in styles of communicating, do you think it would be easier for men or for women to lie undetected? Why?
2. What effect do you think the intention to lie would have on the choice of channels an individual would use to communicate?
3. Are proxemics, kinesics, or paralinguistic cues more useful in detecting a lie? Identify which ones and explain why they would be useful.
4. Discuss the role that cross-cultural differences play in the detection of deception.
5. You want to tell a very big lie and get away with it. What information would you use from the chapter to help you? Do you think you could get away with it in person? On a polygraph?

CHAPTER 5

Influence Processes in Groups

What Would YOU Predict?

Robert is standing in line in the fast-food restaurant, waiting to buy lunch before his two o'clock class. He's allowed plenty of time; he missed the rush at noon and still has an hour to eat. He's next to be served when another student, a stranger to Robert, hurries up to him, saying, "Please may I get in line in front of you? I have to buy lunch." Will Robert let him in line, or make him go to the end?

Each day all of us make hundreds of decisions regarding our behavior. We decide what to wear, what to eat, where to go, what to do , and with whom to associate. While at least some of these decisions can be considered to be independent of other people, most of what we do is, in fact, affected by those around us—the groups to which we belong. In this chapter we will examine the relationships between our own preferences and the extent to which these preferences and our behaviors are influenced by others. Some of these mechanisms of influence are quite subtle, such as our conformity to norms. Others are very explicit and blatant, as when a soldier is given an order by a superior officer. Americans in particular like to think we are the captains of our own fate and make independent decisions. The reality is that most of the time we don't.

POSSIBLE INTERACTIONS BETWEEN ATTITUDES AND ACTIONS

This situation described above is known as **interdependence,** which can be simply defined as situations in which the outcomes we experience are affected both by our own preferences, opinions, and choices as well as the preferences, opinions, and choices of others. When you decide what to wear in the morning you may choose to wear your favorite blue sweater to class—which may seem to be clearly based on your own preferences. Or maybe not. Maybe you favor that sweater because someone special (who happens to be in that class) told you it makes your eyes look really blue. But you probably choose not to wear a tuxedo or evening gown to class at least in part because that would violate the norms of the group with which you will be interacting. And, as we discussed in Chapter 1, violation of norms can endanger our status or membership within the group.

When you go to the store for bread for a sandwich for lunch, it may be because your parent or roommate or partner asked you to do so and your role relationship with that individual gives them the right or authority to make such requests of you—with a reasonable expectation on their part of compliance on your part (either based on status or affection). When you stay up late studying group dynamics when you would rather be out partying, it may be because you wish to study, but very likely it is because a teacher told you there would be an exam on that material the next day and you know that if you do not master the material, you will probably not receive the grade you desire. Thus we are not alone in determining our own behavior.

In situations of interdependence there are four possible combinations of our own desires and those of the others involved in the situation. As can be seen in Table 5.1, all but one of these combinations allow for several possible behavioral responses.

This taxonomy is based on Forsyth (1990) and will be the basis for the remainder of this chapter, including mechanisms and techniques for avoiding behavioral influence.

TABLE 5.1. Possible Interactions Between Attitudes and Actions

Behavioral Response (public)	*Personal Opinion (private)*	
	Agree with Other	Disagree with Other

Agreement	I Consensus
	     Conversion
		II Conformity
		      Compliance
		      Obedience

Disagreement	III Counterconformity
	      Reactance
		IV Independence
		      Ways to avoid influence

Within the context of these choices we will examine the classic and more recent research on these phenomena and the effects of such individual difference characteristics as age, gender, status, and cross-cultural influences. We will see, however, that in a number of topic areas there has been very little published research on the effects of these characteristics. We will also examine several examples of these phenomena in current American society, including the standoff between the Branch Davidians and the forces of the American government in Waco, Texas, in 1993, and how influence processes affected the mass suicide in Jonestown, Guyana, in 1978.

CELL I: PRIVATE AGREEMENT/PUBLIC AGREEMENT—CONSENSUS AND CONVERSION

Consensus

The simplest case in this quadrant is the situation in which we initially agree with the attitudes, opinions, or behaviors of others and this private agreement is matched by public behavior which confirms this agreement. For example, suppose I feel that a particular candidate would be the best choice for senator in the election, my friends agree, and we all vote for this individual. There is no necessity for persuasion , pressure, or even discussion because we were all of one mind from the beginning. In other words, we began the discussion with **consensus** as to the most appropriate behavior.

This, of course, is not always the case. Perhaps I begin by believing that the incumbent in the office deserves a second term and therefore I plan to vote for her. When I mention this to my friends, however, they tell me they disagree and begin to present information and arguments as to why I should change my mind. If they are successful in convincing me of the error of my ways so that in fact I do vote for another candidate because I have truly come to believe this person would make a better senator, the process known as **conversion** has occurred.

How did you vote in the last presidential elections? How did you decide to vote for your candidate? Were you persuaded by others? By campaign ads? By the candidate himself? Was conversion a factor in your decision?

Conversion

There are a number of mechanisms through which conversion can occur: we can obtain new information; we can be persuaded by others to change our minds; and we can be affected by our relationships with the relevant others which pressure us to convert in order to protect the relationship.

Information

The acquisition of new information may or may not affect our attitudes, beliefs, or behaviors. If we consider this information to be credible and it contradicts information upon which we had based a behavior, we may change our mind.

French and Raven (1959) and Raven (1965) presented a taxonomy of methods of interpersonal influence intended to provide a classification for any such interaction between individuals. ("Power" in this context is defined as the ability to influence the behavior of others.) The original model presented in 1959 consisted of five **power bases: reward, coercive, expert, legitimate,** and **referent.** However, it soon became clear that there was a loophole which was closed in 1965 with the addition of *informational power*. We will discuss the five power bases in our discussion of leadership and power in Chapter 8; for the moment we will focus on informational power.

"Informational power, or persuasion, is based on the information, or logical argument, that the influencing agent can present to the target in order to implement change" (Raven, 1992). **Informational power** is the weakest of the power bases, which means it is the least likely to change behavior. If I provide you with a piece of information that is irrelevant to you or that you feel lacks credibility, you are likely to ignore me and I have not wielded any influence over you. If I inform you that the local hardware store is having a sale on chain saws and you live in an urban apartment, you probably will not rush off and buy one. However, if I mention that there is only one day left to register for classes for the fall semester and you rush off to register, I have had power over your behavior. Or, if we are serving on a jury together and I remind you of a piece of evidence I considered to be particularly relevant but which you had not factored into your decision and this re-evaluation results in your changing your vote—again, I have influenced your behavior. It is extremely important that you understand that when we are discussing conversion the target of influence has actually changed his mind. He is not just "going along"—we have a believer.

The Process of Persuasion

The process through which we come to change our minds, the process of **persuasion,** can be considered using a six-step model (Zimbardo & Leippe, 1991, based on Hovland et al., 1951, 1953, 1957; McGuire, 1968; and Sherman, 1989).

These steps are:

1. Exposure (encountering the message)
2. Attention (focusing on the message)
3. Comprehension (understanding the message)
4. Acceptance (believing the message)
5. Retention (attitude change)
6. Conversion of attitude to behavior

Exposure. We are constantly bombarded with messages from the environment. In order to function in the world, we cannot process or react to all of this information. Thus we limit the messages to which we are exposed. Sometimes we make these choices ourselves; for example, if we are pro-choice regarding reproductive rights we will generally not choose to attend a pro-life rally. We will instead generally choose to expose ourselves to information that is consistent with our already existing attitudes and beliefs. This helps validate our beliefs and comforts us with the evidence that others have the same fine judgment we ourselves possess.

Actually, however, we do not have the control we believe we have over our access to relevant information. Often our **exposure** is governed by others—the gatekeepers in our lives and society. Even when we deliberately expose ourselves to a message, the content of the message has often been determined by these gatekeepers. Gatekeepers for information for children start with parents, continue with educators, and as adults, gatekeepers include the media and the decision makers in society.

When you pick up a newspaper or turn on your television to watch the news you can count on the fact that you will not be exposed to everything that happened on the entire planet that day. When you pick up this text you can be assured that not everything in the universe relevant to group dynamics will be revealed to you.

STOP Tonight watch news reports on two different television stations. Be sure they cover the same area, either local or national news. Do they report the same stories? Are duplicated stories in the same order? (Order of presentation often indicates importance.) Do they use different adjectives or take a different slant on the stories? Was one more liberal or conservative than the other?

Given that everything cannot be reported, communicators prioritize the events and information and present that which they consider important. On a day where there has not been a lot of activity the media consider important, but there are thirty minutes of newscast to fill, we will be exposed to "human interest" stories to help fill the time. On a "slow news day" we are much more likely to be exposed to a story about animals or children than on an eventful day (as defined by the media). In a text on group dynamics written by an author who is a practicing group therapist, you may be exposed to many more applications relevant to that particular topic than if the author was particularly interested in the group dynamics of juries, or hospital operating teams, or social groups such as sororities.

The determination of what makes a message "important" deserves consideration. After all, communicators are human beings and thus affected by the same factors influencing judgment as are we all, including cultural myths and individual knowledge and bias. There is also a growing consciousness that journalists are like everyone else in the sense that they have attitudes and values about all sorts of subjects (Lichter, Rothman, & Lichter, 1986). Whether the various media chose to cover the State of the Union speech by President Clinton in 1997 or to cover the simultaneously breaking story of the verdict in the civil trial of O.J. Simpson, they were dependent at least to some extent upon the judgment and decisions of others in terms of the information they themselves received, and made decisions as to how much as well as what information to pass on. Herman and Chomsky (1988) have developed a model of news construction that discusses the "filters" that are employed by the media. "These filters are said to impede objective news reporting and force media outlets to promote culturally edited or 'politically correct' renditions" (Wright, 1995). Personal experience as a reporter for such shows and television stations as CNN, "ABC World News This Morning," "Good Morning America," and print media such as the *Village Voice,* the *Baltimore Sun,* and the *Cleveland Plain Dealer* (among others) leads Dan Gifford (1997) to say:

> *Speaking as a former television reporter, twisting stories is easy. One can keep stories and unfavorable facts off the air; interview photogenic, articulate people backing the favored view; and use of words, tones of voice and facial expressions to signify favor or disapproval. These techniques are used in print as well.*
> **(Gifford, 1997, p. 799)**

In the case of the siege and subsequent conflagration involving the Branch Davidians at Mt. Carmel in Waco, Texas, in 1993, Attorney General Janet Reno was faced with the difficult decision as to when and how to end the extended standoff after a failed attempt by the Bureau of Alcohol, Tobacco, and Firearms (BATF) on February 28, 1993, to arrest their leader, David Koresh, on a number of potential charges. After this disastrous attempted raid, in which six Davidians and four BATF agents were killed, Koresh and a number of followers barricaded themselves in the compound and refused to either come out themselves (although some women and children were allowed to leave) or to allow entry by the forces of "law and order." This situation continued until April 19, 1993, when with Reno's agreement the compound was stormed, resulting in the deaths of an additional 74 Davidian men, women, and children (Wright, 1995).

In order to make this decision, Reno was dependent upon conflicting sources of information regarding at least four key issues: (1) whether the group was in fact in possession of illegal firearms; (2) whether or not child abuse was in fact occurring within the compound; (3) whether the group would commit mass suicide if further intervention was attempted; and (4) whether the chosen method of entry would harm the individuals within the compound.

The arrest warrant for Koresh was based entirely on the belief that the group possessed illegal weapons. Suspicions were based on the fact that the Davidians had *bought a number of legal weapons and legal gun parts which, with the help of a few parts they had not purchased, can be converted into machine guns.*

(Moore, 1995, p. 52)

Such weapons must be registered, and the question (and basis for the warrant) was whether these weapons had been converted and thus required registration (Williams, 1995). At the trial, "prosecutors could not call even one gun dealer who could provide evidence of illegal purchases of guns" (Moore, 1995). The raid was based on law enforcement assumptions regarding the presence of automatic weapons.

Reno was being informed both that the children within the compound were being abused, and that there was no evidence to support such charges. (The charges were primarily being brought by individuals who had chosen to leave the group and thus may have suspect motives in making such charges. As we saw in Chapter 3, the mechanism of cognitive dissonance often leads individuals to remember negatively groups they have chosen to or been asked to leave in order to justify that departure.)

Children's Protective Services (CPS), a division of the Texas Protective and Regulatory Services had conducted a two-month investigation of allegations of physical and other forms of child abuse and decided to terminate the investigation for lack of evidence (Smith, 1993; *Houston Chronicle*, October 10, 1993). Even after this decision was made by her organizational supervisors, however, Joyce Sparks, the individual CPS caseworker who had led the investigations, was alerting various state and federal agencies, including the BATF and FBI, and freely circulating anecdotal evidence about sexual abuse and unsubstantiated rumors about physical abuse (National Public Radio, Ellison & Barkowski, 1995).

The Branch Davidians perceived themselves as a legitimate religious group—albeit one with an apocalyptic vision, one that believed in and prepared for the imminent end of the world. The religious implications of this belief system were not considered legitimate by the FBI or BATF who failed to accept the offered assistance from religious experts on such groups, such as James Tabor who believes that the ultimate outcome of the standoff was preventable (Tabor, 1995), but became inevitable because

even a cursory examination of the FBI construct of mass suicide suggests that they viewed it an inherent and static predisposition, rather than a sect's possible response to a dynamic and shifting situation.

(Hall, 1995, p. 230)

In this instance, Reno was not faced with conflicting information, she was faced with only one (possibly incorrect) side of an argument because potentially important information was withheld.

Finally, Reno was concerned about the final assault plan first introduced to her. She was particularly concerned about the approach the proposed assault would take in terms of the damage that might be caused to the individuals within the compound . (The proposed plan involved insertion of tear gas into the compound for 48 hours, after which if there had been no response a tank would begin "disassembling the structure" [Rogers, 1993, p. 256].) Reno was not informed that only a few months earlier (January 1993) the United States (along with 100 other countries) signed an agreement banning use of the proposed chemical substance (CS gas) (Moore, 1995, p. 293). Information was also not shared about the potentially serious medical effects of the gas itself; nor the fact that the manufacturers of the gas had issued a warning that the burning of such gas emits toxic fumes; nor about the fact that the delivery method itself could be highly dangerous and . . . "could suffocate a child or person with respiratory problems if sprayed directly into their face" (Moore, 1995, p. 296).

STOP Given the conflicting and missing evidence and information provided, what decision would you have made? Would you have made the same decision as Reno and sent in the military at that point in time, allowed the standoff to continue, or perhaps sought out another alternative such as the intervention of experts in nontraditional religions?

Does it make a difference in your decision if you know that subsequent congressional hearings held on the events at Waco questioned not only the decision itself but also the handling of the matter by the BATF and FBI? What about the fact that Carol Moore who is cited numerous times above is considered quite controversial by the federal government and that her findings were co-published with the Gun Owners Foundation? Or that apparently Reno was not informed by the FBI of the offers of aid by the religious experts? Or that based on the media coverage most Americans supported the need for the final raid?

Clearly our decisions and opinions are colored to a large extent by the information to which we are exposed. (A CNN/Gallup poll immediately after the Waco incident found that 73 percent of those Americans polled felt the use of tear gas in this situation was "responsible" and 93 percent blamed Koresh for all of the deaths [Wright, 1995].) Information, then, passes through a series of filters before we are offered the opportunity to filter it ourselves.

In the United States, this potential distortion of information provided to the public is probably unintentional and can be counteracted by being aware of potential bias and seeking out multiple sources of information and opinion as expressed in the media. (Even individuals who are perceived by others as highly biased, however, such as the moral majority, perceive themselves to be at least one of, if not the only source of truth and may discourage searches for alternative information.) This lack of intentional censorship is not necessarily true around the world where the media are very closely controlled by the government.

Lack of censorship is not even necessarily historically true within the United States. There was a time when fictional novels, which are now considered by some to be great literature, were routinely banned based upon their content (generally sexual in nature). Novels such as *Ulysses* by Joyce or *Tropic of Cancer* by Miller were "banned in Boston" (typically one of the more conservative cities in the United States) which generally led to an instant increase in sales. And the controversy about what constitutes pornography and the extent to which we can ban messages still rages within the context of the First

Amendment to the Constitution (e.g., see Gillespie, Jacobs, French, Shange, Dworkin, & Ramos, 1995).

Attention. In order for the messages to which we have been exposed to begin the process of conversion, we must notice them. Even the environment we have controlled to fit with our values, beliefs, and prejudices is too full of information for us to ever hope to systematically evaluate it all. So again we filter out information through a process the social psychologists refer to as **selective attention.**

Basically this process involves our seeing and hearing—and attending to— those messages that validate our already existing ideas. We are not only more likely to notice confirming information, we process this information more quickly (Dovidio, Evans, & Tyler, 1986), and we are entirely capable of interpreting messages as confirming—even if this involves distortion of the information (O'Sullivan & Durso, 1984). For example, if we believe the stereotype that individuals who are overweight are lazy (one of the few currently remaining socially acceptable prejudices [Crocker, Cornwell, & Major, 1993]), then even if a member of our group is extremely industrious, and is overweight, we will tend not to notice her contributions; will attribute them to someone else; or if absolutely forced to acknowledge her contributions, we will label her an exception to the rule. This leaves our prejudice safely in place for use on future occasions.

What affects whether we notice and pay attention to a message? A primary consideration is the *salience* of the message. Salience is related to personal relevance. If we believe that a message is personally important to us for some reason, we are much more likely to pay attention. An extended family watching the news together might have the following set of reactions: the college student pays close attention to the report on rising tuition costs; her brother, an expectant parent, is much more interested in the story on a recall of infant car seats; and their father, who is within a year of retirement, is riveted to the story on the failing Social Security system.

As mentioned in the example on the Waco standoff, Attorney General Reno was particularly interested in information regarding the safety of the children regarded by the government as hostages in the situation. A question that might be raised would be whether Reno's gender made the safety of the children particularly salient to her and whether a male attorney general would have been more concerned with other issues—such as the allegedly illegal cache of guns and ammunition. Certainly sex-role stereotypes adhered to by many in this country might suggest this argument.

Comprehension. Even once we have paid attention to a message, we must understand the message for there to be any effect on our position, attitude, or behavior. A communicator who overestimates or underestimates my knowledge of a subject runs the real risk of my not understanding what is being conveyed. Examples must be understandable to the targeted individuals and salient to their interests. Thus messages aimed at children are likely to be more effective if they are syntactically simple, presented by other children, and use games or toys or school in explanations or examples.

This creates a problem for some experts in terms of their ability to effectively convey a message to individuals substantially less sophisticated or knowledgeable than themselves. As discussed in Chapter 4 on communication, experts often overestimate the sophistication and knowledge level of the audience. Since admitting to a lack of understanding is embarrassing for many people, individuals will tend to avoid asking questions that might be crucial to their understanding.

The language of the message must be an appropriate level (particularly for written communications). Generally, for written communications, comprehension is enhanced when a complex message is presented in written rather than oral form (Zimbardo & Leippe, 1991). This is one of the reasons that (rather than depend entirely upon our own brilliant lectures) most instructors require you to acquire (and to read) a textbook to help you comprehend the material.

Comprehension of a persuasive message is also influenced by the ability to create messages that possess validity, strength, and compellingness to the audience—or message quality (Zimbardo & Leippe, 1991). Knowing one's audience allows you to determine their prior knowledge regarding an issue and the strength of their existing attitudes. Attitudes that are long held and well thought out are more difficult to change than are weak attitudes. In other words, you are more likely to be able to convince me to try a new toothpaste flavor than you are to change my mind about my position on allowing women into combat positions in the military. Knowing the audience also allows you to craft messages that are "strong"—that seem to make sense to the audience and add new information to the issue in question (Morley, 1987).

Acceptance. Having been exposed to, paid attention to, and understood the message, the next step in the process is the question of **acceptance.** Will I come to believe the truth of the message? Acceptance is strongly affected by two factors of the message—the **source** and the **content.** Since comprehension is so strongly associated with content, the previous discussion dealt with content issues. Therefore we will focus on characteristics of the source of communication.

In order to be maximally persuasive, the source of an attempt to create attitude change should be credible. We should have faith that whatever this individual or group is telling (or trying to sell) us is correct. The selection of a credible source of persuasion may make or break any influence attempt.

STOP If you were a police officer responding to a call from a store owner accusing a teenager of shoplifting, whose account would you be more likely to believe—that of the shopkeeper or the teenager who says they just forgot to pay before trying to leave? What if the alleged perpetrator was the daughter of the mayor of the town and the mayor was a political rival of the store owner? Does that affect your decision? Discuss the difference (if any).

Credibility of source rests primarily on at least two bases: the expertise or competence of the source and the trustworthiness of the source (Hovland & Weiss, 1951). If an individual is an expert, or is perceived by the target to be an expert, then more attitude change will be obtained.

Often the issue of expertise can be troublesome. It is not at all unusual in criminal trials for both sides of the case to produce "experts" whose testimony completely contradicts each others'. This was true in the 1995 criminal case in which O.J. Simpson was accused of the murder of his ex-wife Nicole Brown, and her friend, Ronald Goldman. Both the prosecution and the defense brought forward supposed experts in DNA analysis (a technique by which bodily fluids or tissues can be identified as to their probability of belonging to a particular individual). Although the prosecution firmly believed that the evidence should convict Simpson, a conviction was not obtained.

The question remains whether jurors were unable to determine which expert was "correct" or were merely so confused by a potentially unclear presentation of the scientific evidence that they could not eliminate reasonable doubt as to Simpson's guilt. Perhaps comprehension and thus acceptance could have been improved if the scientific witnesses had been more aware of the fact that most of the population is not familiar with the scientific and statistical nuances they were trying to convey. It is also, of course, possible that jurors comprehended but rejected the prosecution witnesses' evidence. Whatever the reason, Simpson was acquitted at the criminal trial.

Trustworthiness of source is the second criterion that impacts on the power of the source of persuasion. Whenever someone wants to convince us of or sell us something, we are justified in wondering how that individual or group will prosper should we adopt their position. Clearly politicians have something to gain by convincing us of their trustworthiness—our vote. Advertisers of products have the incentive of financial gain possible if we buy their message—and their product.

Thus we may be much more likely to trust the source who does not appear to have any vested personal interest in or anything to gain from our adopting their position. In the 1970s, the National Organization for Women (NOW) used television to recruit membership in the organization. NOW was perceived by some then (as now) as having a very radical political agenda concerning women's rights, including at that time the passage of the Equal Rights Amendment to the Constitution. A woman as spokesperson—any woman—could easily have been perceived as having a potential for personal gain should the organization become strong and influential. Therefore it was an extremely wise choice to use a man, actor Alan Alda, to serve as the spokesperson. Many individuals would be likely to see him as having nothing directly to gain and therefore might see him as more trustworthy.

Finally, **likeability of source** is an important consideration in the impact of persuasion. As we shall see in our discussion of balance theory, it makes people quite uncomfortable psychologically to find they agree with their enemies. This is one of the reasons that advertisers carefully choose spokespersons who are perceived as likeable by the public. Basketball player Michael Jordan has served as spokesperson for a number of products—probably in large part because of the general perception of him as a likeable individual.

Fellow basketball player Earvin (Magic) Johnson was retained as spokesperson for several companies even after disclosing his infection with the HIV virus (a disclosure that would cost many their jobs), probably again largely because of his extreme popularity with sports fans. It is also interesting to consider that the method of acquisition of his AIDS infection (heterosexual activity) may have protected his popularity and visibility as compared with multiple Olympic gold medal-winning diver Greg Louganis, whose HIV infection was contracted through a homosexual partner. Louganis virtually disappeared from advertisements once this fact became known.

Retention of Message. Once we've made our pitch, how can we be certain that an individual will remember what we've said long enough to consider and perhaps change their own opinion or attitude? One approach described by Zimbardo and Leippe (1991) is to "hit it again, harder, again and again" (p. 179). (Ever wonder why the same television commercial plays so many times in one evening?!) Will repetition necessarily help comprehension? No, but repeated exposure to a message increases the likelihood of **retention of message** and that the target will go through the cognitive work necessary to analyze the position. If it makes sense and is not too discrepant from their original position, the target may adopt the new, desired attitude.

Conversion of Attitude to Behavior. Since LaPiere's classic 1934 study on the connection of racial attitudes to prejudicial behaviors, the problem of attitude-behavior connection and the **conversion** to behavior has been an important topic for research. LaPiere journeyed to 250 restaurants and hotels, with a Chinese couple. They were denied service only once. LaPiere subsequently wrote to these establishments stating he would be traveling with a Chinese couple and that he hoped there would be no trouble in obtaining service in their establishment. At that time, racial prejudice was not only socially acceptable in the United States, it was the law of the land. Only 128 of the establishments bothered to respond to LaPiere's communication (slightly over 50%). Of those who did respond, 92 percent stated there would be serious problems, and asked that the visit not take place. LaPiere cited this as evidence that there is not a connection between attitudes and behaviors.

Subsequent research has found that increasing the specificity of the attitude measured can dramatically increase the connection with the behavior observed (Davidson & Jaccard, 1979; Schwartz, 1992). Recent positions on the issue of the connection between attitudes and behavior focus on the intention to behave in a particular fashion that is influenced only partially by attitude (Fishbein & Ajzen, 1975).

Influence by Others

As we discussed in Chapter 2, we are attracted to and likely to form groups with individuals who are readily accessible to us (proximity) and who we perceive as being similar to us in some way. Once we have established these bonds with others, the tendency to wish to maintain these relationships can affect our beliefs and attitudes. This effect is independent of the persuasion tactics discussed above since in this case it is the presence and the quality of the relationship itself that affects our attitudes and behaviors—often at a nonconscious level.

The overreaching explanation for this phenomenon is known as **balance theory** (Heider, 1958). Balance theory proposes that humans are uncomfortable with inconsistency. (Cognitive dissonance, already defined and discussed in

Chapter 3, is an example of a more specialized type of balance theory than the general theory we're about to consider. While cognitive dissonance focuses on what happens within the mind of one individual, general balance theory focuses on interpersonal relationships.) When I find that my best friend and I disagree on a topic of importance to us both (the relevance of religion to everyday life, for example), the relationship will be thrown into a state of unbalance and we will both become uncomfortable.

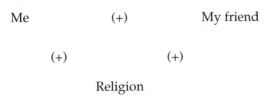

In the illustration of the situation above (illustrated from my perspective), there are attitudinal bonds connecting me and my friend, my friend and the attitudinal object (in this case, religion), and me and the attitudinal object. If all of these bonds are positive (as indicated by the sign in parentheses), we are comfortable and our friendship is reinforced.

If we disagree with each other about religion, then the bonds are positive from me to my friend and toward religion, but her bond with religion is negative and the relationship becomes unbalanced. After all, if she is wonderful enough to be my friend, how can she be silly enough to disagree with me?! (Of course, she's thinking the same thing!) In order for us to return to our comfortable friendship, something has to change. And there are three possibilities.

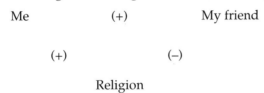

First, I can try to persuade my friend that her attitude is wrong. If I succeed, this situation is balanced (all positive signs). My friend and I agree. As long as we agree it doesn't matter whether we both like or both dislike the attitudinal object. Thus I could also reconsider my own attitude toward religion and decide that she's correct and again, this brings my friend and myself into agreement and balances the situation.

Finally, I could decide that I really can't be friends with someone who has attitudes so very different than my own and I could dissolve the friendship. Any of the three changes would serve to rebalance the relationship.

STOP Do you and your best friend have significantly different attitudes on some issues? Are they attitudes about which you feel strongly (such as religion or sports), or are they minor issues such as your favorite flavor of ice cream? How do you handle these differences? Do you agree to disagree? Do you argue? How have these differences affected your relationship? Have you ever lost a relationship because of attitude differences?

If I care for my group members, friends, fellow gang members, or family members, there are strong pressures to push me to agree with their attitudes. So if I discover that my decision to vote for a particular candidate is in disagreement with that of my club members, I may very well change my mind and believe and vote as they do. Again, conversion has occurred.

Pressure is also exerted if I discover that any enemy and I agree about an attitudinal object. How can we be enemies if we both have the good judgment to share an attitude? In this case, again I can: (1) change my mind toward the attitudinal object (disagree with my enemy—which represents a balanced situation), (2) try to change his mind (less likely since we're enemies and therefore unlikely to be in close communication), or (3) decide he's not such a bad guy after all and change my attitude toward him.

The bottom line for balance theory is that in a model with three objects if you have either all positive bonds or two negative bonds the situation is balanced. Any other combination of attitudes is unbalanced and should result in some shifting of attitudes.

What about the effects of gender or other characteristics on influenceability? Gender has been found to have a small effect, with women being slightly more influenceable or persuadable. Eagly and Carli (1981) used **metanalysis** to look at the phenomenon. Metanalysis is a statistical procedure that allows researchers to compare the results, including the direction and size of the results, across studies. Their analysis found that only 1 percent of influenceability was accounted for, or associated with, the gender of the subject. Thus 99 percent of the variability in amount of influenceability must be explained by and associated with factors other than gender.

One of these factors is the *involvement* of the individual with their position. As mentioned before, individuals who have minor investment in a position are much more likely to change their minds than those extremely committed to a cause. Therefore an individual who is slightly uncomfortable with the idea of gun control would be more easily convinced to switch to a more accepting position than would an individual who has actively campaigned for the passage of legislation to limit access to guns such as the "Brady Bill" (named after President Ronald Reagan's aide who was permanently disabled in the attempted assassination of Reagan in 1989).

So far we have explored the situations in which we privately hold, or come to hold the same position as that of the group and our behavior is consistent with that agreement. Sometimes, however, we may mildly or even actively disagree with the group on an attitude or belief yet go along with the group's behavior. In the next section we'll consider factors that might result in such actions.

CELL II: PRIVATE DISAGREEMENT/PUBLIC AGREEMENT—CONFORMITY, COMPLIANCE, AND OBEDIENCE

The second cell in our matrix of actions and attitudes contains three situations: *conformity, compliance,* and *obedience*—which represent increasing pressure brought to bear by others on the individual to behave in a certain manner. The difference between the three is the extent and nature of the pressure. Conformity involves implicit pressure brought to bear by others, compliance results from requests for behavior, and obedience occurs in reaction to demands for behavior.

Conformity.

The classic study of **conformity** was conducted by Asch in 1946. Subjects were led to believe they were participating in a study on perception and asked to compare stimulus lines to a set of standardized lines, identifying for the experimenter which comparison line was closest in size to the stimulus. When subjects arrived at the study they found a number of other students already occupying all but the end seat in a row of chairs. The number of other students (who were actually confederates of Asch's) varied.

After explaining the experiment to the subjects the first stimulus lines were presented. The experimenter began at the opposite end of the row from the naïve subject and asked each student to identify the "correct" line. On 12 of 18 trials (beginning on trial number three) the confederates had been instructed to unanimously give an incorrect response. This left the poor naïve subject as the last to respond. Would the subject go along with the crowd, or would he (all the subjects were male) give a deviant, however correct, response?

 If you were a subject in the Asch study described above what would you have done? Would you have gone along with the group, or would you have given the correct answer?

Surely all of you reading this are positive that *you* would always give the correct response, regardless of what the others said. However, Asch found that approximately three-fourths of subjects went along with the rest of the "subjects" at least once, and conformity was obtained on roughly one-third of the critical trials. Apparently it doesn't take much indirect pressure to cause people to go along with the group.

Two important issues Asch explored as factors affecting the extent of conformity were the number of confederates used in a trial (group size), and the effect of **unanimity of majority** within the group on level of conformity by subjects. Varying the number of confederates from one to over ten, Asch found that the amount of conformity to a unanimous majority increased from less than 5 percent with one confederate to approximately 13 percent with two confederates to over 30 percent with three confederates. Then the dramatic increases in amount of conformity stopped. He had found what is known as a **ceiling effect.** In other words, it appeared as if the amount of conformity had reached some sort of upward boundary. Thus it appears from this study that it really does not take much implicit pressure to cause individuals to conform to a group.

The unanimity of the incorrect majority was another critical factor in affecting the amount of conformity. When even one of the confederates gave the correct response or a different incorrect response than the unanimous majority, even if that still left the supposedly critical number of three confederates agreeing on an incorrect response, the naïve subjects were significantly less likely to give an incorrect response themselves. Having some social support, however little, makes a big difference in our ability to behave independently of the group.

Why do people conform? It appears three basic factors are at work (Forsyth, 1990) and they are: (1) *normative influence*, (2) *informational influence*, and (3) *interpersonal influence*. Since we have discussed **interpersonal influence** in the form of persuasion, we will focus on normative and informational influence.

Normative Influence

Much of our behavior is governed by the *norms* of the group which are the unwritten rules of behavior discussed in Chapter 1. Why do people conform to the norms of a particular group? Because of **normative influence,** they wish to be perceived as a member of that group and accepted by that group. Violation of group norms can lead to reduced status or to rejection by or ejection from the group. Norms for acceptable physical appearance are often used as a vehicle to indicate group membership: in the 1970s the Hippies were identifiable by their long hair, beards (on the men), and flowing clothing; Punks in the 1980s were identifiable by their multiple earrings, black leather clothing with lots of zippers, and shaved heads or multicolored hair; and Goths in the 1990s were softened Punks, wearing black lipstick, nail polish, and eye makeup and flowing black clothing reminiscent of the Renaissance (or a vampire movie).

At the first university where I was employed, I taught in both the psychology and the business administration departments. The faculties and students of the two groups had very different norms for acceptable clothing. The psychology group, including the faculty, attended class in jeans and very casual clothing. Business students and faculty alike, however, wore more businesslike attire to classes (including ties for the men and suits and heels for the women). Whenever I appeared in one of the departments in the "wrong" clothing, there was sure to be some comment made to remind me I was breaking a norm.

Members of the Amish community are closely controlled by rules and norms.

Sometimes extreme conformity to the norms of a group occurs when the group feels they are under some sort of attack. Hostetler (1993) writes of the phenomenon of **overconformity** sometimes found among the Amish, a religious group that lives a very simple, nontechnological life (Old Order Amish often may not have electricity in their homes and must use straight pins rather than buttons to fasten their clothing, which may only be one of a limited number of colors) and finds itself increasingly encroached upon by the rest of society.

An Amish adult man who overconforms to the rules will let his hair grow longer than the Ordnung *requires just to "play it safe." Older members and ministers frequently adhere to stricter practices than is required, just for the sake of avoiding any possible criticism. Some of the aged Amish persons of very conservative groups have observed that the hair is worn longer today than it was fifty years ago.*

(Hostetler, 1993, p. 369)

Informational Influence

Informational influence is directly related to our discussion of the fact that group membership satisfied individuals' needs for information, discussed in Chapter 2. When we're deciding whether to spend the money to see a new movie, we might poll our friends or check with a movie critic to decide whether we should go ahead with our plans. Informational influence causes us to reinterpret, or reconsider the meaning of key aspects of an issue (Campbell, Tesser, & Fairey, 1986).

Effects of Diversity on Conformity

The issue of conformity is an area where there has been investigation of the effects of culture, status, and gender. Various reviews of Asch-type conformity studies have been conducted (Mann, 1980; Smith & Bond, 1994) and found that levels vary a great deal across cultures. Conformity among the Bantus in Africa and teachers in Fiji was higher than found by Asch in the United States with conformity found on more than half of the critical trials. In Germany, Japan, and Belgium, conformity levels were generally lower—around 20 percent.

This figure for the Japanese might be viewed as surprising given that Japanese culture places much more emphasis on the importance of groups and is thus considered a **collectivist culture.** Triandis (1994) explains this finding based on the concept of behavior toward **in-group** versus **out-group.**

The definition of an in-group differs across cultures. In some cultures the in-group is very narrow (e.g., the family, southern Italy in the 1950s), and no other collectives are important; in others there are several important collectives, and some are very broad (e.g., in Japan the whole country is one of the collectives).

(Triandis, 1994, p. 113)

Triandis finds that the type of culture or society impacts strongly on conformity behavior. Crowded, hierarchical cultures generally socialize their children to conform, as do the lower social classes of industrial societies (Kohn, 1969). On the other hand, hunters, food-gatherers, and the upper social classes in industrial societies tend to socialize children in the direction of self-reliance and individuality.

In Japan, confederates in the conformity studies were considered out-group members.

> *When members of a collectivist culture are said to be more conforming, that refers explicitly to their conforming to in-groups. Such people in fact are likely to conform less to out-groups than are members of **individualistic cultures.***
>
> *(Triandis, 1994, p. 230)*

This effect was sufficiently strong in Japan that 34 percent of subjects actually gave **anti-conformity** responses—incorrect answers—when the majority was actually giving the correct response.

The effects of *status* on tendency to conform follow our commonsense hunches: individuals with low status are more likely to conform with or defer to individuals of higher status. Strodtbeck and Lipinski (1985) found that juries were more likely to choose individuals of higher socioeconomic status as foremen. Higher status individuals are more likely to prevail in juries in their opinions, with the correlation in one study between an individual's opinion on the case before deliberations and the ultimate decision by the jury being $r = +.50$ for high status individuals and $r = +.02$ for lower status individuals (Strodtbeck, James, & Hawkins, 1957).

The effects of gender on conformity seem to be somewhat complex.

> *For many years, social psychologists maintained that women were far more influenceable and conforming than men. Most recent research concludes that gender differences may be statistically significant, but they are small in magnitude.*
>
> *(Matlin, 1997, p. 250)*

In addition, more recent research, including Eagly and Chrvala (1986) found that large gender differences in tendency to conform existed only in college students who were 19 years old and older. Younger students of both genders conformed more than older students (perhaps reflecting status differences).

Eagly and Wood (1982) provide two reasons why women might be more easily influenced. Traditional gender-role socialization has trained women to be more compliant and men to be more persuasive and influential. Also, women have traditionally had lower status in our society and, as mentioned above, lower status individuals are more likely to conform.

However, in conducting metanalysis of the body of research on conformity behavior, Eagly and Carli (1981) made an interesting discovery. They found that male researchers found larger gender differences in influenceability and conformity than did female researchers. Hall (1978) in a metanalysis on the ability of subjects to guess emotion found that male researchers found smaller gender differences than did female experimenters. Thus it appears that the gender of the authority figure reinforces culturally accepted sex-role stereotypes and affects the direction of results. If the gender of the experimenter affects the results to such an extent, one might wonder about the robustness of the actual differences independent of context.

 Have you ever made any changes in your appearance or behaviors in order to be accepted by a particular group? At what age were you most likely to make these changes? Discuss the reasons for your answers.

Compliance

Compliance occurs when we acquiesce to the request of another for a particular behavior. The difference between conformity and compliance is that in compliance the source of the pressure for the behavior is clear and explicit. Someone has made it clear that they wish to control, or at least influence, our behavior. While we may be unaware of the subtle pressures toward conformity, we are aware in the situation of potential compliance that we have a choice.

One factor affecting whether or not we respond to a request is based upon our perception of the legitimacy of the request. Does this person have the authority or right to influence our behavior? Another of the bases of power developed by French and Raven (1959) and Raven (1965) is the power base known as *legitimate power*. **Legitimate power** rests on the agreement between the target of influence and the individual seeking to exert influence that their roles within the relationship give permission for such influence attempts. When your supervisor at work asks you to stay a few minutes late to complete a project, you will probably do so—because that is part of the authority granted to supervisors by their role. You would probably be much less likely to comply with the request of a stranger under most circumstances—unless, of course, that stranger could lay some other sort of claim on you.

We are likely to help little children to cross a busy street even when they are strangers because we perceive them as having the legitimate right to request help because of their relative helplessness. So high status is not necessarily the

Individuals who claim to be nonconformist to society usually simply conform to another set of norms.

issue. The determination as to who has a right to expect compliance depends upon our social contract with that individual.

Some situations are likely to elicit compliance with a request based upon social norms. This may seem paradoxical—behavioral change based upon an implicit pressure to comply in response to a direct request—however, in American culture there are a number of social norms that pressure us toward compliance to requests. One is the norm of polite behavior. When someone makes a request we should, when possible and appropriate, comply. Another is the norm of reciprocity, which requires that when someone has allowed us to influence their behavior (perhaps through doing us a favor such as providing us with notes for a class we've missed), we "owe them one." Or to put it more directly in terms of compliance, they now have the right to expect that they have a future opportunity to even the score.

STOP How would you feel if someone did you a huge favor anonymously (e.g., paid a year's worth of your tuition), and no matter how hard you tried you couldn't determine their identity? Would you feel happy about the favor or unhappy that you couldn't reciprocate and restore equity to the situation?

The justification given for requested compliance in some cases need not be particularly compelling. Often when asked to do someone a favor we respond automatically, a situation referred to as **mindlessness** (Langer, Blank, & Chanowitz, 1978).

Langer's classic study (Langer et al., 1978, experiment 1, p. 637) involved the conditions under which a student waiting to use a photocopy machine would allow a stranger (a confederate of the experimenters) to use the machine first. There were three conditions which varied the extent of the justification given for the request (intended to vary the extent of the legitimacy of the request).

In the first condition the confederate (both male and female confederates were employed) approached the machine and said, "Excuse me. I have five pages. May I use the Xerox machine? I'm in a rush." This was perceived as the legitimate condition which should result in compliance. In the second condition—which was seen as the control condition—the phrase about being in a rush was eliminated, thus removing the need for allowing the confederate to move ahead in line.

The experimental condition involved giving what might initially sound like a reason (such as being in a rush or needing to eat lunch), but upon evaluation was nonsense. In this condition the individual said: "May I use the Xerox machine, because I have to make copies?" Of course. Why else would you use a copy machine?

If real justification for compliance is necessary, then you would expect that more subjects would comply in the first or real information condition; few in the "no reason" condition where no justification was offered; and very few in the third condition where there was actually just as little justification offered as in the control situations. That was not what was found, however.

Sixty percent of subjects complied in the "no reason" condition (surprisingly high, but perhaps in response to the cultural norm of being a "nice guy"). Over 90 percent of subjects complied in the real information condition AND in the nonsense information condition—and there was no significant difference in compliance rates between the two conditions. Later research on the phenomenon has supported these initial findings (Folkes, 1985; Langer, Chanowitz, & Blank, 1985).

What about you? This situation was depicted at the beginning of the chapter. Did you predict that Robert would give up his place? If not, don't worry. This finding is counterintuitive until you think about it. How often do we stop to analyze carefully what is asked of us in a relatively trivial situation?

So it would appear that compliance is like conformity, a relatively easy response to evoke, at least in many situations. It would appear that who asks, the situation in which the request occurs, and to some extent the justification provided for the request are among the important factors in obtaining compliance.

Obedience

Obedience is behavior in response to an increase in the pressure to change behavior. We no longer have implicit pressures or requests, we now have demands or orders that we are to behave in a particular fashion (e.g., a sergeant orders a private to dig a latrine, or a parent orders a child to clean her room). Clearly these two examples are situations in which the identity of the person making the demand will affect obedience based upon their authority to make the demand. So once again, legitimate power comes into play.

 From whom are you willing to take orders? Compare with your group members or classmates the number of people who have this much power over your behavior. Why these particular people?

A number of studies have shown that the identity of the individual making the demand and their relationship with the target is crucial. A truly disconcerting study investigated the power of doctors to make inappropriate demands of nurses. Experimenters called nurses' stations in hospitals and identified themselves as a physician—an imaginary identity concocted by the experimenters. This supposed doctor ordered the nurse to give a totally inappropriate injection to a particular patient on the floor. A confederate of the experimenters was placed outside the door of the designated patient's room. There were no written orders, and the nurse could not possibly have had any information about the physician since there was no such physician on staff. The majority of nurses receiving the calls were stopped at the door—they had been intending to follow the "doctor's" orders!

The power of certain uniforms also confers legitimacy to demand obedience. The military has an elaborate system of designations worn on the uniform to indicate to other military personnel whether or not obedience is required. For civilians, police uniforms often elicit obedience not only because of the legitimacy factor, but also perhaps because of the implied potential for coercion (another of French & Raven [1959] and Raven's [1965] power bases) (Bushman, 1988; Geffner & Gross, 1984).

The classic study of obedience was conducted by Milgram at Yale University in the 1960s. Subjects were recruited to participate in what they believed to be a study of learning. Naïve subjects were paired with a confederate and the confederate was always assigned the role of learner while the subject played the role of "teacher." The teacher was to read a list of pairs of unrelated words to the learner, then test the learner by providing four alternatives from which to select the correct response (sort of a verbal multiple-choice test).

For each mistake the learner made, the teacher was to administer a shock, increasing the intensity of the shock with each mistake. Shocks were administered by a piece of equipment with a set of toggle switches—the switch at the lowest end identifying the amount of electricity associated with that switch as 15 volts and the highest end (moving up on 15-volt increments) as 450 volts. Labels above the switches ranged from "Slight Shock" at the lowest end through "Severe Shock" to "XXX" at the extreme high end. Once pushed, the toggle switch would remain in an intermediate position so the teacher could identify the next higher switch to be used for the next error.

The condition that elicited the highest amount of obedience involved taking the learner to another room where he was strapped into a chair and attached to the shock generator. The teacher then went into an adjoining room to begin his role in the experiment. An experimenter sat in the same room as the teacher during the experiment.

Just before the teacher and experimenter left the learner in place, the learner explained he had a mild heart condition and asked about the danger involved in the shocks. The experimenter responded, "Although the shocks can be extremely painful, they cause no permanent tissue damage" (Milgram, 1963, p. 19). After the teacher and experimenter exited the room, the learner/confederate quickly released himself from the chair and set up equipment that would provide standardized feedback during the study to the naïve subject/teachers.

Before conducting this experiment, Milgram checked with 39 psychologists and psychiatrists as to their expectations for the teachers' willingness to administer the increasingly high levels of shock. None expected any of the subjects to proceed to the highest level. Most felt that the majority of subjects would quit at about the 150-volt level.

As the experiment progressed and increasingly high levels of shock were supposedly being administered, the learner began to protest. If subjects continued with the experiment at the urging of the experimenter, at the 315-volt level the learner stopped responding altogether.

315 volts?! Hadn't the experts said that most subjects would stop by 150 volts? In this condition of highest obedience, not one of the 40 subjects stopped at that level. In fact, 26 of the 40 subjects continued right to the end of the shock board and had to be stopped by the experimenter.

What would you have done as a subject/teacher in the Milgram study? Do you know? Why do you think individuals were willing to hurt someone on orders from a stranger?

Why would these people behave in such a barbaric manner? Even though they were in reality not hurting anyone by administering massive shocks, during the experiment they believed they were. Were they terrible people? Viewing tapes as well as reading transcripts of the study shows that teacher/subjects were under tremendous psychological pressure. There were tension-generated giggles and rivers of perspiration and numerous expressions of concern for the learner—even while continuing to administer shocks. A number of factors, which Milgram varied in different conditions of this study, may provide clues regarding the factors affecting levels of obedience.

First, as discussed previously, the perceived legitimacy of the source of the demand affects obedience. In this case the study was being conducted by a prestigious university and overseen by an experimenter in a white laboratory coat (a uniform of sorts). The experimenter was also physically present. And the learner was physically absent—so the teacher was not actually witnessing the potential damage he was inflicting on the learner. When Milgram ran this study from a storefront without identifying Yale as the source, obedience was only somewhat diminished. Obedience was dramatically diminished, however, when the location of the experimenter and the learner were manipulated.

Manipulation of the experimenter's presence—moving him farther away and eventually replacing him with a tape recording that subjects played for instructions—resulted in greatly reduced levels of obedience. So did moving the learner closer to the teacher—into the same room in one condition, and in another condition forcing the teacher to hold the unwilling learner's hand on the shock plate in order to receive punishment. (Obviously the subjects were very naïve about the potentially shocking effects of such an act.)

Having the learner out of sight may have allowed teachers to make use of a variation of a social psychological phenomenon known as **deindividuation.** In this state, "The individual becomes less aware of his or her own personal values and behavior, and instead focuses on the group and the situation" (Diener, 1984). In this case, teachers no longer had to react to or even think of the person they were hurting as a person experiencing pain that they (the teachers) were inflicting. Instead it likely became possible to think of the shocks as just part of the study to which the learner had agreed, and to think of the learner as just another part of the experiment—not as a suffering individual. Subjects might also have been able to think of themselves as just a part of the experiment, under the controlling responsibility of the experimenter and larger context of the experiment. A number of the subjects actually asked the experimenter who would take responsibility if the learner was injured. Once the experimenter explained he would take responsibility, it seemed easier for the teacher/subjects to continue.

One way to achieve the state of deindividuation is to actually hide your identity from others. The Ku Klux Klan members all wear robes and pointed hats with masks to ostensibly cover their identity. Frequently these masks are not worn, but even when they are, such physical characteristics as height and weight and voice often disclose the identity of the individual. However, the illusion of being unidentifiable because they look like everyone else allows individuals to think of themselves just as part of a larger group and not an individual who must take responsibility for their individual actions. This act of sharing the blame with others so as to reduce one's own guilt or shame is known as **diffusion of responsibility.**

Cultural Impacts on Obedience

Just as we find cross-cultural differences in the rates of conformity, such differences are also found in obedience studies of the type described before (see review by Smith & Bond, 1994). Germans generally show an even higher rate of obedience than in the Milgram study—at 85 percent. A study conducted in Holland by Meeus and Raaijmakers (1985, cited in Smith and Bond) and in Spain by Miranda et al. (cited in Smith and Bond) found the highest rate of obedience—over 90 percent. The Spanish study was conducted on students and the Dutch study on a sample from the general population.

Australians, on the other hand, demonstrated only about 40 percent obedience in the most extreme conditions (Triandis, 1994). However, in three studies conducted in Australia cited by Smith and Bond (1994) using students and including the study cited in Triandis (all conducted by Kilham and Mann, 1974), male students showed a rate of obedience of 40 percent in one study and 50 percent in another, while in a replication using female students, a rate of only 16 percent obedience was obtained. Milgram, in a replication of the original study using female subjects, found that American women were just as obedient as their male counterparts. Obviously, cultural differences affect the behavioral characteristic of obedience to authority.

Certainly we have a horrifyingly real-life example of obedience to authority in the November 18, 1978, mass suicide at the People's Temple compound in Jonestown, Guyana, on the orders of Reverend Jim Jones, leader of the group (Hall, 1987). Over 900 people lined up to drink poisoned Kool-Aid upon these orders. That the suicides were committed for the most part voluntarily is supported both by audiotapes of the event and the pattern of the bodies on the ground. On the tapes a few people dare to question what is happening but are quickly shouted down by others. Also, the cyanide was quick-acting so Temple members were asked to wait to drink until they were far enough away that their collapse would not block traffic and prevent others from receiving their cups of poison. The bodies were found in unnervingly neat rows.

Why should Jones have such power? Jones was a master at creating situations and training his followers for obedience to his commands. He had moved his people physically several times—from the Midwest to Ukiah, California, to San Francisco to an isolated compound surrounded by jungle in Guyana. Each move severed contacts of members with their extended families and the final move limited their contact with the outside world—making them entirely dependent upon Jones for both information and resources. They were encouraged to denounce and deny their family connections—even those between husband and wife, parent and child, further encouraging dependence.

To further break any relational bonds between group members and anyone other than himself, Jones ordered group members to have sexual relations with others than their spouses (mostly himself) and demanded that parents sign over legal custody of their children to him. Cutting all ties to the outside world included signing over all earthly possessions to Jones. Thus group members had no one to turn to and nowhere to go.

Jones created a new "family" and established himself as "father" of the group. Playing upon his role as minister, he even went so far as to fake miracles so that followers would believe in his divinity (Kilduff & Javers, 1978). Those who didn't believe, those who expressed doubt, were punished. Those who left the group often were found mysteriously dead from apparently other than natural causes.

Finally, Jones had reframed (redefined) the concept of suicide from that of death to merely "stepping over" into a better place, and enacted rehearsals of the event as tests of faith. These enactments were an exact duplicate of the real event—except that the punch didn't contain poison—and were intended and served to desensitize the citizens to the idea of death.

On the day of the actual suicide, a mission from San Francisco containing Congressman Leo Ryan and the families of several group members who had come to Guyana to investigate conditions in the compound were ambushed on the way to the plane to return to the United States. A group of armed men from Jonestown intercepted the party at the landing strip, killing Ryan, three newsmen, and one of the defectors; and wounding an additional eleven people (Internet, www.mayhem.net/Crime/cults.html).

At Jonestown Jones had frequently cited the example of Masada in biblical times where an entire Jewish community chose suicide as the more noble alternative to inevitable slaughter by their enemies when it became apparent that they could neither escape nor defeat the Roman army surrounding the city. He had also preached that the jungle surrounding Jonestown was teeming with armed CIA agents whose intent was to ruin their paradise. Receiving news of Ryan's death, Jones announced that the compound would be taken by the CIA. All it took on the crucial evening to set the final tragedy in motion was one final command to emulate the biblical tragedy.

CELL III: PRIVATE AGREEMENT/PUBLIC DISAGREEMENT—COUNTERCONFORMITY AND REACTANCE

The behaviors in this cell might at first appear to be quite counterintuitive or strange. Why would someone who actually shares consensus with the group risk the potential disapproval and sanctions of the group by violating their own position? While the behaviors involved in counterconformity and reactance appear the same, the motivations behind them are quite different. One (counterconformity) may actually benefit the group, while the other (reactance) may cause problems for the group.

Counterconformity

Counterconformity is a reasoned action with a means to an end. There is thought and deliberate intent involved. One example of the use of counterconformity may be to slow down a group that is plummeting toward what at least one group member considers a premature decision. While agreeing with the inevitable decision, the individual wants the group to pay more attention to alternatives and be sure that they have considered carefully their actions (Forsyth, 1990). An example was shown in the murder trial of suspected serial killer Juan Corona in the 1970s cited by Forsyth. After the trial, one of the jurors admitted that in the initial balloting he voted to acquit—fully believing in Corona's guilt—in order to force the jury to slow a rush to judgment.

A second situation in which counterconformity might be experienced is when an individual wishes to prevent what is known as the **mandate phenomenon** (Clark & Sechrest, 1976). This is the situation in which overwhelming support from a group causes an individual to attempt to acquire more power, influence, or resources by capitalizing on their popularity. A mandate can certainly be inferred when a quick, unanimous decision is made on the part of a group. In an election for leader of the group, even one dissenting vote (while not changing the outcome) may provide notice to the victor that she does not have unlimited license with her behavior.

Reactance

While counterconformity is reasoned and has an intended benefit for the group, **reactance** is a much more emotional, knee-jerk reaction without regard for the consequences. The theory of reactance was introduced by Brehm (1966) to help explain why some people just seem to need to be "contrary" and to do exactly the opposite of what the group wishes. (Reactance is the basis for the "pop" psychology term *reverse psychology*, the phenomenon in which we ask someone to do the exact opposite of what we want, knowing this will trick them into doing exactly what we DO want.)

Reactance appears to be based upon the idea of individual freedom. When individuals feel that their freedom is being impinged upon by other individuals of the group, the best way to show that they are really independent is to do the reverse of what is being requested. In a way, this is equivalent to the toddler who, while experiencing the "terrible twos" says no to just about everything suggested. Children in this stage have been known to say no to wanting a cookie while in the act of reaching for it. For these children, their resistance is a way of differentiating themselves from their parents—and of announcing their supposed **independence.** Similar defiant behavior by adolescents also serves the purpose of declaring independence from parental control.

Research on the theory of reactance has found two situations in which reactance is most likely to appear. The first is when an individual's choice appears to commit them to further, potentially unknown consequences (you agree to pick up something from the grocery store for a neighbor not realizing you have just assumed the role of official shopper for the individual); or when

> . . . a concern with freedom is aroused when situations or other people seem to threaten the view that people have of themselves as choosing to react to the environment rather than as determined by it . . .
>
> *(Kiesler, 1978, p. 223)*

Kiesler goes on to elaborate on this second point by identifying four situations in which reactance is most likely to appear based upon the source of the pressure for behavior. These are: (1) strangers or members of an out-group; (2) potential competitors for resources; (3) "people who are either incompetent or relatively low in social desirability" (p. 225); and (4) people who lack sufficient power or status to legitimize their demands.

There are obvious potential implications of reactance for our behaviors within groups. Individuals may be differentially defensive of their perceived independence, and the leader must be careful not to push past limits. Second, individuals or leaders who wish to avoid creating reactance must be accepted in-group members with sufficient perceived competence and legitimacy to influence others' behavior.

CELL IV: PRIVATE DISAGREEMENT/PUBLIC DISAGREEMENT—INDEPENDENCE AND WAYS TO AVOID INFLUENCE

Independence

Independence is a highly valued commodity in the United States. As we've seen, however, it's also not a tremendously common commodity. We are pressured, directly or indirectly, into many of our behaviors. Assuming that we do not wish to be susceptible to influence, are there techniques that can be used to increase our ability to remain independent? Zimbardo and Leippe (1991) list four:

> *They can be (1) encouraged to commit themselves to their existing attitudes, (2) given knowledge, (3) induced into practicing counterarguing persuasive attacks, or (4) forewarned about impending attacks on their lifestyle or attitudes.*
>
> **(Zimbardo & Leippe, 1991, p. 229)**

The first and fourth strategies are somewhat general in that they can be used against pressures to conform, to comply, or to obey. The second and third strategies are most effective and applicable in the situation of attempted persuasion to conversion.

Commitment to a position can be increased if individuals decide to stand firm on a position and can be even stronger if that individual makes such a commitment publicly. Hearing yourself make such a statement to an audience can trigger cognitive dissonance (Festinger, 1957). So if I announce to an audience at a Weight Watchers meeting that my goal is to lose 50 pounds, I'm going to be extremely cognitively uncomfortable if instead I gain or fail to meet my goal. Ability to withstand change influences is most likely to be true when the commitment I've made is linked directly to my values (Lyndon & Zanna, 1990).

Also to be considered in the case of a public commitment is the concept of saving face. People who do not live up to their public commitments may face ridicule and/or pity from group members. So once we announce a position or a planned behavior, we have pressure not only from ourselves, but also from others to hold true to that commitment.

Ways to Avoid Influence

Knowing in advance that someone is going to attempt to change my behavior allows me to prepare myself. The knowledge that someone is about to try to limit my independence may well trigger reactance on my part. At the very least, it will allow me to prepare defensive tactics. One of these tactics might be for me to collect more information on my position. This allows me to counterargue more effectively (Wood, 1982). In addition, watching myself scurrying around collecting additional arguments or support for my position could trigger cognitive dissonance. Surely I wouldn't devote this kind of time and energy unless I was really committed!

Finally, I can make use of what McGuire (1964) referred to as an **inoculation defense** strategy. Simply stated, inoculations in the medical sense introduce a small amount of the bacteria or viruses for the disease we wish to prevent. The immune system develops antibodies to protect us from the disease should we be exposed to a large number of the germs.

Psychological inoculation works in somewhat the same way. A mild version of the anticipated pressure is placed on the individual, who is encouraged to resist. This should be relatively easy since the influence is deliberately weak. This essentially provides practice in resistance. If the individual has trouble resisting even this dramatically reduced amount of pressure, coaching or further information can be provided.

Of course, independence may not always be what it's cracked up to be. If we were to resist all types of persuasion or pressure toward behaviors, we would end up spending most if not all of our time alone. We would not be able to attain or maintain membership in groups. And as we discussed in Chapter 1, human beings are (for whatever of the reasons discussed) pack animals. We are not happy alone—so moderation in independence (as in so many things) is probably the most desirable state.

Summary

We have talked about a number of ways that individual, private attitudes, thoughts, and behaviors interact with the attitudes, thoughts, and behaviors of those around us. We have seen that pressures can be indirect or direct, but either way are often quite difficult to withstand. We have discussed the reasons people would not want to withstand the pressure from others. And we have discussed factors such as gender, status, and cultural factors that serve to mitigate influence on our behavior. In all, we have seen that it is probably true that most of our behaviors are an interaction between ourselves and our social environment.

Key Terms

acceptance
anti-conformity
attention
balance theory
ceiling effect
coercive power
collectivist cultures
compliance
comprehension
conformity
consensus
content
conversion
counterconformity
credibility of source
deindividuation

diffusion of
  responsibility
expert power
exposure
independence
individualistic cultures
informational influence
informational power
in-group
inoculation defense
interdependence
interpersonal influence
legitimate power
likeability of source
mandate phenomenon
message content
metanalysis

mindlessness
normative influence
obedience
out-group
overconformity
persuasion
power bases
reactance
referent power
retention of message
reward power
selective attention
source
source of message
trustworthiness of
  source
unanimity of majority

APPLICATION

Getting to Heaven's Gate

On Monday, March 25, 1997, Rio DiAngelo sent an e-mail message to the group known as Heaven's Gate, a group with whom DiAngelo no longer lived in their Rancho Santa Fe home (near San Diego) but with whom he continued to keep in close touch. He received no reply, which was unusual. The next day he received a package from Fed-Ex containing a letter explaining that Do (born Marshall Herff Applewhite in 1931) and the group had "exited" their "vehicles" (Miller, *Newsweek*, 4/14/97). DiAngelo knew immediately what this meant. He announced to his boss that the group members were dead and proceeded to the house where thirty-nine individuals, ranging in age from 26 to 72 years old, were found lying dead. Each member was wearing a pair of new Nike tennis shoes and the group's unisex uniform and lying under a purple cloth shroud. Two had plastic bags over their faces. All had packed bags under their beds containing clothes, toiletries, and money.

Applewhite was so capable of
influencing his followers that they were
willing to commit suicide to comply.

The house was scrupulously neat. The "exits" apparently had taken place over a period of three days, starting Friday, March 22. Each wave made their exit by eating pudding or applesauce lethally laced with phenobarbital followed by a drink of vodka. To speed the death, a plastic bag was placed over the head. (This is a formula recommended by the Hemlock Society in the book *Final Exit* written by the group's founder Derek Humphrey. When interviewed, Humphrey admitted that the recipe appeared to have been taken from the book, but insisted that the book is intended only for the terminally ill, not as a cookbook for suicide. When interviewed after the incident, Humphrey was quoted by CNN in their U.S. news page on the Internet as saying, "I regret it—a serious misuse of my book. Just like guns are misused for murder, my book has been misused here.") After each wave of departures, group members removed the bags and cleaned the individuals and their surroundings. There was no one to remove the bags from the heads of the final two. Once the police became involved and the news media got the story, much attention was paid to the case for weeks, trying to determine the identities of the victims, the reason for their apparent suicides, and more information about what immediately became identified as the Heaven's Gate cult.

What is a cult, and how are their ideas spread? Not surprisingly, there is no consensus regarding a definition of a cult, either within psychology or religion, or even the popular vernacular. Any group with ideas out of the mainstream is likely to find itself labeled with this term. This means that such disparate groups and some religious groups such as the Church of Jesus Christ of Latter-Day Saints, Wicca, Santeria, and Scientology may have received the label ("Harmless Cults", www.religioustolerance.org, Internet), as have groups such as the Church Universal and Triumphant, David Koresh's group in Waco, Jim Jones' People's Temple, and the early Christians. As can be seen, groups identified as cults are often religious in nature or have a specific philosophical belief system by which they abide. They often develop norms, attitudes, and behaviors that are deviant from the dominant culture. In order to avoid "contamination" some may cut themselves off from the dominant culture which also allows for what is often very strict control over the members.

A new "science" known as memetics is based upon an epidemiological approach to the spread of a cult's (or any) ideas (Cowley, *Newsweek*, 4/14/97). In his 1989 book, *The Selfish Gene*, Dawkins "proposed thinking of culture as a Darwinian struggle among 'memes,' or mind viruses. . . ." The best fitting ideas at any given time are passed on, while others die off. Lynch (*Thought Contagion*, Basic Books, cited in Cowley) gives the example of how a taboo on birth control will result in a larger number of children being born who will then carry on the idea.

In a process much like the social psychological concept groupthink (Janis, 1967) (to be discussed in detail in Chapter 6), unorthodox groups ("abnormal" by the definition of the dominant culture) often withdraw from the culture and decide that only they are worthy and candidates for heaven. Apocalyptic "memes," such as the idea that the world will end at the end of the millennium, can cause a group to frantically recruit their loved ones into the "chosen" ranks before it is too late. Signs or signals that the end is near can further speed up the process. As we will see later, the Heaven's Gate group believed they had received such a sign.

Unfortunately, as the Heaven's Gate tragedy reminds us, hosts who swallow both the heaven-is-ours and the end-is-near memes may conclude the end is theirs to hasten—and hasten it.

(Cowley, p. 14)

The Heaven's Gate group was formed in 1975 by Applewhite and a nurse named Bonnie Lu Truesdale Nettles. Various stories of the circumstances of the couple's meeting have surfaced in the press. Applewhite's version as appearing on CNN's Web page on March 28, 1997, was that he was in a hospital in Houston where he had a near-death experience. Nettles was a nurse on the staff who convinced him they could move on to better things. By March 29, CNN reported that group members said the two had met in a psychiatric hospital where Applewhite was trying to overcome his homosexual urges. In that same article, it was reported that Applewhite had told his sister the hospitalization had been for a heart problem. However they met, Applewhite and Nettles remained together in what was apparently (again according to Applewhite quoted by CNN on 3/29/97) a nonsexual relationship until her death in 1985. During that time the two adopted a number of different names—from "The Two," to "Bo" and "Peep," to "Do" and "Ti." During this time they moved around the country collecting the members of their group.

The beliefs of the Heaven's Gate group appear to be an unusual combination of Christian beliefs and UFOlogy. In several places in materials taken from the Website maintained by the group, Applewhite makes biblical references and talks about entering the Kingdom of Heaven. He speaks of some individuals who have "developed enough" to become "containers" for souls deposited on Earth two thousand years ago. Souls that have evolved sufficiently may move on to the "Next Level," but must be accompanied by a "Next Level Representative." Applewhite believed that Jesus was the first such representative, and that he himself was the current incarnation. He believed that the group would be picked up by a spaceship and taken to "Next Level" where they would join Nettles. There may be some significance in the fact that there were 39 who "exited." An early disciple of the group as quoted in *Time* (Chua-Eoan, 4/14/97) thinks that numerology played a role in the choice of the number: 3 plus 9 equals twelve (the number of Jesus' disciples) and 1 plus 2 equals three—the number of the Trinity. Applewhite most emphatically stated he did not believe the group to be committing suicide. Suicide, he said, was "to turn against the Next Level when it is being offered" (Heaven's Gate Website 4/1/97).

The timing of the departure appears to have been triggered in part by the appearance of the Hale-Bopp comet and a report on a Website constructed by Art Bell, a radio talk-show host who claimed that an object was trailing Hale-Bopp and that it was a spaceship full of aliens (Jaroff, *Time*, 4/14/97). Being in the business of creating Websites and being highly computer literate, it is probable that the Heaven's Gate group heard of this claim and believed that the time had come.

During the years waiting for the vehicle to take them to the next level, the Heaven's Gate group lived a life that is very typical in many ways of that of groups described as cults. Individuals were to drop their previous identity and adopt oneness with the group and its beliefs. Upon entering, group members dropped their birth name and were assigned a new name consisting of "a three-letter prefix followed by 'doti' or 'ody' (a play on the founders, Do and Ti)" (Isikoff, *Newsweek,* 4/14/97). Male or female, hair was cut extremely short (even by male hairdressing standards) and uniform, unisex clothing was adopted. This was intended to help "get control of the vehicle" because Applewhite believed that there was no gender at the Next Level so sex, sensuality, or any gender-identified behavior or decoration became taboo. So strong was this inhibition that eight of the male members of the group were found, upon autopsy, to have been surgically castrated. Applewhite was apparently the third of the group to undergo the surgery.

On the Heaven's Gate Website was a listing of the rules that group members were required to follow "to maintain the purity of their 'vehicles.'" Major offenses included any type of sensuality or arousal, breaking any rule, and lying. Minor offenses included "trusting my own judgment—or using my own mind," "having likes and dislikes," and "exaggerating vehicular symptoms." Each group had a "check partner" to make sure the rules were followed. Instructions were believed to be from Nettles to Applewhite (she was apparently always the stronger of the two and group members believed she died because "her mind was so powerful it 'short-circuited her vehicle'" [Isikoff, *Newsweek,* 4/14/97, p. 34]) while Applewhite would communicate the instructions to a group of "overseers"—individuals who had been with the group a long time. There were seating charts for meals and even television watching. There was a list of acceptable (such as *The Sound of Music,* the "X-Files," and "Chicago Hope") and forbidden (such as *Golden Eye* and *Multiplicity*) viewing materials. In other words, all decisions were made for the group members.

Perhaps DiAngelo should have realized that Applewhite felt the time had come to join Nettles on the spaceship trailing Hale-Bopp; however, he didn't. In the weeks before the suicides began, the group went on what might have been a sentimental journey for Applewhite, visiting the site of his first recognition of his calling and other places the group had lived over the years. Several group members traveled to Tijuana, Mexico, where they obtained the phenobarbital. The group went to San Diego to see the Wild Animal Park and Sea World and went out several times to dinner (Miller, *Newsweek,* 4/14/97). Then the suicides began on Friday and were completed on what is known in the Christian religion as Palm Sunday—the day of Jesus' joyous entrance into Jerusalem a week before his crucifixion and subsequent resurrection. The choice of dates would seem to be more than mere coincidence.

So now is the Heaven's Gate over? At least two individuals have survived the mass exodus. DiAngelo believes that he was allowed to leave the group to take a full-time job and live outside the group so he would be left to spread the story. Another individual calling himself "Rkk" reported to *Newsweek* (Miller, *Newsweek,* 4/14/97) that he had also received a packet from the group containing videotaped good-byes. He apparently could not live by the regimentation that was required of the group and left at the end of 1996. He stated, however, that he would have gone with the group "in a microsecond" (Miller, *Newsweek,* 4/14/97, p. 36).

Perhaps Lynch (of "meme" fame) has made a chillingly accurate prediction.

Let's say 100 million people were exposed to the Heaven's Gate meme as a result of the 39 suicides. If one in a million of those people contracted the meme, the suicides would have yielded 100 new infections.

(Quoted by Cowley, **Newsweek,** *4/14/97, p. 14)*

Discussion Questions

Apply the concepts from the chapter to consider the following questions:

1. Identify at least one example for each of the following terms from the information on Heaven's Gate: conversion, conformity, obedience, and independence.
2. Attempts have been made to portray the members of the Heaven's Gate group as losers—as stupid people without lives. Many, however, were college educated. And all worked in the Website creation business of the cult. Why are so many people anxious to believe the worst about these people?
3. Eight male members of the group chose to be surgically castrated. Although Apple-white was not the very first, it was his idea and he was one of the earlier members to undergo the procedure. He did not order others to undergo the surgery, but they did. Why would the members choose to have themselves transformed in this fashion? What type(s) of influence were at work?
4. Members of the group were very closely controlled in their everyday lives—from assigned seating to approved video. How can you reconcile this with the fact that members had outside contacts in their computer business?

CHAPTER 6

Group Productivity

- **Introduction**
- **Group Problem Solving: Steiner's Model of Effectiveness**
- **Potential Productivity**
  - *Characteristics of Tasks*
  - *Types of Tasks*
- **Productivity Inhibitors**
  - *Groupthink*
  - *Group Polarization*
  - *Coordination Problems*
  - *Social Loafing*
  - *Free Riding*
- **Productivity Enhancements**
  - *Synergy*
  - *Nominal Group Techniques*
- **Mixed Blessings**
  - *Brainstorming*
  - *Social Facilitation*

APPLICATION: Managing Effective Meetings to Improve Productivity

What Would YOU Predict?

Luis, Jeremy, Elizabeth, and Anika are in a classroom group for their marketing course. Luis, Jeremy, and Elizabeth are senior marketing majors. Anika is a sophomore sociology major. Their group task is to turn in a marketing analysis of a new product. As the group progresses how do you think the group will allocate the work on the project? Would it be different if Anika was an accounting major?

INTRODUCTION

As long as there has been study of groups, there has been the basic question of whether it is more productive and efficient to employ individuals or groups in problem-solving and decision-making situations. Although the distinction between problem solving and decision making is in a sense artificial, the discussions have advanced separately in the literature and research. In this chapter we will discuss a classic model of factors that affect the decision as to whether an individual or a group will be more productive in a given situation, and in

Chapter 7 we will discuss the process of decision making within the group once the decision has been to employ a group for the task.

GROUP PROBLEM SOLVING: STEINER'S MODEL OF EFFECTIVENESS

The decision as to whether to employ an individual or a group on a task is always based upon a guess. Since we can't predict the future or the outcome of the task with perfect accuracy, we are forced to fall back upon models of probable outcomes using individuals versus groups. Which is more likely to succeed? And how do we define success?

Clearly there are a number of criteria that could be employed. Is time an element? Is there only one correct choice in the situation? Is the issue the amount of work that can be accomplished or the quality of the finished product? All of these questions would factor into the question of how much productivity could be anticipated in the best of all possible worlds. We don't live in that world. So the best we can do is to identify the issues that will impact upon the situation and make our best judgment from there.

> *Optimal group productivity is rarely attained . . . for potential productivity is reduced by losses due to faulty social process, especially motivation losses and interpersonal-coordination losses.*
>
> **(Davis, 1969, p. 48)**

Steiner (1972) developed a model that allows for the prediction of potential group productivity. But there are other intervening issues that affect the amount of actual productivity we can expect to see on a task. Besides the questions posed above, what about the impact of group dynamics on the task? Will the use of a group enhance productivity, or will the dynamics of the group potentially inhibit success on the task? Thus Steiner's model can be expressed as the equation below:

ACTUAL PRODUCTIVITY = POTENTIAL PRODUCTIVITY −
GROUP INHIBITORS + GROUP ENHANCEMENTS

We will structure the remainder of this chapter around this equation. First we will discuss the factors that affect *potential productivity*, such as *characteristics* and *type of task*. We will then focus on those aspects of group dynamics which can, as Davis (1969) suggests, detract from that potential productivity. Davis fails to mention the fact that there are aspects of the group that make it superior to an individual under some circumstances. Such aspects as *synergy* and *nominal group techniques* can improve task performance. And, finally, (not represented in the equation) are two very important issues in productivity that serve as mixed blessings. *Brainstorming* and *social facilitation* may improve upon productivity, or detract from productivity. After deliberating these issues, we will use the application portion of this chapter to discuss what is often one of the most unproductive aspects of groups: the meeting. It **is** possible (believe it or not) to hold a useful, efficient, and productive meeting if you keep the issues from the chapter in mind.

The primary determinant of **potential productivity** is the task upon which the group or individual will work. Thus Steiner (1972) states:

> *The nature of the task determines whether a particular kind of resource (knowledge, ability, skill, or tool) is relevant, how much of each kind of resource is needed for optimal performance, and how the various relevant resources must be combined and utilized in order to produce the best possible outcome. . . .*
>
> *(Steiner, 1972, p. 273)*

Characteristics of Tasks

When examining tasks, there are two basic aspects that will influence whether a group or individual represents the probability of highest productivity. These are the structure of the task and the type of result that is desired. The structural aspect of the task that is of concern is the *divisibility* of a task. Can the task be broken down into smaller units, or must it be done as a whole? If the task is indivisible, it is known as a **unitary task,** as opposed to a **divisible task.** If we can break the task into smaller components, it is possible that these components might be done in parallel, thus saving time on the project. An individual would have to work through the components in a linear fashion, thus taking longer on the task.

For example, if I want my house painted, I could hire a single individual who would go from room to room, or I could hire a team, each of whom could be working at the same time. Assuming an adequate skill level from each, I would have my redecorating accomplished more efficiently by a group. Painting a portrait, however, is a unitary task. Although I could, in theory, divide the features and assign them to different artists, there are two problems. First, no time would be saved since there's limited room in front of a canvas. Second, it is highly unlikely I would be able to find artists whose styles were exactly the same, so my portrait, while interesting, would probably not be what I had hoped.

The type of result required is the second aspect to be considered as we start defining types of tasks. Do we want quantity or quality? If you shuddered at the term "quantity" (and as conscientious students you well might), let me give you an example. Suppose I'm running for mayor of my town. I want to put a flyer touting my virtues in as many home mailboxes as I possibly can on the day before the election. There's no art or skill required in stuffing a mailbox. So the more, the better. This is known as a **maximizing task.** "Maximizing tasks make success a function of how much or how rapidly something is done" (Baron, Kerr, & Miller, 1992).

When quality is the important aspect we refer to the task as an **optimizing task.** If we as a group are preparing a grant application for federal funds to study the spread of athlete's foot in high school shower rooms and only one grant will be funded, we want the best possible product. "Optimizing tasks make success a function of achieving some correct or optimal solution . . ." (Baron et al., 1992).

Think of the many tasks required of you in your life. Identify three maximizing and three optimizing tasks. Compare your lists with others in your group or class. Which tasks do you tackle alone? Which ones with help? Why?

As I'm sure you've deduced from these examples, unitary tasks pull toward the use of an individual. Divisible tasks pull toward groups. Maximizing tasks such as a tug-of-war lend themselves well to groups. With optimizing tasks the issue is not so clear. The quality of individuals available, the time constraints, resources, and group dynamics or process all may affect the decision. In fact, these constraints play a role in every determination about using an individual or a group because:

Unlike task demands and resources, process cannot be measured or evaluated before work begins. Process consists of the actual steps taken by an individual or a group when confronted with a task. It includes all those intrapersonal and interpersonal actions by which people transform their resources into a product, and all those nonproductive actions that are prompted by frustration, competing motivations, or inadequate understanding.

(Steiner, 1972, p. 274)

Types of Tasks

We can take all of the above concerns and create a taxonomy of **types of tasks** and evaluate each for their potential for the highest level of productivity, considering both the group and the individuals. The first task is known as the **additive task.** Additive tasks are divisible and maximizing. The outcome is the sum of the contributions of the members. For this type of task, individual differences in capability are essentially irrelevant.

The group *always* does better than the individual. Let's take an example of a prom decorating committee. They've decided to fill the ballroom up with balloons. On the day of the dance Patrice blows up 250 balloons, Jack blows up 500, and Dominic blows up 300. Even though Jack has clearly made the greatest contribution to the total, the group as an entity has blown up a total of 1,050 balloons. No one is hurt or disadvantaged by using the group, and each individual in the group is helped. Even with motivation or coordination losses, for additive tasks it is still best to go with a group.

The second type of task is known as a **compensatory task.** This is an example of a divisible-optimizing task. An example of this task is when a jar is presented full of jelly beans or pennies or whatever and the task is to guess the correct number. Since the guess must be made in the absence of knowledge of the correct number, guesses by individuals will vary widely in accuracy. Some individuals will be quite accurate, others quite inaccurate.

If you choose an individual for this task you are taking a chance that you have happened to choose someone who will be accurate. When a group performs this task the accurate members tend to balance out the wildly inaccurate members by averaging their guesses and the group is more likely to come up with a more accurate guess. This, of course, helps the inaccurate members, but tends to disadvantage the individual who was extremely accurate at the start. Most of the members have been helped rather than hurt by membership in the group.

Another important aspect enters the decision about whether or not to use an individual or a group in this situation. If your most accurate member is also the most articulate and persuasive, you're in luck. But what if someone who is extremely far from the correct response is more influential?

Many of you will be familiar with the various group exercises that revolve around a survival group. The group is stranded somewhere (the desert, the moon, the Arctic) with a limited list of resources. Each individual first ranks the importance of the articles for survival of the group. Then the group meets and comes to a consensus list as to the items' importance. Differences between the individuals' original rankings and the group's ranking help identify the persuasive members. Finally, a list of the correct order of importance as identified by experts in the area is read. Comparisons can be made between individuals' original rankings, the group's rankings, and the expert rankings.

I participated in an Arctic survival exercise in a graduate school course in the Northeast. I had been raised in southern California so knew nothing about cold weather survival. My original rankings were dismal. However, because I was a member of the faculty in another department and the other group members were MBA students, I apparently had an amount of influence that was wildly inappropriate. Looking at the accuracy of the group rankings at the end of the exercise, one group member suggested the group would have been better off if they had weighted me down with rocks and sunk me with the airplane!

Several members of our group had answers that were highly accurate. But since the rules stated the group had to stay together, they let me talk them into a situation which in "real life" would probably have cost them their lives. So in deciding whether to go with a group or an individual in a compensatory task, be very sure you know about individuals' characteristics and levels of competence before making your decision.

The **disjunctive task** is a task where there is a single correct, verifiable answer such as puzzles, riddles, or math problems. Thus disjunctive tasks are examples of optimizing tasks. There are, however, two separate types of disjunctive tasks, and correct identification of which type you are dealing with may strongly influence your choice for an individual or a group solution. The first type is known as the **"eureka" disjunctive task** (Lorge, Fox, Davitz, & Brenner, 1958). For this type of problem the correct answer is immediately obviously correct. Thus only one person in the group must solve the problem. Once one person has the solution, all will concur that the task is completed. An example of a "eureka" disjunctive task is the following (borrowed from Forsyth, 1990):

What is the next letter in this sequence? O T T F F S S __. Got it? (Answer is at the end of the chapter. Don't peek.) Remember that if anyone in the group gets it, the entire group has been successful. So the more the merrier. For this type of task you will again always do better with a group. The best member is not disadvantaged, and everyone else is helped.

The other type of disjunctive task is the **"non-eureka" disjunctive task.** Again, we have a single correct answer that can be verified, but it is not immediately obvious when the correct response has been discovered. I'll paraphrase an example of a classic exercise I use in class.

> Joe Doodlebug is a strange insect. He can hop, but he can't fly, swim, run, or do anything else but hop. He must always face north. He can only hop in the cardinal directions (north, south, east, west), not any of the diagonals. His hops can range in size from 2" to 3'. He must hop four times in any one direction before changing directions. One day he's hopping around and his master places a pile of food directly to his west, five feet away. Joe's hungry. He looks at the food and says, "I MUST jump four times to reach the food." Why 4 (no more, no less) times?

This problem is extremely frustrating for groups. In each class a number can never come up with the correct solution (again at the end of the chapter—same rules). Yet, as I walk around the room listening to the groups as they work on solutions, I frequently hear a group member state the correct answer only to be shouted down (sometimes literally) by their fellow members. What's going on here?

Earlier research on "non-eureka" disjunctive tasks suggested that the groups should solve the problems correctly based on the **truth-wins rule** (Forsyth, 1990), which is what happens in the eureka disjunctive tasks. The obvious truth wins. But this does not always hold for the non-eureka disjunctive tasks (Bray, Kerr, & Atkin, 1978). For this type task, the group only comes up with the correct answer if a significant number of the group also reach the same conclusion. This is known as the **truth-supported-wins rule** (Laughlin, 1980; Laughlin & Adamopoulos, 1980; Strasser, Kerr, & Davis, 1980; Laughlin & McGlynn, 1986; and Hastie, 1986).

Without an obviously correct answer, it takes persuasion to convince members who have come to alternate conclusions that others have the correct answer. And again the level of persuasiveness is often a significant component of whether the group ever solves the problem. When I give the answer in class to those groups who have been unable to solve the problem, there is usually a frustrated groan because someone in the group at one point suggested the correct response but was dismissed by the other group members.

A very serious real-life example from Kiesler (1978) shows how a group individual can identify a correct response to a situation but be ignored with devastating results:

> *An article by Sam Adams, who worked as a CIA intelligence analyst during the Vietnam War, provides a good example of how competent people in an organization may come up with verifiably correct answers to a relatively simple question but not have their answers accepted in the organization because of political and social considerations such as those listed above. Adams' job was to estimate Vietcong military strength. After examining military documents carefully and comparing field reports with official ones, he realized that the strength of the Vietcong had been seriously underestimated (600,000 versus the official count of 270,000). Excitedly, he wrote a report to that effect and told everyone in his office. Nothing happened. No one responded. His numbers, he*

was finally told, were not acceptable to the military, and it was their responsibility to release official figures. When Adams wrote more memoranda, documenting his estimates with data and demanding a response, the secret CIA estimate was finally revised, but still the military insisted that the official (public) estimate had to remain under 300,000. Low estimates provided support for public statements by the White House that there was light at the end of the tunnel. The CIA organization thus complied with military demands and did not communicate its own estimates to the administration. It was not until many months later, after a devastating offensive by the Vietcong, that the official estimates of its strength were revised.

(Kiesler, 1978, pp. 305–306)

Conjunctive tasks require the entire group to complete the task before the job can be considered completed. Again the issue of divisibility creates two different types of conjunctive tasks. For one the individual is the best use of resources; for the other, either an individual or a group may be used. An example of a unitary conjunctive task would be a mountain climbing team; the summit is not conquered until each and every team member has reached the top. Or a relay race which isn't won until the last member of the team crosses the finish line. If you have a four-person relay team, three of whom hold world-competitive times in the event and one person who can barely run the distance, you're not going to win many races. If you have a mountain climbing team and have been unfortunate enough to include a total novice climber, you are going to move at the speed of this member. In other words, in a unitary conjunctive task the group performs at the performance levels of the weakest member. Everyone else is disadvantaged. Clearly, unless you can have a group composed of extremely highly skilled members, a group would only serve to frustrate the individuals who could have clearly done better by themselves.

Some conjunctive tasks can be divided. If your group is preparing a presentation for being awarded the contract for a new Vietnam War memorial in your town, you can take the task and divide it up into pieces. What you are doing is turning the task into a compensatory task. Each person is given that portion on which they can do the best job and other phases of the task are given to the least-skilled individual—for instance, making copies and passing out the presentations at the meeting. The job is done, all have participated, and damage by the least-skilled member is contained.

In our chapter opener example, Anika may be detrimental to her group—she doesn't possess the same relevant skills as the other members. However, perhaps Anika is an excellent writer and editor. Others could provide the content, and she could prepare the document. The situation might very well be different if Anika was an accounting major. Since every marketing analysis requires a financial analysis, she would possess skills important to, even though different from, the other group members.

Gender differences have been reported in task solutions in groups. Wood (1987) examined the results of 52 studies of sex differences in performance. She was interested in possible differences in two factors: task content and interaction style. Studies that found men were "better" in the group were found to have a content that played into the typical skills, interests, and abilities of men.

Men tended to adopt a task-oriented interaction style and outperformed women when a high rate of task activity was important to success. Women tended to outperform men when group success depended on a high level of social activity (Wood, Polek, & Arken, 1985). As has been seen in other areas of group dynamics, extraneous factors such as gender may interact with more relevant factors in groups.

PRODUCTIVITY INHIBITORS

Groups, as groups, can make some terrific decisions and be wonderfully creative in problem solving. However, groups, as groups, are also prone to certain types of influences that may affect the quality of their productivity. In this portion of the chapter we will discuss five: (1) *groupthink*, (2) *group polarization*, (3) *coordination problems*, (4) *social loafing*, and (5) *free riding*. All can quite effectively sabotage a group. Luckily, understanding these phenomena makes it more possible to prevent their occurrence.

Groupthink

Groupthink is a term coined by psychologist Irving Janis in 1982. He:

> invoked the term . . . to refer to a kind of pathology that often occurs in group decision making, a pathology that arguably contributed to high stakes foreign policy disasters such as the Bay of Pigs invasion, Argentina's decision to initiate the war in the Falkland Islands or Lyndon Johnson's escalation of the Vietnam war. (Baron, Kerr, & Miller, 1992, p. 171)

Groupthink occurs in groups whose level of cohesiveness has grown too high. These group members respect each others' opinions to the extent of rejecting out-group members who might disagree. The leadership style and advent of a crisis mentality stifle group dissent so that norms are adopted by the group that violate the norms of the larger environment. These are sometimes referred to as **runaway norms.** The groups develop a superior attitude and believe that outsiders are stupid and evil. This in turn justifies and encourages their isolation from the larger environment, insulating them from any questioning or criticism of their norms or decisions. The leader is often a strong individual whom the others wish to please, further smothering any dissent. Hearing none, each member assumes that all the others represent a united front. Even if a single individual member has doubts, they are not expressed, partly because of self-doubt ("If all those other people, who are smart and whom I respect, agree, I guess I'm wrong") or because the leader has chastened any individual so unwise as to express disagreement that all the rest of the members can anticipate a similar fate should they express dissent.

Cross-cultural research on groupthink indicates the phenomenon occurs in other cultures, though perhaps not to the extent as in the United States. In the Netherlands groupthink was increased by the homogeneity of group member backgrounds, ideologies, and gender (Kroon, Van Kreveid, & Rabbie, 1992). In another study, a network analysis of the central social circles (CSCs) of national political subcultures of Australia and the United States was used to model the CSCs sociometrically. The CSC of the United States was elitist while that of the Australian group was pluralistic in design. The United States rated higher in the incidence of groupthink (Bovasso, 1992).

On January 28, 1986, the space shuttle *Challenger* was scheduled to begin a very special mission. For the first time a teacher, Ms. Christa McAuliffe, was included in the crew and would be beaming down lessons from the shuttle. The *Challenger* was the second of the space shuttles and had flown nine successful missions since 1982. The morning of the launch was unusually chilly for Florida. After many serious discussions between NASA officials, it was decided that because of all the media hype the mission should go on. NASA officials estimated that the chances of failure of the space shuttle was 1 in 100,000. However, only 73 seconds after launch the *Challenger* exploded, killing all seven members of the crew.

What happened? Could this tragedy have been avoided? On January 28, 1986, NASA appointed the Rogers Commission to examine the circumstances of the explosion. On that commission was physicist Richard Feynman. He believed the NASA figures estimating the probability of failure of a shuttle to be overly optimistic, and placed the probability closer to 1 chance in 100.

> *Feynman also learned that pieces of rubber used to seal the solid rocket booster joints, called O-rings, failed to expand when the temperature was at or below 32 degrees F (0 degrees C). The temperature at the time of the Challenger liftoff was indeed 32 degrees F.*
>
> **(www.Feynman.com, p. 1)**

Feynman's explanation for the disaster was unfortunately elegantly simple. The O-rings are used to seal the joints of the solid rocket booster (SRB). Upon launch, the material in the SRBs expands and pushes against the joints. Failure of the O-rings allows a leak. Photographs of the *Challenger* immediately after launch clearly show this leak. The leaking fuel ignited, heating the fuel tank, which then exploded. This explosion in turn released liquid hydrogen which exploded the booster and then the *Challenger* itself (www.Feynman). Given the temperature at the time of takeoff, the disaster was virtually a foregone conclusion. Yet some of the best scientific minds in the country allowed the launch to occur.

STOP Where were you when the *Challenger* exploded? What were you doing? This event stands out in the memory of the current generation as clearly as did the Kennedy assassination in the minds of a previous generation. If you were watching the launch (it was being widely televised), how did you feel when you realized the shuttle had exploded? If you are too young to remember, ask older siblings or your parents.

The *Challenger* disaster is a classic example of groupthink. What steps could have been taken to prevent this tragedy? The best way to prevent the development of groupthink is to be aware of the conditions under which it thrives, and create norms inconsistent with the development of groupthink. Rather than limiting contact with the outside environment, outsiders should be brought into the group on a regular basis. This serves to keep the group in touch with outside norms and to allow the expression of divergent opinions.

Rather than discouraging dissent, the group should require that whenever a member presents an idea to the group they must present the advantages AND the drawbacks associated with the idea. This creates the norm of healthy criticism and skepticism. Increasing each member's accountability for the outcome decreased groupthink more in male groups than in female groups in the Netherlands (Kroon et al., 1992). If necessary, a group member can be asked to play the role of **devil's advocate.** This person becomes responsible for finding fault with each idea presented to the group. It is wise not to allow one person to become fixed in this role as eventually the group will simply view this person as a grumpy curmudgeon and ignore what might be important criticism.

Finally, the leader should not express an opinion until the group members have already expressed their own. This will at least force those who wish to fawn over the leader to guess her position on the issue. With the creation of an open, critical, grounded group, the phenomenon of groupthink is unlikely to occur.

Group Polarization

Group polarization is another inappropriate decision-making strategy that may develop as part of a group's dynamics. Unlike groupthink, however, although the existence of the phenomenon is well established, it is difficult to predict the effect on the group decision and the bases are not well understood. There are several competing explanations for the phenomenon.

The first indication of a tendency for groups to make more extreme decisions than individuals (to polarize) was discovered by Wallach, Kogan, and Bem (1962), and was referred to as the **risky shift.** Individuals would fill out questionnaires making decisions on situations which required a choice between two behaviors. The choice with the highest reward was also the choice that was the least likely to succeed—in other words, the riskiest. After filling out the questionnaires, the participants would meet in five- or six-person groups. The group was required to make a choice between the same two behaviors. There was a tendency, which was slightly larger for the males, for the group to shift to the riskier decision. Examination of the specific questionnaire items, however, identified some in which the shift occurred in the more cautious direction. When Moscovici and Zavalloni (1969) found shifts in both directions the term "risk shift" was dropped and the term "group polarization" was adopted. Cromwell, Marks, Olson, and Avary (1991) found that thirty active American burglars, when evaluating sites for potential crimes, showed a cautious shift when these evaluations were made in the presence of co-offenders.

That the phenomenon occurs is clear. What is unclear is what causes a shift in which direction. A number of explanations have been offered, including *diffusion of responsibility, familiarization theory*, and *persuasive arguments theory* (Vinokur & Burnstein, 1978). As discussed in Chapter 5, **diffusion of responsibility** is the effect found when there are others around who can act in a situation so the individual doesn't feel the personal responsibility for action (Latane & Darley, 1970). In this instance the additional risk accompanying the riskier choice is spread out across the group members and no single individual is responsible. There is always someone else to point to. While this seems a plausible explanation for the shift in the risky direction, it is difficult to see how it can be applied to those situations where the group shift is in the cautious direction.

When miniskirts first hit the scene in the 1960s they were considered totally shocking. Then, as they appeared in magazines, on television, and in movies and started to appear in stores, they stopped seeming quite so extreme. Soon everyone (even lots of people who shouldn't have) was wearing them. This is the basic principle behind **familiarization theory.** When the risky behavior is first proposed it is perceived as extreme and radical. As the group discusses the alternative, however, they become more familiar with the idea and as they hear the idea endorsed by others the alternative becomes acceptable. This effect was found in Germany where groups' repeated attitude expression enhanced group polarization (Brauer, Judd, & Gliner, 1995). Again, however, it is difficult to explain how this would result in a cautious shift.

The **persuasive arguments theory** is very similar. Group members who are initially attracted to the risky position talk everyone else into taking the risk. The basis of this theory that differentiates it from the familiarization theory, however, is the importance of the group discussion. It's the persuasion of the group that causes the shift. Polarization occurs, though, even when there is no discussion, when each individual presents their positions, then the group decides without any give-and-take (Myers, 1978; Goethals & Zanna, 1979). Pavit (1994) found that the choice of a risky versus a cautious group shift was based on the proportion of arguments known by individuals on each side, but that individuals only argued their chosen side during discussion, thus attempting to persuade others.

It appears that both normative and informational pressures are involved in group polarization. Since we don't know for sure why it happens, it's very hard to identify solutions. Probably the best use of the information on group polarization is to consider the possibility and the acceptability of an extreme decision (either way) when a decision must be made. If an extreme decision is unacceptable it would be wisest to assign the task to an individual to perform.

 Have you ever been in a group that demonstrated a risky shift? What was the behavior involved? How was the group convinced to go along with the idea? Which of the theories discussed seems best to fit your situation?

The phenomena of groupthink and group polarization appear to be losses due to the use of groups that are the result of the intellectual or interactive process of the group. Other losses due to group process are based in other areas. The larger the group, the less effective the group tends to become (Steiner, 1972; Ingham, Levinger, Graves, & Peckham, 1974). There have been two explanations offered for this effect: problems with coordination within the group and motivational problems resulting in group members' failure to work at optimal capacity. We will discuss these phenomena now.

Coordination problems may occur in a group when they are performing an additive task that requires them all to do exactly the same thing at the same time, such as raising a sail on a ship (Davis, 1969). The **Ringelmann effect** is named for a French professor of agricultural engineering whose research involved the additive effect of participants pulling with maximum effort on a rope (1913). Each individual's peak capability was measured, then the individuals pulled at the rope together. The total measured pressure was less than the sum of the parts.

This was not because individuals had decreased effort. The problem was in coordinating so that the maximum effort of all occurred at the same moment. This problem is not going to be equally serious for all types of tasks. For intellectual tasks it is not necessary that every group member think at exactly the same second. But for successfully competing in the World Cup yacht race, winning might depend heavily upon the ability of the crew to coordinate their physical movements.

There are a number of ways this can be accomplished. Anyone who has ever seen an old Viking movie, or any movie about Cleopatra on her barge, or any movie about chain gangs working on the railroads will remember that in each case there was some method of developing a rhythm so that individuals knew when to exert maximum effort. There are entire genres of songs which were developed to help in this task.

> *Music more than anything else gave their actions the joint effort that was needed. The rhythms of the shanty expedited work on the sailing ships—the hauling of ropes, the turning of winches, the heaving of the anchor. The railroad man drove his spikes, laid his ties, and dragged his rails to tunes whose music and words grew out of the work itself. The principle still exists. The sailing ships are gone, and the era of laying new rail lines has come to a halt. But during the way, factory workers in many countries found their speed stepped up, their nerves quieted, and their efficiency increased if they worked to music which was rhythmically stimulating.*
>
> *(Boni, Lloyd, & Provensen, 1947, p. 129)*

College (and Olympic) competitors in crew events depend upon the rhythm provided by the coxswain seated at the front of the boat to coordinate their oar strokes.

This is not to deny that coordination is also an issue in nonphysical tasks. However, here the coordination has more to do with meeting a schedule for project completion than with temporally coordinated movements. Coordination may also be an issue in arranging any activities, such as meeting times, when the group must choreograph their work.

Reduction of effort in a group can also be considered as a motivational issue. Latane, Williams, and Harkins (1979) developed a task in which they were able to separate coordination and motivation. When coordination was not an issue, the group output was still less than the sum of the individual outputs. This leads us to the discussion of the possible sources of motivational losses in groups which might detract from potential productivity.

Social Loafing

Social loafing is the term applied to one of the motivational aspects of reduced effort on the part of individuals in groups. Since we find the reduction in productivity in groups even when coordination is not an issue, we must look for other possible explanations. Two probable contributors to this effect are *diffusion of responsibility* and *deindividuation*. In this application, diffusion of responsibility occurs when there are a large group of people to accomplish a task and the individual contributions of each are not identifiable.

To go back to our example of blowing up balloons for prom decorations, if there are twenty of us huffing and puffing, who's going to know if I slack off and only do a few. It's not as if we were each putting our names on them. Who will know? I'll contribute, but since the end result is the sum of all our work, why work too hard?

Deindividuation is also a term we have discussed in a previous chapter. To remind you, **deindividuation** is the feeling of loss of personal identity. With this comes a feeling of a diminished responsibility to follow social norms (Dipboye, 1977). Thus it appears that the combination of anonymity of contribution and lack of accountability together work to create the social loafing effect. In order to look for solutions to this problem it would be useful if we could find groups that do not experience social loafing.

Are there group conditions where social loafing does not occur? People in groups who are personally involved in a task tend not to slack off. Brickman, Harkins, and Ostrom (1986) found that when students thought they were working on a problem that was relevant to their particular institution they did not exhibit levels of social loafing that were seen in groups who thought their work would be used by institutions elsewhere. This same effect of high involvement in task—reducing social loafing—has been found by others (Zaccaro, 1984). Williams, Harkins, and Latane (1981) found that telling group members that their output would be identifiable eliminated the social loafing effect.

Groups in which individuals know that they will be held responsible for their output (Harkins, 1987) or where trust in co-members is high also do not experience the effect (Jackson & Harkins, 1985). Finally, more difficult tasks appear to elicit less social loafing (Jackson & Williams, 1985).

All of the studies cited in support of the phenomenon of social loafing involved American participants. Cultural differences have been found. The United States is an extremely individualistic culture where focus is on oneself and not necessarily on the group. Since the focus is exactly the opposite in collectivist cultures—the focus is on the group as opposed to the individual—we might expect to find different results. In fact, in China (a collectivist culture) increased rather than decreased effort was found in groups (Gabrenya, Wang, & Latane, 1985). A metanalysis of cross-cultural research on social loafing supports the above reported finding (Karan & Williams, 1993).

Free Riding

Although on the surface, the phenomenon of **free riding** looks like social loafing, most believe the motivational basis is different (Olsen, 1965; Kerr, 1983).

Both represent a tendency to do less when one can benefit from others' work. Where, then, is the difference? There is none, according to Kidwell and Bennett (1993). They believe that shirking, social loafing, and free riding are not distinct phenomena, but all have in common the propensity to withhold effort. Others believe that the difference resides in whether the individual feels her contributions will have any effect on the outcome of the group.

> *Although both processes link social conditions (e.g., group size, group task demands) to the instrumentality of task effort, they are concerned with somewhat different outcomes—reductions of effort have a less direct impact on the chances of group success when free riding is possible; reductions of effort have less direct impact on the chances of receiving salient personal and social evaluations when social loafing is viable.*
>
> **(Baron et al., 1992)**

Greater cohesiveness in groups reduces the tendency to free ride since greater cohesiveness is associated with a greater identity with the group and more concern for the group's success (Chapman, Arenson, Carrigan, & Grzckiewicz, 1993). Free riding can also be reduced by providing incentives for contributions, making contributions to the group by the individual indispensable, and by decreasing the costs associated with contributing to the group (Shepperd, 1993).

STOP Did you vote in the most recent election? Many people don't. If you didn't vote, why not? Did you feel your vote wasn't important? Do you think that free riding is a plausible explanation for the fact that so many eligible voters don't take advantage of the opportunity?

An interesting study on the effects of gender in the feminist community in the United States examined the "Woman's Encampment for a Future of Peace and Justice" held in Seneca, New York. The encampment based its organization on "feminist process" which included voluntarism, shared leadership, and consensus decision making. The use of voluntarism (making individual contributions dispensable) created a problem with free riding. Some of the women did more of the work and suffered burnout and resentment against those who didn't carry their weight in the group. The assumption that women are "naturally cooperative" and thus would not indulge in free riding was not supported (Schwartz-Shea & Burrington, 1990).

Group participation doesn't always reduce productivity; there are a number of situations that occur in groups that cannot be created by the individual. We refer to these as *productivity enhancements*.

PRODUCTIVITY ENHANCEMENTS

In our discussion of types of tasks, we identified most types of tasks as offering a higher level of potential productivity if given to a group to perform rather than to an individual. Then we spent pages discussing how working in groups can reduce potential productivity. Where does that leave us? Are there any factors that can enhance group productivity? Glad you asked.

Synergy

While the individual alone has only their own resources, abilities, knowledge, and energies upon which to draw, the effective group develops a special type of group energy known as **synergy.** Cattell (1948) was the first to discuss this special force and called it "syntality" or the commonality of the group.

> *Syntality, however, has a more basic level; that is, it is composed of something. That something is what Cattell calls synergy, or the total amount of energy available to the group for group activities.*
>
> *(Baird & Weinberg, 1977, p. 7)*

Cattell believed that the group created this energy (which we are referring to as synergy) through the process of communication and that synergy was necessary for the success of the group. If you have ever been involved in a lively group discussion, or watched any of the news programs on which the "talking heads" pontificate to the rest of us about the government, the economy, etc., you have witnessed synergy. An isolated individual does not have the opportunity to draw the energies from others. While synergy may not occur in all groups, successful groups learn how to interact in such a way as to be more, rather than less, than the sum of the parts.

Nominal Group Techniques

The term *nominal group* is somewhat paradoxical. If you take the term at its purest meaning, it refers to a group that exists in name only. The group does not engage in fact-to-face interaction. There are actually several levels of nominal groups. The most detached form of nominal group is known as the **Delphi technique.** This method was developed by the Rand Corporation "think tank" in the 1950s as a tool in planning (Francis & Melbourne, 1980). Experts in the area of concern are identified. They need not be in the same location—they in fact do not know each others' identities. Group members fill out a series of questionnaires on the issue under consideration. The results are tabulated and the group receives the document containing data from all group members. Only facts are presented, no feedback or opinions (supporting or otherwise). The panel members report on the document and any other questionnaires that might be relevant and again the material is centralized, and the feedback provided to all. Although this could theoretically go on forever, generally the process goes through three rounds before a final report is prepared.

In many ways one could hardly call this a group as compared to the type of group we have been discussing thus far in the book. However, there are some real advantages to this technique that have only been enhanced by technological advances. The fact that the group members do not know each other prevents bias and the need to become ego defensive about one's own ideas. The group can have as many people as desired (or can be afforded). Because the group will never meet in the same location, experts from anywhere can be recruited. You don't have to make do with some local "experts" who will not be likely to provide the same quality of information.

A downside? But of course. Several. First, if you are going to hire the top experts in a field you can expect their time will be quite expensive, if they are available at all. Second, this method can be time consuming. Advances in technology have practically eliminated all of the delays other than actually getting the panel members to respond. *Electronic mail* is almost instant. *Teleconferencing*, in which individuals have immediate electronic access to each other loses the advantages of anonymity bestowed by the Delphi technique. However, as we shall discuss, teleconferencing has made the possibility of even global meetings a possibility.

Intermediate in immediacy between the Delphi technique and face-to-face groups is what is known as **nominal group techniques.** In a way this label is unfortunate because the group does interact, but in a very formalized manner. These groups are actually a hybrid between actual nominal groups (such as in the Delphi technique) and interactive groups. There are four stages to nominal group techniques (Delbecq & Van de Ven, 1971). In the first, the leader of the group introduces the problem written out on a blackboard (or a flip-chart or a projected computer monitor). Group members sit silently and write ideas about the problem for approximately fifteen minutes. The second stage is a round-robin of sharing ideas. These are listed under the statement on the board. The third stage involves group discussion of each item, focusing on clarification not evaluation. Finally, group members rank their five favorite solutions independently, writing them on an index card. The leader collects the cards, averages the "votes" and informs the group of the decision. In a later elaboration, Delbecq, Van deVen, and Gustafson (1975) added a fifth and sixth step. These involve the group to a greater degree. In the fifth step the group discusses the vote, and in the sixth step there is the option to reconsider and vote again. Even though the group does interact to some extent, there is not the free flow of praise or criticism that characterizes interactive groups. The process is somewhat distant.

Groups can be more productive than individuals under certain conditions.

Technological advances have made the Delphi technique much more effi-cient and attractive than in the past. It is also possible to meet face-to-face with individuals from all over the world. What effect does this have on productivity of groups? The preliminary research is provocative. In comparing face-to-face and dispersed groups meeting electronically, Burke and Chidambaram (1995) found that face-to-face groups had more effective leadership and coordination, suggesting the possibility of the Ringlemann effect being greater in electronic groups. However, cohesiveness of group and equality of participation did not differ across the types of group. In another study, the use of electronic brainstorming (a phenomenon we'll discuss momentarily) overcame the problems of free riding, evaluation apprehension, and production blocking (Siau, 1995).

Now we must deal with the middle ground, the area of techniques I refer to as mixed blessings. These techniques can enhance or detract from group pro-ductivity, depending upon how they are employed.

MIXED BLESSINGS

There are two techniques in particular that may either help or hinder a group's productivity. It depends upon the techniques employed and the situation in which the processes are being conducted. These are *brainstorming* and *social facilitation*.

Brainstorming

You probably recognize the term "brainstorming." Unfortunately in many fields terms that began as jargon with a very specific meaning escape out into the ver-nacular. Brainstorming is one of those terms. Teachers from kindergarten to uni-versity, organizations from businesses to charities, "brainstorm" ideas. Actually they don't. Brainstorming is not what most people think. It is not just sitting around throwing around ideas. It is a very specific technique with very clear

Technology has introduced new techniques of group interactions.

rules. Done the usual way, groups actually produce fewer and lower quality ideas when they brainstorm than if the members each went off on their own or used nominal group techniques.

 Have you ever been in a class or a meeting where you were asked to brainstorm? Did anyone bother to train you in the technique? If not, what's the difference between what was called brainstorming and just having a "bull session"?

The major difference between the incorrect and the correct procedure is the separation of the generation of ideas and the evaluation of those ideas. If, in the usual situation of brainstorming I offer an idea to the group and I get criticized or ridiculed, I learn quickly not to contribute creative, unique ideas—or maybe not to contribute at all. So do the others who witness my humiliation. The entire process changes from creative to inhibiting.

The formal process of **brainstorming** has been attributed to Alex Osborn (1957). The process takes place in two separate meetings. The first meeting is devoted entirely to the generation of ideas. There are four rules that are to be strictly observed (Brilhart, 1986). First there is to be no criticism or evaluation of any kind of any of the ideas. Second, the wilder and more creative the ideas, the better. Third, quantity is encouraged. A quota might even be established (Callanan, 1984). Finally, building upon the ideas of others is encouraged.

The actual meeting should be as informal and comfortable as possible. It is often advisable to remove the group from its usual setting to a neutral location. All ideas are recorded using audiotape. If the meeting has developed the synergy desired, it will not be possible to take notes, and nothing dams up creativity more than having to stop and repeat an idea so someone can write it down. The leader's job is to try to encourage everyone to participate and not allow anyone to dominate the group.

When ideas seem to be slowing down, a moment of silence should be called. This allows ideas already presented to percolate down and perhaps stimulate new ideas. The group continues until no one has any more ideas, no matter how impractical or expensive, or illegal or extreme they may seem. Often the truly bizarre ideas are the ones that strike a spark in someone else.

The tape recording is taken away and transcribed. All ideas are listed without any identification of their originator. The purpose of the second meeting, which will obviously have to wait until a transcript of ideas is ready, is to evaluate the ideas. The same group may meet again, or another group can take over for the evaluation phase.

There are definite advantages to this lapse in time. People will have time to digest the meeting and perhaps integrate or elaborate on ideas that were presented. Also, people will tend to forget who said what. In the usual form of brainstorming all sorts of group political agendas can prevent an effective meeting. If two individuals dislike each other, they may attack each others' ideas on principle. If my ideas get attacked, I may feel sufficient ego involvement to need to defend them (even if I've decided later they were "dumb").

Change in personnel for the second meeting might also be an advantage. When the group deals with a list of "anonymous" ideas or ideas generated by another group, the effects of egos and feuds tend to dissipate. The ideas can be taken at face value and the advantages and disadvantages of each considered.

So brainstorming can be a double-edged sword. If done correctly, it is an extremely useful tool in helping the group generate alternatives, and the more alternatives generated the better the eventual solution is likely to be. Done the usual way, the group will present fewer, more conservative, safer ideas and the group will have wasted its time.

Social Facilitation

Social facilitation is the second of the techniques that may help or hinder a group. Social facilitation was actually one of the earliest group phenomena discovered and explored in 1898 by Norman Triplett. He conducted studies of the speed at which individuals wound balls of string and rode bicycles and discovered that people appeared to work more effectively in the presence of other people. Because the behavior increased, he dubbed the effect "social facilitation."

The phenomenon became an instant star in the firmament of research topics. The effect was examined using other species: dogs running, chicks eating, ants moving more sand (Zajonc, 1965). The effect was explored on different types of tasks—tasks in which participants worked side-by-side (*co-action tasks*) and tasks of one individual who worked while watched by others (*audience tasks*).

In the midst of all this research a stumbling block was discovered: sometimes the presence of others facilitated performance and other times it impaired performance (Allport, 1924). And no one could find the pattern until 1965, when Robert Zajonc unveiled his theory. (The pronunciation of this name is one of the great mysteries of social psychology—it is pronounced like the word "science" only starting with a z!)

Before we can explore the theory, we need to define a few terms. In any situation, we have a choice of responses. If I put a bowl of food in front of a hungry dog, he can eat, howl, bark, lay down, shake hands. . . . You get the picture. One of these behaviors is the most likely. This is known as the **dominant behavior.** In the example the dog is most likely to eat. All the other behaviors possible that do not occur are **nondominant behaviors.** That's our first important distinction.

Also important to Zajonc's theory is the comparison between simple and complex tasks. Simple tasks are those that are so mindless (such as eating) that they take no learning and can be done correctly the first time. For simple tasks, then, the dominant response is to perform the correct behavior. Aha! Social facilitation has occurred. For complex tasks (such as a tennis serve, or solving a calculus problem, or playing a Mozart concerto on the violin) learning and practice are necessary before we can perform the behavior.

Thus for *unlearned* complex tasks, the dominant behavior is going to be impaired performance. After we have practiced our serve or the music piece and learned it well, the dominant behavior will shift over and our dominant response will be to perform the task well.

Remember when you learned to drive a car? Remember how you had to think about every little movement you had to make to stay on the street? Driving is a very complex behavior. Now, after years of driving, your performance is probably almost automatic. Think about the effect a car full of your friends (or maybe even worse, the evaluator at the Department of Motor Vehicles) would have had on your driving your second time behind the wheel. Now you can drive with anyone in the car and carry on conversations without it interfering with your driving.

If you understand this example, you understand the pattern. No wonder it took over sixty years for someone to figure it out!

Simple task = dominant response = facilitated behavior

Complex task/learned well = dominant response = facilitated behavior

Complex task/unlearned = dominant response = impaired behavior

Maybe some of you can relate to an embarrassing story about myself. In high school I played the piano for years and was considering going into music in college. I was offered an opportunity to audition for a scholarship to a prestigious university. I was pretty sure I didn't want to be a musician, but decided to try anyway. First, I had chosen popular music rather than classical. Second, I had not bothered to memorize the piece. Third, and most important of all for this example, I had not practiced sufficiently (unlearned complex task).

I did fine when alone in a practice room at school or home. But when I went up on that stage into the spotlight with my music in hand and an audience of other potential scholarship recipients I fell apart, which is exactly what the theory of social facilitation would predict. Needless to say, I didn't major in music.

Why does this happen? There have been a number of potential explanations offered. Some would appear more useful than others, but all have some empirical support. Zajonc's explanation and several others depend upon physiological mechanisms. Several others depend upon cognitive explanations.

Zajonc (1980) believes that the *mere presence* of another member of our species creates a general elevated drive/arousal state. This hypervigilance does not interfere with our ability to do simple or learned tasks—it's what athletes refer to as being "psyched." However, it will interfere with complex, unlearned tasks which require attention on our part. Cottrell (1972) believes that this increased *drive state is learned* from our rewarding or punishing experiences with others. The "mere presence" position of Zajonc would mean that we should get the effect even if the others are ignoring us or blindfolded. Such an effect was found by Robinson-Staveley and Cooper (1990). Baron, Moore, and Sanders (1978) believe the increased drive state is created by *distraction* created by the presence of another.

Again, there's only a problem if we need to be paying attention to what we're doing. For any of these physiological theories to be supported, there should always be a measurable increase in some physiological measure that indicates increased drive. Glaser (1982) reported over sixty-one social facilitation studies since 1965 that failed to find any measurable increase in physical arousal.

Two other explanations for the phenomenon of social facilitation depend on thinking. Duval and Wickland (1972) posit a **self-awareness theory.** As we are performing the behavior we evaluate ourselves against how well we think we should be doing. If we are doing poorly on this comparison we become rattled which further impairs our performance. Bend (1982) suggests that **evaluation apprehension** is the culprit. In this case we don't worry about our own evaluation of our performance, we worry about what others think of us. These make sense for human beings.

But remember that we find social facilitation in ants, chicks, and dogs (among other species). I personally find it difficult to imagine an ant becoming self-conscious in the presence of others. We haven't spent nearly as much time or examined as many theories of causation as we might because the bottom line is this: who cares? Social facilitation is a very robust phenomenon that can be used in groups to enhance performance (the well rehearsed theatrical troupe) or impair performance (the football team that has not practiced together).

Summary

In this chapter we have examined the many factors that affect group productivity. We have discovered that the actual productivity in any situation depends upon a combination of the potential productivity of group or individual performance upon different types of tasks, and whether the use of groups will impair or enhance the potential productivity. The determination of which to use depends upon the structure of the task and whether the group will be more likely to benefit the individuals involved, or harm the individuals involved. The type of outcome also influences our choice of group or individual. Once in the group we must be vigilant for such phenomena as social loafing and free riding, which may harm the productivity of the group. We can also take advantage of several techniques, including brainstorming, which enhance group productivity. We have also discovered that we have probably never really brainstormed in our lives.

Note: I promised you the answers to the disjunctive-type problems. Here they are:

O	T	T	F	F	S	S	E
n	w	h	o	i	i	e	i
e	o	r	u	v	x	v	g
		e	r	e		e	h
		e				n	t

AND . . . Joe Doodlebug had just taken ONE jump to the east when he spied the food. Since he must jump four times IN ONE DIRECTION before he can change directions, he had to complete the series—making three jumps more to the east, then one long jump back west to the food.

Key Terms

additive task
brainstorming
compensatory task
conjunctive task
coordination problems
deindividuation
Delphi technique
devil's advocate
diffusion of
 responsibility
disjunctive task
divisible task
dominant behaviors
"eureka" disjunctive task

evaluation apprehension
familiarization theory
free riding
group polarization
groupthink
maximizing tasks
nominal group
 techniques
nondominant behaviors
"non-eureka" disjunctive
 task
optimizing tasks
persuasive arguments
 theory

potential productivity
Ringelmann effect
risky shift
runaway norms
self-awareness theory
social facilitation
social loafing
synergy
truth-supported-wins rule
truth-wins rule
type of task
unitary task

APPLICATION

Managing Effective Meetings to Improve Productivity

Everyone hates meetings. Most meetings are boring, time-consuming, and un-productive. Most people feel they could be using the time spent in these meet-ings in a more productive manner. And most of the time they are absolutely correct. In this application we're going to pick the brains of the experts (Callanan, 1984; Frank, 1989; and Miller & Pincus, 1997) to help you manage meetings so that they are actually a help rather than a hindrance to group pro-ductivity and to group cohesiveness.

We can break down the effective meeting into three separate processes: preparation, the meeting itself, and effective follow-up. With careful planning, the group leader can manage these processes so that group members won't dread and/or avoid meetings. There is one initial question that must be ad-dressed before actual preparation begins. That is, do we need this meeting? "Meetings held on a routine basis—weekly, bi-monthly, monthly—are generally tedious and wasteful" (Frank, 1989, p. 28).

In other words, don't have a meeting unless there's a good reason to meet. There may be more group-effective ways to handle the situation. If all that is required is information dissemination, electronic mail or memos are much more effective. You say that people won't read them? Then you may have a problem with cohesiveness in the group and that's where your energies should be directed. If individuals refuse to keep themselves informed on the group progress and process, they may have to be worked around. All meetings, then, should have an objective. Miller and Pincus (1997) recommend having a meet-ing when:

(1) The interaction of opinions is necessary to create an idea, plan, or project.
(2) Group dynamics are essential to the accomplishment of the purpose.
(3) Time restrictions limit other options.

(4) The subject is sufficiently complex as to require interaction and explanation.
(5) The boss says to hold a meeting.

(Miller & Pincus, 1997, p. 28)

If you decide you MUST have a meeting, make sure you have the time to prepare and enough lead time so that everyone essential to the meeting can attend. Again, in some groups if you wait until everyone can attend you might never meet. But a single individual's or a subgroup's apparent unwillingness to cooperate with the group is a problem with conflict that must be settled. If not, the specter of escalating conflict looms large enough to threaten the group's essential ability to function. If you must have a meeting with as many group members as you determine to be a quorum, and you are missing group members, understand that you are in danger of these individuals coming back to haunt the group in the form of sabotage or attempted blocking of group decisions made in their absence. It should be made clear to the group that if sufficient advance notice is made and individuals miss the meeting they may not retroactively interfere with the group.

You've determined that you do need to have a group meeting. When? The obvious answer from above is when everyone can attend. This may place some serious constraints upon time available. This leads to calling evening or Friday meetings, times that will dramatically reduce group effectiveness. If at all possible, "avoid scheduling a meeting on holidays, long weekends, and at the beginning or end of the week" (Miller & Pincus, 1997, p. 22). Just as people are warned not to buy a car that comes off the production line on a Monday or a Friday because of the level of defective cars constructed on those days, people need time on Monday to get into the week, and on Friday (especially if your meeting is scheduled as the last item in each member's working day) people are anxious to finish up their work and leave.

You should also consider the demographics of your group. If many people have families and are responsible for their children, allow them time to transport kids from school to appropriate care. Then start the meeting. Think hard about having evening meetings. Many individuals resent time taken away from their "real life" and families. Generally, "morning meetings are more productive than those scheduled late in the day" (Miller & Pincus, 1997, p. 22).

Also to be considered is the length of the meeting. Generally, meetings that run longer than two hours have either been run inefficiently or have tried to take on too much for one meeting. Allow a ten-minute bladder break for each hour the meeting will run.

Detailed advanced preparation is essential for the effective meeting. An agenda should be prepared and distributed with sufficient time for group members to prepare their expected contributions to the meeting. This prevents rambling and off-the-cuff soliloquies during the meeting. The agenda should include the objective of the meeting, the issues to be discussed, the time of the beginning and end of the meeting, the location, and exactly what is expected in terms of member preparation (e.g., "Please be prepared to offer several ideas about how we might market Imperial Widgets," or "Please be prepared to report your progress on the annual report," or "Please be prepared with specific suggestions for curricular change").

The physical setup of the meeting is also an important part of meeting preparation. Try to hold the meeting in a "neutral space," especially if there are any conflicts over group control issues or if there is an "old guard" securing a home court advantage by virtue of seniority. If at all possible, use a round table. Next best is a square. A rectangle encourages dominant people to take seats at the end or the middle of the side with the fewest seats.

There is a well-established "head of the table effect" (Porter, 1980) which identifies irrelevant status attributed to a male at the head of the table, and sabotage status of a female at the head of the table in a gender-mixed group. The person seated at the leader's direct right has the lowest positional power at the table as this is where the secretary traditionally is located. To avoid this chore, avoid this position. Individuals will also usually try to sit directly across from their adversaries and with members of their subgroups. Try changing seating patterns at each meeting. This tends to break up coalitions. Intermixing the factions rather than allowing them to sit across from each other can also disrupt the dysfunctional norms sufficiently to allow for an effective meeting.

The meeting should start on time. Late arrivals should be noted in the minutes. Individuals who appear late should be quietly briefed on where the group is in the agenda, but should not be allowed to drag the group back to an issue they have missed. The meeting should be kept moving. Some sort of format rules should be established.

There is more and more a move to claim to use *Robert's Rules of Order*, however, in actuality these rules are only resorted to when conflict arises. Either the group uses them ALL, or none should be used. Otherwise it's equivalent to choosing to obey some laws (e.g., stopping at red lights) and ignoring the others (e.g., making harassing telephone calls). Because of the exquisite detail with which every portion of the meeting is constrained, consensus in the group dynamics community discourages their use for a group smaller than twenty for the following reasons:

> . . . no fewer than 7 pages are used to describe how the group member "obtains the floor," including suggestions for proper phrasing of the request, appropriate posture, and timing.

> But they are not without certain drawbacks. Robert purposely designed them to "restrain the individual somewhat," for he assumed that "the right of any individual, in any community to do what he pleases, is incompatible with the interests of the whole" (Robert, 1915/1971 in Forsyth, 1990). In consequence, the rules promote a formal, technically precise form of interaction, sometimes at the expense of openness, vivacity, and directness. Additionally, the rules can create a win/lose atmosphere in the group, for members expect to debate differences and to solve these disagreements through voting rather than through a discussion to consensus. Lastly, groups using the rules can become so highly structured that little room is left for group development, interpersonal adjustment, and role negotiation. Because, in a sense, the rules take the dynamics out of group dynamics, group members should remain ever mindful of their weaknesses as well as their strengths.

> **(Forsyth, 1990, p. 290)**

Suggested rules by which meetings should be conducted include civility (which includes stopping any personal attacks [Miller & Pincus, 1997]) and brevity. Frank (1989) suggests either timing each speaker in terms of the time available, or establishing rules such as allowing a speaker to speak on each issue only twice.

The time is here. Deal with one issue at a time, in the order appearing on the agenda. Resolve that issue and move on. Keep the conversation relevant. It is appropriate for the leader to interrupt irrelevant conversation if necessary (Miller & Pincus, 1997). As a point is completed, summarize the decision, identify and assign activities following from the decision to group members.

If your group consistently stalls at problem solving and cannot make progress, consider the following questions posed by Frank (1989, pp. 39–40):

1. How did we do this in the past?
2. How effective was it?
3. How do we do it now?
4. How effective is it?
5. How might we do this in the future?
6. How effective might that be?

For problem groups, perhaps a meeting where the task of each member is to prepare answers to the above questions IN ADVANCE in respect to a particular issue might nudge the group in a more effective direction.

An effective leader is essential to facilitate effective meetings. The basic role of the leader is to facilitate interaction in the meeting and keep the tone and interactions civil. The leader should control the process rather than the content of the group discussion. The leader should also be sure that all relevant information is being shared with the group as a whole and not held captive by a subgroup (knowledge is power). Suggest that members take general notes to help them remember the content of the meeting and to verify subsequent minutes of the meeting.

There are some difficult situations that are predictable during group meetings. These must be dealt with as they occur. We'll discuss: (1) late arrivals; (2) side conversations; (3) emotional participants; (4) ditherers; (5) blockers; and (6) deadlocks.

The late arrival of a member to a meeting for which they have been given the time appropriately in advance is at best a distraction and at worst a disruption. This may be intentional. As little attention as possible should be paid to this individual. As mentioned before, DO NOT allow this individual to drag the group back to reconsider issues and decisions already completed.

Side conversations may also be an attempt to try to establish power within the group. They are distracting to others, and if not stopped are contagious. Handle these as teachers have learned to over the years. Stop and stare at the offenders. They will usually stop. If they don't, you may request that if they have something important that they share it with the group, discuss the matter after the meeting, or leave temporarily and discuss the matter in the hall—with the full understanding that whatever they miss will not be reprised for them.

Emotional participants are difficult to deal with. Emotional participants are not contributing to the advancement of the task focus of the meeting. "Recognize that logic loses to emotion" (Frank, 1989, p. 132). Do not criticize the emotional individual, but make them aware of the fact that they are not functioning rationally, they are interfering with the group meeting, and ask them to get back to the point being discussed. This may be an attempted manipulation of the group. If so it is even more important that the hijacking is stopped. Or the individual may simply be emotional. If you feel the source of the emotionality is important enough for the group to deal with it, put it on the agenda of ANOTHER meeting. And keep moving.

I used the term "ditherers" for people who ramble on and on with no organization and repeat themselves constantly. Limits such as suggested for time or amount of permitted participation may help. Or you might ask the individual to write a summary of their position and distribute it to the group. (This is often a sign that the individual has not bothered to prepare in advance, or may be a ploy to hijack the meeting.)

Blockers disagree with everything. They are using the meeting for their own ends, not for the good of the group. Ask the individual to explain how what they are saying is relevant to the discussion of the group. If they can't, ask them to stop. "If all else fails, ask him to leave the meeting and suggest a private conference with you later in the day" (Miller & Pincus, 1997, p. 77).

Sometimes the group just locks up and can't go any further on an issue. The group moves around in circles. If this happens, have each side summarize their position, then put the matter to a vote. Then go ahead and assign tasks based on the group decision.

A few "don'ts" for leaders. Don't try to dominate the group. Try not to interrupt a group member unless it is really necessary. And don't get personal with group members and don't allow others to do so. Insist on professional conduct. One final word about conflict. It's OK. Better ideas are generated when there's room for constructive discussion. (If you have problems with conflict, read the relevant portions of Chapters 3, 4, 9, and 10.)

The ending time has come (as stated in the agenda). If you have not covered everything, you might briefly ask the group to consider why, particularly if there was a reasonable agenda. You may need shorter agendas in the future, or better control of the meeting. At the end, summarize the decisions reached, be clear about the assignments made during the meeting, THANK the participants, and adjourn. Very often at this point an individual will suddenly have something they feel vital for the group to consider. This is akin to the therapy client bringing up the most important issue five minutes before the end of the session. If someone brings up new material at the end, cut them off. Suggest that the person submit the issue for discussion at a future meeting.

The last important task is follow-up. Minutes should be taken during the meeting and distribution should be a priority. Don't hand them out the day of the next meeting, give individuals plenty of time to consider them. All participants should receive copies. The minutes should identify issues discussed and decisions made. All assignments should be identified. Any deadlines should also be clearly indicated. Allow time in the next meeting for discussion of any errors (perceived or real).

And there you have it—Meeting 101. These tips won't get you past every potential hurdle in groups, but they should help. Organization and focus are the most important issues in keeping a group involved in meetings that will produce positive results.

Discussion Questions

Apply the concepts from the chapter to consider the following questions:

1. How can you use these principles to enhance creativity in group meetings?
2. What effects might you expect from social facilitation on the meeting process?
3. In what ways might meetings reduce group productivity?
4. Discuss how you could make maximal use of teleconferencing to increase productivity at meetings.
5. Identify the last three meetings you attended. Were they necessary? Were they effective? What changes could have improved productivity?

Decision Making

What Would YOU Predict?

You are serving on a jury in a criminal trial. When you and the other jurors take your first vote, the result is split right down the middle with half of you believing in the defendant's guilt, and half of you believing the defendant to be innocent. What actual decision will the jury most likely make?

INTRODUCTION

Groups deal with all sorts of decisions. They may be as simple as what time the group should break for the evening or as difficult as determining the sentence of an individual convicted of murder. In this chapter we will examine a number of theories that have been developed to explain the process by which these decisions are reached. As we saw in Chapter 3 on the development of groups, here too we will find a number of theories that differ from each other only slightly.

DECISION-MAKING MODELS

Each decision model has something important to contribute to the study of decision-making groups. We will examine a number of these theories, then, after determining the various types of decisions and how the type might affect which approach would be optimal, we will create an integrated theory by combining the best ideas of the theories discussed. Finally, we will look at groups whose entire reason for existence is to make decisions: juries. A great deal of research, both analogue (using mock juries) and interviewing actual jury participants or examining court records (we can't use the actual courtroom as an experimental laboratory) has identified the ways in which these groups are typical of other decision-making groups as well as ways in which they are distinctive.

A Basic Template

The very most basic model of decision making is also the simplest. It can serve as the template upon which we will elaborate in additional theories. This theory identifies five steps through which the group must pass before a decision is complete. They are: (1) definition; (2) identifying constraints; (3) generating alternatives; (4) selecting the best alternative; and (5) follow-up (Francis & Melbourne, 1980). This is a bare-bones approach to making decisions because it does not include a number of steps which we will introduce with other theories. It is important, however, in that it gives us a skeleton upon which to hang subsequent ideas. We will "flesh out" this theory as we move along.

Rational Decision Models

The entire concept of the **rational decision-making model** is based upon an ideal. The steps as defined above are adhered to, in principle, but elaborated upon. At the stage during which alternatives are generated, this model requires that we identify first ALL possible alternatives to this situation, and identify ALL the possible consequences of each and every alternative.

While laudable in intent, this theory in practice is impossible. First, human beings are limited. We often can't identify all the possible alternatives to a problem. We couldn't even if we had all the time in the world—which we usually don't. Even if we could generate a list of all the possible alternatives we again run into trouble trying to predict all of the possible ramifications of each one—positive and negative. This is because all alternatives have multiple attributes.

There is no perfect solution to any problem. There is simply the acceptable, or "least bad" solution. And, as fallible human beings, we are not going to be able to be perfectly rational in valuing the alternatives. Our choice of "favorite" will often be influenced heavily by politics or our own values. We often aren't even aware of how much or the ways in which our basic values affect our evaluations and perceptions of the world. Therefore, we don't usually make the best possible choices, or realize that the decision to which we have come is, in fact, not the best choice (Fischoff & Johnson, 1990).

Does this mean we abandon this theory as useless? Not at all. Early in the discussion I referred to this theory as an ideal. Keeping it in mind will push us to try to identify as many alternatives as we possibly can—perhaps through the process of brainstorming. It will also keep us cognizant of both the advantages and the disadvantages of any single solution and push us to look for as many of both as we can identify. This should certainly contribute to or result in the best possible decision within our powers, given the constraints of time and other resources under which we operate.

Let's look at a real-life application of this model. Each morning when you get up you have to determine (unless you wear some sort of uniform) what you will wear for the day. Let's keep it relatively simple and say you need to choose a shirt, a pair of pants, socks, and shoes. To employ the rational decision-making model optimally, first you must consider each and every one of your shirts. What are their advantages (they're warm, or you like the color) and their disadvantages (they're dirty or torn)? Then you have to decide on the pair of pants. Now you not only have to think about the advantages and disadvantages of the pants in isolation, you have to consider how they work (or don't work) with your choice of shirt. Socks might be easy, but again, they need to "go" with the previous two selections, as do the shoes.

Theoretically, we should identify every possible combination of clothes in our wardrobe and the advantages and disadvantages of each. If we really did this, we'd probably never get dressed! So although this theory looks good on paper, we just don't have the resources or the luxury of employing the theory in its entirety.

 How do you go about making decisions? Do you flip a coin? Do you make lists of advantages and disadvantages? Does your approach differ depending upon the importance of the decision (who to marry compared to what kind of ice cream to order)? Compare your approaches with your group members or classmates.

Utility Models

The major additional contribution of the **utility models** lies in helping us identify which of our identified alternatives is the "best." The models provide a systematic way to identify and evaluate our options (Dipboye, Smith, & Howell, 1994). First, we identify what attributes of any alternative are most important to us. In other words, we establish some criteria—in advance—defining the most critical advantages and disadvantages. Once we have these criteria established, we can identify options which will fit within our parameters.

Finally, we examine the alternatives for how much the valued attributes are offered by the alternative and the costs or disadvantages incurred by each alternative. By establishing our criteria before we even begin identifying alternatives, we can automatically eliminate some potential alternatives and we can try to prevent individual agendas or politics or status from swaying the group.

Let's consider a group that is to make the decision as to who will build the new city hall. The committee should meet first and identify their criteria. The committee decides that first and foremost they want an imposing structure in stone with a flight of stairs to the front doors and some sort of unique entry. When they are examining bids by architects and contractors, cost may fall by the wayside in deciding who will be awarded the contract. If, however, money is tight, then the most acceptable design that costs the least money will be the choice of the group.

Optimizing Model

Harrison (as cited in Robbins, 1989) has elaborated upon the basic utility model. Harrison does not begin in the middle of our basic template—generating alternatives. First, he suggests we must ascertain the need for a decision at all. Individuals often get caught up in the need to "do something" in any given situation. This is known as an **activity trap.**

 What is the best thing to do if you get lost in the woods and you can't find your way back to civilization? What behaviors are most likely to enhance your chances of survival and rescue?

If we discover we are lost in some woods, most of us want to do SOMETHING, so we flutter about, trying to remember whether streams run north or south or whether moss grows on the east or west of trees. In all this moving about, it is very likely that we will keep moving away from those searching for us. The best thing—and the very hardest—is to just sit down, build a fire if it's cold, and wait. Each time we move we make it harder on our searchers. (So, of course if you don't want to be found, just keep moving!)

There are many times when we examine a situation, we assume some sort of solution or action is needed when actually the best thing to do may be to do nothing. Each time we intervene in a situation, with the very best of intentions of improving the situation, we take the risk of making the situation worse. If there is a very small problem (unless it's a conflict as we'll discuss in Chapter 9) we have much more room to worsen the situation than we have room for improvement.

So we're going to need criteria for when it is appropriate to intervene and when it is better to keep our hands off things—at least for a while. One way of deciding suggested by the **optimizing model** is to look at the disparity between the present situation and the situation as we would like it to be. If there is a large difference, then an intervention is probably warranted.

Once we have decided that we do have a decision to make, the optimizing model suggests that we identify our decision criteria. What are the characteristics we value? When we have identified these desired characteristics, we assign a weight to each. Is it more important to us that our decision be inexpensive, or fast? If we decide we're looking for a quick response, that will certainly affect our identification and evaluation of the alternatives, which are our next two steps. Based upon our weighted criteria we can choose the solution that is "best" according to our needs.

Intuitive Model

All of the models examined so far strive to be very logical and objective in making our decision. Some psychologists feel we've gone overboard in trying to keep the personal judgments of group members out of the decision process (Johnson, 1993). If all decisions could be made based solely on logic we could have computers make all of our decisions. Clearly that is not an option. One of the advantages of a group in the decision-making process is the richness of resources that group members bring to the group. The **intuitive model** is growing in acceptance.

Sometimes a decision logically appears to be the direction to go, but our gut says "no." People used to attribute intuition primarily to women, but most people know when something just doesn't feel right. We may not be able to articulate our concerns but they are very real. We should recognize that people contribute their innate humanity to the decision-making process and try to identify just what feels "wrong" about our apparently optimal solution.

Communication Focused Model

Watzlawick, Weakland, and Fisch (1974) are researchers and experts in the process of communication. Their model (which curiously enough doesn't have a special name, so I created one) continues to add important steps and considerations into the process of decision making, particularly when the decisions to be made involve having to work with people rather than technology or organizational or group structure. The major contributions of this model are the emphasis on defining both the problem and the desired changes in behavioral terms (what needs to be done to create the change), and to examine past attempts at problem solving in the group context.

The first step of the model is to define the problem in objective behavioral terms. Who is doing what that is problematical? Exactly what are the problem behaviors? Are people social loafing? Has groupthink become a problem?

The second step is to identify solutions previously tried by the group to solve this problem. Were they successful? Did they create more problems than they solved? Were they efficient when considered from a cost-benefit analysis perspective? This step may help the group recognize a pattern of either effective or ineffective past problem solving. Identification of either pattern can help move the current process in a more productive direction.

Once the analysis of past decision-making behavior has been completed, the next step in the model is to identify the desired changes in objective behavioral terms. What do we want, specifically, to see? Do we want our group members to show up at group meetings on time? Do we want group members to complete assigned tasks within the time allotted by the group? It is much easier to create a change in an individual when they know what to do. It is often easy to think that people know what we want. That's not ever a safe assumption unless we have been explicit. Rather than risk change to an even more problematic behavior, communicate the desired behaviors. Finally, the last step of the model is to make a plan to create the desired change. How will we create the new behavioral patterns?

Let's stop for a moment and assess our progress. We've been through a number of theories of how to make decisions. Each one contributes to the collage of an integrated model we're going to create. So far we have the basic structure. We've added the factors of logic and objectivity, as well as values. We've realized that before we fling ourselves into the process we should be sure there's a need for the process. And we've recognized that when the decision involves changing individuals we must think in behavioral terms.

Believe it or not, we're almost there. We'll only examine one more model of decision making. But then, before we can create our own model we'll pause for a moment to look at different types of decisions. The type of decision path we identify in any situation will help us to recognize the aspects of the decision which require most attention. Back to the last model of decision making—the spiral model.

Spiral Model

All the models we've examined so far have been linear. In a straight line we move from Point A (having a decision to make) to Point B (making the decision) to Point C (implementing the decision) to Point D (evaluating the decision). Scheidel and Crowell (1964) suggest that decisions are often made employing a less direct process of decision making they've labeled the **spiral model.**

A new idea is suggested to the group. The group discusses the idea, develops, changes, and revises it. The idea then becomes the basis for a new approach by the group. Other new ideas are presented which go through the spiral, or "reach testing" process described above and then are accepted as the basis for the next increment forward toward a decision. This constant backtracking, according to Scheidel and Crowell is at least one of the reasons that groups take so much time to reach decisions.

TYPES OF DECISIONS

Not every decision-making situation is the same. Life's never that easy. Because groups are faced with different types of decisions it is important to recognize the various different approaches possible and to determine whether one approach is universally optimal or whether the approach should be tailored to the type of problem.

Poole and Doelger (1986) suggest that there are three types of activity going on in decision-making groups at all times. The first is *task process activity*—movement toward accomplishing the group's objective. Then there is activity regarding *relational character issues*. These two should by now sound very familiar. They're the basic group issues we defined in Chapter 1, task and social issues in the group. To our basic duo, Poole and Doelger add one additional activity. That is the *topical focus* of the group. Is the group on task, or have they moved off to discussing or doing something else?

Fisher and Stutman (1987) believe that groups move along the three threads at different rates and switch focus at different times. These moments of changing focus are termed **breakpoints,** when one communication segment ends and another begins. The intention to switch is signaled by a "routing statement" made by one of the group members. An example would be a group whose task is to choose a speaker for commencement exercises. Once they have reached consensus on their choice (task process activity), someone might ask what the group members are planning to wear to commencement. This would move the group off their topical focus and into discussion irrelevant to their charge.

In addition to the three types of activities that go on in the decision-making group, there are also various types of decision paths. The three major types of decisions that must be made are defined by Poole and Roth (1989). Each type dictates the most efficient and effective type of approach to be used. The types are: (1) *unitary paths;* (2) *complex decision paths;* and (3) *solution-oriented paths.* The unitary path is not frequently encountered. This path is most appropriate when the group is highly cohesive but has unclear goals. This path might be useful when a group of close friends wants to plan some sort of social occasion (not knowing what type) but keeps getting pulled off task by relational character issues (in this case gossip and chitchat). The point is to keep the group on task until a decision is made.

The second decision path is much more frequently encountered and is more appropriate. The **complex decision path** is employed when there is a pattern of cyclic problems and solutions. The group must keep moving through the decision-making cycle as solutions to old problems contribute to new problems. It is particularly useful when the questions dealt with by the group have moral implications and a plethora of potential opinions and solutions. This is by far the most complex of decision-making situations a group can face.

An example of this style might be a city council that decides that the public schools in the city are too homogenous as to socioeconomic status. They direct the school board to come up with a plan to integrate the schools. The school board examines a number of alternatives, then implements busing. However, once at their new schools the children remain in segregated groups and do not mix. The school board must come up with a program or series of techniques that will bring the children together. They decide on emphasizing sports—as it has been found that creating common goals that require cooperation to achieve help create cooperation. But funding the sports programs means that the art department's funding must be slashed. Parents complain. You can see the circular nature of the process as each decision creates the need for another.

The final path, the solution oriented path, does exactly what the name implies. The thread of task process activities is emphasized. The group focuses on confirming a solution but does not take the time and effort to define the problem well. This lack of specificity could be problematical. It is akin to having a physician start medical treatment without a careful diagnostic review.

However, this path is most useful where the group has clearly defined goals and the task with which they are confronted requires little creativity or innovation in the decision. The problem, then, is so straightforward, the criteria so clearly defined, and the necessary steps to solution so direct that the group can afford to act almost like a computer and just feed in information and come out with a solution.

We're now ready to put together the most useful pieces of the models described into one, unified, integrated model of decision making. You may have noticed that there have been far fewer italicized and boldface terms thus far in this than in previous chapters. That's because although I wanted you to know where the ideas in our finished model originated, I'd really rather you concentrate your energies on the completed model.

AN INTEGRATED DECISION-MAKING MODEL

Our finished model is going to add an additional step to our original template. So our steps will be: (1) problem identification; (2) identifying alternatives; (3) discussion of alternatives; (4) choice; (5) implementation of decision; and (6) evaluation of the decision.

Problem Diagnosis and Creation of Decision-Making Structure

In step one we will have two important tasks to accomplish. The first is to identify the decision that must be made (including the need for a decision). The second will be to establish the structure the group will use to move through the rest of the model. One of the best ways both to help in the identification of a problem and to help us evaluate our decision later is to start with data collection.

What is going on now that is deemed problematical? If we feel that the group is not sufficiently productive, just how productive are they? Collect information. You may be surprised and discover that things are not as bad as originally thought. Or they may be worse. Recall that Harrison defined a problem as a discrepancy between the situation as it now exists and the desired situation. This data we have collected provides us with a *baseline* of information defining the present situation.

Next we must define the situation we would like to have. Is there a discrepancy? Is the ideal situation possible? Everyone would like 100 percent productivity from a group, but no one can seriously expect to attain that goal. So we ask ourselves several questions. Do we need a decision in this situation? Is a solution possible as the situation is defined? Can we make a change without significant probability of worsening the situation?

We now need an **operational definition** of the problem. This is simply a fancy way of saying we want to make a diagnosis of the problem that will point to the operations necessary for solution. Correct **problem diagnosis** is crucial. If you are informed that you have the flu when you really have lyme disease, the treatment provided (decision made and solution provided) might be very appropriate for flu, but it won't do you a bit of good. In other words, you can do all the right things, but if you're addressing the wrong problem you're wasting your time and other resources.

What's contributing to the problem? Probably several things. Try to identify as many as possible. If there are five pressures creating the problem, solving one or two will probably leave the problem relatively untouched. This is called *overdetermination*.

Be thorough and ask questions about when the problem started. How did it start? What were the environmental conditions when the problem started? What individuals were involved when the problem began or when it was noticed? This is analogous to your physician doing a battery of tests to be sure of a medical diagnosis.

 Making the diagnosis is only part of the important initial phase of the group. Many groups don't even take the time to carefully diagnose the problem. Think back to problem-solving groups in which you've participated. Did you generally take the time to define the problem carefully? If you didn't, what do we know about groups that would suggest an explanation to this phenomenon?

Once you've identified the problem, there is one more stage of this initial step to be taken before you forge ahead. Now is the time to decide just how you will proceed. Make assignments for tasks. Make schedules. Decide in advance your method for determining when a decision has been reached. Will you vote? Will you require unanimity? It is best to make these decisions now before anyone has a political agenda to protect.

By making the rules of the process now, you ease functioning later. It is much easier, for example, to solve a conflict if you already have established rules. Otherwise you have to make up the rules in the maelstrom of the conflict, when objectivity is likely to be at an all-time low. Additionally, creating structure now reduces role ambiguity in the group.

So to summarize. At the end of step one we will have identified whether a problem exists, and whether we should move any further in the process. We will have gathered as much relevant data as possible to be sure that our diagnosis is correct. And we will have laid the ground rules for the remainder of the process. On to step two.

Identification of Alternatives

Now that we have decided what is going wrong and in need of repair, we generate **identification of alternatives** for solution. Again turning to Harrison, before we start generating alternatives, we should decide on the important criteria that should be satisfied by the "best" solution. We should also identify the negative side effects that are acceptable and those which cannot be tolerated. Weighting these criteria now will help avoid future conflicts.

We use whatever methods of generating alternatives we desire. Now might be a good time to go back and look at the sections on brainstorming and nominal group techniques in the previous chapter. We want as many potential ideas as possible. If you are choosing a car to buy you want to look at as many models as possible. If you only look at one or two you are far less likely to satisfy all your criteria for the "best" car for you.

A warning. The **implicit favorite model** (Power & Aldag, 1985) appears on the surface to be going along with the model suggested, but in fact is a way to sabotage the process. Individuals start the process with preferred alternatives. These preferences may be unconscious, but they affect the process of identifying and weighting criteria.

If I have a personal favorite, I'm going to make sure that the criteria that describe my choice are listed and heavily weighted in the process. This is a way of allowing subjectivity to enter the process and possibly negatively impact the alternatives that are available for the group to consider in the next stage of the model.

For each of the alternatives identified, be sure to list all the pros and cons. These will be essential in the discussion and decision stages of the model. There is also one alternative that should be on every list of alternatives—that alternative involves doing nothing. Remember activity traps. Sometimes the best thing to do is just sit back and keep an eye on the situation. You can always move later if it is warranted.

Discussion of Alternatives

During this stage of the model you are going to probably reach your first potential points of disagreement and/or conflict. If you've set up your structure early and identified and weighted the criteria for the ideal solution, you dramatically reduce the probability of any real problems at this stage. But do expect some disagreement. As we saw in Chapter 3, when the group members know that they will be challenged they bring in better thought-out alternatives and the group process will take these better ideas and improve upon them.

However, we also discussed how some groups try to avoid conflicts. Janis and Mann (1944) have identified a number of avoidance techniques found in groups. Each of these may make the group members more comfortable, but they will also reduce the quality of the group's eventual decision. A technique familiar to us all (especially if you're reading this the night before the exam) is **procrastination.** We delay taking any action as long as possible. Why?

There are at least two possible reasons a group might employ this technique. First, this limits the time available for a decision. There simply may not be enough time to get into prolonged discussions comparing ideas. Thus the time for conflict is compressed or eliminated. Second, if there is some sort of time constraint on the task, procrastinating long enough may cause you to miss the deadline. For example, if your group is working on a grant application and you can't get it together to meet the due date, then you have no decisions to make.

STOP Do you have a problem with procrastination? Has this been a problem in groups in which you've participated? What steps could the group take to reduce this problem?

187

CHAPTER SEVEN

Decision Making

Bolstering is a technique that is almost procrastination in reverse. The group quickly latches on to the first acceptable alternative without bothering to evaluate a number of alternatives. Then whatever time is left is employed in rationalizing and justifying the decision. **Cognitive dissonance** plays a role here. We're a smart, creative group. Why would we make a dumb decision? Since we have made decision X it must (by definition) be the best. Of course when we're not in the throes of having to make a decision, this appears ridiculous, but at least for Americans, cognitive dissonance has been shown to have a powerful effect on our behaviors.

As we have discussed, any decision not employing the rational decision-making model is by definition imperfect. The term for this choice of an acceptable, but not best alternative is **satisficing.** Is this a good thing? No. Do we do it all the time? Yes. I'm repeating it here to remind you that ignoring alternatives, or limiting the scope of your search for alternatives is going to result in a less than ideal solution. So even though you will never make a perfect decision you should strive to make the best decision possible.

Many decisions are multifaceted. There are a number of decisions that make up the whole. One way of avoiding dealing with potentially conflicting opinions on the "big picture" is choosing a smaller, less controversial decision and spending your group time on this decision. This is known as **trivializing.** For example, your daughter wants to date the tattooed, unkempt high school dropout who sells drugs. Rather than arguing whether you will allow her to socialize with this person the family fights about curfew times instead. Or, she wants to marry him and the family focuses on and argues about the color of the bridesmaid's dresses. You are, in a way, procrastinating because you know that the big picture is going to generate a great deal of conflict, which you are unwilling to face.

One final issue in the evaluation of alternatives involves ethics. Just because a decision is legal doesn't necessarily mean it is ethical. President Clinton committed adultery. Even if we find this behavior distasteful, cheating on your wife isn't illegal. However, the Articles of Impeachment voted on by the House of Representatives focused on whether he committed the crime of perjury, which is illegal. Ideally, groups wish to make decisions that are both legal and ethical.

Certain questions can be asked to help determine whether your alternatives are legal and ethical (Kallman & Grillo, 1996). First, is it legal? With laws as complicated as they are today, it is best to check with an attorney if there is any question. Once the question of legality is dealt with, we face the more ambiguous issue of ethics.

Does anyone want to keep this decision secret? Why? What would your mother think if she knew you'd made this decision? How would you like to turn on your television and see your name linked with the decision on the national evening news? Does your instinct make if feel "funny" or "wrong"? "Does the situation 'smell'?" (Kallman & Grillo, 1996, p. 9). If any of these questions when applied to your preferred alternative make you cringe, perhaps reconsideration is appropriate.

Finally, what about the consequences of the decision? There are three levels to consider. **Egoistic decisions** involve maximizing the good for myself or at least incurring the least harm to me. **Utilitarian decisions** involve the good of the group or the least harm to the group. And last, **altruistic decisions** are best for the group although potentially incurring some harm to me.

But these levels still only focus inward toward the group. What about the consequences for the larger society or environment? Deciding to buy up rainforest land and cutting down the trees for profit could certainly benefit my group in terms of money, but ultimately harm the larger environment and society at large. What are the potential larger ethical issues?

Well, it's time. You've generated all of the alternatives you can and evaluated their positive and negative attributes. Time for a decision.

Choice of Most Appropriate Alternative

Before we begin to discuss how to choose the best decision alternative, let me remind you again that this process will be much smoother if you have taken the time earlier to determine how you're going to know when a decision has been made.

At first that may sound silly, but there are lots of ways to make a decision. Will the leader decide? Will you vote? If so, how many votes does it take to "win"? These approaches to deciding the "winner" are known as **decision criteria.** Let's examine the possibilities.

One way the group could make a decision is to delegate the authority to the leader or to a subgroup of some sort. This potentially leaves out the inputs of the group. This may anger the group, depending upon the type of decision. Usually for small, routine decisions groups are delighted to allow the leader to decide when to order more letterhead or other such tasks. But for large, important decisions it is usually wise to include the group. Their support will be important in the implementation and success of the choice.

A typical approach to decision making is to vote. Each person states their preference and a winner is identified. But wait. How many votes does it take to make for a winner? That's not a trick question. There are several levels of decision criteria that might be employed.

Typically groups use the **majority wins** approach. If there are five group members and three prefer one alternative, it's over. But what if those two other group members really hate the decision? They may not only fail to help, they may have a vested interest in seeing that the decision is not successful (so they can be proven correct). If you need support from the group, a "majority wins" criterion may leave you with 51 percent of the group supporting your decision and the other 49 percent at best lacking support and at worst representing a threat to the decision.

So you can raise the level of the decision criterion by demanding a two-thirds majority for winning. In a group of nine, at least six people must vote for the same alternative. So what's wrong with this? You've definitely got more support for the decision. But wait. Suppose you have a group of twelve. This would require at least eight people to vote the same direction. Suppose seven vote the same way. That's not enough votes. So the minority of five has ruled the group. This possibility of minority rule should be considered before adopting a two-thirds majority decision criterion.

Or we could make it even more complicated. We could demand that in order for an alternative to be accepted it must receive a unanimous vote. This is known as **consensus.** The clear advantage of consensus is that at least publicly everyone has expressed support. And having publicly supported the decision they will have to face embarrassment at the least if they fail to rally around the decision. However, consensus can take a very long time to achieve. It requires much discussion and persuasion. That's not always bad as we will see in our discussion of juries. But not all groups have the luxury of time required to allow for the group to reach consensus.

The last decision criterion we will discuss is used in situations where it is clear to all that there are conflicting political interests which will potentially affect the voting procedure. Some people will vote for a less than optimal alternative because it fits with their political agenda. In this case we can use the technique of **averaging inputs.**

One approach is that used in the nominal group technique. Group members vote for their top five alternatives and the averages are taken to determine the winner. Or the technique can be employed as it is in international athletic events such as the Olympic Games.

At issue in the Olympics is not just who are the best athletes, but which country can win the most medals. Therefore judges have at least implicit pressure to favor athletes from their own country (or from countries that share their political ideology) for events where subjective judgments are called for, such as diving, gymnastics, or ice skating. A panel of expert judges is chosen to represent the world community. After each athlete performs, each judge rates the individual on a predetermined scale. The scores are then displayed. The highest and lowest scores are dropped from the decision and the others are summed. Although this can't remove all of the nationalism from the judging, at least the most extreme cases are eliminated from the decision.

 Averaging inputs is not only appropriate for the Olympics. Can you think of other situations in which it would be appropriate? Do you think this method would work in "beauty pageants"? What others come to mind?

Implementation of Decision

This step might seem a little strange to find in a decision-making model. After all, the decision's already been made, hasn't it? Yes, but the changes implied or demanded by the alternative chosen must be put into practice. And in our final step of evaluation we can't evaluate whether an idea was any good if we can't see how it was acted upon.

Part of the decision-making process, then, is establishing the plan for **implementation.** Who will be responsible for what tasks? What will be the time frame for implementation? How will the change be introduced? Where will the necessary resources be obtained? (As you can probably see, these issues should have been considered in the process of evaluating each alternative.) The best ideas not put into place are as bad as no attempt at change at all.

Evaluation of Decision

We've made our choice and we've overseen the implementation of the decision. Now it's time for **evaluation of decision.** This will help us in our future decision-making endeavors. We can identify what we did well and what could stand some work for the next time.

Our first step in the evaluation process takes us back to the first step in the model. We need to collect information on the situation as it now exists. Before we start collecting the data we should allow for some time to pass. Implementation takes time, and changes need time for assimilation into the system. Even when individuals welcome change, it may take them some time to adapt to a new environment or hone new skills. So we must wait a reasonable amount of time for the changes to become established. Then we'll collect the same data we did at the beginning of the process and compare the situation as it now exists to the baseline data. Are things any different? If the answer is no, the first place to check is implementation.

Was the decision carried out as intended? If not, you have no information on the quality of the decision itself. If you discover that implementation proceeded exactly as planned, the next area to check was your initial diagnosis of the situation. Maybe you were treating the wrong area. In that case we would not expect to see any change in the original problem.

Once we've established that things are, indeed, different at this point in time, we need to examine this difference. Are things better? Have they changed in the way we wanted? Are we closer to the ideal than before? Where have we fallen short? If things are a little bit better, maybe we failed to identify all of the sources of the problem. Or maybe we need to be more forceful in the implementation of our decision. What if things are different, but worse than they were? Then we really need to reevaluate our decision and make some alteration. In fact, we must start the entire cycle again.

Let's fantasize about a best of all possible worlds and assume that everything is almost exactly as we had hoped when making our decision. Now we should look around the larger context in which our situation exists. Have we created any unintended side effects either within the context of our situation or outside in the larger environment? Are these good things? Or have we solved the problem in the design department only to create an overwhelming problem for our sales staff? Everything and everyone exists in context. We must be sure that we have not solved one problem only to create another. But if we have created another problem, we can start through the model again.

Decision making is usually a cyclical process in long-term groups. We're very seldom perfect the first time around making a decision. The new conditions resulting from our original decision become the basis for the next trip through the model. Hopefully, as we carefully evaluate each decision made by the group we become more proficient by improving our technique.

FACTORS INFLUENCING THE DECISION-MAKING PROCESS

What role do gender and culture play in the process of decision making? Sex-role stereotyping would certainly assume that men and women would favor different approaches to the process. Actually, as it turns out, the actual sex of the individual is less important in influencing decision style than is sex-role identity (e.g., masculinity or femininity).

> *The words masculine and feminine do not refer in any simple way to fundamental traits of personality, but to learned styles of interpersonal interactions which are deemed to be socially appropriate to specific social contexts, and which are imposed upon, and sustain and extend, the sexual dichotomy.*
>
> *(King, 1995, p. 72)*

It is, of course, certainly true that sex and gender identity are strongly correlated. King (1995) administered the **Bem Sex-Role Inventory (BSRI)** (a standardized measure of gender identity) and the **Decision Style Inventory (DSI)** to managers to measure the relationship between the two measures. The DSI differentiates between four styles of decision making: *directive, analytical, conceptual,* and *behavioral.*

The directive style is task related, control oriented, realistic, direct, pragmatic, and decisive. These are the "General Pattons" (King, 1995, p. 76) of the managerial world. The analytical style is more focused on problem solving and dealing well with ambiguity. This style is often used by researchers and analysts. The conceptual style is oriented more toward people than tasks. These are the dreamers. Finally, the behavioral style is employed by managers who are people centered but also pragmatic. These are the "people" managers.

Past research with the DSI had found women more likely to be behavioral or conceptual than directive or analytical in decision-making style. Since both of these styles are people oriented we might expect women to be more effective in this realm. However, King did not find this pattern. Perhaps times have changed. King did find that women managers were more likely to be masculine on the BSRI than men managers, and the men were more likely to score high on femininity than the female managers. This could possibly be the result of only extremely masculine women choosing a nontraditional career such as management, or a "hardening" effect of the environment, or something else entirely. King concluded that perhaps the strongest influence in decision making between managers is their communication styles and patterns.

As we have discussed in several contexts, collectivist cultures value interdependence, embedment in their in-groups, and require in-group harmony. Self-sacrifice for the good of the group is considered natural. Individual and group goals are more often consistent in collectivist cultures than in individualistic cultures. Thus one would expect less contention in the decision-making styles of collectivist groups. This has been found to be the case. Collectivist cultures' decisions are more often by consensus than by other means (e.g., the Japanese *ringi* **method** [Triandis, 1994]).

JURIES AS DECISION-MAKING BODIES

Juries are an important part of the American judicial system. A group of individuals together determine the fate of those accused of committing crimes. Their entire reason for existence is to make decisions. We will look now at the unique factors affecting juries as groups. Finally, in the Application section for this chapter we will look at the effects of these issues on the two trials of O.J. Simpson—the criminal trial where he was accused of murdering his ex-wife Nicole Brown and her friend Ron Goldman, and the civil trial where he was accused of the wrongful deaths of these individuals. We will also discuss the differences in the rules and contexts of civil and criminal trials in the United States.

Scientific Jury Selection

The expectation of most American citizens is that if they are accused of a crime they will be tried before a jury of their peers. Our images of the ideal juror include both the impartial juror (which requires ignorance of the individual defendant and the circumstances of the crime) and the knowledgeable juror who is familiar with the defendant, the crime, and the community. The second, a true peer, is often believed to be preferable because they can more accurately represent the "conscience of the community" and apply the law in ways that are appropriate to "the community's moral values and common sense" (Abramson, 1994, p. 18).

These two images, however, are often at odds with each other. If we choose the entirely impartial juror, we must choose from those who are basically oblivious to the goings-on in the world around them. How can they represent

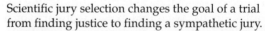

Scientific jury selection changes the goal of a trial from finding justice to finding a sympathetic jury.

the conscience of the community if they are not informed as to the community mores, norms, and values? Given we can't have both, do we prefer the blank slate or the informed, conscious juror? Which truly represents a jury of one's peers?

Since composition of the jury may potentially have profound effects on the outcome of the case, selection of the jury is an important consideration. In some jurisdictions it is relatively easy to dodge jury duty. In 1988 in Massachusetts, 31 percent of those called were disqualified or excused (Abramson, 1994). In 1986 I was called for jury duty in the state of Delaware. I was to report on the date that my obstetrician expected me to give birth, and feeling that going into labor in the jury box was less than desirable, we filed for an excuse. I was astonished when the excuse came back. It was good for eighteen years. So at least at that time in Delaware, anyone (any woman?) with a minor child could be excused from jury duty until that child reached adult status.

In some states jurors are called from the voter registration lists. This eliminates a significant number of the population. Other states call from the records of driver's licenses. Again we may be limiting the pool of potential jurors. It is also true that in many states it is relatively simple to prove that you are indispensable at work and are thus excused. This is more likely to occur in professions that require a higher level of education such as physicians and teachers.

If it is so easy to dodge serving on a jury for personal or professional reasons, are juries equipped to deal with the complexities of the law in the courtroom? Many think not. As late as 1960, federal courts did not randomly choose jurors. They impanelled "blue ribbon" juries of those they felt were intelligent, educated, and sophisticated enough to serve as effective jurors. With the recent increase in the technological evidence that is often presented in court (e.g., DNA evidence), this may become more of a concern.

Thus the beginning of **scientific jury selection.** Individuals trained in psychology and group dynamics serve as consultants to the attorneys of whomever can afford to help choose the most sympathetic jury. Jury consultants help with the selection of jurors by directing attorneys' questions during jury selection, by conducting community surveys on attitudes toward the case and the client, running focus groups, and supervising various alternative possible arguments by the attorneys as to which will "play best." And jury consultants don't come cheap.

In 1994, the American Society of Trial Consultants estimated that there were at least 250 jury consultants in the United States, compared with 25 in 1982. Fees run about $150 an hour; in a high-profile case, Litigation Science's fees range from $10,000 to over $250,000 per case.

(Abramson, 1994, p. 149)

Does scientific jury selection affect the outcome of cases? The jury's out on that one (pun intended). There are some who believe there is no question that there is a biasing effect. The book *American Tragedy* by Schiller and Willwerth (1997) discusses at length the jury consultants' role in the selection of the jury for the criminal trial of O.J. Simpson. There was a profile of the ideal juror and a lengthy questionnaire that potential jurors were required to complete.

Jury Size

The traditional size for American juries has been twelve. In the 1970s, however, the Supreme Court allowed for juries as small as six individuals and for nonunanimous decisions (e.g., Florida and Louisiana). If a state opts for smaller juries, however, the Supreme Court does require unanimity of decision. Immediately concern was expressed that the size decrease would decrease the amount of interaction between jury members and also cause the juries to be less representative. Review of the studies would appear to corroborate these fears (see Nemeth, 1977; and Saks, 1977).

So do these changes affect the outcomes of trials? The answer is clearly yes. Juries can render three possible verdicts: acquittal, guilty, or what is known as a **hung jury.** (A very common misconception is that an **acquittal** is the same as a "not guilty" verdict. Nothing could be further from the truth. In criminal cases jurors must believe the evidence against the defendant to the extent that they have no reasonable doubt that the evidence indicates guilt. If the quantity or quality of the evidence allows for doubt, the jury is required to acquit—whether or not they believe the defendant committed the crime.)

While the ratio of acquittals to convictions is not affected by jury size, the probability and number of hung juries does increase. If a case ends because of a hung jury, the prosecutors must decide whether or not it is worth going through the process again. Cases are often dropped, so in effect the number of acquittals does increase. So a smaller jury works to the advantage of the defendant.

Choice of Foreman

The jury is represented in court by one individual chosen by the jury from within the ranks of the jury itself. This individual is known as the foreman of the jury. The title refers back to the time when women were not allowed to serve on juries. It was believed that because women were so easily persuaded, they would just go along with the male jurors' opinions. It was not until 1972 that federal courts were impelled to allow women to serve on the jury. Before that time they could be dismissed simply because of their sex.

Often the foreman of a jury is chosen based upon some outside status, such as being highly educated. Having served previously as a juror also confers status (Hans & Vidmar, 1986). More recently, however, it appears that whoever speaks up first is likely to be chosen foreman. In several recent celebrity trials the "foremen" were women.

Jury Nullification

Juries seldom understand the variety of factors they may use as they make their decision. Most judges will instruct the jury as to the law(s) of which the defendant stands accused and will explain the possible sentences and the criteria for conviction or acquittal. Often judges refrain from instructing juries on an additional fact that can completely turn a case around.

Jurors are not required to apply the law in deciding the case. This process is known as **jury nullification.** At present this option is quite controversial as at gested in the *Yale Law Journal* that as a step toward righting the wrongs done to the African-American community over time, African-Americans should not be convicted—even when the evidence indicates guilt beyond a reasonable doubt. He believes that African-American jurors have a " . . . moral responsibility . . . to emancipate some guilty black outlaws" (quoted in Goldberg, 1996).

The reason judges hesitate to explain this option to juries is the fear that they actually might exercise this right. Jury nullification is a narrow right. "The crucial significance of this restriction is that juries can nullify only to acquit, never to convict" (Abramson, 1994, p. 67). That is, they can refuse to convict a defendant even when the evidence would appear to call for conviction, but they can not convict someone unless they believe beyond a reasonable doubt that the evidence indicates that the defendant is guilty.

STOP How do you feel about jury nullification? Do you see a difference in the use of jury nullification as a chance for the jury to make a statement about what they perceive as a "bad" law or a law being inappropriately applied and the use of jury nullification to right past discrimination? If jury nullification is to be used as a tool for delayed justice, what other groups might claim that the process should be used in their trials?

Types of Evidence: Polygraphs and Eyewitnesses

There are two types of evidence that have been shown to be particularly persuasive to juries in coming to their decisions—polygraphs and eyewitnesses. Unfortunately, these are two types of evidence that are very likely to be inaccurate.

The **polygraph,** also known as the **lie detector,** does nothing of the sort. There is no direct way of measuring a lie. What the polygraph measures are the physical reactions of the individual being tested to their answers to questions, including changes in heart rate, blood pressure, skin conductivity, skin temperature, as well as breathing rate and sweating.

In the usual testing procedure there are four sensors placed on the subject of the test. Pneumatic straps are placed around the person's chest and stomach areas; a blood pressure cuff is placed around the arm, and metal electrodes are placed on the fingers (Ekman, 1985). A physical reaction assumes that the subject feels uncomfortable about lying. Most of us are raised with the admonition to tell the truth, so do react when lying. That's those of us who internalize the societal norm.

We have two types of error that can be made with the polygraph. The first is that it can call a truthful individual a liar—in other words, they "failed" the test. This is called a **false positive.** The other type of error is when a liar is not detected. Although they have been lying we say they have "passed" the test. This is called a **false negative.** The problem with polygraphs as evidence in the courtroom is the fact that there are such high levels of both false positives and false negatives that we can't with any degree of certainty identify whether the person is being truthful.

A perfectly innocent person being subjected to a polygraph exam is often quite nervous. All the physiological indicators of this nervousness can be interpreted as a lie by an inexperienced polygrapher. False positive rates have been measured as high as 55 percent (Lyken, 1987). For this reason a federal law was passed in 1989 barring the use of the polygraph in hiring decisions with the exception of very few professions.

Equally frightening in the context of the courtroom is the possibility of false negatives. In this case a guilty individual would be identified as truthful and possibly go free. There are individuals in our society—known as sociopaths—who do not internalize the rules about lying. To the sociopath, anything that is beneficial to themselves is good. Therefore a lie in self-protection is nothing. Serial murderer Theodore Bundy passed a number of polygraph tests in a number of states although he eventually admitted committing a number of murders (the exact number still unknown at the time of his execution in Florida). And, as one of my students once stated, "If a person can commit murder with no regrets, what's a little lie?"

The percentage of false negatives in some studies is as high as 31 percent. It is for the basic inaccuracies of the polygraph that this evidence is inadmissible in courtrooms. Then why discuss this test? Often attorneys have their clients undergo a polygraph test. If the results are negative they keep them quiet. If the client "passes" the test, it usually appears in the media to which potential jurors are exposed.

The second type of inaccurate evidence is **eyewitness identification.** This evidence is admissible in court, and has been shown to be very persuasive to juries. However, this evidence is also often tainted.

STOP Let's imagine a situation in which you witness a crime. You're at the local convenience store in the evening buying some milk for tomorrow when the door bursts open and two armed individuals start shouting demands for money. Imagine your stress level. Are you going to be hurt? Or killed? Where is your attention going to be focused? On the weapon? In trying to find a place to hide? Are you going to take the time to memorize the faces of the intruders? What if you're the clerk with a gun in your face?

In order to remember something, two things must happen. The memory must be recorded, and the memory must be available to recovery. We do not record information well under stress. And the memory can be changed simply by the questions we are asked after the fact (Loftus, Miller, & Burns, 1987). Also, research has shown that individuals of different races are more likely to accurately identify a member of their own race than of another (Milpass & Kravitz, 1987).

Thus eyewitness evidence can be quite shaky. Attorney Barry Scheck of Yeshiva University in New York and associates have founded a project known as the Innocence Project. They go back and examine cases where scientific evidentiary technology was unavailable at the time of the trial. As of 1998 they have had thirty-five men released from prison, some from death row, a number of whom had been convicted based on identification by eyewitnesses.

Decision-Making Processes

The major focus of research on juries is on their decisions. Unfortunately it is quite rare to have access to the actual deliberations of a jury, so most research in this area depends upon comparing theoretical models to the outcomes of "mock juries" in what is known as analogue research or to the outcomes of actual trials. The theoretical starting point is based upon the concept of majority rules. If more than half (seven people in a twelve-person jury) vote for conviction, the jury convicts. And if more than half vote for acquittal, the jury acquits. The only time this model would predict a hung jury (no decision) would be when the jury started out split exactly down the middle with six for and six against conviction.

According to Zeisel and Diamond (1978) based on the outcomes of actual trials, we can only predict a final verdict with certainty when the jury starts out unanimous in their decision. A minority of one (either way) will only slightly affect the outcome (1% to 2% of cases). So forget the classic movie *Twelve Angry Men* in which a jury which starts out 11 to 1 for conviction is persuaded by the one holdout to acquit. That only happens in Hollywood. If you have one juror against the others, the most probable outcome is that the holdout will be persuaded to conform to the others. Only approximately 1 percent of the time does the holdout maintain that stance and hang the jury.

Equal initial factions are in reality most likely to eventually reach a decision. Only approximately 12 percent of these cases end in hung juries. There is a slightly higher probability (46% compared to 42%) that these trials will end with an acquittal.

This last finding leads us to the phenomenon of the **leniency bias.** There is a hesitancy both in criminal trials (Kerr & MacCoun, 1985) and in mock jury situations (MacCoun & Kerr, 1988) to convict defendants unless there is an initial overwhelming majority in favor of conviction. When the jury starts out with equal factions, the juries are more likely to acquit (46%) or to hang (43%) than to convict (11%). Thus in the jury on which you were placed at the beginning of this chapter, the eventual outcome is likely to be acquittal.

 What explanations can you provide for the leniency bias? Why would juries give the benefit of the doubt to the accused in criminal trials? Would you? Discuss this with your classmates.

It is clear from this research that minority opinions affect the outcomes in groups—in this case, juries. But the majority generally carries the decision. Larger factions are more likely to have their arguments heard. (Remember that in the Asch study of conformity it required only one break in a unanimous majority to profoundly reduce conformity effects.) Not only are larger factions going to hold the floor for a larger proportion of the time, there is also a difference in the ways they present their opinions. Minority opinion holders are more likely to be more tentative and less likely to be forceful in bringing up their opinions (Kerr & MacCoun, 1985). "Apparently, faction size not only affects what is said and how it is said, but how it is heard and interpreted" (Baron, Kerr, & Miller, 1992).

Who Needs Juries? Let the Judges Decide

Jury trials are expensive and disruptive to the lives of the individuals required to serve on the juries. Why not just allow judges, who after all are often attorneys themselves and well schooled in the law, just make the decisions? Wouldn't that be more efficient? One way to consider this question is to compare the decisions on actual trials made by the jury as compared to how the judge would have ruled. Precisely such research has been conducted (Kalven & Zeisel, 1966). Since criminal and civil trials operate under different sets of rules, outcomes of 3,576 criminal trials and 4,000 civil trials were examined.

In the criminal trials, judge and jury agreed on the appropriate outcome 78 percent of the time. They were more likely to agree when the outcome was conviction. When the verdict was guilty, there was a 64 percent level of agreement. When the actual verdict was acquittal, there was agreement only 14 percent of the time.

What of the 22 percent of the cases on which there was disagreement? Juries were seen to be more lenient than judges. Of the 22 percent of cases where there was disagreement as to the appropriate verdict, in 19 percent the jury acquitted when the judge would have convicted. Only in the remaining 3 percent did the jury convict when the judge would have acquitted. Again we are seeing the leniency bias.

What of the civil trials? Civil trials potentially affect the defendants' wallets, not their freedom. Of the 4,000 cases examined, there was again agreement between judge and jury 78 percent of the time. Again there was more agreement when the case went against the defendant in favor of the plaintiff, although the difference was smaller than that seen in criminal cases. In the civil trials, 47 percent of the agreement was in finding for the plaintiff (the equivalent of a guilty decision), and only 37 percent in findings for the defendant (the equivalent of an acquittal). This pattern matches that found in criminal trials.

When the judge and jury disagreed (as they did on 22 percent of the cases), in 10 percent of the cases the judge would have found for the plaintiff (equivalent to conviction) when the jury would have found for the defendant (equivalent to an acquittal). In the remaining 12 percent of the disputed cases, the judge would have found for the defendant (the equivalent to an acquittal) while the jury would have found for the plaintiff (equivalent to conviction).

The difference in direction in the disagreements reverses for criminal and civil cases. In criminal cases, juries are overwhelmingly more lenient than the judges (19% to 3%). In the civil cases, the juries were slightly more likely to rule against the defendant, although the difference was quite small (12% to 10%).

So what do all these numbers mean? If I were to take up a life of crime I'd certainly prefer to retain the jury system (with all of its flaws) if I'm committing crimes that would land me in criminal court. In civil trials I'd rather go with just the judge. However, notice that in both types of case, in more than three-quarters of the cases the judge and jury do agree and are more likely to rule against the defendant.

Effects of Juror Characteristics on Jury Processes

What effects (if any) do the individual personal characteristics of jurors have on the outcome of trials? Several prominent attorneys believe they do, including Alan Dershowitz (1996) who stated in reference to the O.J. Simpson criminal case that "different jurors, exposed to the same evidence but with dissimilar life experiences, might have voted to convict" (p. 98).

We do know that race is an important factor in the criminal justice system from the initial encounter to the commutation of the death penalty. We know that African-Americans are overrepresented in our prison systems. We know that African-Americans are more likely to acquit than whites. We know that both races are more likely to acquit defendants of their own race. Mostly white juries impose the death penalty more frequently on African-Americans who kill whites than on whites who kill African-Americans.

The whole concept of the death penalty jury requires some explanation. In the process of choosing the jury where the attorneys and judge question potential jurors known as voir dire, they are allowed to exclude anyone who may have a built-in prejudice or opinion that would affect their judgment on the case. In cases where the potential consequence of a guilty verdict might be the death penalty, a **death-qualified** jury must be chosen. Anyone who opposes the death penalty on principle is automatically excluded from the jury pool. Death-qualified juries are more likely to convict than are juries on non-capital cases. And women and African-Americans are more likely to be excluded from death-qualified juries (Abramson, 1994).

Just recently, the issue of the death penalty for female prisoners received a great deal of attention when the state of Texas planned to execute the first woman since the Civil War. Carla Faye Tucker had been convicted of a particularly savage murder she committed in her teens under the influence of drugs. Her childhood background was dismal, including prostitution while still in her teens.

While in prison, Carla Faye underwent a spiritual conversion and became a born-again Christian. As her death date approached, the entire country was in upheaval over whether she shouldn't be allowed to live since she had undergone such a transformation. Very little was said about the numerous men who have also probably undergone rehabilitation in prison. There was question, however, whether her conversion to another religion would have made her a less attractive martyr. The fact that juries don't want to sentence women to execution has been a fact in this country. The execution of Carla Faye, however, may change that.

Summary

Groups make decisions on all sorts of matters. In this chapter we have examined a number of basic decision-making models and theories which we have integrated into a single, elaborated model. We have discussed the importance of proper diagnosis of the situation, proper structure applied to the group from the earliest stages of the process, the generation and subsequent evaluation of alternative solutions. We've also discussed a number of ways the choice can be made, and the importance of follow-up by means of checking on implementation and proper evaluation techniques. Finally, we discussed a particular type of group—the jury—whose sole function is decision making in a very important venue. We examined ways in which all the group dynamics we've discussed to this point in the book apply, or differ, in these special groups.

Key Terms

acquittal
activity trap
altruistic decisions
averaging inputs
Bem Sex-Role Inventory
  (BSRI)
bolstering
breakpoints
cognitive dissonance
complex decision paths
consensus
death-qualified jury
decision criteria
Decision Style Inventory
  (DSI)

egoistic decisions
evaluation of decision
eyewitness identification
false negative
false positive
hung jury
identification of
  alternatives
implementation
implicit favorite model
intuitive model
jury nullification
leniency bias
lie detector
majority wins

operational definition
optimizing model
polygraph
problem diagnosis
procrastination
rational decision-making
  model
ringi method
satisficing
scientific jury selection
spiral model
trivializing
utilitarian decisions
utility models

Did O.J. Simpson murder his ex-wife Nicole and Ronald Goldman? The criminal trial jury said "no," while the civil trial jury said "yes."

An Analysis of Two Trials: Simpson and Simpson

On October 3, 1995, 95 million Americans watched their televisions with bated breath as the jury in the O.J. Simpson criminal trial presented their verdicts.

> *Superior Court of California, County of Los Angeles, in the matter of the State of California versus Orenthal James Simpson, case number BA097211. We the jury, in the above-entitled action, find the defendant, Orenthal James Simpson, not guilty of the crime of murder . . .*
>
> **(Schiller & Willwerth, 1997, pp. 866–867)**

Simpson sagged in relief against his defense counsel. After a trial lasting slightly more than a year, it was over. He would not be spending any more time in jail or going to prison. He had just been acquitted of murdering his ex-wife, Nicole Brown and her friend Ronald Goldman.

But it wasn't really over. The families of the victims brought civil charges against Simpson and on Tuesday, February 4, 1997, the jury brought back guilty verdicts against Simpson for "willfully and wrongfully" causing the deaths of both Brown and Goldman. The court awarded the families $8.5 million dollars in compensatory damages, and $25 million dollars in punitive damages (Schiller & Willwerth, 1997).

How can it be that a person in the United States can stand trial for the same crime twice? The concept of double jeopardy is well established in this country. This states that you cannot be tried a second time for the same crime. However, we have two tiers in the judicial area of the criminal courts: the criminal and the civil.

> *The burden of proof in a criminal case is "beyond a reasonable doubt," while the burden of proof in a civil case is "by a mere preponderance of the evidence."*
>
> **(Dershowitz, 1996, p. 39)**

Thus an individual can be tried twice, using different criteria, and the verdicts may differ between the two trials as they did for Mr. Simpson.

And, of course, the punishments differ dramatically between the two court systems. In the criminal system the potential punishments include fines, incarceration, and even—for some crimes in some states—death. In the civil courts, the punishments are usually financial in nature. Thus criminal punishments are by nature more severe and an incorrect decision more serious. As Dershowitz states (1996, p. 41):

> *But in criminal cases, we prefer the type of error under which a possibly guilty defendant would go free to the type of error under which an innocent defendant would go to prison or be executed.*

In this Application we will look at the topics we discussed in the chapter section on juries to try to explain the differences in the outcomes of the Simpson trials. We will discuss the role of scientific jury selection (which played an extensive role in both trials), the types of evidence presented in each case, and the effects of the juror characteristics on the outcomes of the trials.

When the Simpson defense team was organized for the criminal trial, they wasted no time in hiring one of the country's preeminent jury consultants— Dr. Jo-Ellan Dimitrius of the Social Research Laboratory at San Diego State University (Schiller & Willwerth, 1997). Dimitrius moved quickly to conduct surveys to evaluate the public perception of their client. Before the trial only 20 percent of her sample believed that Simpson had not committed the murders, but an additional 50 percent did not want to believe that Simpson was responsible. This gave hope then, that a jury might be impaneled that wanted to be given evidence that would allow them to acquit Simpson.

Focus groups conducted by Dr. Dimitrius provided the team with the profile of their ideal juror. On August 27, 1994, three focus groups were run with twenty-five people per group. It became clear that there was one group who believed in Simpson's innocence most strongly—"black middle-aged women" (Schiller & Willwerth, 1997, p. 243).

While the prosecution would focus on the fact that there was some evidence that Simpson had battered Nicole Brown during the marriage and thus was predisposed to violence and possibly murder, battering was not the issue for these women. "The gut issue was Nicole. This white woman had lived *their* fantasy. She had things they should have had" (Schiller & Willwerth, 1997, p. 244). Thus Dimitrius identified the ideal juror as a middle-aged, divorced, black woman.

To this end a questionnaire was developed for potential jurors consisting of 302 questions. The attorneys would evaluate responses to these questions to determine whether or not to challenge any of the potential jurors. The defense team decided that they would hope for a jury with four black jurors. They eventually got nine.

This final jury developed over the course of the trial. Because of the sensational nature of the media coverage, Judge Lance Ito sequestered the jury. This means they were kept in a hotel and not allowed to go home during the trial. Supposedly they were not to be exposed to any media coverage, although both sides later admitted to hoping that during "pillow talk" during conjugal visits from spouses, some of the information being presented in the media would leak.

During the year-long trial five of the original jurors were replaced with alternates. Three of the deputies watching the jurors at the hotel were dismissed. And apparently, the group dynamics of the jury definitely included formation of coalitions:

> *When we sat down, an amazing thing happened: There was an immediate separation of the races. It was so impromptu, happening so naturally, that I'm convinced to this day it was not preconceived on anyone's part. One minute we were a melting pot; the next three separate tables, islands segregated according to race. Black jurors at one table. Black alternate jurors at another table. Whites and Latinos at yet another table.*
>
> *(Knox & Walker, 1998, pp. 80–81)*

That paragraph was taken from a book written by one of the expelled jurors describing the jury during meal times. It was clear that these subgroups did not choose to mix. The female foreman of the jury described how these groups not only ate together, but also remained separate when exercising and going on trips provided by the court while matters were being discussed outside their presence. The final jury that deliberated the criminal case consisted of ten women and two men; nine blacks, two whites, and one Latino. Three of the jurors were in their twenties, three in their thirties, two in their forties, two in their fifties, and one each in their sixties and seventies.

The prosecution case depended heavily upon the history of physical abuse administered by Mr. Simpson upon his wife; scientific DNA evidence to prove that the blood of the victims was in Mr. Simpson's car and home, and that Mr. Simpson's blood was at the murder scene (Ms. Brown's home); and other physical evidence such as a pair of gloves and a knit hat that allegedly linked Mr. Simpson to the murder scene. Unfortunately, race became a central issue when it was discovered that one of the officers at the scene, Mark Fuhrman, had made racist remarks on tape to a screenwriter. Fuhrman had been at the murder scene, and it was suggested by the defense that perhaps he had a role in planting incriminating evidence.

Whether or not you followed this trial that was covered heavily by television media, the book by the expelled juror is dramatic reading, as well as a good lesson in group dynamics. The trial was not only influenced by the race of the jury and the evidence admitted (and that refused), it was also influenced by the composition of the teams of attorneys.

The defense team was headed by African-American attorney Johnnie Cochran. It is believed by many whites that Cochran made race an issue in the trial in numerous ways. His final arguments were heavily based in style after the typical revivalist minister. He also developed an extremely adversarial (even more than one would expect) relationship with the African-American attorney for the prosecution, Christopher Darden. There was much macho posturing and many attempts at one-upmanship. The remainder of Simpson's team consisted of extremely well-known attorneys, including Barry Scheck, who was mentioned previously as an expert on DNA evidence.

All was not well in the Simpson defense lineup with continuing disagreements as to who should lead the team, but they were relatively successful at keeping these conflicts out of court. They were uncovered at length by almost all involved in books published subsequent to the trial.

The prosecution team was headed by a white woman attorney, Marcia Clark. It also initially contained a white male, Bill Hodgeman, who was hospitalized for chest pains during the early portions of the trial and did not return to the team. And, of course, there was Christopher Darden.

When both sides had rested their cases, it took the jury only hours to reach a decision. As the jury filed in the next morning to present their decision, the prosecution knew it was in trouble. The jury was dressed up. As one of the assistants to Clark commented after the trial, "I did not like this jury, and I sensed that they did not like us" (Goldberg, 1996, p. 42). This would certainly make sense based upon the preliminary information gleaned by Dimitrius. If the jury resented Simpson's white wife and saw him as a persecuted hero, why would they not resent a white woman prosecution attorney and a black man who was "breaking ranks" and trying to tarnish their hero?

The defense itself presented four explanations for their loss in the criminal trial: (1) the jury just didn't accept the domestic violence angle presented; (2) the media coverage; (3) Simpson's celebrity status; and (4) race.

Race certainly played a role in the public reaction to the verdicts. A *Newsweek* poll taken after the verdict indicated that while 85 percent of African-Americans agreed with the verdict, 32 percent of whites did not. A poll conducted by the *Washington Post* after the verdict stated that 63 percent of whites thought the jury was biased in favor of Simpson, and that 70 percent of white respondents believed Simpson was guilty (Dershowitz, 1996). Interviews with the jurors indicated that they did not necessarily consider Simpson "innocent," they simply felt that the evidence did not reach the level of certainty required in a criminal trial. The families of the victims were enraged and immediately filed civil charges.

The two trials took place in different courts. The criminal trial took place in downtown Los Angeles, the civil trial took place in Santa Monica. The demographics of the two areas are quite different—thus the makeup of the pools of potential jurors is quite different. Attorneys Lambert and Petrocelli rated potential jurors as they went through jury selection on a scale from 1 to 5 with jurors at the low end being basically sympathetic to Simpson and the jurors at the high end basically sympathetic to the families. The jury that was impaneled had all received 3's from the attorneys (Schiller & Willwerth, 1997).

The jury for the civil trial was quite different demographically from the criminal trial. It consisted of six female and six male jurors. The racial composition was one African-American/Asian, nine whites, one Latino, and one Asian-American. This jury was slightly older than the first jury. Two were in their twenties, four in their thirties, three in their forties, one in their fifties, and two in their sixties.

In a civil trial, the witnesses make statements (known as depositions) under oath before the trial begins. Any discrepancies between what is said in the depositions and what is said during the trial is grounds for a perjury charge. Simpson himself did not take the stand during the criminal trial, but he was deposed and testified during the civil trial. There are some who believe he was not allowed to testify in the criminal trial for fear he would incriminate himself. These same people believe that this is what happened in the civil trial.

Also evidence was admitted during the civil trial that had not been available during the criminal trial (e.g., the Bruno Maglia shoes). It had also appeared in the press (although not admissible in either trial as evidence) that Simpson had "failed" a polygraph test taken after the murders.

The prosecution in the civil trial carefully studied the transcripts from the criminal trial in an attempt not to make the same mistakes. Apparently they were successful. It took the jury in the civil case a week (from Tuesday, January 28 to Tuesday, February 4) to find Simpson guilty of causing the deaths of both Nicole Brown and Ronald Goldman.

Discussion Questions

Apply the concepts from the chapter to consider the following questions:

1. In trying to achieve the jury most sympathetic to Simpson in the criminal trial, what sorts of questions do you believe appeared in the juror questionnaire?
2. In California, the death penalty is an option in a murder trial. Yet the prosecution chose not to press for the death penalty (a decision that must be made before jury selection for obvious reasons). Why not? Might a death-qualified jury been more likely to convict?
3. The criminal jury took less than a day to acquit Simpson while the civil jury took a week to convict. Why do suppose it took so much more time?
4. Discuss possible ways that jury nullification might have played a role in the criminal trial.
5. Discuss the "fairness" of the process of scientific jury selection. Does it advantage one side over the other? How? If it results in an uneven playing field, what can be done—or should anything be done?

CHAPTER 8

Leadership and Power

What Would YOU Predict?

Sarah, a 24-year-old recent MBA; Chou, a Laotian engineer; Ronald, a personnel manager who is known for his charisma; Anita, a sales representative who requires a wheelchair for mobility; and Edward, a Harvard PhD in research and development are all chosen to sit on Acme Corporation's Grievance Board. Who would you expect to become the leader of this group?

Abraham Lincoln, Catherine the Great, Napoleon, General Colin Powell, Alexander the Great, Jesus, Gandhi, Henry VIII, Richard III, Martin Luther King, Jr., Mao Tse Tung, David Duke, Adolph Hitler. What do all these people have in common? They are known as exceptional leaders. We mentioned the role of leader in Chapter 1 as an extremely important role that must be filled in the successful group. In this chapter we are going to explore the characteristics of the individuals and the groups they lead that are most likely to result in a successful group. We will first define the idea of leadership. As you would suspect, there is some disagreement over this definition, but by putting together a number of different definitions we will come to understand just what we mean in the rest of the chapter when we discuss leaders. Next we will take a model of leadership developed by Campbell, Dunnette, Lawler, and Weick (1970) and bend it until it is almost unrecognizable from the original to discuss the various traits, skills, and behaviors of leaders including their use of power. We will examine the effects of group culture upon leadership and the conditions under which leadership becomes more or less important for the success of the group. Then we will separately consider the issue of leader effectiveness. A large part of the research in this area has focused in this area. Finally, we will discuss the many effects of gender and culture on all aspects of leadership—from definition to effectiveness. As our application we will analyze the leadership of a criminal named Charles Manson (nobody said "good" leaders are "good" guys!) who masterminded multiple murders in the late 1960s.

WHAT IS A LEADER?

A **leader** is a person who takes care of the behaviors that are entailed in the role of leader. No more. No less. These behaviors include those associated with task accomplishment and with the social issues in the group (yes, again!). But as before, you will see that there are many approaches to defining the **role of leader** and the *process of leadership.*

> *A leader is an individual who is perceived by group members as having a legitimate position of power or influence in the group. The leader can be assigned or designated to that position. Or, the leader may emerge from within the group's interactive process or even by group election.*
>
> **(Fujishin, 1997, p. 112)**

> *Learn to lead in a nourishing manner.*
> *Learn to lead without being possessive.*
> *Learn to be helpful without taking the credit.*
> *Learn to lead without coercion.*
>
> **(Heider, 1985, p. 19)**

I chose these two quotes over many others because between them they describe many of the behaviors and factors of leaders we will discuss in this chapter. In the first we are reminded that one cannot be a leader without fol-lowers. As with all other roles, the role of leader is reciprocal. So if you wish to be a leader, you must function in such a way that people either choose to or are forced to follow you. The first quote also reminds us that the role of **group leader** is a recognized, or legitimate, position within the group structure. And this role confers upon the leader the right to expect that he or she will be able to direct the group and its members. There are several ways an individual may become a leader. An outside agency may appoint or assign the role, or the group itself may make the decision as to who will occupy the role.

The second quote is taken from a modernization of the Taoist religion. It reminds us of the most appropriate leader behaviors from a spiritual perspective. As we shall see in the section on **leader effectiveness,** not everyone agrees with these behaviors. However it does show us that the topic of leaders and leader-ship have been under consideration for thousands of years.

Why is it I keep differentiating between leaders and leadership? Leaders are people. Leadership is what leaders do. Again two positions:

> *Leadership is the process of influencing the task and social dimensions of a group to help it reach its goal.*
>
> *(Fujishin, 1997, p 112)*

> *We define leadership as <u>interpersonal influence</u>, <u>exercised in situation and directed</u>, <u>through the communication process</u>, toward <u>the attainment of a specified goal or goals</u>. Leadership always involves attempts on the part of the <u>leader</u> (influencer) to affect (influence) the behavior of a follower (influencee) or followers in <u>situation</u>.*
>
> *(Tannenbaum, Weschler, & Massarik, 1961, p. 24)*
>
> *(emphasis in original)*

Actually, here the second quote simply fleshes out the first. Leadership involves influencing the behaviors of the group. It also is focused toward the attainment of the group's goal. The medium of the influence is communication. And the context (situation) is always relevant to the performance of leadership.

Is there a distinction between leaders and **managers?** Psychologists tend to do research on leaders, and business and management types (often with the same training) do research on managers. I see very little difference between leaders and managers, except that they are not necessarily connected at the hip. One can lead and not be a manager. And managers don't always lead effec-tively. Perhaps Bennis (1989) stated it best:

> *I tend to think of the differences between leaders and managers as the differ-ences between those who master the context and those who surrender to it.*
>
> *(Bennis, 1989, p. 44)*

I believe that Bennis is simply more eloquently making the same distinction I did. We will continue to discuss leaders and leadership in this chapter, but it applies as well to managers as they seek to "master the context."

This quote again highlights that all leaders are not equal. Bass (1960) distin-guished three types of leadership. In attempted leadership, the leader accepts the task of changing group members' behavior and can be observed in the process of the attempt. In successful leadership, the group members change their behavior as desired by the leader. Finally, in effective leadership, the changes in the group members' behavior will cause the members to be more satisfied, better rewarded, or more successful.

HOW DO YOU GET TO BE A LEADER?

This issue was addressed in the first definition of a leader. Either an outside agency confers the position of leadership, or the group chooses or allows an individual to take on the role. The leader who has the advantage of being legitimized by an outside authority or is chosen by the group has an easier time enacting the behaviors of leadership than does an individual who takes over the position without any prior legitimization. We call these **emergent leaders.**

Emergent leaders have not been conferred the permission or authority to lead the group. They simply take on the role. Thus they must prove themselves to a far greater extent than chosen or **appointed leaders.**

On what bases are people either chosen or allowed to become leaders in groups? A number of theories have been developed to explain this phenomenon as we shall see later in the chapter, however, recent work focuses on what are known as **implicit leadership theories** (Lord, Foti, & De Vader, 1984). Implicit leadership theories are the templates we all carry around in our heads as to what constitutes a leader. To a certain extent these are idiosyncratic based upon our own experiences with leadership situations. These theories cause us to identify those individuals who we feel would make good leaders, and are subsequently used as the basis of our evaluation of a leader's success. For example, based upon what he said in his first campaign, I voted for President Clinton because he "fit" my concept of someone who would be a good leader. His subsequent behavior, however, did not live up to my expectations, so that when the second election came around I did not vote for him again.

STOP Make a list of the characteristics you feel make for a good leader. Which do you feel are most important? Can you identify any leaders (past or present) who fulfill your expectations? Compare your list with classmates—especially those of the opposite sex. Are your lists similar? Different? In what ways?

Some individuals believe that these implicit theories are so powerful as to overwhelm most of the classic research on leadership by underestimating the extent of our own subjectivity. Bresnen (1995) believes that leadership is a "socially constructed phenomenon" based upon implicit leadership theories.

If there are specific characteristics that are commonly employed when we evaluate a subordinate for promotion, or a candidate for election, certain people are going to be placed at a distinct disadvantage. We will discuss the effects of the expectation of masculinity—a frequently identified characteristic of leaders—later in the chapter. One characteristic that pops up often in the choice of leaders is charisma. Unfortunately, however, we don't know much about this trait. Although many people can identify charismatic leaders off the tops of their heads (e.g., Jesus, or Gandhi, or Martin Luther King, Jr.) there have been major problems in trying to study this phenomenon (Behling & McFillen, 1996). This is believed to be based on the fact that there has not been sufficient development of a conceptual framework of the concept to guide the work, nor has there been much attempt to operationalize just exactly what is meant by charisma.

One attempt to examine the phenomenon focused on Malcolm X as a charismatic leader. The charisma of Malcolm X for Black Muslims was perceived as an interaction between the "personality traits, and intellectual, moral, and emotional predispositions" of those followers who identified with Malcolm X and projected their frustrations with the white culture onto him (Corsino, 1982). This fits well with other explorations of **charismatic leadership** which are left saying that there is a timing associated with charismatic leadership in which an individual with a particularly attractive set of characteristics emerges in a group at a time of crisis or heightened feelings (e.g., dissatisfaction or perceived discrimination).

By the way, in our opening vignette example I would probably expect Ronald to become leader. He possesses charisma and his field is closest to the area of the task in which the group will be involved.

Emergent leaders have a number of issues that can be ignored by legitimized leaders. One is the question of when to make the move to lead. Timing is critical. A leader without followers is by definition not a leader, and either too early a move or too late a move can jeopardize the willingness of group members to follow an emergent leader.

One of the behaviors included in the role of leader is to enforce group norms. A group will not accept an individual as an emergent leader until she has proven that she herself understands and follows the norms of the group. Thus she must be a member of the group for a sufficient length of time to demonstrate this knowledge. You can't just walk in and take over a group and expect that they will welcome you with open arms.

But you can't wait too long, either. Roles tend to harden (like cement) over time. The individual who waits too long to make a move to lead will likely not be taken seriously. This can be seen as a particular problem of first-level supervisors in organizations who have been moved up from operative status. His peers are unlikely to relate to him as anything other than a peer. So it becomes a very difficult job. The higher-level supervisors have one set of expectations for the role, and the past peers have another. We discussed this in Chapter 1—we have a case of intra-role conflict.

There's no way to teach the timing of emergent leadership. It's an art rather than a science. However, often a crisis or some unusual circumstance offers the opportunity to the individual so inclined to make their move. And the person so-inclined is often one of the more dominant members of the group (Megargee, Bogart, & Anderson, 1966).

Another issue that emergent leaders face is that the lack of outside legitimization may make it difficult to convince other group members to take them seriously as leader. They are perceived as lacking the authority to lead. The primary way around such a problem is to take charge of the group's resources.

Once these resources are in the hopeful leader's control, they can be used to demonstrate power and to "buy off" anyone who was hurt in the process. Once you control the "goodies" of the group, members are much more likely to take you seriously as leader.

A MODEL OF LEADERSHIP

Campbell, Dunnette, Lawler, and Weick (1970) presented a model of leadership which takes into consideration all of the complexities of the leadership situation. Stripped to its essentials, their basic model shows individual characteristics of the group members contribute to the leader's behaviors, which in turn contribute to the product efficiency of the group. All of these factors are influenced by the group environment (culture) in which the group is functioning and by the extent and effectiveness of feedback. In other words, the basic model looks like this:

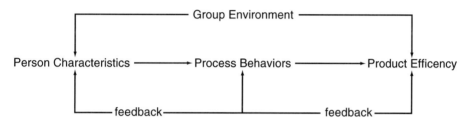

We're going to use this as our starting point, but we're going to take each section and expand and alter it beyond Campbell and others' (1970) recognition. We have already discussed feedback models and importance in Chapter 4 on communication, so we will not repeat the information here. We will start with the *person characteristics* and expand this category by discussing leader traits and skills AND the characteristics of the group members being led. Under *process behaviors* we will discuss the topics of power and influence tactics. We will consider the various theories of leader effectiveness as well as aspects of the task that contribute to *product efficiency* as we discuss productivity. Finally we will discuss *group climate (group environment)* and its effects on the people, the process, and the outcomes of the group.

Person Characteristics

As I've pointed out a number of times, groups are made up of individuals, and the characteristics including traits and skills of all members are important in the eventual productivity of the group. **Person characteristics** of the group members will influence the leader's behavior and the leader's behavior in turn will influence group members.

Traits and Skills of Leaders and Subordinates

Let's look first at the leader. A number of models of the important traits of leaders have been proposed. DuBrin (1992) listed quite a number of **traits** that should be possessed by the potentially successful leader. These include power motives, achievement motives, problem-solving ability, self-confidence, initiative, trustworthiness, vision, insight, flexibility, rationality, and credibility. Landy and Trumbo (1980) presented a list of important supervisor traits that included possession of upward influence within the organization, a similarity of attitudes to higher-level leaders, and similarity of behavior to higher-level leaders.

While DuBrin's list looks exclusively at the characteristics that might be important for success as a leader—particularly an emergent leader—it would appear that Landy and Trumbo are presenting a list of characteristics that might make an individual a very likely candidate to be appointed or assigned a leadership position by someone higher up in the organizational hierarchy.

DuBrin (1992) also listed a number of skills that are important for the successful leader. These include competence, sensitivity to people, good work habits, supportiveness, high expectations, and skill at providing feedback. We are not going to spend time discussing each of these traits or skills (and for heaven's sake don't memorize them!) because when empirically tested, the trait approach is relatively disappointing in its ability to predict effective leaders. The **behavioral approach to leadership** is relatively more successful, so we'll spend more time there. Hollander and Julian (1969) believe this relative ineffectiveness of the *trait* versus the *behavioral approach* is because most research has failed to differentiate between "leadership as a process and the leader as a person" (p. 437).

But what of the other group members? Certainly their characteristics affect the behaviors that the leader is most likely to employ. These characteristics can also affect how easy or difficult a group will be to lead (as will the characteristics of the task as we shall discuss productivity later in the chapter). Landy and Trumbo (1980) have listed the following as important subordinate characteristics: level of expertise, job experience, competence, knowledge of job, and job level.

Each of these will affect the expectations of the leader. Clearly we will expect more of experienced, competent, knowledgeable group members and expect that they will require less "leadership." Also as each of these increases it becomes easier to lead the group and requires a different set of leadership behaviors or tactics for task success. As we have stated above, however, the examination of traits and skills of the leader and group members is less predictive of the eventual success or failure of the group than is the behavior of the leader (Landy & Trumbo, 1980). So we'll turn now to leader behaviors.

The Behavioral Process of Leadership

Leaders make use of many different **process behaviors** to influence the behaviors of group members, but the goal is always the same—to influence or change the behaviors. Leaders can lead by example, thereby providing members a role model. This is in effect what the potential emergent leader does when he follows the group norms initially before making the grab for leadership. However, while leaders are expected to enforce the norms of behavior for the rest of the group, leaders have more flexibility in their behavior regarding norms than do other group members.

Have the leaders in groups in which you have participated always followed group norms completely? If you have been a group leader, did you toe the line? If not, can you think of reasons why the group allowed this behavior?

Power and Influence

Once a leader is firmly in place, she begins to collect what are known as **idiosyncrasy credits.** These can be thought of as units of permission to break the norms. They are accumulated by the leader as long as she "plays by the rules" in following the group norms. Think of these credits as analogous to money in a savings account at the bank. As long as you don't spend any of the money or credits they continue to increase. However, you can spend whatever credits or money you have.

Spending credits is accomplished by breaking the norms of the group. And, just as with a bank account, you can spend all the credits in one extravagant eccentric display of behavior, or you can deviate more frequently in smaller ways. Either way, when the credits are spent, the leader must go back to following the norms as any other group member does. If you "overspend" either with your bank account or with your idiosyncrasy credits, you're in trouble. A leader who overspends may well jeopardize their status as leader—because groups expect their leaders to enact and enforce norms. So if the coffer is empty, the leader must toe the line again for a while until more credits are established. So rank hath its privileges!

Other behaviors that leaders can employ in influencing group behavior include the use of humor, influence through charm and appearance (both men and women use these), demonstrating technical competence in the group task, providing feedback to group members about their performance in the group, ingratiating themselves with group members (although this behavior tends not to be employed much by strong leaders), maintaining high expectations for the group, demonstrating the ability to bounce back quickly from setbacks, using rational persuasion, making inspirational pleas (pumping up confidence, making emotional requests, and appealing to members' values), and making personal appeals to group members (Dipboye et al., 1994; Yukl & Bruce, 1992; and DuBrin, 1992).

All of the above influence tactics fall under the larger umbrella of the use of power. Power can be defined a number of ways. We can have **power over**—the ability to force others to change their behaviors. We can have **power from**—the ability to ignore or resist influence attempts. We can also have the **power to**—the freedom and ability to do what we please. As we discuss leadership, the first two types become the most important. Thus all leadership behaviors are acts of power.

What types of power do you have? In what contexts? Where are you most powerful (in terms of influence)? Do you have more "power over," "power from," or "power to"? What most strongly limits your power?

The Modified French and Raven Model

Although there are several paradigms in the literature examining the phenomenon of power, the most commonly used and researched is the model first introduced by French and Raven in 1959. Although it has been modified as the research continues to develop (e.g., Raven, 1965; Raven, 1992), it remains the most commonly used paradigm (see, for example, Johnson, 1976; Podsakoff & Schreisheim, 1985; Hinkin & Schreisheim, 1990; Schreisheim, Hinkin, & Podsakoff, 1991; Oyster, 1992; and Hogan, 1993).

The model seeks to create a typology of power use that is exhaustive. That is, all attempts by one person to influence another can be categorized in one of the **power bases.** The original model consisted of five power bases: *reward, coercive, expert, legitimate,* and *referent* powers (French & Raven, 1959). However, there was a loophole that was plugged by Raven in 1965 with the addition of *informational power.* In 1992, Raven expanded the categories further:

> *Reward: Personal/Impersonal*
> *Coercive: Personal/Impersonal*
> *Informational: Direct/Indirect*
> *Expert: Positive/Negative*
> *Legitimate: Formal*
> > *Legitimacy of reciprocity*
> > *Legitimacy of equity*
> > *Legitimacy of Dependence (Powerlessness)*
> *Referent: Positive/Negative*

(Raven, 1992)

Now that you have the history, what do these terms mean? Which types of power are most effective, and what potential side effects can be incurred by their use? The six power bases can be thought of as consisting of three sub-groupings. Reward and coercion are both based upon resources. Informational and expert power are based upon knowledge. And legitimate and referent power are based upon the relationship between the leader and the person who they are attempting to influence (usually referred to as the **target**).

Reward and coercion are exactly what you would guess. Reward involves offering some sort of "goodie" in exchange for a particular behavior, while coercion involves threatening negative results for a particular behavior. In **reward power** the group leader might offer a member a larger share of the group reward for additional work, or a boss might offer a bonus for the salesperson bringing in the largest number of new accounts. In **coercive power,** the group leader might threaten expulsion from the group for continued absences from group meetings, or a boss might threaten to withhold a raise from a worker unless the quality of work improves.

These two power bases are the strongest. That means you are most likely to get what you want if you use the bases. However, they come with multiple strings attached. First, they aren't necessarily as easy as they might appear. There are a number of conditions that must be met before they can be effectively employed. Second, there are side effects associated with the use of these bases that may be troublesome or helpful in the future.

If you are going to successfully employ reward or coercion, you must choose your reward or threat carefully. First you must determine that your target either desires or wishes to avoid the outcome you are offering. Perhaps a tangible reward is not as important to your target as your good wishes.

It doesn't matter what you, as the wielder of influence likes or dislikes, the target must be considered. For example you would probably be much more effective in offering extra television time or a chocolate chip cookie or a hug to a school child as a reward than a big, steaming plate of spinach. Maybe you love spinach—if so, bon appétit. But it probably won't get you very far as a reward in this case.

You should also be sure that you are using a large enough reward or threat. If you ask workers to double production or you'll dock their pay a dime a day, don't expect much response. Your threat isn't "worth it."

Since both reward and coercion are resource based, it should go without saying that you had better have access to the necessary resources. And beyond that, the target must believe you have access. If, for example, you are unfortunate enough to be the supervisor of the boss's lazy daughter in your work group, threatening to fire her may be useless if she believes that Daddy won't let you do that. In addition to possessing the requisite resources, you must be willing to follow through on your promise or threat—and the target must believe you're serious. Parents sometimes threaten to "break your neck" if their kids don't stop some annoying behavior. Could an adult break a child's neck? Sure. Would they under most circumstances? Of course not. And the kids know it. So their behavior is unlikely to change.

So an important principle in the use of reward and coercion is this: DON'T BLUFF. If you have no intention of going through with the threat you may find yourself in the nasty situation of having your bluff called and looking the fool. And losing any credibility you might have had with the target, at least for a while. So think before you use these, particularly coercion.

I mentioned strings attached to the use of these two power bases. These involve the peripheral feelings that are created in the target. Rewards make us feel good. We like people who are nice to us. Thus the use of reward actually results in the side effect of having the target feel more positively toward the leader. We don't like people who threaten or hurt us. Thus the use of coercion often results in very negative feelings on the part of the target toward the leader.

Who cares? You should. For several reasons. First as we will see shortly, being disliked by your subordinates limits your ability to use other power bases. Second, often a threat will stop the behavior—but only in your presence. Tell a child not to eat cookies before dinner or they will be punished and you will probably not see them do it again. But the cookies will keep disappearing. You've driven the behavior underground and lost control of it entirely.

Informational power and expert power are based upon the leader's possession of knowledge that the target does not possess. Informational power is the weakest of all the power bases. **Informational power** involves providing the target with a single fact or piece of information that may or may not be relevant to their behavior. If I mention to a class that the campus police are ticketing all illegally parked cars on campus, I will probably have a strong impact on their behavior. However, if I mention that they're showing an "X-Files" rerun that evening and my students are not "X-Files" fans they won't watch the show and I've had no impact whatsoever.

In neither case do they see me as godlike and powerful. I simply knew something they didn't. If they tell me there's a sale at the shoe store and I rush out after class to buy shoes, they've influenced (had power over) me. Do I see them as controlling my behavior? Not a bit. If they'd told me there was a sale at the sporting goods store it wouldn't have affected my behavior in the least!

Expert power is a whole different ball game. When we are the target of **expert power** we allow our behavior to be influenced because we believe that the person exerting the influence has more knowledge, education, or training than we do. This effect may be perceived as much stronger because of the magnitude of the difference between target and leader. The expert is respected for their superiority.

There is a possible downside to expert power. Hovland, Janis, and Kelley (1953) referred to this as the **boomerang effect.** We discussed this response earlier as *reactance* (Brehm, 1966). When an individual tries to convince us that he or she knows more than we do we may rebel and do the opposite of what is suggested. So if we are to use expert power effectively we must be careful not to appear to be condescending or arrogant.

Legitimate and referent power are both based upon the relationship between the target and the leader. **Legitimate power** has a number of facets. Most commonly we think of legitimate power as equivalent to **authority** or **position power.** In other words, we have the right to influence others because of our reciprocal relationship. Leaders can influence followers, teachers can influence students, parents can influence children, police can influence the populace—not because of what they can offer us or how much they know, but because that's the social contract.

In order for this to work, both parties must agree to the terms of the contract. Otherwise the strength of legitimate power breaks down. Parents who had no trouble influencing their four-year-old child may discover that when the same child reaches her teens, as far as she's concerned, they no longer have the right or authority to control her behavior. Catholics are willing to listen to the edicts of the Pope regarding extremely private behavior, but Methodists could care less about what he has to say.

Two of the other faces of legitimate power rest on social norms. The first is the **norm of reciprocity.** In our society we expect that if we do a good deed for someone, that person "owes us one." Have you ever received an unexpected Christmas present from someone for whom you have nothing? This situation is extremely embarrassing to all concerned because the norm of reciprocity has been violated.

The norm also holds true for negative events. When we feel someone has caused us damage, we often at least fantasize about how to "get back" at them, whether we actually do or not. Thus if the norm of reciprocity is violated we can legitimately influence someone to redress the situation.

The second social norm that affects use of legitimate power is the **norm of equity.** We have a societal expectation (realistic or not) that things should be "fair." Thus if we have more than others, we can be expected (based on the norm) to share the wealth through volunteering or giving to charity. This also influences individuals to work for social causes such as civil rights when we perceive a certain group as having received fewer societal benefits because of their race or other characteristics beyond their control. We have been influenced by the "legitimate" expectation that fairness is appropriate.

The final face of legitimate power is the **legitimacy of dependence.** There are certain people who strongly influence our behavior through an appropriate expectation that we will take care of them. We gladly help a small child or an elderly individual across the street because they actually need our help to be safe. Even though we don't perceive them as powerful, they have influenced our behavior. In such situations and others such as aging parents or the ill, it is acceptable for the powerless to make demands on our behavior.

Sometimes, however, people make demands on us based upon a faked helplessness. Imagine that you're driving to work or school one day and you see a disabled vehicle beside the road (with a flat tire) and the driver standing beside the car wringing their hands and crying. Will someone stop to help? Maybe. But certainly more probably if the "victim" is a woman rather than man.

Even though any physically able adult is capable of changing a tire, stereotypically women aren't expected to know about such "guy things" as cars. And they're certainly given permission to cry in more situations than are men. In this case the individual is manipulating the legitimacy of dependence to their advantage. Very often this involves sex-role stereotypes. So I'm not just going to pick on women. Men who are very intelligent and capable when it comes to other machines have been known to at least feign ineptitude at the sight of a stove or a washing machine. What happens? Often someone else (probably a woman) will cook and do the laundry because nurturing and household drudgery is "women's work."

If I'm sounding a bit caustic at this point it is because while I believe it is absolutely appropriate and necessary to help those who truly need our help, I resent being manipulated by someone who could take care of themselves. My favorite science fiction writer, Robert Heinlien (1987), said that every adult should at the very least be able to change *both* a tire and a baby. My point is that feigning helplessness is not a way to enhance the perception of yourself as a powerful, competent adult.

 Have you ever made, or do you know someone who makes, use of the legitimacy of dependence to influence others? "Guilt tripping" can also fall into this category. How do you feel when someone tries to use this technique on you? Compare notes with someone of the opposite sex.

Referent power can be both positive and negative. It is based upon liking, admiring, and/or identifying with the leader. It can be based upon friendship. Your roommate asks to borrow your car Friday night and you lend it because he's your friend. Or your boss asks you to work over the weekend because of a sudden deadline shift and you do so because she doesn't make such demands unless they're absolutely necessary and you know she'll be in there every minute, too. Or a professor you particularly admire suggests that you consider going to a particular graduate school because he attended that school, so you apply. The negative side is that if the leader trying to use referent power is someone you don't respect or like, it won't work.

Referent power also plays a large role in advertising. Right now Michael Jordan, the basketball player retired from the Chicago Bulls advertises a large number of products in the media. He is perceived not only as successful, but also as a very nice guy. Kids want to be like Michael Jordan. So he advertises everything from underwear to cereal and children clamor for the products because they believe that by using the products they can be like their hero, Michael Jordan.

Let's examine the process of the use of power from the perspective of the leader. Raven (1992) presents a model with five steps in the influence process. First is the motive to influence. Why is it that the leader feels influence is necessary? Second is the assessment of the power bases available to the leader. What resources are available? What is the cost to benefit ratio of each power base? And what about negative side effects? The third step involves setting up the target. This may involve setting the stage or doing a preliminary favor (which would then make it easier to invoke the norm of reciprocity). Fourth is the choice of power base to use (which is also, of course, affected by the issues in the second step). The fifth and last step in the model is an evaluation of the effects of the influence attempt. Did it work? Were there side effects? The answers to these questions provide feedback to the first two steps of the model for use in future situations.

So what effects does the leader's power style have on the group and its productivity? Several recent pieces of research have sought to connect these two phenomena. Oyster (1992) surveyed members of the National Association for Female Executives as to the traits, behaviors, and power styles of their best and worst bosses.

In response to criticism of earlier studies that asked individuals to rank order the frequency of power styles (Schreisheim et al., 1991), a forced choice measure was created in which all possible combinations of the power bases were paired and the respondents were asked to indicate which most accurately described the bosses' typical behavior. Thus counts could be made which could be converted to rank orders.

It was found that bad male bosses and bad female bosses were "bad" in the same way—their style of power usage. The same held true for good bosses. "Bad" bosses were most likely to use coercive power, next most likely to use legitimate power, and least likely to use referent power. "Best" bosses used referent power most often, informational power next most often, and coercive power least often. (For you statistical buffs, the Spearman Rank Order Correlation was $-.72$, significant at the .0001 level. For the rest of you, this means that the order of frequency of use of the power bases was almost perfectly reversed between the two types of boss.)

STOP Do you think these findings are surprising? What expectations did you have for power use differences between male and female bosses? Have you ever had a female boss? Discuss with your class or group members your best and worst experiences with bosses and their uses of power.

This might be interesting, but what does it have to do with performance? Hogan (1993) studied employees of a national chemical company looking for the connection between perceived power use by a current supervisor and the performance ratings received by employees. Hogan also developed a new measurement system in which three-item subscales were developed for each power base and which were all significantly intercorrelated.

After receiving the rating scale from the employee, Hogan contacted the employee's supervisor (with the employee's permission) and requested a copy of the employee's most recent performance evaluation. The company in question rated employees on three characteristics: quality of work, quantity of work, and teamwork.

It was found that high ratings on quality of work were significantly related to higher use of reward and referent power and negatively related to use of coercion. Quantity of work was also negatively correlated with the use of coercion. In other words, supervisors who had been identified as using coercion frequently rated the employee as having done a lower quantity of work.

Teamwork ratings were positively rated with the use of reward, informational, expert, and referent power, and strongly negatively related to the use of coercion on the part of the supervisor.

So that completes the connection. Supervisors who use coercion are perceived as bad bosses. These bad bosses rate their employees as lower in all three evaluation categories than supervisors who use referent power (Oyster's "good" bosses) who rate their employees higher in quality and teamwork. So it would appear that style of power use at least affects the perception of productivity in the group.

Leadership Effectiveness

The final third of the original model was labeled by Campbell and others (1970) as **product efficiency** and we have been referring to it as **productivity.** We are going to consider two aspects of this factor: both the theories of leadership effectiveness that have been developed over the years, and the task traits that might affect the productivity of the group.

Much of the research on leadership effectiveness has focused on what I refer to as the "either/or" models of leadership. Two styles of leadership are compared to determine which is "better." And in many of these theories, individual leaders could be either/or one type of leader. The more recent scholarship has been somewhat more sophisticated in the examination of leadership effectiveness.

Theory X and Theory Y Leaders

One of the earliest studies of leadership effectiveness was conducted by Douglas McGregor (1960). Even more than a theory of leadership, these leadership styles were perceived as a pervasive world view held by the leader. **Theory X** leaders were described as having a somewhat misanthropic view of the world. They believed that people don't like to work, and thus must be forced to work (coercion). They also were perceived as believing that people don't want to think or make decisions—they just want to be secure. (Sounds a lot like our "bad" bosses, doesn't it?)

Theory Y leaders were described as having a much more positive perception of human beings. They believe that work is just as much a normal human activity as play or rest and don't believe that people must be coerced into work. They should, however, be rewarded when they achieve on the job. Finally, Theory Y leaders believe that people are eager to use their intellect and to make decisions and ask questions on the job.

Clearly these two perceptions of subordinates would indicate very different behavioral styles for leaders. Interestingly enough, both lead to **self-fulfilling prophecies.** The Theory X leader would feel she must always be present or the workers would slack off and not do their jobs. If forced to leave, the probability is that the workers would take a break. Arriving back on the scene and seeing the workers slacking off, the leader would say, "See, I told you. I have to be here or they won't work," not realizing that her own behavior is creating the situation. The Theory Y leader is much more relaxed about supervision, expecting that if people are resting they will get back to work eventually. So if he leaves, the workers' behavior probably won't change much at all. Upon his return he says, "See, they don't need me to hang on their shoulders to do a good job." Again, a self-fulfilling prophecy.

Which type of leader is more conducive to productivity? Independent research by Lewin, Lippitt, and White (1939) found that **autocratic leaders** (equivalent to Theory X) had higher productivity in terms of quantity, but lower levels of quality than democratic leaders (equivalent to Theory Y). In terms of social needs of the group, the **democratic leader** won hands down. Not only did the participants prefer the democratic leader, they liked each other better under democratic leadership!

The Ohio State Model

Ohio State research conducted during the 1960s (e.g., Fleishman & Peters, 1962; Fleishman & Harris, 1962) investigated the behavioral dimensions that were associated with leadership using a process known as **factor analysis.** This procedure (done by computer) takes a large number of initially separate terms and identifies which ones are rated similarly, thus sorting them into internally related categories. Starting with over 1,800 items, ten different categories were constructed. Questionnaire items were constructed for the dimensions which were administered to groups in industrial, educational, and military sites.

Factor analysis on these data identified two dimensions of leadership: *consideration* and *initiating structure*. **Consideration** is based upon the relationship between the leader and follower and is characterized by mutual trust, respect for ideas presented by subordinates, and concern for subordinates as individuals with feelings. **Initiating structure** is based much more on the task aspects of the group and reaching the group's goal. Again we trip over this same differentiation between task and socioemotional issues we first discussed in Chapter 1. Here again we also have an either/or approach to leadership. The question the research continued to follow was which style was most effective? Which affected productivity most positively?

Fiedler's Contingency Model

Fiedler (1967) began with the intention of identifying the "best" of the two leadership styles: **relationship-oriented** or **task-oriented.** He studied various already existing groups and identified which were successful and which were unsuccessful. Then he identified the style employed by the leader. No nice, neat pattern emerged. No one style was represented in all successful groups.

Upon examining the data further, however, Fiedler realized there was a pattern, albeit not the one he had expected to find. For the first time someone began to consider the situation in which the leadership was occurring.

Fiedler identified three important dimensions of the situation that affect the ease of leading the group. The first was the **structure of the task.** Groups performing highly structured tasks are much easier to lead than groups with unstructured tasks. For example, if I were asked to lead a group in constructing a table, it would be relatively easy because we all know what a table is, and generally how it should look. On the other hand, if you were appointed to head a commission to develop a source of power separate from internal combustion or solar power, where would you start?

The second important dimension dealt with **leader power.** Was the leader recognized as such by the group? How much power, and what types did the leader have at their disposal? A well-respected leader with lots of resources will have a much easier time of bringing the group to success than will a leader who has little respect and no resources.

Finally, the last dimension dealt with the **relationships within the group.** Do people like each other? Do they cooperate well with each other? Do they like the leader? A group full of dissension is far more difficult to lead than a group where there is a high level of positive feelings and cohesiveness.

If you take these three dimensions and rate situations on each, assigning either a + for positive conditions, or a − for negative conditions, you identify eight types of groups:

$$+++ \quad ++- \quad +-+ \quad +-- \quad -++ \quad -+- \quad --+ \quad ---$$

where the first symbol identifies the structure, the second the leadership, and the third the relationships. Fiedler found that the successful groups in each type had in common the style of the leader. Thus the most effective leadership depended upon, or was contingent upon the situation. Thus the name of the theory: **Fiedler's contingency theory.** In the most positive of conditions, task-oriented leadership was most likely to result in a successful group. The same was true in the worst of all possible worlds at the other end of the spectrum (although very few of these groups were successful at their tasks). In the middle of the spectrum it appeared that a key ingredient in the best type of leadership had to do with the relationship dimension of the group. Under conditions where relationships were problematic, a relationship-oriented leader was more likely to be successful. So Fiedler's first important finding was that there is no one best style of leadership, that the situation influences the best style.

The second important finding in Fiedler's research was that through effective leadership the leader could move the group from one position on the spectrum to another. In a group where relationships were difficult a relationship-oriented leader would be best. However, if she was any good, she would improve the relationships in the group to the point that the type of group changed. Perhaps into a type of group for which a task-oriented leader would be best.

Unfortunately, Fiedler was an either/or theorist in another way. He believed that leaders could either be relationship-oriented OR task-oriented, which becomes a problem in the example. When the group changes do we change leaders? That's possible in a mature group that has moved to the stage of development where division of labor is sensible. But it would create havoc in an immature group. So what are we to do?

The Managerial Grid

Enter Blake and Mouton (1964) and the **managerial grid.** They believed that each person is probably better at and more comfortable with either a leadership style that focuses on **concern for people** or a **concern for production.** (Are we seeing a pattern here?) They would measure individuals on each of these dimensions and place them on a scale from 1 to 9, with the lower score indicating the less facility with the style. By creating a matrix with concern for people on one axis and concern for production on the other, they came up with an 81 square matrix. Each individual would be placed in the matrix based on their scores on both scales. Blake and Mouton's goal was to train leaders to balance their skills in both areas, and to move them as far as possible up the balanced scale, with the ideal being a leader who is maximal in both styles, the 9,9 leader.

Of course this is an ideal. But it gets us out of the corner into which Fiedler painted us. IF leaders have both sets of skills, and IF through their leadership they move the group to another spot on Fiedler's spectrum, then the leader can simply shift leadership style to that which is most effective for the group at that moment. So a good leader recognizes that there are different skills necessary at different times and is capable of using the currently most effective style.

Path-Goal Leadership

The **path-goal model** of leadership developed by House (1971) is a contingency model that is also based upon different types of leadership styles. House identifies four types of leader: the **directive leader,** the **achievement-oriented leader,** the *supportive leader,* and the *participative leader.* The first two are reminiscent of the task-oriented or orienting structure type leader; the second two remind us of the relationship-oriented or consideration type leader.

House's basic premise is that success for the group will depend upon proper choice of leadership style, and that the "best" style is dependent not only upon situational factors (those that Fiedler identified), but also upon characteristics of the other members of the group. This theory, like that of Blake and Mouton, assumes that individuals are capable of adapting their behaviors to the most appropriate style.

Just as you thought the theories couldn't get any more complex, along come Vroom and Yetton (1973) and the **normative model** of leadership. The theory was further updated by Vroom and Jago (1978).

This theory identifies five different leadership types, based upon the amount of control over group decision making and problem solving the leader reserves for herself and how much she allows the group. The autocratic-type leader has two levels, as does the **consultative-type leader,** while the group-type leader has one level. In all but the last the leader ultimately makes the decision. The determination of which style is most appropriate is determined by going through a complex decision tree (see Figure 8.1).

This model has twelve contingency variables that help determine the most appropriate leadership style. It also mechanizes the process to the point that less subjectivity and intuition are required of the leader.

We haven't, of course, covered all of the leadership effectiveness theories out there. You've gotten what I think are the more important and relevant theories. What I hope you have gotten from this discussion is that different situations call for different types of leadership styles and behaviors and that flexibility and the ability to identify the best style at any one time are critical for effective leadership. Having identified the importance of the situational variables in the effectiveness of a leader, we will turn to the task variables that both influence the appropriate leadership style and the probability of a successful outcome.

Task Traits Affecting Leadership

It's easier to succeed at some tasks than at others. Certain tasks, by their very characteristics are more difficult. In a truly difficult situation leadership becomes a much more trying and problematic task. Landy and Trumbo (1980) identified a list of task issues that affect productivity. The first is **time pressure.** Putting together a prize-winning grant proposal is much easier in a week than it is in a day. The same is true for an "A" paper in a course on group dynamics. No matter how good the leader or what style he adopts, severe time urgency is bound to negatively affect productivity.

Physical danger is also going to reduce the productivity of a group. A mountain-climbing team racing another team to the top of Mt. Everest is going to need to be cautious in order to avoid disaster. So is a group publishing a politically radical newsletter in a politically repressive country where they may need to disappear at a moment's notice or at least keep looking over their shoulders as they work.

Another task issue is the **permissible error rate.** A group planning a party can afford to have someone forget to buy ice. A surgical team doing heart transplants cannot afford to make any errors. Perfection is extraordinarily difficult for human beings to attain.

The extent of *external stress* can also make leadership more difficult. As I write this book the economies of a number of countries, such as Japan, are undergoing severe turmoil. Trying to lead the country, or even your own cabinet under such conditions is much more difficult than when the economy is stable and favorable.

FIGURE 8.1. The highly complex leadership decision-making tree of the Normative Model.

QR	Quality requirement:	How important is the technical quality of this decision?
CR	Commitment requirement:	How important is subordinate commitment to the decision?
LI	Leader's information:	Do you have sufficient information to make a high-quality decision?
ST	Problem structure:	Is the problem well structured?
CP	Commitment probability:	If you were to make the decision yourself, is it reasonably certain that your subordinate(s) would be committed to the decision?
GC	Goal congruence:	Do subordinates share the organizational goals to be attained in solving this problem?
CO	Subordinate conflict:	Is conflict among subordinates over preferred solutions likely?
CO	Subordinate information:	Do subordinates have sufficient information to make a high-quality decision?

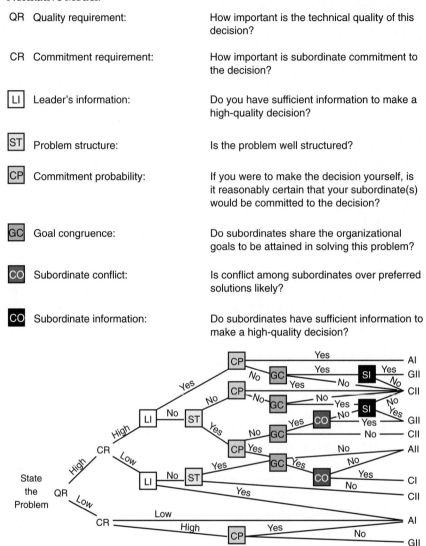

The extent of the group's **autonomy,** the **scope of the task,** and the **level of ambiguity** of the task all can contribute to improving or damaging productivity. If the group is given very little room to make decisions (low levels of autonomy), then they are not really free to operate in an optimal manner. The Gay Student Union that wants to participate in the newspaper of a Catholic high school will probably find very little opportunity to make their own decisions. Rebuilding a city or rebuilding a monument are tasks with a very different scope. Generally, the broader the task, the more difficult to achieve optimal productivity, especially if there are other factors such as time pressure. Finally, is the city to be rebuilt as it was, or do you want a new design? If the group is not told, they may have to guess—which leaves substantial room for disaster.

Finally, the *importance of the task* and the *meaningfulness of the work* affect productivity. In these cases, however, the higher the level, the more likely that productivity will be enhanced rather than impaired. A group of laboratory technicians working on a cure for AIDS or cancer would probably perceive their task as both important and meaningful and would likely become quite personally involved in the success of the group at their task. It would probably be much more difficult for one of fifty file clerks in a large organization to feel their work was either important or meaningful.

Effects of Group Climate

So now we've looked at the personal characteristics of both the leader and the group members, the behaviors and power use of the leader, and the product efficiency. We're not done with the model until we examine the context in which the leadership opportunity is occurring. The **group climate** is the shared meanings the group creates.

Reviewing the literature on climate, Campbell, Dunnette, Lawler, and Weick (1970) found five common factors of climate across the research. These were **individual autonomy** within the group; *degree of imposed structure* from above; **reward orientation** (how are the goodies distributed); the *amount of consideration, warmth, and support* shown by the environment; and the **level of cooperativeness** and quality of relationships.

So there we have our elaborated model. At this point you probably understand just how difficult it can be to lead effectively. It often has very little to do with you as the leader, but is affected by the environment or the task or the group members you are expected to lead to success.

But this entire chapter to this point has assumed that a leader is necessary to a group. Is that true? I often find my students denying the existence of a leader in the group as if they were protecting someone from a shameful label.

SO WHO NEEDS LEADERS ANYWAY?

There are some situations that require leadership more than others. In an extremely small group, or a group of highly trained professionals, or a group with a very routine task, leadership may not be very important. The term **neutralizers** was coined by Bass (1990) to describe characteristics that make leadership unnecessary or obsolete. As you can see in Table 8.1, Kerr and Jermeir identified characteristics of the subordinate, the task, and of the organization that will substitute for leadership.

Life Cycle Theory of Leadership

There is one theory that posits that the need for leadership depends upon the level of maturity of the group and its members. Hersey and Blanchard's **life cycle theory of leadership** (1969) can be seen in Figure 8.2. There's a lot going on in this model. Along the bottom of the figure you can see the changes in what Hersey and Blanchard refer to as *readiness*. Each of the four levels of readiness are associated with specific leader behaviors, which decrease in directiveness as the group matures.

The theory combines the idea of task-oriented leadership and relationship-oriented leadership into four leadership behaviors: *Telling* (S1) which is high task and low relationship. This style involves very directive behavior and is appropriate for groups who are at level R1—unable and unwilling. *Selling* (S2) combines high-task and high-relationship behaviors and is paired with groups who have reached the unable, but willing stage of development (R2). *Participating* (S3) is low-task and high-relationship behavior in which the leader begins to share decision making with the group which has matured to the R3 level of readiness—able and unwilling. Finally, when the group reaches the highest

Table 8.1. Substitutes for Leadership

Characteristic:	Will Tend to Neutralize	
	Relationship-oriented, Supportive, People-centered Leadership: Consideration, Support, and Interaction Facilitation	Task-orientated, Instrumental, Job-centered Leadership: Initiating Structure, Goal Emphasis, and Work Facilitation
Of the subordinate		
1. Ability, experience, training, knowledge		X
2. Need for independence	X	X
3. "Professional" orientation	X	X
4. Indifference toward organizational rewards	X	X
Of the task		
5. Unambiguous and routine		X
6. Methodologically invariant		X
7. Provides its own feedback concerning accomplishment		X
8. Intrinsically satisfying	X	
Of the organization		
9. Formalization (explicit plans, goals, and areas of responsibility)		X
10. Inflexibility (rigid, unbending rules and procedures)		X
11. Highly specified and active advisory and staff functions		X
12. Closely knit, cohesive work groups	X	X
13. Organizational rewards not within the leader's control	X	X
14. Spatial distance between superior and subordinates	X	X

Source: From "Substitutes for Leadership: Their Meaning and Measurement," by S. Kerr and J. M. Jermeir (1978). *Organizational Behavior and Human Performance, 22,* pp. 375–403. Copyright © 1978 by Academic Press. Reprinted with permission.

level of maturity (R4), the leadership style is **delegating** (S4) in which the leader steps back and allows the able and willing group to essentially lead themselves. This theory, then, posits a strong need for directive leaders early on, with the need for leadership declining as the group's level of maturity increases.

GENDER AND CULTURAL EFFECTS ON LEADERSHIP AND POWER

A common thread in implicit theories of leadership is the characteristic of masculinity. What does this mean for women in leadership positions? Unfortunately, nothing good. In this section we will examine the research on women in leadership in the United States, the effects of various cultures on leadership, and the interaction between gender and leadership across cultures.

In the United States, sex-role stereotypes are important in the studies of women as leaders. The appropriate characteristics of women are seen as incompatible with those expected of a manager or leader (Schein, 1973; Heilman et al., 1989). Lower expectations are held for female leaders, which may negatively affect their ability and opportunities to advance. The mismatch goes so far that women in traditionally male jobs (such as leaders) are often referred to as "gender aliens" (Bailyn, 1987). Supporting evidence was collected by Lips (1985)

FIGURE 8.2. Situational leadership model.
Source: *Napier, Rodney W. and Matti K. Gershenfeld,* Groups: Theory and Experience, 5th edition. *Copyright © 1993 by Houghton Mifflin Company. Used with permission.*

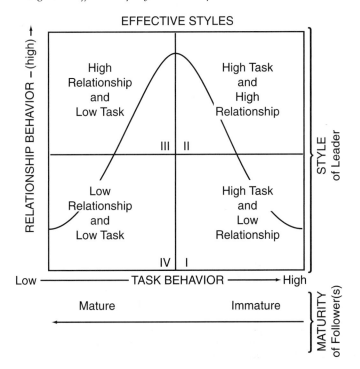

who asked college students to identify the most powerful person they knew. Ninety-one percent of the men and 69 percent of the women named a man.

The almost automatic status differential between women and men is one of the keys to understanding why the image of a powerful woman causes discomfort in so many people.

(Lips, 1991, p. 20)

This discomfort is shared or at least recognized by women as well as men. Even when in a leadership position, women tend to try to avoid the label of "leader." They tend to refer to themselves as **organizers** or **coordinators** instead (Andrews, 1992). That is, of course, if women are perceived as leaders at all.

A 1965 survey in the *Harvard Business Review* of 2,000 business executives found that 31 percent believed women to be "temperamentally unfit for management." Thus people often ignore cues to leadership status they would use to identify men as leaders. The position at the **head of the table** is usually associated with leadership. Porter and Geis (1981) found that in all-male, all-female, and gender-mixed groups with a man at the head of the table, the person at the head of the table was identified as the leader almost all of the time. When the woman was at the head of the table in a mixed group, more than half the time the male closest to the head of the table was identified as leader instead.

And what of uniquely female characteristics such as pregnancy? Corse (1990) found that both men and women were uncomfortable with the idea of a pregnant leader, and expressed very stereotypic views. The pregnant leader was perceived as passive and nurturing and, perhaps because she dared to violate expectations for leader behavior, she was seen as rigid, mean, hostile, and aggressive. Consistent? No. But then those who violate the norms tend to get punished. And what nastier epithet to throw at an expectant mom than hostile, mean, and aggressive?

So what if the woman leader tries to "look the part"? Is it really true that "clothes make the man," or in this case, the woman? Temple and Loewen (1993) compared perceptions of women portrayed as managers wearing or not wearing a jacket. Women wearing the jacket were perceived as having more expert and legitimate power than women without the jacket. This fits with the

Women must work harder than men at being recognized as effective leaders.

conventional wisdom that suits are an important indicator of status and with the "dress for success" research of Molloy (1993).

 Do women and men leaders behave differently? Should they? What do you think?

While it is encouraging to see more women in leadership positions than in the past, many women are required to "act like a man" in order to succeed.

(King, 1995, p. 67)

The research has actually found very mixed results. Let's first examine the research that indicates that certain behaviors are perceived as differentially appropriate for male and female leaders.

Hackman, Hillis, Paterson, and Furness (1993) found that masculinity was perceived as an effective demeanor for both male and female leaders. Feminine behavior was only effective for male leaders. In particular, female participants were more critical of females who appeared feminine than were male participants. What behaviors are perceived as masculine or feminine? Cann and Siegfried (1990) found that the consideration style of leadership from the Ohio State studies was perceived as feminine and the initiating structure style was perceived as masculine.

Oyster (1992) found that while there was no difference in the probability that a "worst boss" was identified as male or female, there was a significantly higher than chance probability that a female boss would be rated as "best boss." And recall that these best bosses excelled in referent power. In another study on the interaction between leadership type and power, Tavistock study groups' consultants were compared with trainers of T groups. There was an interaction between gender and type of power. Female leaders of T groups were rated least competent and least potent. Male trainers were the most positively valued (Morrison & Stern, 1985).

In a study of West Point cadet ratings of leadership ability, Rice (1984) found that males were rated higher during two of the three rating periods. Physical ability and performance were the characteristics most directly correlated with leadership. Both of these, of course, are perceived as masculine behaviors. Also, the military environment tends to be particularly tough on females.

What about the studies that find no differences between the behaviors or perceptions of female and male leaders? A comparison of direct versus indirect power use by female and male leaders conducted by Sagrestino (1992) found that the type of influence used was more important than gender in rating leaders. Direct strategies were used by experts and indirect strategies by novices, but there were not gender differences. Oyster (1992) also found that "good" bosses and "bad" bosses were identifiable by power use pattern rather than gender. And Hawkins (1995) found no differences in the production of task-related as compared to relationship-related communication between female and male leaders.

So what do these contradictory results mean in practical terms? In other words, how should one behave as a leader if one happens to lack the Y chromosome? Obviously our culture is in a state of flux regarding that matter. The fact is that more and more women are entering the work force and are moving up into leadership positions. Perhaps a critical mass of female leaders will help settle the question. However, not everyone believes that simply bringing women into nontraditional leadership positions is even a sound idea.

> *Bringing more women into politics will not translate directly into a proportionate amount of female power and influence. In fact, a powerful backlash may occur when women exceed a certain critical mass in a highly masculinized institution such as legislative politics.*
>
> *(Duerst-Lahti & Kelley, 1995, p. 189)*

What about cultural differences in power and leadership? Given what we already know about different values across cultures, we should expect to find not only differences based on culture alone, but also the collision between culture and gender. In fact, that is exactly what we often find. But we also find situations where we do NOT find differences we might expect.

In terms of cultural differences, interesting comparisons can be made between research conducted in Europe as opposed to the Far East. Western nations tend to be more individualistic in nature and Eastern nations more collectivistic (Triandis, 1994). Chilladdinai, Malloy, Imamura, and Yamaguchi (1987) compared the preferred leadership style of Canadian and Japanese male athletes. The Japanese preferred the more supportive relationship-oriented style of leadership more than did the Canadians. Japanese five-year-olds were observed while playing, then their behaviors were factor analyzed. Two factors emerged: consideration (equivalent to relationship-orientation) and facilitation of play. The child in the central role in the group (identifiable as the leader) showed more leadership behaviors based on consideration. No differences were found on facilitation of play (Fukuda, Fukuda, & Hicks, 1994).

In the Far East there are three distinct streams of preferred leadership style. In East Asia there is a split between a preference for participative and direct leadership. In South Asia there is a preference for remote, directive leadership. And in Southeast Asia there is a preference for autocratic leadership (Swierczek, 1991). This is supported by findings by Hui (1990) that autocratic leadership is reinforced in Chinese society, and that in India participative leaders are perceived as weak and indecisive (Padaki, 1989). However (isn't there always a "however"?), other research on the dichotomy from the Ohio State research has found that the most desirable leaders are high in both characteristics in India (Sinha, 1980), Taiwan (Cheng & Yang, 1977), and in Western cultures (Tjosvold, 1984).

As in the United States, the combination of gender and leadership can prove to be problematic in other cultures. Bhatnagar (1988) identified the social problems facing professional women in the workplace as social isolation, difficulty finding mentors, token status, sex-role stereotyping, and discrimination—problems similar to those faced by American women in the workplace. In research comparing two European countries, Bruins, den Ouden, Depret, and Extra (1993) found that when participants in the Netherlands and Poland were shown an organizational chart with themselves at the bottom and asked to nominate someone for an open leadership position at the top of the chart, Dutch males strongly overnominated themselves. Dutch females nominated themselves, another female, or the person just under the open position in the hierarchy.

Other research on the topic conducted in the Netherlands tested the gender-role congruency hypothesis (Rojahn & Willemsen, 1994). Males rated leaders in incongruent gender roles (either considerate men or task-oriented women) as less effective than those leaders who lived up to the sex-role stereotypes. This same male preference for congruency between gender and stereotypical behavior was found in Australia (Onyx, Leonard, & Vivekananda, 1995) in that powerful women were seen significantly more positively by women than by men.

Thus it would appear that sex roles play an important role in the perception and acceptance of leaders around the world. As America becomes more and more diverse culturally, and the workplace equalizes in terms of gender, it will be most interesting to see how these issues are resolved.

Summary

In this chapter we've explored the many facets of leadership. We've talked about the role of leader and the task of leadership. We've discussed the paths individuals take to become leaders, and the traits, skills, behaviors, and styles of leaders. We've also identified situations where leadership is not as important, and the life cycle theory of leadership that identifies not just characteristics but also maturity that might neutralize the need for leadership. Finally we discussed the extensive research on the effects of and interactions between gender and culture on the behavior and perceptions of leaders.

Key Terms

achievement-oriented leader
appointed leaders
authority
autocratic leadership
autonomy
behavioral approach to leadership
boomerang effect
charismatic leadership
coercive power
concern for people
concern for production
consideration
consultative-type leaders
coordinators
delegating
democratic leadership
directive leader
emergent leaders

expert power
factor analysis
Fiedler's contingency theory
group climate
group leader
head-of-the-table effect
idiosyncrasy credits
implicit leadership theories
individual autonomy
informational power
initiating structure
leader
leader effectiveness
leader power
legitimacy of dependence
legitimate power
level of ambiguity
level of cooperativeness

life cycle theory of leadership
managerial grid
managers
neutralizers
normative model
norm of equity
norm of reciprocity
Ohio State research
organizers
path-goal model
permissible error rate
person characteristics
physical danger
position power
power bases
power from, over, to
process behaviors
product efficiency
productivity

Key Terms (continued)

referent power	reward power	task-oriented leadership
relationship-oriented leadership	role of leader	Theory X
	scope of the task	Theory Y
relationships within the group	self-fulfilling prophecies	time pressure
	structure of the task	trait
reward orientation	target	

APPLICATION

Leadership Gone Awry: Charles Manson and "Family"

Charles Manson did not enter the world under the most auspicious of circumstances. He was born on November 12, 1934 in Cincinnati, Ohio to a sixteen-year-old, unmarried prostitute. His mother continued in her profession and Manson was convicted for the first time when he was five years old for helping his mother "roll" (steal from) her customers while they were otherwise distracted. His mother committed him to reform school at the age of 11 years old. He then spent the next twenty-one years in and out of penal institutions (Boar & Blundell, 1983). In the intervals between incarcerations, Manson married, fathered a child, divorced, and entered into other common law relationships.

Manson was released from prison in 1967, the height of the "hippie" movement and he went directly to the Haight-Ashbury neighborhood of San Francisco, the epicenter of the movement. He quickly warmed to the lifestyle, particularly the use of drugs and the freely available sex. He began to attract a group of followers, particularly women. Many of these people came from upper middle-class backgrounds but were attracted to the excitement and danger of the hippie world. They included Mary Brunner (by whom he fathered a

Charles Manson used coercive and referent methods of leadership in convincing his "family" to commit murder.

child), Catherine Share, Patricia Krenwinkle, Lynne Fromme, Susan Atkins, Ruth Moorehouse and her father Dean, Paul Watkins, and "Tex" Watson. The group revolved around Manson, sex, drugs, and rock and roll. Manson played the guitar and wanted to become a rock star.

Eventually the group evolved into what they referred to as a family. The characteristics of the "family" were similar to those in other groups identified as cults: (1) the leader was a charismatic figure; (2) the members have a cause which justifies their existence and is supported by violence; (3) the cause is based on an irrational philosophy of the need to protect whomever the group identifies as the "underdog"; (4) they were mostly middle class and white; (5) the violence of the group was purposeful; (6) the women were key in the violence (as they were in the Weathermen and the Symbionese Liberation Army that kidnapped heiress Patty Hearst); (7) the members were rigid and immature; (8) the followers and leader formed a symbiotic relationship; and (9) the group was emotion oriented.

Tiring of San Francisco, Manson and his group bought an old school bus and toured the California coast, went to Texas, then settled in the Los Angeles area where Manson might have a better shot at stardom. Upon reaching Los Angeles, Manson met Dennis Wilson, a member of the singing group the Beach Boys and the group actually lived with Wilson for a brief time until Wilson threw them out. They then moved to the outskirts of Los Angeles to Spahn Ranch.

The family was extremely structured. The few male members were the "deputies" for Manson. They took care of the vehicles and procured women for Manson. They also stole and faked identifications to make money. Lynne Fromme ("Squeaky" as she was known) was the head of the women. The group lived communally and the women played very traditional, subservient roles. They cooked and sewed for the group and were physically punished if they did not behave as Fromme or Manson wished. Their level of status can be inferred from the fact that the men were fed first, then the dogs were fed before the women were allowed to eat (Livsey, 1980). The women had to have sex with whomever Manson chose. None of the members were allowed to use contraception, alcohol, or wear glasses. The group generally avoided "hard" drugs, preferring hallucinogens and stimulants.

In his quest for rock stardom, Manson actually managed to meet Terry Melcher—a record producer (and Doris Day's son). However, by February of 1969 it was clear that his singing career was not to be. Just as the group lost that cohesive factor and began to splinter, the Beatles singing group released their "White Album." Manson announced to the group that the songs were coded messages that ordered him to start a race war in the United States which he would call "Helter Skelter" (Bugliosi, 1974). After starting the war, the group would escape to the desert and wait while society destroyed itself. For this they needed money. Their first move in this direction was to murder Gary Hinman for his money. This they used to accumulate food, maps, and weapons for their exodus to the desert.

In order to ignite the race war, Manson planned several spectacular murder sprees. On Saturday, August 9 and Sunday, August 10, 1969, they were carried out. Manson accompanied the group to the first location, but did not actually enter the house or physically commit the murders. The house belonged (coincidentally?) to Terry Melcher. Melcher, however, had sublet the house to producer Roman Polanski and his wife, Sharon Tate. Because Polanski had to be out of the country on business and Tate was eight months pregnant, she had a number of friends with her at the house that night. Members of Manson's group murdered Tate, Abigail Folger (of the coffee family), Voytek Frykowski, Jay Sebring, and Steven Parent. The bodies were found stabbed numerous times and with rope around their necks. Tate's child did not survive. On the front door in blood was written the word "PIG" (a common epithet for the police at the time).

The next evening, Rosemary and Leno LaBianca were the designated victims. They, too, were savagely murdered. On the walls of their home, in their blood, were written: "Death to Pigs," "Rise," and "Healter Skelter" (misspelled that way).

The two murder sprees put Los Angelenos into a state of terror, but did not instigate the race war Manson wanted. On August 16, the police raided the Spahn Ranch and arrested Manson, Atkins, Watson, Leslie van Houton, Krenwinkle, Robert Beausoleil, and Steve Grogan. A number of the "family" escaped arrest. On August 26, "Shorty" Shea, a ranch hand at Spahn Ranch was found murdered—apparently because he was believed to be the individual who alerted police.

To this day, Manson, Atkins, van Houton, and Krenwinkle remain in prison, having been given life sentences for the crimes. Watson spent a lesser sentence in prison. Fromme is also in prison for a subsequent attempt to assassinate President Gerald Ford. Manson periodically comes up for parole and each time announces that he will repeat his behavior if released. Parole appears unlikely. But Manson still claims innocence:

> *Everyone says that I was the leader of those people, but I was actually the follower of the children . . . I didn't break God's law and I didn't break man's law.*
> **(Bugliosi, 1974, p. 500)**

Discussion Questions

Apply the concepts from the chapter to consider the following questions:

1. Manson denies that he was the leader of the group. What evidence can you cite to identify him as the leader of the "family"?
2. Using three of the leadership effectiveness theories presented in the chapter, discuss Manson's leadership of the family.
3. What effects of the group culture do you think were most influential in the behavior of Manson and his group members?
4. Which do you think were more important to Manson's leadership—his traits or his behaviors?
5. Speculate on the types of power that were typically employed in the Manson family.

Intra- and Intergroup Conflict

What Would YOU Predict?

Danielle and Tammy are in a group whose goal is to plan the senior prom for Magoo High School. Danielle wants to have a romantic theme, and Tammy wants to have a patriotic theme. Danielle is very used to getting whatever she wants. Tammy really doesn't care that much about the theme—she's on the committee so she can put it on college applications. What techniques will the two girls use to resolve to deal with this conflict?

INTRODUCTION

Although we have dealt with conflict indirectly throughout this text, it is now time to turn our undivided attention to the phenomenon. We will start by defining exactly what we mean by, and our basic assumptions about conflict. We will examine sources and levels of conflict as well as the positive and negative results brought about by conflict. We will look at process dimensions of conflict such as stages and escalation, and discuss ways to handle conflict appropriately. After discussing the cultural effects on conflict and conflict resolution, in the Application section we will look at the conflict in the United States military created by the question of homosexuals serving in the military.

235

There are many types of conflict. We can have **individual conflict** (e.g., a clash of motives); we can have **interpersonal conflicts** within the group, **intragroup conflict** (such as **autistic, contingent,** and **escalating conflict** discussed in Chapter 3); we can have conflict between groups, **intergroup conflict,** or we can have **interorganizational conflict** (DuBrin, 1992). In this chapter we will focus on intragroup and intergroup conflict. In each case, many of the basic principles are the same.

Schmidt and Kochman (1972) define two basic prerequisites for conflict: (1) **goal incompatibility,** and (2) perceived opportunity for *interference* or blocking. The first prerequisite assumes we are dealing with what is known as a **zero-sum** situation. In a zero-sum situation, if I win, you lose. And the amount I win is the total you lose. An example is the game of poker. If I leave the table with $10 more than I sat down with, the other players are leaving with a total of $10 less. Conflict can arise, then, when we both can't get what we want in a situation. There's a happy winner and a resentful loser.

The important word in the second prerequisite is "perceived." Do I think that by my actions I can prevent you from winning the situation? Whether or not my perception is accurate is less important than my belief.

There are both objective and subjective aspects to the prerequisites. Usually goal incompatibility is fairly objective in that it can be verifiable. If not verifiable, the tendency to conflict will be strongly influenced by group culture or climate that encourages or discourages this behavior. A good example of the model is the game of football. The goal is to win the game. Only one team can win so we have a verifiable situation of goal incompatibility. And not only do the teams try to make as many points for themselves as possible, they try to prevent (block) the other team from scoring.

Dipboye, Smith, and Howell (1994) use a similar definition for conflict. It is defined as:

> . . . *activities that are incompatible in that one activity obstructs, interferes, impairs, or in some other way lessens the effectiveness of another activity.*
> **(Dipboye, Smith, and Howell, 1994, p. 195)**

As we continue our discussion, we will make several basic assumptions about conflict (O'Connell & O'Connell, 1997). First, conflict is inevitable. We cannot have individuals interacting with each other who think precisely alike at all times. If we did, we wouldn't need a group for anything. The second basic assumption is that if not recognized and dealt with, conflict has a tendency to go underground only to emerge in ways that can have serious consequences for the group.

In Chapter 7 when we discussed decision making I said that the possibility of simply doing nothing should always be considered. Not with conflict. Ignoring conflict is akin to ignoring that little fire in the wastebasket under your desk. Not only is it not going away, it's going to get worse. Finally, we will work from the assumption that handled correctly conflict keeps the group fresh and creative, creating better and more innovative ideas and solutions.

SOURCES OF CONFLICT

Conflict has many potential sources, within and between groups. In this chapter we have already identified goal compatibility and zero-sum thinking as sources. In Chapter 3 we discussed false perceptions as the source of autistic conflict, and in Chapter 4 we identified communication difficulties as providing for potential conflict.

We can also have conflict as a result of **scarce resources.** If there is a limited amount of money available in an organization (and there seemingly always is), departments within the organization will find themselves in conflict over who can get the money they need to operate. Within a group, two individuals may come into conflict over the scarce resource of the role of leader. And when there's any prize to be won, there's usually only one blue ribbon.

Personality clashes may be the source of conflict, as can **whistle-blowing, job discrimination, sexual harassment, separation of knowledge and authority, ambiguity about power,** and **status incongruities** (DuBrin, 1992). Some roles or jobs such as auditors or safety inspectors have **conflict-prone responsibilities** as part of their role (Brilhart, 1986). And the idea of relative deprivation (Bernstein & Crosby, 1980) can result in both intra- and intergroup conflict. Most of this list can deal with both intragroup and intergroup conflict. Rather than just leave it at a list, let's examine each one separately.

Personality clashes are inevitable in some groups. You are not going to like everyone you meet, and everyone you meet is not going to like you (sorry). However, in a situation that requires interdependence, such as a group, you must behave in a professional manner and be sure that your disagreements are based upon the group task and not just sniping at each other. And recognize that just because you disagree with someone, you don't automatically or necessarily have a personality conflict with them. One of my colleagues had a characteristic which I respected greatly. He disagreed with me about almost everything we discussed in meetings. However, once the meeting was over he was able to leave the disagreements behind and resume a collegial relationship.

A jockey urges his mount on to win the race,
thereby attaining the scarce resource of first place.

Not everyone can do that. Some people hold grudges. This is not good for the group. By refusing to work well with others, the individual is depriving the group of their resources. Such a group has problems with social issues and should work to solve them.

Whistle-blowing and job discrimination are most likely to occur in formal groups such as those in the work setting. Whistle-blowers are individuals who identify some inappropriate behavior and convey the information to an authority. Children call them "tattletales," and you can remember how popular they were. On a sports team, one of the players might sell the play-book to another team. One of their teammates finds out and tells the coach. Or an employee of the State Department discovers that a colleague is selling classified information to another government and reports the behavior to a superior.

Whistle-blowing is actually a noble behavior, but if a whistle is blown, expect it to create conflict. In the scandal over President Clinton and Monica Lewinsky, his popularity ratings held up very well (still above 50%). Ms. Lewinsky, on the other hand, had popularity ratings down almost in the single digits, even with people who believed the allegations. Why? She rocked the boat. Whistle-blowers call our attention to matters that cannot be ignored and are unpleasant to handle. So we tend to blame the bearer of bad news rather than the creator of the situation.

STOP Since whistle-blowing results in attention to group problems, what steps can you think of that could be taken to prevent the usual punishing reaction to whistle-blowers? How do you think whistle-blowers should be treated? Have you ever blown the whistle? What happened to you?

Job discrimination is another situation that is more likely to occur in formal settings; however, it is not limited to these environments. If a group will not consider an individual as leader, even though the person is capable, experienced, and good with people, simply because this person uses a wheelchair for mobility, that's discrimination. If a woman is not considered for a promotion because she's pregnant, or over 40 years old, or a Vietnam Veteran, that's discrimination. And all the examples given are illegal. But you can be certain that the individual being discriminated against is at least not going to be a happy camper, and may well create a conflict within the group trying to receive fair treatment.

Sexual harassment can, unfortunately, occur in any group setting. There is no agreed upon definition of sexual harassment, so this can be a particularly problematic area. Some behaviors such as a leader demanding sexual favors in order for the target to remain in the group are clearly inappropriate (and illegal). But sexual harassment can be much more subtle and can happen to men as well as to women. Generally, sexual harassment is an individual in a position of power using that power (even implicitly) to bully a person of lesser power in a sexual manner. Many organizations consider even consensual relationships between a superior and a subordinate, or a professor and a student, inappropriate. There is always the question of whether the subordinate would have said yes if they were on an equal level.

Conflicts over power such as the separation of knowledge and authority, ambiguity about power, and status incongruities can also occur in any type of group. When the individual in the position of authority knows less about the task than other members and is leading the group in an inappropriate direction, members will be most unhappy, and may rebel—causing conflict. Ambiguity about who has the power to do what in a group is a form of role ambiguity that can become quite serious. This can be a problem when several people believe they have the power and have incompatible goals and ideas or when no one wants the power and the group stagnates.

Status incongruities are also known as **rank disequilibrium** (Rubin, Pruitt, & Kim, 1994). When one group member feels that another group member is getting more authority and power than they deserve, they make what Rubin and others (1994) refer to as **invidious comparisons.** This problem exists when:

> *. . . there are multiple criteria for assessing people's merit or contributions, and some people are higher on one criterion and lower on another criterion than others. In our society, for example, both experience and education are sources of on-the-job status. People with experience tend to believe that experience makes the most relevant contribution, whereas people with education tend to believe the opposite. When these two kinds of people have to work together, each is likely to feel more deserving of rewards than the other, and conflict is especially likely to develop.*
>
> **(Rubin et al., 1994, p. 19)**

While the examples discussed above are primarily involved in intragroup conflict, many of them can also play a role in intergroup conflict. Countries go to war with each other for scarce resources such as food. Clashes between groups can be based on characteristics other than personality, such as religion (e.g., Northern Ireland, the Middle East, and what once was the country of Yugoslavia), or race, or social class.

A theory known as **realistic group conflict theory** (Sears, Peplau, & Taylor, 1991) is based on real competition between groups. As each wave of new immigrants has come to the United States, they have been discriminated against—often by individuals who fear that these "foreigners" will take away their own jobs. And, unfortunately, individuals with low levels of education and skills may well have realistic concerns in this area. New immigrants may be willing to work for lower wages simply to have a job, which might lower the wages for all of those who work in a particular job classification—regardless of whether they are immigrants or native-born Americans.

A classic example of conflict based on whistle-blowing has occurred between the United Nations and the country of Iraq throughout most of the late 1990s. The United Nations set up a group to inspect sites suspected of harboring materials or facilities to manufacture "weapons of mass destruction." If these were found, the United Nations was to be informed and (at least theoretically) something would be done. Iraq resisted mightily the inspection attempts. Thus the role of the inspectors clearly had conflict-prone responsibilities attached. On several occasions they were ejected from the country, and on other occasions Iraq's refusal to cooperate resulted in air-strikes by American planes.

Based upon international agreements such as the North American Free Trade Agreement (NAFTA), unions and management in several organizations (including General Motors) have come into conflict about what can be perceived as job discrimination—the importation of jobs to other countries where wages are cheaper, thus putting American workers at a disadvantage and causing the loss of some American jobs. Sexual harassment as alleged in the Clarence Thomas/Anita Hill conflict has been the basis for conflict between men and women "into conflict," and Republicans and Democrats reacted to the Clinton case almost entirely based upon party membership—also creating conflict.

Ambiguity about who has the power to make a decision regarding an abortion for a pregnant teenager below the "age of consent"—the girl herself or her parents—has brought groups into conflict. The conflicts are based not only on authority, but also on the controversial nature of abortion itself.

Relative deprivation is the feeling that compared to someone else, you're not getting enough (Bernstein & Crosby, 1980). There are basically two levels of relative deprivation that will determine the level at which the conflict will occur. **Egoistic deprivation** is when we feel as an individual that someone has more of something we should have. An extreme example of egoistic deprivation is the number of murders that have occurred between teenagers because one teenager wants (and can't afford) the other's expensive shoes or coat. The perpetrator feels deprived and seeks to redress the situation by committing the murder and theft.

Fraternal deprivation (Runciman, 1966) is the comparison of our group to another and feeling deprived. The threat doesn't even have to be to a group to which we directly belong. In the troubles in Northern Ireland, when an Irish Catholic is killed, American Catholics grieve. Fraternal deprivation can be the source of conflict between men and women, or can be the basis for the formation of unions and sympathy strikes. Others "like us" are not getting what they deserve compared to another group. Fraternal deprivation can also be a source of conflict between races.

Intergroup conflict between the races has been and continues to be a serious societal problem in the United States. Over time racial groups have continued to remain separate—first through the mechanism of slavery then the motive changed to:

> . . . one based in the sociopolitical reasoning of the labor market and the role of education in supplying needed human resources.
>
> **(Wilson, 1987, p. 173)**

We could carry this list out a great deal further—in fact there are entire books written on the sources of conflict—but we have identified many of the sources of conflict which you are likely to encounter. Most of the examples given above result in negative outcomes. Let's now summarize the negative results of conflict and turn to consideration of the positive results of conflict.

Negative Results of Conflict

As we have seen, there are a number of potentially negative effects of conflict. Conflict consumes group time and attention. There's a cliché used in the business world that states: When you're up to your ass in alligators it's hard to remember that your goal was to drain the swamp. Conflicts can serve as the alligators. As long as you are having to deal with them you can't get on with group business.

Conflict can result in extreme **demonstrations of self-interest** at the expense of the group when an individual feels wronged and withdraws from or tries to sabotage the group. Prolonged conflict between individuals can harm them both *emotionally and physically* (as we'll see in Chapter 11), and might result in a prolonged schism in the group. In some settings, such prolonged and serious conflicts within a group might result in **legal action** (as in a sexual harassment situation).

Conflicts can also result in such **loss of trust** that individuals begin to give the group (or one group gives another) *false information*. And negative attitudes can form that appear to outsiders as a *distortion of reality*. During the Cold War, America referred to the Union of Soviet Socialist Republics as the "evil empire." Iraqis now refer to the United States as the "great Satan." Both of these are probably the result of the prolonged conflicts between the nations. So it sounds pretty bad. Conflict can cripple or destroy a group. Are there any benefits to be obtained from conflict?

 Before I list them, can you make a list of the possible beneficial outcomes from conflict that the group might experience? Have you ever experienced conflict in a group that improved the group in some way?

Positive Results of Conflict

Yes, Virginia, conflict can result in positive outcomes. There can be an upside. During conflict, **talents and abilities** may emerge from group members that they have not demonstrated during more peaceful times. Someone who has not been active in the group may step forward to help settle the conflict. Conflict may lead to *innovation and change* within the group and its members. If old policies or norms are creating repeated conflict, the group has the opportunity to reconsider and create more appropriate structures.

Regardless of how the conflict is handled, the observant group member(s) may identify useful methods that will help to prevent a reoccurrence of the conflict. The conflict may clarify problems within the group(s) by providing **diagnostic information** about unresolved feelings and issues in the group. And, finally, if the conflict is dealt with successfully, resolution of the conflict can lead to *unity* or *re-unity* (DuBrin, 1992).

CONDITIONS DISCOURAGING CONFLICT

It is possible to create conditions that discourage conflict within or between groups, although as we have just seen this might not always be a good idea. While this prevents the negative effects, it also prevents the positive effects. It also assumes that groups cannot develop skills in handling conflict that would result in positive outcomes so they are more likely to be harmed than helped by conflict.

The first technique to avoid conflict is to *avoid ambiguity about norms.* When there is consensus about the appropriate behaviors, conflict is less likely to occur. To prevent invidious comparisons or feelings of relative deprivation, *information can be withheld* regarding resources or attainments (Rubin et al., 1994). Perhaps if Iraq did not know how many other countries possess nuclear weapons they would not feel the need to have their own. Keeping the information secret, however, can often be easier said than done.

A large corporation with whom I have worked claims that all salary information is secret—that individuals do not know the salaries of their co-workers. Bunk. The only individuals in the company who claim to believe that are those at the upper, policy-making levels. In reality, in this company people not only know each others' salaries and the size of their raises and bonuses, they also know the size of each others' workloads. And this does lead to invidious comparisons. If a reward system is managed in an equitable manner, it makes no sense to even try to keep it secret. If those with the largest workloads, or the most dangerous jobs, or the highest level of achievement receive better outcomes, the reward system can work in favor of the organization by serving as a motivator for workers. Having a strict status system with the possibility for social mobility (in which anyone can advance) will also prevent conflict.

Another way to keep groups from conflict is to keep them *physically or psychologically separate* from each other. Sometimes this happens deliberately on the part of group members. Major and Forcey (1985) found that men compare their salaries only with their male peers when asking for a raise. (And a good thing, too, since women tend to make less than their male peers, and probably the reason for the phenomenon.) Schelling (1978) found that African-American students and white students separated themselves by race in college dining halls.

However, other research has shown that prejudice and hostility between groups can be reduced by *decreasing or eliminating the importance of group boundaries* (Miller & Brewer, 1984; Gaertner, Mann, Murrell, & Dovidio, 1989; and Worchel, 1986). The problem is that it is almost impossible to reduce group boundaries.

> If we view group membership as an important part of individual identity, this homogenization of groups will prove uncomfortable and threatening in the long run.
>
> *(Jones, 1972, p. 87)*

What then is the alternative? Worchel (1986) suggests that we not only recognize, but even **emphasize group differences.** The aim is to focus on the unique skills and experiences of group members and how they can be combined to solve mutual problems. There has not been much research in this area, and even Worchel admits trying to mix the groups against their will might blow up in your face.

A final tactic for discouraging conflict is to *create physical and/or social barriers to communication* between groups (this one doesn't do well within groups).

Again, this often happens naturally as we discussed in Chapter 2. People are usually most attracted to and comfortable with others who are similar. This attraction leads to creation of proximity and separation from others who are perceived in some way "different."

STAGES OF CONFLICT

The severity of conflict between and within groups can be gauged by identifying the stage of the conflict in a model presented by Pondy (1967). Pondy identifies five stages: (1) *latent conflict*, (2) *perceived conflict*, (3) *felt conflict*, (4) *manifest conflict*, and (5) *conflict aftermath*. **Latent conflict** is when the conditions for potential conflict exist, such as a scarcity of resources, but the situation has not yet been recognized by the group(s). For example, a budget crisis at a university might result in a rebudgeting which reduces the amount of money available to fund campus clubs. However, the administration has not yet notified the groups of the newly created shortage. Or two members of a group were counting on having access to the same computer at the same time to write up their contributions to the group class assignment but they haven't compared notes on scheduling yet.

Perceived conflict occurs when the potential for conflict is recognized by one or both participants. North Korea suffered a drought in the late 1980s that destroyed crops and left the people starving. One solution to the problem would have been to overrun South Korea and take their food. In the late 1990s both the South Korean army and American military forces in South Korea spent the majority of their time on alert status. South Korea perceived the threatened conflict.

Felt conflict is when tension is building, but there is no overt struggle. The clubs have been notified by the administration of the budget cuts. Or the group members have compared schedules and discovered they both want the computer at the same time. The situation may move on to manifest conflict—which is what most people have in mind when they think of conflict.

Manifest conflict is when the struggle has started and the behavior of the participants makes the conflict visible to others. In other words, the fight's on. Or, more hopefully, the strategies for dealing with the conflict are being put in place. The behaviors that are employed by the groups can result in either positive or negative ramifications of the conflict.

The final stage, **conflict aftermath,** is the time after the conflict has ended either through resolution or suppression. The mood and affect of the group will probably be very different depending upon which of the two has occurred. Changes have occurred in the conditions which precipitated the conflict and the groups can go on to new or further conflict (in the case of suppression), or cooperation and cohesion in the case of resolution.

ESCALATION OF CONFLICT

Once a conflict begins, it has a tendency to increase in intensity—to escalate. First we'll discuss the ways in which conflicts escalate, then we'll examine the psychological mechanisms that push for escalation in conflict.

The tactics employed in dealing with the conflict tend to move from **light to heavy.** The interactions between the participants tend to start out gentler and kinder and to move up to threats. The *motives* of the participants may also change. Initially each participant probably just wants to do well, then they decide they want to win. After a while, the participants may want to see how much damage they can incur on their opponent.

The size of conflicts escalates at three levels. Conflicts often start over *small, concrete issues* but as the conflict continues, larger more general concerns are included. Conflicts tend to move from small in terms of the **number of issues,** but continued conflict results in more issues being included. And finally, the conflict may start out relatively small—between two people or groups—but as the conflict continues each side brings in **reinforcements.** (This model was presented by Rubin et al., 1994.)

Let's follow an example through the levels of the conflict using what might be a familiar example—parents and a teenager in conflict over the state of the teenager's bedroom. Moving from light to heavy, Mom may start out gently suggesting that the room might use some tidying up. If the room doesn't change, Mom may offer a reward for a clean room. If it still doesn't change, she may threaten to go in herself and dispose of everything on the floor.

Both sides start out just wanting to get their ways, but after a while both become angry and the mother invents punishments while the teenager piles it on deeper in her room. The conflict started about a messy room, but if it continues it may become an issue of lack of responsibility and over-strict parenting (depending on the participant). And even though the conflict started about one chore not being taken care of, as the conflict escalates, Mom may begin to mention other things that aren't being done by the teen. And, finally, while it began between Mom and her daughter, the mother may enlist the father's aid and the daughter may recruit her sisters for support.

STOP Have you ever had trouble with roommates? Has something like this ever happened to you? You begin to discuss with your roommate your problem with her inability to keep the kitchen clean. Using the above discussion, write the outline of the probable advancement of the argument.

There are a number of psychological mechanisms that push for conflicts to escalate. When I am in conflict with you I will probably try to convince you I'm right and you're wrong. This process of attempted persuasion often actually makes the conflict worse in a number of ways. In order to convince you, I'll marshal all my strongest, most compelling arguments. They may not impress you, but I will often become even more solid in my position. I *convince myself!*

Cognitive dissonance can also play a role in the reaction to the persuasion process. (Recall that we are in a state of cognitive dissonance when our values, attitudes, beliefs, and behaviors are inconsistent with each other. We seek to reduce this discomfort by altering one of the inconsistent factors to regain consistency.) As I watch myself expending all this time and energy trying to convince you I think, "Gee, if I'm willing to invest this much, I must REALLY believe in my position." And by trying to convince you that you're wrong, I may cause you to feel that I'm trying to control you and limit your independence and thereby invoke **reactance** on your part.

What if while we're arguing I realize I'm wrong. Am I likely to admit it? Possibly. If I feel you will humiliate me or make fun of me for backing down I may continue to represent a position even I no longer sponsor. Always allow your opponent a graceful way out. Most people do not want to **lose face.** This is particularly true of individuals in Asian cultures.

The **norm of reciprocity** also plays a role in conflict. Just as this norm requires that I return a favor done for me, it also pushes me in the direction of retaliation for what I perceive is a wrong done to me. This is the biblical "eye for an eye" concept. It's also known as revenge.

People involved in conflict are often angry. This anger results in an altered perception of the "opponent." It is easier to attack an enemy or a thing than it is Suzy Brown who lives next door, so we stop thinking of her as a person with feelings and needs and start thinking of her as a thing through a process known as **deindividuation.** This is one of the reasons for racial epithets. It's much easier to demonize or hurt a "nigger" or a "spic" or a "slope" or a "mackerel-snapper" or a "kike." (Sorry for the offensive words, I tried to be an equal opportunity offender.) It's even easier to hurt a thing if we can deindividuate ourselves—move away from our personal identity.

The members of the Ku Klux Klan wear pointed hoods as a largely symbolic disguise. Wearing the hoods they can maintain at least the fiction that they are not functioning as John Brown, but as part of a group. Also as part of a group we do not have to take the personal responsibility for any damage we inflict in a conflict. **Diffusion of responsibility** allows us to blame the group as an entity and avoid personal blame.

Finally, the causes I attribute to your behavior may cause me to escalate the conflict further. People are not comfortable when they don't understand the reasons for a phenomenon (in nature or in the behavior of another). Thus even if we don't know for sure, we assign, or attribute, a cause to the behavior. This is known as **attribution theory,** from the work of Heider (1958).

We tend to attribute behavior to one of two basic causes: **dispositional** (internal) or **situational** (environmental). If I am working in a group and one of the members is late, I can either assume she's just irresponsible (internal attribution) or I can wonder whether she had car trouble (environmental attribution). If I make the internal attribution I'm more likely to become angry at her wasting my time than if I make the external attribution. So internal attributions for negative behavior are likely to escalate a conflict.

Unfortunately, it has been found that when evaluating other people's behavior, we have such a common tendency to underestimate the impact of the environment and make an internal attribution that the phenomenon is known as the **fundamental attribution error** (Ross, 1977). We're particularly likely to make this mistake when we are in the midst of a conflict. (This is, by the way, a particularly American phenomenon, probably because Americans are so individualistic and believe so strongly in personal responsibility, [Deaux & Wrightsman, 1988].)

Well, it's happened. Despite all our best efforts to the contrary, we're in the middle of a manifest conflict. What shall we do? What we want to do is solve the conflict with a result that will be sufficiently satisfactory to all the participants that the peace will hold stable, at least for a while. Individuals who feel they lost in a conflict situation are potentially dangerous. They not only have no vested interest in maintaining the calm, they may have an agenda that involves sabotaging the solution so they can prove themselves right, or at least have another chance of winning.

The *dual concern model* as a method of conflict style developed out of the managerial grid (1964) discussed in Chapter 8. It has been adapted by a number of authors, including Blake and Mouton, 1964; Ruble and Thomas, 1976; and Van de Vliert and Prein, 1989. The dual concern model creates a grid with one axis representing *concern about one's own outcome* in the conflict, and the other axis representing *concern about the other's outcome*. These are seen as separate, not the ends of a single continuum running between selfishness at one end and cooperativeness at the other (Thomas, 1976). Using this grid we can identify four types of tactics used to deal with conflict as seen below.

Concern about Self	Concern about Other	Tactic
Low	Low	Avoiding
Low	High	Yielding
High	Low	Contending
High	High	Problem solving

As we would expect, *avoiding* means the conflict is simply not important enough to continue the conflict. Neither party particularly cares about getting their own way, so there is no point in continuing the conflict. **Yielding** doesn't have to be total surrender of one's own interests, but it involves at least settling for less than originally desired. The quality of the relationship between the parties may strongly affect the choice of yielding. If I don't particularly care which movie to see but my husband has a strong, clear choice I will give in to make him happy.

On the other hand, if the potential adversary is someone with whom I have a history of conflict, I am unlikely to want them to win so I will be more likely to emphasize my own self-interest and have a very low level of interest in seeing my opponent win. In that case I will end up fighting for my own outcomes and engage in the behavior of **contending.**

In the final situation, where my concern for my own outcomes is equal to my concern about my opponents' outcomes, I will be inclined to engage in problem solving. Problem solving seeks to find a solution in which all participants feel they have achieved at least some of their desired outcomes. In other words, everyone feels like a winner. Thus everyone has an interest in maintaining the solution that has been reached.

By the way, in our opening prediction, Danielle had very high concern for her own outcome and little concern for Tammy's. Tammy has low concern for her own outcome and low concern for Danielle's outcomes. So Danielle is likely to contend, and Tammy is likely to avoid.

How good are you at solving conflict? Do you find that you are usually playing a particular role in the conflict resolution situation, such as the mediator, or are you more likely to be one of the combatants? List three ways you could reduce a growing conflict in a group in which you were a member.

Conflict Resolution

We can't eliminate conflict altogether and we shouldn't. We have seen that there are some potentially very positive outcomes from conflict successfully resolved. However, conflict is an inevitability so we must learn to manage conflict appropriately.

Miles (1980) presents a model with four general strategies for resolving conflict. The best approach is based on the source of the problem. You can change: (1) the issue, (2) the individuals, (3) the relationships, or (4) the organizational structure or context. Changing the issue involves problem solving. The components of the conflict must be identified and solved separately to the maximal satisfaction of all involved. Changing the individuals can be done literally through moving people into or out of the group, or through training of some kind. For example, Lublin (1991) estimates that eventually 90 percent of the top 500 companies will offer sexual harassment training to reduce the incidence of this behavior. Below we will examine a conflict-solving communication model that works quite well in resolving conflicts.

Changing the relationships involves negotiating and bargaining which we will discuss at length. And finally, changing the organizational structure or context involves the use of a third party. We will also discuss the use of third party interventions. One method of trying to change individuals is to go through training in the problematic area. One common problem in many conflicts is the difficulty in communicating appropriately during the conflict. It's very possible that individuals will become angry during the conflict and, unfortunately, people can't listen or problem solve when they are angry.

When we're angry we often become more concerned about "scoring points" off our opponent rather than solve the conflict. And when someone feels blamed or accused they will tend to become defensive and will at least psychologically retreat from the situation. Again, no solution. Again and again I have mentioned that group members must behave appropriately during conflict. Now I'm going to present a model of communication to be used during conflict situations developed by Bower and Bower (1976) which is simple, direct, and very effective.

There are four steps to the **DESC model:** (1) **D**escribe, (2) **E**xpress, (3) **S**pecify, and (4) **C**onsequences. For each of these steps you prepare one or two sentences in what the Bowers refer to as a DESC script. If you try to deliver a long speech, chances are good you'll never get through, you'll be interrupted and thrown off track.

In the Describe step you describe in objective, concrete terms the specific problem you have with the other person's behavior. Use examples, specifying a time and place or the frequency of an action. Be sure to keep your description at the level of behavior. Don't try to read someone's mind. You don't know what's going on in someone's head any more than they know what's going on in yours. Try to be as dispassionate as you can. If you find yourself becoming angry, terminate the session by informing the other person that you are too angry to continue, but that you need to discuss this matter after you've cooled down. Often the fact that you have become that emotional will make the other party aware of just how strongly you feel about the issue.

By the way, don't blame your anger on someone else. Despite the way the English language is structured, people don't "make other people angry." Anger is our own personal response to someone's behavior. The same action that might cause you to feel anger might make me laugh. So be sure to take responsibility for your own emotions. This also prevents the other participant from feeling blamed.

Let's look at a bad then a good example of a Describe step. One of your group members has been late for three of the last four meetings of the group and the group has wasted a lot of valuable time waiting for him. You decide you need to confront him. You could say, "You inconsiderate bastard, you're always late. You're too irresponsible to be in this group!" That should help considerably (sarcasm intended). First, calling names helps nothing and shifts the group member into defense/attack mode. Second, the words "always" and "never" are dangerous. They're very seldom accurate. Finally you've twice tried to identify the motives of the group member. You've called him inconsiderate and irresponsible. Maybe John's late because he lives across town taking care of his disabled, widowed mother and has to take three buses to get to meetings and is at the mercy of the transit system.

Let's try it again. "John, you've been late three of the last four meetings of the group. When you're late we have to sit and wait for you." If you've accurately described the behavior, John is unlikely to argue. If he denies being late this may be someone with whom you cannot reason. But at this point John has no reason to become defensive (that you've created).

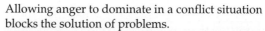

Allowing anger to dominate in a conflict situation blocks the solution of problems.

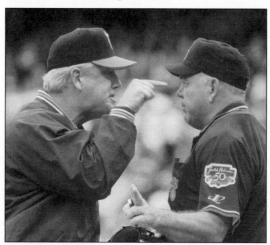

Next you Express your own, personal feelings in reaction to the behavior described in the first step. Express them calmly and as positively as you can. Make sure you direct the feelings at the behavior and not at the person. Don't say, "John, you jerk, you make me so mad when my time is wasted. How can you be so selfish?" Again you've attacked John by trying to read his motives. You've called him names, and you've been negative.

How about: "John, I would feel so much better about you and this group if we were able to be more effective with our use of time. Your lateness upsets me." Already you've offered him some incentive to change. And expressed yourself in a nonblaming manner.

In the **Specify** step you explicitly, concretely explain what behaviors you want instead of what you're getting. Don't assume that just because you've expressed dissatisfaction the other person can read your mind as to what to do instead. This, by the way, is another reason not to use words like "irresponsible." If you use that phrase to me I have no idea what you want me to do instead of what I'm currently doing. If you say, "Carol, I want you to start being on time to meetings." I know exactly what you want. (Whether I decide to comply is a separate issue we'll talk about soon.)

Ask for only small changes and don't ask for more than one or two changes at a time. No matter how nicely you put it, if you complain about sixteen things I'm doing wrong I'm going to feel attacked. Also, even with the best of intentions I will probably not be able to keep all sixteen in mind at once. So start off first with the most important change. Others can follow.

Also understand that if you have been in conflict with a person for an extended period, you are contributing to the problem. It takes two to tangle. Consider the role you have been playing in the problem. Ask what behaviors you could change that would facilitate the change you're requesting. Suddenly it's "our" problem to solve together, not a situation of blame and innocence. So don't say, "You'd better clean up your act, pal." How about instead, "John, I'd really like you to start being prompt about meeting times. Is there anything we, as a group, can do to help you?"

Now John may confess there's a problem with the times you've been scheduling the meetings (don't blame yourself—he should have spoken up before) and his problems with the buses. Maybe simply changing the times of the meetings will solve the conflict. Or maybe a group member lives near John or at least near one of the bus stops he uses and could give him a lift.

Finally, you need to express the Consequences of the changes in John's behavior. Don't be embarrassed to talk about consequences. All behavior has consequences and it's only fair to let people know what they might be. Try to present a positive incentive first. If that doesn't work you can always threaten later. So don't say, "John, if you're late again we're going to throw you out of the group." If it's a class or work group maybe your instructor or supervisor won't let you throw him out (I wouldn't). Besides, everyone's late sometimes, so why be so Draconian with John? You might be the one late to the next meeting. And imagine the fun he could have then.

How about, "John, if you're on time we can get the meetings started on time and we can all get out of here earlier. We may even need to have fewer meetings." If that doesn't motivate him to change, I don't know what will.

Don't expect you'll win all the time. Some people will simply not stand still to listen to you, or they will deny, or they will attack you and your motives. But at least this model gives you a framework. You can plan in advance what you want to say. (And it works great in multiple situations—such as returning merchandise or dealing with the auto mechanics who ripped you off in repairing your car.)

Negotiations and Bargaining

A good way to make changes in relationships within and between groups is the process of **negotiation** and **bargaining.**

> *Successful problem solving can lead to three broad classes of outcomes: compromise, agreement on a procedure for deciding who will win, or integrative solution.*
>
> **(Rubin et al., 1994, p. 170)**

Is one of these alternatives preferable? Yes, the **integrative solution.** The integrative solution is best because:

> *(1) If both sides are resisting, resolution may be impossible unless you can find a way to "join the two parties" interests.*
> *(2) When both parties feel they've benefited, solutions are more stable.*
> *(3) Integrative solutions strengthen relationships between the parties.*
> *(4) Integrative solutions contribute to the broader community of which the parties are members.*
>
> **(Rubin, et al., 1994, p. 172)**

The integrative solution is the search for the win/win solution that will at least partially satisfy all parties to the conflict.

Why isn't **compromise** the best alternative? In compromise you go to the middle ground between the two parties' desired outcomes. So if a couple wants to go out to dinner and she wants Chinese and he wants ribs, the compromise would be to go to a burger joint. Who won? No one. Neither party is likely to be happy with the outcome. If we are talking about a more "serious" issue such as labor/management negotiations, then a compromise that truly pleases no one may be inherently unstable. Compromise isn't always bad. If the parties are really determined to reach some sort of agreement and time pressures are high, compromise may be acceptable. At least it's better than a *stalemate* in which no mutually acceptable position can be identified.

Besides compromise and integrative solutions, Rubin and others (1994) identified "procedures for deciding who will win." What exactly does that mean? These are arbitrary, nonintegrative solutions. For example the parties could *toss a coin,* or *choose a number.* In a group where grade points must be divided, the largest number could be given to the *member who "needs" them the most.* Or, as we discussed in Chapter 7 on decision making, the parties can **vote.** Just make sure that the **decision criteria** have been put in place before the vote occurs.

Integrative solutions that search for a win/win solution will depend upon the basis of the conflicts. There are a number of standard procedures that can be used, depending upon the situation. Here, again, there are entire books on this topic so we will only discuss a few of the many possible alternatives.

One technique is **expanding the pie.** This is used when faced with a resource shortage. There is not enough of some resource to go around. This problem is often faced by government agencies who award grant monies for research. Since the 1970s most agencies receive far more requests than they can fund. So there is competition for the dollars. One alternative is to determine how much too much is being requested (e.g., you have requests for 110 percent of the money available). Then you simply make an across the board cut and each applicant is cut an equal percentage of the request.

The National Institutes of Health (NIH) used this technique when I worked as the administrator of a research laboratory in the 1970s. Everyone was cut 10 percent. Not surprisingly, everyone the next year simply asked for 10 percent more than they needed, thus making the problem worse. So if you're going to expand the pie, make sure that requests are actual.

One way is to require bids or brochures for requested subcontracted work or equipment. Another is the process known as **zero-based budgeting.** Many budgets for the next year simply take the current year's budget and increase the request by the amount necessary to increase salaries. Zero-based budgeting requires a newly justified budget each year. Once you know how short on resources you really are, then you can look for additional resources so that all requests can be satisfied. The NIH might go to Congress and ask for additional moneys.

If the money is not forthcoming, then the technique of **costcutting** might be employed. In costcutting, all of the requests would be evaluated for quality and only the "best" receive resources. The other parties (the "losers" if you will) are compensated some other way—perhaps by giving them priority on the next round of applications.

Another integrative solution is known as **logrolling.** Logrolling is a version of "you scratch my back and I'll scratch yours." Logrolling works most effectively when there are multiple issues involved in the conflict, but can also work under some circumstances when only one issue is the focus of the conflict.

Let's use the example of a union and management negotiating a new labor contract. Under discussion are both salaries and benefits. The sides have come to a stalemate. They aren't willing to compromise. Each party is asked to identify the issue on which they are most determined to win. Which issue do they feel is most important? Often the parties identify different issues. Thus labor could win on salaries and management could win on benefits. Even though each lost on one issue, it was an issue of lesser importance. And no one rational above the age of two expects to get everything they want all the time.

Suppose, however, there is only one issue. Here we have to determine whether the parties will be in a long-term relationship or whether this will be their only conflictful interaction. If the relationship is short-lived, some parties may be tempted to cheat. An example of one-issue logrolling happens all the time in the legislative branch of our state and federal governments. Representative X has a bill coming up for vote on Monday that she REALLY wants to pass.

She goes to Representatives A, B, and C and promises that if they vote for her, she will promise to vote with them on their next bill. Since they will be in a long-term relationship, Representative X doesn't dare go back on her word to Representatives A, B, and C if she ever wants to pass another piece of legislation. However, if the two parties are unlikely to ever be dealing with each other again, the temptation to cheat may be too strong.

Bridging is a technique in which neither party gets what they originally requested. So why is this an integrative solution? Each party is required to identify the underlying interests of their initial demands. What did they really want? Let's look at an adult with an aging parent who calls at all hours of the night and day with little tasks that need to be attended to such as changing a light bulb or finding the television remote control. The son wants his mother to leave him alone. Probably the mother just wants to be sure that she will get attention from her son. The son probably just wants to not have his life constantly interrupted.

A bridging solution would be to arrange for the son to spend one evening a week with his father doing chores, and having his parents over for dinner each Sunday. While not what they originally requested, each side got what they actually wanted.

GRIT (Graduated Reciprocation In Tension) is an intergroup integrative solution method developed by Osgood (1962). This method's effectiveness depends upon both parties feeling bound by the norm of reciprocity. One side unilaterally makes a small concession to the other with the assumption that the other side will reciprocate. Then the original party makes another small concession and the conflict spirals down to nothing.

So you can't make everybody happy all of the time. But the closer you can come to this ideal in a conflict solution, the more probable it is that a stable solution can be reached.

Third Party Intervention

The use of **third party intervention** to solve conflicts should be a last resort. An internal decision between the parties is preferable because the parties will be more likely to honor a solution they hammered out themselves, and because they can't run to an outsider every time there is conflict. The introduction of a third party also changes the dynamics of the conflict (Kressel & Pruitt, 1989; Pruitt & Carnevale, 1993).

 When you were a child did you occasionally fight with your siblings or neighbor children over toys? How did the conflicts get solved? Did you settle the problems yourselves, or did someone's parent become involved? Which type of settlement was more satisfactory? Why?

The third party can come from within the group in an intragroup conflict or from one of the groups involved in an intergroup conflict—which means that they are generally a nonspecialist who has allegiances to one of the parties involved. This **emergent third party** may not be as effective as a **contractual**

management conflict specialist. What is essential is that both parties to the conflict must trust the third party and believe in his competence or the entire process will be a waste of time and energy (Deaux & Wrightsman, 1988).

The third party can control a number of structural aspects of the confrontation process.

> *The possibilities for such modification include structuring communication between the principals, opening and neutralizing the site in which problem solving takes place, imposing time limits, and infusing additional resources.*
> **(Rubin et al., 1994, p. 203)**

Whether the third party encourages the participants to meet face-to-face depends on the level of the conflict. For low-level conflict, direct contact is preferable. However, when conflict is intense it is best to keep the parties separated. The term used in political settings is **shuttle diplomacy.**

Besides choosing a neutral site for negotiations, the third party can determine whether the site is open or closed to outsiders. Generally it is wise to keep the site closed until a solution seems imminent. Outsiders, whether merely interested parties or the press, can offer the platform for posturing and stall the solution process.

The third party can also identify issues and determine the sequence in which the issues will be discussed. It is usually best to try to find an "easy" issue first as this will tend to set the norm of agreement in motion. The third party also works to *increase the motivation on each side to reach an agreement, encourage opportunities for face-saving, defuse emotions,* and *encourage momentum.* All of these tasks are probably easier for an outside party to accomplish.

There are three levels at which the third party can operate. These are the *inquisition process, arbitration,* and *mediation,* presented in decreasing order of control exerted by the third party. To be perfectly honest, I have never actually known of an instance when the **inquisition process** has been used, but as it continues to appear in the literature (e.g., Deaux & Wrightsman, 1988), I continue to teach the process.

Does the phrase Spanish Inquisition ring a bell? If it doesn't, shame on your high school history teacher. Go look it up. The Catholic Church tortured confessions out of thousands of people before killing them. The conflict management method of inquisition doesn't result in death for anyone, but the control rests entirely in the hands of the third party.

It is determined in advance that both parties will agree to abide by whatever decision is made by the inquisitor. The inquisitor then approaches each party and asks specific questions. The sides don't get to argue their case, they can only directly respond to questions. They are not allowed to suggest solutions unless specifically requested. After gathering information, the inquisitor goes off and makes a decision based on his/her own judgment and conveys the decision to the parties. I think the reason that I have never heard of this situation actually occurring is that most parties to a conflict are unwilling to completely give up any power over the outcome.

There are two levels of **arbitration:** binding and nonbinding. In **binding arbitration,** both parties agree that they are required to follow the arbitrator's decisions. In *nonbinding arbitration* they are only required to listen to the arbitrator's suggestions but may reject them. In arbitration each party gets to make their case for the arbitrator, including stating their preferred outcomes. The arbitrator makes a decision using this information, but may not necessarily choose the preferred outcome of either party.

Mediation is a much less intrusive process than either inquisition or arbitration. The mediator's role is to work with the parties to help them come to their own solution. The mediator facilitates the discussions but otherwise does not provide any personal input. A new procedure that has been introduced is **mediation/arbitration** (Pruitt, McGillicuddy, Welton, & Fry, 1989). The parties start out with mediation with the understanding that if mediation fails, the parties must move directly into binding arbitration. The method tends to be effective because the parties are worried about losing control if the mediation fails.

Two other new third party strategies are **problem solving** and *designing dispute resolution systems.* Problem solving works much like mediation with the mediator educating disputants on new ways to deal with issues. The parties are taught new techniques with the intention that they will be able to employ these techniques when future problems arise (Deaux & Wrightsman, 1988).

Designing dispute resolution systems involves establishing a structure for use in conflict resolution (Ury, Brett, & Goldberg, 1988). Procedures are established specifying who will participate, the timetable for negotiations, and procedures if negotiations fail. Participants are encouraged to problem solve and avoid power tactic such as threats. **Cooling-off** periods may be called if participants become too emotional. Disputants are taught negotiation skills and encouraged to start with low-cost procedures and only move to high-cost procedures as a fallback position.

In each chapter of this book we have seen that gender and culture have significant impacts upon the ways in which groups interact and function. Conflict and conflict resolution preferences are no exception as we will see in the next section.

CULTURAL EFFECTS ON CONFLICT AND CONFLICT RESOLUTION

The research on gender and cross-cultural conflicts and conflict resolution have focused more on resolution and culture. Gender either does not play a significant role, or has simply not been frequently used as a variable in the research.

Two studies where gender did appear to be an important consideration examined interactions with culture regarding preferences for conflict resolution. Gire and Carment (1993) examined the differences between male and female Canadian students (from an individualistic culture) and Nigerians (from a non-Asian collectivist culture). Women showed a much greater preference for negotiation while the men showed a greater tendency to use threats. There was also an effect for overall culture in that the Canadians preferred negotiation while Nigerians as a group seemed not to have a preference between negotiation and arbitration. Itoi, Onbuchi, and Fukuno (1996) compared American and Japanese males and females on their preferred method of conflict resolution after they were given a scenario in which they had accidentally harmed someone. The Japanese women were more likely than any other group to apologize. Individualistic Americans in general preferred justifications while Japanese (collectivistic) were more likely to prefer mitigating accounts such as apologies or excuses. Itoi and others (1996) suggest that gender differences in conflict management styles are cultural products.

One aspect of conflict not mentioned in the body of the chapter is the tendency to use **adjudication** as a solution to conflict, or other legal means such as **contracts** to avoid conflict. Americans like to use contracts. They feel that a signed contract is an indication of commitment. Japanese, on the other hand, dislike contracts because they feel that requiring a signature indicates a lack of trust (Sullivan, Peterson, Kameda, & Shimada, 1981). In general the United States shows a strong preference for adjudication—Tanaka (1972) found 18 attorneys per 10,000 people in the United States, 4 per 10,000 in West Germany, 2 per 10,000 people in France, and 1 per 10,000 people in Japan. Leung and Lind (1986) found that American college students preferred adversarial adjudication over inquisitional adjudication. Chinese college students showed no preference.

The continuing difference between individualistic and collectivistic cultures appeared again in the research on preferences for competition or collaboration and compromise in conflict resolution. Cushman and King (1985) found that Americans prefer competition while Japanese and Yugoslavians (non-Asian collectivist culture) prefer collaboration and compromise. The French and Brazilians also like competition and confrontation in negotiations (Campbell, Graham, Jolbert, & Meissner, 1988). The Indians were found to be even more competitive in bargaining than Americans (Druckman, Benton, Ali, & Bogen, 1981). Americans (Graham, 1981) and Germans (Schmidt, 1979) prefer to keep negotiations impersonal. Japanese and Malaysians prefer establishing personal relationships (Moran, 1985; Renwick, 1985).

A number of studies have examined the underlying assumptions of GRIT—that the norm of reciprocity would result in reciprocal concessions in negotiations. North Americans and Arabs do reciprocate concessions. The Norwegians are even more willing to reciprocate than are the Americans. The Russians, however, prefer to start extreme and resist making concessions, which are seen as indicators of weakness (Glenn et al., 1977).

It should be clear to you by now that culture plays an important role in every aspect of group dynamics. It surely is no wonder that multinational organizations spend a great deal of time and energy training employees who must deal with individuals from other cultures in the nuances of the differences. I leave it to your imagination the probable interactions at the Yalta conference during World War II when FDR represented the United States, Stalin represented the Russians, and Churchill represented the United Kingdom in negotiations.

Summary

In this chapter we have looked at the important phenomenon of conflict within and between groups. Because conflict is an inevitable outcome of human interaction, it is important to understand the sources of conflict, the pressures that tend to escalate conflict, and the most appropriate methods for solving conflict.

While the pressures escalating conflict tend to remain fairly constant despite the issue in conflict, the most appropriate measures of resolution often depend upon the source of the conflict. If the conflict arises over scarce resources a different solution will be appropriate than when the conflict arises from personality clashes. When groups are mired down in the process of conflict, it becomes important that they recognize this fact and turn to the services of a third party to intervene at one of the levels discussed.

Key Terms

adjudication
ambiguity about power
arbitration
attribution theory
autistic conflict
bargaining
binding arbitration
bridging
compromise
conflict aftermath
conflict-prone
  responsibilities
contending
contingent conflict
contract
contractual management
  conflict specialist
cooling-off period
costcutting
decision criteria
deindividuation
demonstrations of self-
  interest
DESC model
diagnostic information
diffusion of
  responsibility
dispositional
egoistic deprivation

emergent third party
emphasize group
  differences
escalating conflict
expanding the pie
felt conflict
fraternal deprivation
fundamental attribution
  error
goal incompatibility
GRIT
individual conflict
inquisition process
integrative solution
intergroup conflict
interorganizational
  conflict
interpersonal conflict
intragroup conflict
invidious comparisons
job discrimination
latent conflict
legal action
light to heavy conflict
  resolution
logrolling
losing face
loss of trust
manifest conflict

mediation
mediation/arbitration
negotiation
norm of reciprocity
number of issues
perceived conflict
personality clashes
problem solving
rank disequilibrium
reactance
realistic group conflict
  theory
reinforcements
relative deprivation
scarce resources
separation of knowledge
  and authority
sexual harassment
shuttle diplomacy
situational
Specify
status incongruities
talents and abilities
third party intervention
vote
whistle-blowing
yielding
zero-based budgeting
zero-sum

APPLICATION

Conflict and Disarray in the United States Military: Don't Ask, Don't Tell, Don't Pursue

Homosexuality is incompatible with military service. The presence in the military environment of persons who engage in homosexual conduct or who, by their statements, demonstrate a propensity to engage in homosexual conduct, seriously impairs the accomplishment of the military mission. The presence of

such members adversely affects the ability of the Military Services to maintain
discipline, good order, and morale; to foster mutual trust and confidence among
servicemembers; to ensure the integrity of the system of rank and command; to
facilitate assignment and worldwide deployment of servicemembers who fre-
quently must live and work under close conditions affording minimal privacy;
to recruit and retain members of the Military Services; to maintain the public
acceptability of military service; and to prevent breaches of security.

(Department of Defense Directive 1332.14)

The concept of homosexuality is sure to create heated discussions in many situations. As can be seen above, the Military Services deal with the situation by
simply banning such individuals from serving their country. The military is a
world apart, governed by the Military Code of Justice and not the laws that
govern the rest of the citizens of the United States. For this reason this apparent
discrimination is perfectly legal as the military is not bound by Title VII of the
Civil Rights Act of 1964 (USGAO, 1993).

The military emphasizes uniformity. They believe this is necessary to "maintain good order, discipline and combat effectiveness." One of the tactics believed to help maintain good order and discipline is uniformity of dress, even
when it violates what would be a civilian's civil rights. In 1986 this was emphasized by the case of *Goldman v Weinberger* (475 US 503). An Air Force clinical
psychologist who was also an Orthodox Jew was denied permission to wear a
yarmulke in his office as required by his religion.

The orderly outward appearance of military units belies the conflict simmering over the
role of gays in the military.

The military generally managed to keep a peacetime white, male entity until 1948 when Truman signed an executive order racially integrating the armed forces. I emphasize the word "peacetime" because of the list of categories of individuals who have been called into service during time of war who would ordinarily be excluded according to Ray (1993):

> *The military exists only to fight wars and thus LEGALLY DISCRIMINATES BY NECESSITY against many categories of Americans who are properly excluded or are deemed unfit to fight, including those lacking a high school diploma, who are felons, drug users, alcoholics, who are too old, too young, too weak, too large, too small, who have excessive traffic violations, or individuals with a variety of disabilities and medical conditions including the blind, the deaf, the handicapped, paraplegics, epileptics, asthmatics, dyslexics, the near-sighted, homosexuals, transsexuals, the color-blind, conscientious objectors, single parents and women.*
>
> *(Ray, 1993, p. 86)*

Clearly a number of these should be exclusionary criteria and maybe they are all enforced during peacetime, but my father fought in World War II and was totally red-green color-blind, and my ex-husband fought in Vietnam wearing his glasses. Knowing all the gyrations men of my generation went through to avoid Vietnam I'll bet a lot of them would have liked to have known that having too many traffic tickets might have excluded them from the service.

Why traffic tickets? This is believed by the military to indicate seriously poor judgment (Ray, 1993). The military chooses to justify these exclusions with the following:

> *We choose to err on the safe side, excluding groups whose members have poor prospects for success, rather than worry about the infrequent individual who might have done well. This is proper because war is a collective enterprise and success is achieved by military groups, not individuals.*
>
> *(Gregor, 1991, p. 25)*

Such a statement makes it difficult to counter with case examples such as Captain Linda Bray who while participating in the military action in Panama in 1989, led thirty military police into what was a supposedly lightly guarded kennel for attack dogs. After a three-hour firefight she and her battalion secured the kennel (Heinemann, 1996). Apparently they are the exceptional, infrequent individuals who did well.

In 1941, the Committee to the Secretary of the Navy wrote "[If the Navy were integrated] discipline, harmony, cooperation, teamwork, and fighting efficiency could be lowered and morale would disappear" (Blumner, 1996). Truman, however, went ahead and signed the act racially integrating the military, but also signed the Women's Armed Services Integration Act, Public Law 625 on June 12, 1948. Apparently the results have not destroyed the military. By 1989 General Colin Powell, an African-American was head of the Joint Chiefs of Staff and Cadet Kristin Baker was named First Captain at West Point, identifying her as the top cadet of 4,400 students in academic excellence, athletic ability, and military skill (Stremlow, 1990).

During his campaign for president in 1992, Bill Clinton promised to end the exclusion and expulsion of gays from the military if elected. On July 19, 1993, however, he approved a new policy of compromise known as "Don't Ask, Don't Tell, and Don't Pursue." In other words, recruiters were not to ask an enlistee's sexual orientation, homosexuals were not to tell anyone of their orientation, and the military was to stop the witch hunts to find homosexuals and dismiss them from the service and/or arrest and jail them (Servicemember's Legal Defense Fund, 1995).

There has been much social science and medical research into the claims the military makes about the effects that would result from allowing homosexuals to serve. (From purely anecdotal evidence and cases I will cite later it is clear that the military has never been much good at keeping homosexuals who wish to from serving.) Particularly interesting and relevant are the studies of fire and police departments where good discipline, good order, and morale are also critical, as well as the militaries of other nations who do not exclude open homosexuality.

However, the military continues to make a case against the inclusion of homosexuals based upon four points. After listing these points we will examine the research that refutes each one of the points. Here are the reasons given for exclusion:

1. Homosexuals as a group are not able bodied.
2. Almost all homosexuals engage in sexual practices which are inherently degrading or humiliating and are rarely practiced by heterosexuals.
3. One-third of all cases of child molestation involve homosexual acts, even though as we have noted, homosexuals make up less than 2 percent of the population.
4. People won't accept gays as leaders.

Homosexuals aren't able bodied? Since it's not possible to look at an individual and identify their sexual orientation such a statement is absurd. Actually, homosexual men tend to take very good care of their appearance, including working out regularly to remain attractive to partners (Shilts, 1994). Perhaps the reference is to the fact that the HIV/AIDS pandemic entered the United States through the male homosexual community. Currently, however, the fastest growing group of AIDS patients are college-age women who are exposed to the virus through heterosexual intercourse.

The sexual practices that were referred to in the statement that heterosexuals find inherently degrading and rarely practiced by heterosexuals include mutual masturbation, oral sex, and anal sex. Mutual masturbation is engaged in by most heterosexuals—it's called foreplay. In terms of oral and anal sex, these behaviors are more common among those who attend college and more common among whites. The figures for participation (not identifying sexual orientation) can be seen below:

	Oral Sex		Anal Sex
	Active	Passive	
Men	77%	79%	26%
Women	68%	73%	20%

Source: Michael, Gagnon, Laumann & Kolata, 1994

So it's untrue that most heterosexuals abhor these behaviors. And these are the most common types of sex engaged in by homosexuals.

Interestingly enough, for the civilian population homosexual sodomy (all the aforementioned fall under that term) is illegal in only five states: Montana, Nevada, Kansas, Texas, and Arkansas. Eighteen states and the District of Columbia have laws making heterosexual sodomy illegal: Rhode Island, Maryland, Virginia, North Carolina, South Carolina, Georgia, Florida, Alabama, Tennessee, Kentucky, Michigan, Minnesota, Missouri, Louisiana, Oklahoma, Arizona, Utah, and Idaho. (Are you a felon?)

As to the charge that one-third of child molestation cases involve homosexual acts, that doesn't mean that homosexuals are necessarily committing these acts. In fact, most pedophiles are heterosexual and "many are married fathers" (Masters, Johnson, & Kolodny, 1995, p. 459).

The last argument is that people won't accept gays as leaders. I can cite three cases of individuals who had achieved leadership roles in the military. Colonel Margarethe Cammermeyer left the military after 27 years of a distinguished career in the Washington National Guard. During her enlistment period she had won a Bronze Star in Vietnam and been named the Veterans' Administration Nurse of the year. She left the position of Chief Nurse of the Washington National Guard. Before Joseph Steffan was thrown out of Annapolis six weeks short of graduation when his sexual orientation became known, he was the president of the student council in his senior year, president of the senior class, voted most likely to succeed, and was co-salutatorian in the graduating class. Paul Starr served in the Air Force. He was named the Strategic Air Command Outstanding Officer of the Year, Junior Officer of the Year, and Officer of the Year. He was given a less than honorable discharge and a one-year prison term (Humphrey, 1988). Until these individuals' sexual orientations were identified, they were excelling in the military environment. And it is probable that they had not been celibate.

The United States is not the only military which specifically excludes homosexuals from service. New Zealand, Portugal, and the United Kingdom also exclude homosexuals from service. Countries where homosexuals are allowed to serve with some limitations (e.g., no sexual relations on-base) include Belgium, Finland, France, and Germany. Homosexuals are allowed to serve with no restrictions in the militaries of Austria, Canada, Denmark, Italy, Japan, Luxembourg, the Netherlands, Norway, Spain, and Sweden. And there are no reports of problems there (USGAO, 1993).

The United States Government Accounting Office (USGAO) also investigated eight police and fire departments in four cities; all but one practices nondiscrimination on the basis of sexual orientation. The principles of these organizations are very close to those the military claims would be damaged by allowing homosexuals to serve: unit/team cohesiveness, discipline and good order, morale, trust and confidence, and a system of rank and respect. Not only have there been very few problems with the inclusion of homosexuals,

Some other officials stated that they believed exclusionary policies based on sexual orientation are counterproductive and only create further stress.

(USGAO, 1993, p. 42)

Finally the question of security. The military has claimed in the past that homosexuals are likely to be security risks as targets of blackmail. Of course, if they didn't have to keep their orientation secret there wouldn't be any fodder for blackmail. Nevertheless, recently the Chairman of the Joint Chiefs of Staff in a 1992 speech said that he agreed with the Secretary of Defense.

> *He said that the ban on homosexuals serving in the military is not based on a security argument but on his judgment and the judgment of the service chiefs that homosexual behavior is inconsistent with maintaining good order and discipline.*
>
> *(USGAO, 1993, p. 35)*

So what's happened since the new policy which should make it safe for homosexuals to serve their country (as long as they stay in the closet)? Expulsions from the military for homosexuality were 850 in 1996, a five-year high and the highest number since 1987. The Servicemember's Legal Defense Fund (1995) documented 443 specific violations of the policy. Women were particularly targeted. Only 13 percent of those serving in the military are women. They represented 29 percent of the courts-martial for homosexuality. In general, it would appear that the policy is in conflict with the realities of the situation in the United States military.

Discussion Questions

Apply the concepts from the chapter to consider the following questions:

1. What are the basic sources of the conflict between those who feel homosexuals should serve in the military and those who believe they should not?
2. What positive and negative effects on the military do you see resulting from this conflict over the exclusion of homosexuals from the military?
3. Do you think President Clinton's policy on homosexuals in the military decreased or escalated the conflict?
4. Design a program that would reduce the amount of potential conflict should homosexuals be allowed to openly serve in the military.
5. Why do you think some countries have no problems with conflict in the military when gays are allowed to serve?

Social Dilemmas: A Special Case of Conflict

What Would YOU Predict?

Pat is trying to watch Rickie who is three years old, and trying to get the kitchen cleaned up. Pat turns on the television and sets the channel to the public broadcasting channel which is showing "Sesame Street"—Rickie's favorite show. Just then a pledge break comes on asking for contributions to the station. It emphasizes how the channel depends on public funds. Pat has not contributed to the channel, but watches it regularly. Will Pat leave the channel where it is, feel guilty and change the channel to a cartoon station, or call and make a pledge? (Hint: You're sophisticated enough by now for me to throw you a semi-trick question.)

INTRODUCTION

In the last chapter we discussed a range of conflict situations and possible solutions. In this chapter we will focus on a particular type of conflict situation known as social dilemmas. Because these are so commonly encountered in daily life and because the solutions are particularly elusive, we'll spend an entire chapter exploring these phenomena.

WHAT ARE SOCIAL DILEMMAS?

Social dilemmas have been variously defined by individual psychologists (surprise!). But one aspect they all agree upon is the fact that social dilemmas spring from the fact that group members are **interdependent** upon each other for their individual outcomes. In a group, my choices for behavior do not entirely account for my results, because others are also making choices that affect my outcomes. The choices that maximize my own outcomes are not always good for the group. And the group's choices are not always optimal for my outcomes.

Let's examine a number of the definitions presented for the phenomenon of social dilemmas. "A social dilemma is a structure in which **dominating strategies** converge on a **deficient equilibrium**" (Dawes, 1980). In order to make sense of this definition, we need to define several more terms. Dominating strategies are (as in social facilitation) the most likely behavioral choice for an individual. Further, there are several important facets of this term:

> This is a strategy that (1) yields at least as high a payoff for the individual choosing it as any other alternative strategy no matter what others choose, and (2) leads to a higher payoff than any other strategy for at least one combination with others' choices. If dominating strategies exist for all players, then the outcome resulting from their mutual choice is the sole equilibrium in the game; if the outcome is deficient, the game is a social dilemma.
>
> **(Caporael, Dawes, Orbell, & Van de Kragt, 1989, p. 697)**

More simply stated, any of us are more likely to make a choice that both gives us the most "goodies" regardless of what others choose, and gives us better results than any of our other choices when combined with at least one of the plethora of choices of other group members. So I either get the best possible outcome, or have a chance at a better (possibly not the best) outcome with at least one of my partners' choices of behavior. I'm maximizing the goodies I get. But if everyone does this, then there is only one equilibrium or possible outcome of the game. If everyone loses (deficient equilibrium), then we have a social dilemma. More formally stated,

> Social dilemmas occur when the pursuit of self-interest by individuals in a group leads to less than optimal collective outcomes for everyone in the group. A critical assumption in the human sciences is that people's choices in such dilemmas are individualistic, selfish, and rational.
>
> **(Caporael et al., 1989, p. 683)**

This doesn't present a very pretty picture of human behavior. It sounds as if everyone is always out for themselves. However, the term "rational" is used in this context to assume that we will choose the behavior that results in the best outcome for ourselves. And it is more rational to take the most or the best for ourselves, except in situations of interdependence. Because then we depend on others to help us get the best. As Liebrand and Messick (1996) define social dilemmas:

> *Social dilemmas are complex situations in which we can choose what is in our own immediate best interest or what is in the best interest of our groups, which include ourselves as well as others.*
>
> **(Liebrand & Messick, 1996, p. 1)**

Suddenly it isn't so simple. Since we are members of the group, we should have a rational interest in making sure the group attains the best outcomes. But as individuals, perhaps the group's welfare means we as individuals must take less for ourselves. So there's at least the potential for conflict between the individual and collective optimality of the expected behaviors and consequences of two or more interdependent actors. When we have this conflict, we have a social dilemma. Do I behave in my own best interest (which might hurt the group) or do I behave in a way that corresponds with the group's best interest (which might hurt me).

INTERDEPENDENCE

The whole issue of this interdependence of results is known as **correspondence of outcomes** (Kelley & Thibault, 1978). In a win/lose situation—a zero-sum situation—the outcomes of the players are completely noncorrespondent. What is

The American need for the automobile represents a presently insoluble social trap.

best for me is worst for you. Hark back to the example of the poker game in Chapter 9. If I walk away from the poker table with $10 more than I sat down with, that by definition means that other players are walking away with a total of $10 less. I win, you lose. This situation is purely **competitive.**

Participants on sports teams may do quite well individually (a football player makes three touchdowns himself), but if the other team scores four touchdowns (by four different players, perhaps), the team loses. This may be the very best night of his life for the individual who made the touchdowns, but because there is a complete form of correspondence of outcomes, he loses anyway. Either the entire team wins, or everybody loses, no matter how stellar their performance or how great their effort. Thus in this situation the rational choices are purely **cooperative** in nature (Deutsch, 1949).

We enter the world of social dilemmas when there is no complete correspondence in outcomes. These are referred to as **mixed-motive situations** (Schelling, 1960). While in situations of complete correspondence of outcomes it is fairly easy to predict individual behavior, in mixed-motive situations several factors influence which strategies will be employed by individuals. How then, do we predict? We will break down the problem into two constituent parts: the individuals making the choices for behavior and the structure of the situation in which the behavioral choices are to be made.

INDIVIDUAL CONTRIBUTIONS

There are a number of individual characteristics that have been examined to determine their contribution to choices in a social dilemma. Some of the characteristics are **traits,** or stable over time. Others are **states,** which are temporary in nature. An example of a trait might be my level of intelligence. This is usually assumed to be somewhat fixed and if tested today we would expect a high correlation between the same test taken two years ago. Moods are examples of states. I might be extremely happy because I finally got my dog housebroken, or I might be very sad because my father just died. But these by definition don't last over time.

Things get a bit sticky when some behaviors can be either state or trait. Depression, for example can be either trait or state. Some people are just depressed all the time (trait). Others are reacting to an event and will "come out of it" after a period of time (state).

Social Orientations

Social orientation has been explained a number of ways. Some believe it to be a personality trait (Komorita & Parks, 1994) while others consider one's social orientation to be reflective of attitudes, although this explanation is not well supported in the empirical literature (Baxter, 1972). A social orientation is ". . . a social value as a preference for a specific pattern of outcomes, in a setting of outcome interdependence that is consistent over time" (Baxter, 1972, p. 102). This perception of social orientation as a trait is supported by McClintock (1977) and by McClintock and Liebrand (1988).

How to assess an individual's social orientation? The dominant paradigm has been to simulate social situations of interdependence and measure an individual's pattern of choices (McClintock & Van Avermaet, 1982). The earliest measures differentiated between cooperators and noncooperators. The distinctions in social orientation were further differentiated by Kuhlman and associates (Kuhlman & Marshello, 1975; Kuhlman & Wimberly, 1976; and Kuhlman, Camac, & Cunha, 1986).

Social dilemmas are restructured into **decomposed games** in which the individual makes choices of payoffs in a series of hypothetical situations of interdependence. If an individual is consistent in orientation over two-thirds of the choices offered they are classified a *cooperator,* and *individualist,* a *competitor,* or an *altruist* as seen below.

Here's the way it works. Each participant is told that they are to make a choice from A to D. Their outcomes for themselves and for an unknown partner (Other) are indicated below the letter chosen. However, their TOTAL outcome will be a combination of their own and the others' choices.

Sometimes it helps to concretize this and think of the outcome units as dollars (see Table 10.1). Thus if Philip chose alternative B he would be taking $30 for himself and giving Carla (his anonymous partner) $18. If Carla chooses alternative C, she is giving herself $23 and her partner (Philip) $10. The final totals, then, are Philip $40 ($30 + $10), and Carla $41 ($18 + $23).

 So go ahead, which alternative would you choose? Can you explain your reasoning in making the choice? What would you predict others would choose?

Each of these choices has been carefully crafted to separate out the various social orientations. And each orientation perceives a different rational choice. The *cooperator* looks at the table as a series of addition problems. How can the cooperator maximize the outcomes for the team? Alternative A provides the team with a total of $50, alternative B with $48, alternative C with $33, and alternative D with $35. From a cooperator's perspective, alternative A is the only rational choice.

The *individualist* looks at the table as a series of comparisons. For alternative A the individualist makes $25, for alternative B the individualist makes $30, for alternative C the individualist makes $23, and for alternative D the individualist makes $15. For the individualist, the only rational choice is alternative B.

TABLE 10.1. Example of Decomposed Games Used to Classify Social Orientation

	A	B	C	D
Self	25	30	23	15
Other	25	18	10	20

The *competitor* also looks at the table as a series of comparisons, but very differently than the individualist. The competitor wants to do well, but this motive is secondary to beating the partner by the largest possible margin. So you could say competitors examine the differences in their outcomes to the outcomes of their partners and seek to maximize this difference in their favor. So the competitor sees alternative A as a wash—not winning at all, in alternative B the competitor "beats" their partner by $12, in alternative C the competitor "beats" their partner by $13, and (horror of horrors!) in alternative D the competitor gets "beaten" by their partner by $5. For the competitor, then, alternative C is the only rational choice to be made.

Finally, our *altruist* is someone who never thinks of their own welfare first. They ALWAYS think first of their partner's well-being. In the example, there is only one choice in which the other makes more than the individual making the choice—alternative D. That, for the altruist, would be the only rational choice.

A word of caution here. I often put this table on the board before we discuss this topic and ask students to make a choice. After the first few times I discovered I had to really emphasize that a single choice did not categorize anyone, because some students were upset with the labels associated with their choices. So, if you made a choice that makes you uncomfortable, remember that you would have a series of these choices and you would have to be consistent two-thirds of the time to be classified!

Problems arise, however, when individuals are not consistent. As many as 30 percent of individuals are lost to the classification system because of their inconsistent choices (Maki & McClintock, 1983). This problem can be reduced by using individualized regression (a statistical technique) which reduces the lost percentage down to 3 percent (Knight & Dubro, 1984).

Having classified individuals, let's examine three of the different orientations and their consistent tendencies for behavior as well as evidence as to how

While children can be selfish and individualistic, they can also cooperate and share with each other as they play.

these orientations develop. We are not going to have a separate discussion of **altruists** for two reasons: (1) not many true altruists are found in screening; and (2) while the occasional altruistic behavior is perceived as heroic, anyone who consistently puts the welfare of someone else above their own is probably in need of a referral to an appropriate therapist (personal comment).

Cooperators

Cooperators are generally perceived as nice folks. They want to do well for themselves, but their primary concern is the group's welfare. Their first choice in a new situation will be to behave in a manner that will enhance the group's welfare. What if, however, they are paired with an individualist or competitor? Will they continue to make the cooperative choice, or a **defective choice?** Let's go back to the table and do the math. With an individualist, the cooperator will receive $43 ($25 + $18), and with the competitor, the cooperator will receive $35 ($25 + $10). Thus the group (or team in this case) does not do as well as if both had made cooperative choices which would have yielded a total of $100 ($25 + $25 or $50 for each). In each case the cooperator has been "ripped off" by their partner in terms of both individual outcome, and outcome for the group (which would be $35 for the cooperator and $48 for the competitor for a total of $83; and would be $43 for the cooperator and $55 for the individualist for a total of $98).

Cooperators are nice people, but they aren't stupid. They will not allow themselves to be taken in a second time. Therefore if we allowed the above pairs to play a second round of the game, the cooperators would change their strategies in response to the partner's betrayal on the first round. This is known as **behavioral assimilation.** They would behave like competitors on the second round and the results would look like that of Table 10.2.

The reason there is no change in team outcome on the second round for paired cooperators is because there was no defection on the first round. The team outcomes for the second round for cooperators paired with the other two orientations were significantly worse than for the first round.

What if we switched partners after two rounds of the game? What would we expect to see on the first round of the new game? We would expect to see cooperators revert back to their cooperative behavior. Cooperators don't switch to a strategy of defection unless they are provoked.

TABLE 10.2. Comparisons of Cooperators' Outcomes on First and Second Round of Decomposed Games Indicating Behavioral Assimilation on the Part of the Cooperator

	Round 1 Choice	Team Outcome	Round 2 Choice	Team Outcome
Cooperator with competitor	A ($25) C ($10)	$83	C ($23) C ($10)	$66
Cooperator with individualist	A ($25) B ($18)	$98	C ($23) B ($18)	$81
Cooperator with cooperator	A ($25) A ($25)	$100	A ($25) A ($25)	$100

I've implied several times that the cooperators are good guys. They are motivated to help others. What is the source of this motivation? Recall that in Caporeal and others' (1989) definition of a social dilemma they stated that a "critical assumption" was the fact that in social dilemmas people's choices are "individualistic, selfish, and rational" (p. 683). Just how does this square with cooperative behavior?

One explanation that has been put forward is that cooperation is really based on **egoistic incentives** (EIs). The explanation offered by Axelrod (1984) posits the theory that cooperation develops as a result of the positive outcomes that are received by the cooperator when the cooperation is reciprocated. Caporael and others (1989) propose that cognitive and affective factors in cooperation may have evolved "from selection pressures exerted under the small-group living conditions for developing and maintaining group membership" (p. 684). This would certainly be consistent with the discussion in Chapter 2 offered by the sociobiologists which suggests that people form groups because those who didn't were killed off before they could contribute to the gene pool. The flexibility of behavior seen in cooperators can certainly be explained by Tetlock (1990):

> I suspect that there is an Aristotelian golden mean lurking here: Nature has probably smiled especially kindly on those who recognize that their long-term self-interest hinges on the viability of their group, but who also recognize that serious conflicts can arise between individual and collective interests and who appreciate the importance of knowing when to "defect" and how to do so without incurring the wrath of the collectivity. In short, human nature is complex and embodies many, often conflicting motives; evolutionary arguments are necessarily speculative; and agnosticism on the "selfishness" question probably remains the most prudent position.
>
> *(Tetlock, 1990, p. 724)*

Competitors

The portrait painted of **competitors** thus far is not particularly attractive. They sound like Ebeneezer Scrooge-type folks (Dickens, 1991) who just want to be as nasty as possible. But wait. Maybe there's another possible motivation for their behavior. When asked about their perception of the distribution of the social orientations across the population, American competitors assume that everyone is a competitor. If they truly believe this, then competitive behavior can be perceived as a preemptive strike to prevent others from ripping them off first. Thus the disagreeable behavior can be perceived as defensive rather than offensive.

Compared to cooperators, competitors are very inflexible in their behavior. They can be counted on to make the defective choice in almost every setting. And this very behavior results in a **self-fulfilling prophecy.** I as a competitor am paired with a cooperator. As is my bent, I rip him off. His behavior is cooperative. Until we play again, and he retaliates. See—everyone really IS a competitor. The initial cooperative behavior was a ploy to get me to give them a chance to take advantage of me.

Individualists

Individualists on the surface (at least so far in this discussion) appear to be somewhat aloof from social interaction. Although their behavior is negative, at least competitors are reacting to the presence of the other. Individualists on first examination appear to be oblivious to the existence of others.

This is not the case. Individuals think of themselves FIRST. If they have two equally attractive options and one is more advantageous to the partner than the other option, individualists will choose to benefit their partner—but ONLY if they themselves do not suffer in the process.

Thus we can see an interesting difference in the three orientations. Cooperators are responsive to the behavior of other individuals in the environment and will shift their strategies based on those behaviors. Competitors are so worried about getting hurt that their behavior is frozen. Individuals will base their behavior more on the structure of the situation. In other words, individualists will go wherever their own interests are most highly rewarded. This will become very important when we discuss the various situational structures of social dilemmas.

 If placed in a situation of interdependence (e.g., a class group assignment) with a stranger or with your best friend, would you be more likely to defect by not carrying your weight with one rather than the other? Why? What about you—or your partner determines your response?

Other Traits

There have been a number of other personal characteristics that have been examined for their relationship with behavior in social dilemmas. These include *trust, interpersonal orientation,* culture and gender differences.

Trust has been explored in relation to cooperative behavior (see Messick & Brewer, 1983). Higher levels of trust are related to higher levels of cooperative behavior. This should be interpreted with caution, however, because a correlation does not imply causation. Perhaps cooperators are cooperators because they are basically trusting people. Or it might be that trusting people are more willing to cooperate and take a chance on other people. Or there might be some other, separate characteristic that causes both trust and cooperation.

A recent measure of trust is a five-item questionnaire developed by Yamagishi (1986). Each item is a five-point scale. The points on the scale are summed and higher total scores indicate higher levels of interpersonal trust. Yamagishi validated the scale by finding high correlations between scores on his scale and cooperative behaviors.

Interpersonal orientation (IO) is related to the extent that an individual is concerned with the good of the other person in a relationship (see Rubin & Brown, 1975, and Swap & Rubin, 1983). Individuals high in IO are more concerned with the relationship than those who are low in IO. High IOs are sensitive to the ideas of reciprocity, equity, and orientation. Both cooperators and competitors are considered high IO because both are attuned to others. Individualists are considered low IO.

Interpersonal orientation is measured with a scale consisting of twenty-nine Likert-type questions. A high score indicates high IO (although the scale is not high in face validity because some of the items are reverse scored). Scores on IO don't necessarily predict behavior accurately because of the phenomenon of behavioral assimilation on the part of cooperators.

Cultural and Gender Differences in Individual Contributions

As with every other issue discussed in this text, culture affects individual behavior in social dilemma situations. Early speculation and theorizing on the effects of culture (Tajfel, Billig, Bundy, & Flament, 1971; Turner, Brown, & Tajfel, 1979) were based on the concept of in-group versus out-group behaviors. It was hypothesized that those with positive feelings toward out-groups should be more cooperative. Those with negative beliefs about and attitudes toward out-groups should evidence more competitive or individualistic behavior. Thus it was predicted that individualistic cultures such as the United States should show high levels of cooperation, and collectivist cultures such as Japan should be more competitive and individualistic.

Empirical research has resulted in mixed support for these predictions. First of all, age appears to be an important confounding variable. Generally, young children are individualistic. This finding was supported by Kagan and Zahn (1983) who found only age, but not cultural differences in individualism. The development of cooperation (referred to as altruism by Kenrick, Baumann, and Cialdini [1979], but fitting the definition of cooperation as defined in this chapter) has been described as developing through three stages:

> *(1) for primary grade children, altruism is self-punishing; (2) for slightly older children, altruism is used instrumentally to elicit social approval; (3) for adults, the reward value of altruism is internalized, and adults will act prosocially even when no one is looking.*
>
> **(Kenrick, 1989, p. 711)**

Competition in children also appears to increase as they age, leveling off at about sixth grade across cultures. At this point in age, American and Belgian children were found to be less competitive than Japanese or Greek children, with Mexican children showing lowest levels of competitive behavior (e.g., Kagan & Madsen, 1971; Kagan & Madsen, 1972; Knight & Kagan, 1977; Madsen, 1971; Madsen & Shapira, 1970; McClintock, 1974; McClintock & McNeel, 1966; and Toda, Shinotsuka, McClintock, & Stich, 1978). Knight, Kagan and Burul (1982) found that Mexican-American children were more cooperative than Anglo children. Eliram and Schwarzwald (1987) found that Middle Eastern adults were more cooperative than Westerners in rural, but not in urban settings. Liebrand and von Ruden (1985), however, found no cross-cultural differences in social motives between Dutch and American college students.

An interesting study by Knight and Kagan (1977) found a relationship between social orientation in children and level of *self-esteem*. For both

African-American and Anglo children, high self-esteem was associated with competitiveness. For second generation Mexican-American children, only one generation from a more collectivistic culture, high self-esteem was significantly related to cooperativeness. By the third generation, however, Mexican-American children had begun to be acculturated into standard American norms and away from Mexican norms and no relationship was found between cooperativeness or competitiveness and self-esteem.

Gender differences in social orientation appear to be confounded with culture. American girls are more individualistic than American boys (Knight & Kagan, 1981) which might at first appear to be counterintuitive. However, it can be explained by the higher amounts of pressure to conform to social norms placed on girls. Individualism is a basic American norm (Komorita & Parks, 1994). This finding is supported by a failure to find gender differences in individualism in collectivist cultures (Mexican, Korean, Native American) (Madsen & Shapira, 1970; Madsen & Yi, 1975; and Miller & Thomas, 1972). In the United States, women are only slightly more likely than men to cooperate. When they do, women are more likely to justify their behavior as altruistic and principled than are men (Stockard, Van de Kragt, & Dodge, 1988).

We have now examined the first piece of the puzzle in explaining behavior in social dilemma situations. Individuals are predisposed by virtue of their social orientation, their culture, their gender, and other traits to behave in particular ways. However, the social environment certainly places constraints on our behaviors. So we will turn now to the other half of the puzzle—the variations in **structures of situations** of interdependence and the effects of different structures on behavior.

STRUCTURES OF SITUATIONS

While social orientation and other traits play important roles in predicting behavior, the rewards associated with certain behaviors also influence how people behave. The pattern of rewards associated with particular behaviors in various structures of interdependence is known as the **payoff matrix.** Differences in the structures of these matrices identify the situation. A number of different situations (structures) have been studied and will be discussed here, including the prisoner's dilemma, including the variants: the tragedy of the commons, and the chicken game; public goods dilemmas including the volunteer dilemma and a brief discussion of helping behavior in this context; and social traps and social fences.

Prisoner's Dilemma

Prisoner's dilemma is perhaps the most studied format of payoff matrix. Prisoner's dilemma is a two-person situation in which each person has only two choices of behavior: cooperation or defection. Let's look at the payoff matrix for this situation (Figure 10.1).

So what does this all mean? The lower left letter in each square represents the outcome for that combination of choices for person 1. For example, if person

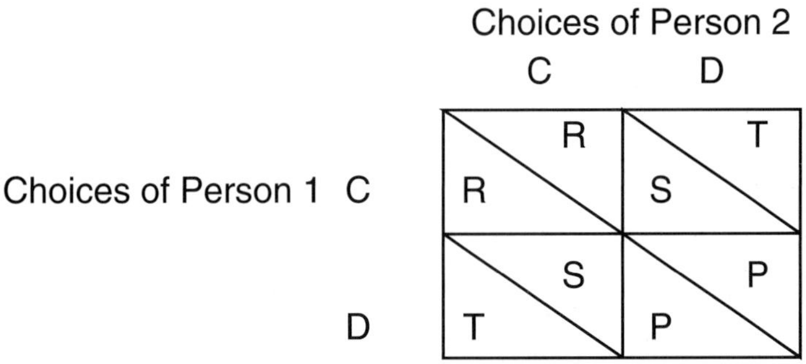

Choices of Person 2

FIGURE 10.1. Payoff matrix in the general form of prisoner's dilemma (Komorita & Parks, 1994).

2 chose D and person 1 chose C, they would end up in the upper right-hand quadrant of the matrix and person 1 would receive outcome S. The values for each letter in the matrix must conform to the following scheme for the situation to represent a **prisoner's dilemma structure:**

R = Reward for mutual cooperation

P = Punishment for mutual defection

T = Temptation to defect

S = Sucker's payoff

with the following restriction: $T > R > P > S$ (Kerr, 1983; Orbell & Dawes, 1981).

Thus the best payoff for an individual in this game is for the partner to cooperate and for the individual to defect (T). Of course, this invites retaliation. And the attractiveness of the temptation depends on the size of the payoff and the individual's social orientation. The worst that can happen to an individual in this situation is the sucker's payoff (S). This is the consequence of being double-crossed after making a cooperative choice. This is the situation that triggers behavioral assimilation in cooperators.

We can identify other situations from this matrix. With the expression $(T − R) = greed$, if the difference is large enough it becomes particularly attractive to defect for the individualist. $(R − P)$ is the size of the incentive to achieve outcome R and avoid outcome P. $(P − S)$ is the incentive to avoid the sucker's payoff. If the game is going to be played over many trials, then an additional restriction must be added: $2R > (T + S)$. Otherwise it becomes a rational choice to simply trade off turns at being ripped off and the outcomes will be equal for the two parties.

Now that we have all the technical aspects nailed down, let me tell you the story that pulls this all together. Bonnie and Clyde decide they're going to rob a jewelry store. They commit the crime, but not being particularly competent criminals, they are arrested after just enough time to stash the goods. The police immediately separate them for interrogation, and they tell them each the same story:

Look, Bonnie, we've got your fingerprints all over the jewelry store so we've got you. You'll spend five years in prison. Unless you tell us where the "stuff" is and implicate Clyde. We've been after him for a while and if we have more evidence on him he'll go to prison for ten years. If you help us and implicate him in the crime, and if we don't get any further evidence on you, we can promise you a one-year term in prison. If you implicate him and give us the loot he'll get twelve years. Think it over.

So now we've got a payoff matrix that looks like this:

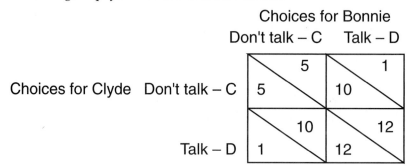

Choices for Bonnie

		Don't talk – C	Talk – D
Choices for Clyde	Don't talk – C	5 / 5	1 / 10
	Talk – D	10 / 1	12 / 12

(Notice that in this example the BEST outcomes are smaller numbers representing time in jail.)

So in this situation, if both cooperate, they'll each do five years in prison and have the jewelry to look forward to upon release. If Bonnie rats on Clyde, she's home wearing the jewelry next year while he cools his heels for ten years. If Clyde rats on Bonnie, he's home in a year decorating someone else. And if they both rat, each will spend twelve years in prison with no loot at the end of the stretch. What's a poor girl to do?

That may well depend upon a number of things. What's Bonnie's social orientation? How much does she trust Clyde? If Bonnie's a cooperator, she considers her outcomes like this: "Hmm. If I and Clyde both keeps our mouths shut we'll be in prison five years, but we'll have the loot. If he talks and I don't, he's out fooling around in a year, while I turn old and gray in the joint. If I talk and he doesn't, I can do a one-year stretch and party wearing the pretties for nine years while he's still in the slammer. But if we both blab, we'll be in for twelve years. What's the best for us as a couple? We should both keep our mouths shut and then we'll get out together and have us some fun." Bonnie the cooperator keeps silent.

Bonnie the individualist looks at things differently. She goes through the same process of identifying her alternatives and decides, "I know that fool Clyde's crazy about me so he'd never talk. If I do, I'm out in a year. The only sane choice is to blab." Bonnie the individualist defects.

Finally, Bonnie the competitor doesn't hesitate for a minute. "Do I think that rat Clyde will keep quiet and risk me getting out ahead of him? No way. How much do you want to know?" Bonnie the competitor also defects. Remember that there is a parallel process going on with Clyde. Their outcomes are interdependent. So, much to our chagrin (whatever happened to true love?), Bonnie cooperates by keeping silent and Clyde sings like a canary; one year for Clyde, ten for Bonnie.

Ten years later Clyde picks up Bonnie at the prison, proclaims his undying love and sincerest apologies and proposes. After the wedding, Clyde suggests a way to add some excitement to their honeymoon. Why not rob a bank? Love may be blind, and in this case it's also stupid, because Bonnie agrees. Neither one has gotten any better at crime while Bonnie was away, but Bonnie remembers all too well her decade in prison.

So this time when presented with the prisoner's dilemma, Bonnie doesn't hesitate a second. And they both spend the next twelve years in prison. That's what behavioral assimilation will do for you.

Chicken Game

Altering the payoff matrix can affect the behavior of individuals, especially that of individualists. Remember that they want the most goodies they can get from a situation. Thus the individualist will be the most sensitive to changes in the payoffs associated with cooperative and defective behavior.

The chicken game alters the payoff matrix so that $T > R > S > P$. Here the temptation to defect (T) is still the strongest value. The worst possible outcome for those involved is the punishment for mutual defection (P). The change from prisoner's dilemma is the positioning of P and S.

The **chicken game** is named after the teenage driving game. Two cars face each other and start to drive straight at each other at high rates of speed. Here the cooperative choice is to swerve away at the last moment to avoid an accident. If both do it, they both live and both have to live with any embarrassment associated with perceived lack of courage (or lack of a death wish). The worst possible outcome is for both drivers to defect and fail to swerve, resulting in a head-on collision. If I swerve away (cooperate) and you keep straight on course (defect), I'm seen as a chicken. And vice versa.

Cooperators would probably swerve anyway. Competitors would probably risk death over dishonor anyway. What we see in the chicken game is that the individualists' best interest is served by the cooperative choice, NOT the defective choice as was true in prisoner's dilemma and the commons dilemma.

PUBLIC GOODS DILEMMAS

Another form of social dilemma is the public goods dilemma. In a **public goods dilemma** there is a resource that is essentially inexhaustible. And individuals can enjoy the resource without having to contribute anything to the resource. Komorita and Parks (1994) used the example of a public television station. These stations are supported by their viewers' contributions. However, it is perfectly possible to watch public television without having to contribute any money. There is the impossibility of exclusion. Noncontributors cannot be shut off.

The individual rational choice is not to contribute, but to watch. But if no one contributes, the station goes off the air. Public goods dilemmas are examples of **continuous public goods dilemmas.** If the station does not receive sufficient money to continue the current level of programming, the number of programs can be reduced, the more expensive programs can be cut, or the number of hours of programming can be reduced. (By the way, Pat sat down and wrote a check after the pledge break. Rickie is only quiet during "Sesame Street." Pat won't risk losing that program.)

Charities are also examples of continuous public goods dilemmas. Charities can only provide help or give away money to the extent that there are contributions. If the Red Cross doesn't have blood, they can't provide it to accident victims. If the United Way doesn't get enough money, flood victims may not get fed or sheltered.

Yet another type of public goods dilemma is the **discrete** or **step-level public goods dilemma.** In this type of dilemma, a certain level of resource is necessary to provide a service at all. If the city wants to purchase a block of land on which to establish a park in honor of Vietnam veterans, they must come up with the total amount of the price or there will be no memorial. In this instance it isn't possible to cut back or otherwise alter the resource. It's all or none. Yet people can still not contribute and use the finished resource.

In my community we have what has to be one of the greatest playgrounds in the world. Architects went to the elementary schools in the city and asked children for ideas as to what would constitute the perfect playground. Then plans were drawn, and the community was asked to contribute not just money, but sweat equity. The original time-line had to be extended because there was a shortage of money and help and it looked for a while as if maybe the project could not be completed. When that possibility became clear, however, sufficient funds and workers materialized. Now anyone can play on an almost square block of castles, rivers, sandboxes (beaches), and other equipment. On a project like this, *free riding* is very tempting. Particularly if it appears that there are sufficient resources being provided without your input. And the larger the group, the stronger the temptation. An interesting gender twist to this effect, however, found by Kerr and MacCoun (1985) is that in a social dilemma both male and female American participants were less willing to attempt to free ride if their partners were female.

A variant of this dilemma is the **volunteer dilemma.** Three friends want to drive to the Mall of America to shop. They can only get there if someone drives. This involves the cost of gas and wear and tear on the car and the energy involved in driving. Everyone benefits by not volunteering unless no one volunteers. Then nobody goes. Everyone loses.

SOCIAL TRAPS

We've explored two of the major types of social dilemmas: the prisoner's dilemma structures and the social goods dilemmas. The final structures we will examine are structured around the conflict between the fact that short-term individual gain produces long-term group losses (Cross & Guyer, 1980; Messick & Brewer, 1983; and Platt, 1973). Cooperative behavior is beneficial in the long term, but requires some sacrifice. Competitive behavior has short-term gains but results in long-term losses. These situations are known as *social traps.*

Tragedy of the Commons

One version of this problem was dubbed by Hardin (1968) as the **tragedy of the commons.** Another story. In colonial times, villages were built in circles around open spaces of ground of which the members of the community shared ownership. Often they grazed their animals on this commons. This was advantageous because it kept the animals in and the predators out. The major difference between the prisoner's dilemma and the commons dilemma is that in the case of the commons we are dealing with a finite resource. As long as the villagers were reasonable about the number of animals they put on the commons, there was plenty of grass for all and everyone profited now and in the future years as the commons replenished itself. This equilibrium point of optimal usage is known as **carrying capacity.** It is possible, however, for too many animals to destroy the commons and turn it into a muddy sinkhole which will not support any animals in the future. The issue, then, becomes managing the resource, and avoiding exceeding the carrying capacity.

So the villagers have a town meeting. It has been determined, they are told, that in order to keep the commons in healthy shape, each household may only graze two sheep per year. The payoff matrix is exactly the same as for prisoner's dilemma. If everyone cooperates the resource goes on undamaged into the foreseeable future (the best possible outcome for all—R). If everyone adds additional sheep, the commons is destroyed which is the worst possible outcome for everyone—P. But what if only some people cheat? Given that each family would like to maximize their outcomes, what is the level of incentive?

> *(1) The positive component is a function of the increment of one animal. Since the herdsman receives all the proceeds from the sale of the additional animal, the positive utility is nearly +1.*
> *(2) The negative component is a function of the additional overgrazing created by one more animal. Since, however, the effects of overgrazing are shared by all the herdsmen, the negative utility for any particular decision-making herdsman is only a fraction of −1.*
>
> **(Hardin, 1968 in Hardin, 1995)**

So all the benefits of cheating accrue to me while I am hurting everyone else, but only a little. The predicted behaviors are exactly the same as for prisoner's dilemma. The cooperator does not add any more animals. The individualist does. So does the competitor. Realizing that everyone else is cheating (the equivalent of round 2 in the example above) the cooperator recognizes the imminent demise of the commons and also adds animals to minimize the personal damage. And next year everyone starves.

Another type of social trap is known as **entrapment.** In entrapment, a group or individual begins a project. Perhaps an American corporation begins building a luxury hotel in Iraq. As time passes and more and more money is invested in the project, relations between the United States and Iraq begin to deteriorate to the point of potential war. The corporation continues to build, hoping things will be all right in the face of evidence to the contrary. Why? They have sunk costs. So they continue to throw good money after bad.

Another example would be an individual who has worked for a company for 19 years. They can retire with full benefits after 25 years. But they hate the job. Still they stay—because to leave means forfeiting the substantial contribution that the employer has contributed to the individual's retirement fund, and will only be paid out after the full 25 years.

Social Fences

The opposite of a social trap is a **social fence** (Messick & Brewer, 1983). Public goods dilemmas are examples of social fences. Behaviors resulting in short-term individual losses produce long-term collective gains. Individuals take money from their own pockets to feed starving children, or support the widows and children of police officers slain in the line of duty, or to elect a candidate to office who they feel will help the country. Short term, they're out-of-pocket. Long term, the collective is better off. Perhaps we could look at taxes as social fences, but somehow I just can't bring myself to do so.

REMEDIES IN REAL LIFE

As different as these three major types of social dilemmas may appear, the solution to all is essentially the same. How can we increase cooperation and discourage defection? The only truly effective approach appears to be altering the rewards associated with cooperative behavior. That's why behaviors differ across games and dilemmas. Defection is encouraged by the prisoner's dilemma type of structure. My best outcome will be achieved if I can sucker you into cooperating while I defect and rip you off. In the public goods dilemma structure, why should I contribute when I can get the resource for free? And finally why should I volunteer when someone else will do so instead?

As much as I wish that socialization could increase the propensity for cooperation, people appear to operate on a more concrete, materialistic basis. What's in it for me? Thus by creating rewards for cooperative behavior you sway the behavior of individualists from defection to cooperation. Cooperators aren't the problem, and competitors will always compete. They can't help it. But if I can make cooperative behavior pay off better than defective behavior in the short term, I have the highest probability of increasing the occurrence of cooperative behavior not only in cooperators, but also in individualists.

Summary

In this chapter we have examined a very particular type of conflict—social dilemmas. In these situations of interdependence we have a potential conflict between what is best for the individual and what is best for the group. Often short-term advantageous behavior results in disastrous future consequences. We have examined the human contributions to these dilemmas in terms of social orientation, trust, interpersonal orientation, culture, and gender. We have also explored the role of the payoff matrix in determining the structure of the dilemma. Finally, we discussed the difficulty in solving this type of conflict and offered a few possible remedies.

Key Terms

altruist
behavioral assimilation
carrying capacity
chicken game
competitive
competitor
continuous public goods
  dilemma
cooperative
cooperator
correspondence of
  outcomes
decomposed games
defective choice

deficient equilibrium
discrete (step-level)
  public goods dilemma
dominating strategies
egoistic incentives
entrapment
individualist
interdependence
interpersonal orientation
  (IO)
mixed-motive situations
payoff matrix
prisoner's dilemma

prisoner's dilemma
  structure
public goods dilemma
self-fulfilling prophecy
social dilemmas
social fence
social orientation
state
structures of situations
tragedy of the commons
trait
trust
volunteer dilemma

(Not everyone who reads this Application will like the political implications of its contents. I assure you, however, that this Application is as thoroughly based in scholarship as are the other ten. If you find the politics disturbing, perhaps this could be the source of a rousing class discussion.)

APPLICATION

Immigration as a Social Dilemma

From the time of "discovery" of the land mass that is now the United States of America by the Vikings or Christopher Columbus (or whatever myth you

Actual photograph of a group of Chinese whose attempt to illegally immigrate to America was foiled by the stranding of their ship.

subscribe to), America has been perceived as an open area, virtually unpopulated and available for those who had the intestinal fortitude and the reason to leave their own native lands. Immigration into the United States continued from both East and West until in 1883 historian Frederick Jackson Turner at the Chicago meeting of the American Historical Society read a paper entitled "The Significance of the Frontier in American History." In this paper he conveyed that an announcement from the Bureau of Census had officially declared the American frontier closed—settlers moving from West to East and East to West had met. No more using up the land and moving on. There was no further room to expand.

Early restrictions on immigration generally excluded only "known criminals, mental defectives and people with serious communicable disease" (Hardin, 1995, p. 2). Chinese had been barred since 1882, and Japanese were barred in 1908. After World War I, in 1924 the National Origins Act was passed which set quotas of immigrants from different nations. Ninety-six percent of the quotas were assigned to European countries, leaving 4 percent for all others not explicitly barred. Immigration from the Western hemisphere was not included nor regulated (Hardin, 1995).

As time advanced, regulations were relaxed. Asians were admitted—the Chinese in 1943 and the Japanese in 1952. In 1965 Congress added legislation in favor of family reunification. If a family member had emigrated to the United States, then other family members could also immigrate. By 1992, other acts of Congress had affected immigration such that the total immigration per year (both legal and illegal) increased. By the 1990s legal immigration had reached a "record 1.8 million admitted in 1991; illegal immigration also running at 300,000 to 500,000 net per year" (Brimelow, 1995, p. xiii).

To give a graphic example of how many illegal immigrants enter the United States from Mexico, on a 14-mile stretch of border between the United States and Mexico in California, in 1992 a total of 565,581 illegals were caught crossing over in this one section alone. Across the entire three-thousand-mile United States–Canadian border in 1992 just over 15,000 were arrested (Brimelow, 1995).

What's the worry? Isn't the United States the country with the Lady holding high her lamp—the Statue of Liberty with lines from the poem by Emma Lazarus inscribed at the base:

"Give me your tired, your poor,
Your huddled masses yearning to breathe free,
The wretched refuse of your teeming shore.
Send these, the homeless, tempest-tost to me.
I lift my lamp beside the golden door!"

(Lazarus, 1877)

Absolutely. But there comes a time when we must wipe our eyes of patriotic tears and take a long, serious look at the effects of essentially unlimited immigration on the carrying capacity of the United States. Our country is a resource that could potentially be taxed beyond its capabilities to provide any quality of life for its residents. Each additional human being on Earth makes use of the Earth's environment, including air, water, and food. "Carrying capacity is inversely related to the quality of life" (Hardin, 1995, p. 82). He goes on to give an example:

> *The present population of India is 600 million, and it is increasing by 15 million per year. The environmental load of this population is already great. The forests of India are only a small fraction of what they were three centuries ago. Soil erosion, floods, and the psychological costs of crowding are serious. Every one of the net 15 million lives added each year stresses the Indian environment more severely.* Every life saved this year in a poor country diminishes the quality of life for subsequent generations.
>
> ***(Hardin, 1995, p. 49, emphasis in original)***

So as we approach the carrying capacity of the United States, what can we do? In 1974, Hardin introduced the analogy of the lifeboat to this social dilemma. Those who have seen the 1997 blockbuster movie *Titanic* can relate to the idea of sitting in an only partially-filled lifeboat and watching others drowning all around.

Hardin offers three alternatives to those in the lifeboat:

1. They can take on everyone who needs help, swamp the boat and everyone will die.
2. Let's say the boat has room for five more people. How do we go about choosing which five? What criteria would be fair, or even moral?
3. We preserve our margin of safety and add no more passengers to the boat—with the attendant need to be alert to those who would board anyway.

At this point we clearly are not able to accomplish alternatives number 2 and 3. Look back to the estimated number of illegal immigrants coming over from Mexico on one short span of border over one year. And it is not only the land borders that are being breached. The photograph that precedes this application is a photo taken on Sunday, June 6, 1993. It is the freighter the *Golden Venture* which beached off Rockaway Beach off New York City carrying over 300 citizens of the Chinese province of Fujian. They had been at sea for three months around the Cape of Good Hope and ended up on a sandbar off New York.

These passengers had indentured themselves to the tune of $20,000 to $35,000 each for the voyage. They would work this cost off at jobs in New York City at wages of approximately $1 to $1.50 per hour. (Wages were so low because all of these immigrants were illegal and if they protested their treatment could be turned in to the Immigration and Naturalization Service (INS) and deported.) This was the 24th ship in two years from China alone that had been intercepted by U.S. officials. These same officials estimate they stop approximately 5 percent of the boats smuggling immigrants (Raspail, 1987).

This photo appeared on the paperback version of a novel by Jean Raspail entitled *The Camp of the Saints* (originally published 1987). This book tells the fictional story of a fleet of over 100 ships loaded with over 30,000 individuals per ship who take leave from the Ganges in India headed for the Mediterranean Sea. The book recounts the debates held in France over how to, or whether to allow the boats to land. Some argue that it is immoral to allow the ships to sink, as they surely will, if they are not allowed to land. Others argue that the traditional way of life will be changed forever by the influx of such numbers of individuals from other cultures with other values. Others argue that the land simply cannot support that many additional people. And the debate rages on as the ships move ever nearer.

America, as a nation of immigrants, is particularly vulnerable to guilt about cutting off immigration. After all, if it had been done before, we ourselves might not be Americans. And what of separated families? And how dare we deny the clearly higher standard of living to those from underdeveloped nations? "The increase in the last decade of the twentieth century exceeds the total population in 1600" (Cohen, 1995, p. 387). The lifeboat is filling up uncomfortably quickly.

Morality aside for a moment, can we practically limit immigration? Do we build an impenetrable wall around the nation, with patrol boats off our shores? Do we shoot down the crowds of people, men, women, children, and the elderly, who race in from Mexico each night? Are there any practical means of stopping immigration? What are the political and international ramifications if we do?

> *Efforts to satisfy human wants require time, and the time required may be longer than the finite time available to individuals. There is a race between the complexity of the problems that are generated by increasing human number and the ability of humans to comprehend and solve those problems. Educating people to solve problems takes time. Developing traditions of stable, productive cooperation takes time. Building institutions with the resources to make educated people into productive problem solvers takes time. Even with educated, cooperative people and appropriate institutions at hand, understanding and solving problems take still more time.*
>
> **(Cohen, 1995, p. 369)**

How much more time do we have?

Discussion Questions

Apply the concepts from the chapter to consider the following questions:

1. What type of structure does the immigration problem represent? Give examples to illustrate.
2. Discuss the concept of lifeboat morality. What is the most appropriate behavior under these circumstances? Do you think social orientation affects this choice? In what ways?
3. Find out in your class how many of the students are descendants of immigrants. How long have their families been in the United States? Does the attitude about limiting or stopping immigration relate to how long the family has lived in the United States? (If there are any foreign students, find out their perspective on this question.)
4. Suppose you were the prime minister of a nation that was losing hundreds of thousands of citizens each year to emigration. How would you feel about that? Would you want to cooperate with the United States in keeping your people home? Why or why not?
5. How much influence do you think politicians' social orientations have on the decisions they make regarding issues such as immigration? Explain.

Stress and Social Change

What Would YOU Predict?

Robert, 33, lives in southern California. The rains of El Niño of 1998 caused a mudslide that totally destroyed his house below. Alex, 35, lives in Des Moines, Iowa. In the winter of 1997, Tanya, his wife of ten years, died of ovarian cancer. One year later, who do you predict will be in better psychological and physical health?

INTRODUCTION

So now we come near to the end of our voyage through the topic of group dynamics. When I submitted the outline for this book to my publisher, I was asked the relevance of this particular chapter to the subject matter. I replied that not only are people a major source of stress in our lives, but that people are often tremendously important in helping us deal with stress. There are also groups whose entire reason for existence places them under extreme stress—individuals such as combat military troops, police officers, firefighters, ambulance crews, etc. The effects of this stress on the group is an important factor in the group's success. Finally, there are a number of types of groups in which change is not simply a side effect of having lived through the maturation of a group. These groups are intended specifically to create change in individuals. The types of people who are interested enough in group dynamics to take a course requiring this text or who choose to read this book are exactly the types of individuals who are most likely to suffer from extreme stress in the workplace and potentially burn out. These are the topics we will explore in this final chapter.

SO WHO CARES ABOUT STRESS?

Stress is a fact of everyday life. All of us are exposed to situations and people who create stress in our lives. So what? Besides being unpleasant to have to suffer through these situations, stress can have some serious effects on our mental and physical health. And the levels of stress are not going down. As the world becomes increasingly technological and complex politically we can look forward to nothing but increasing levels of stress in our lives. Those of us who choose to live in large cities are bombarded with stress on a regular basis. Those who choose to live rurally are increasingly having to deal with the stresses of trying to maintain the family farm against the tsunami of agribusiness as are those who work trying to help people deal with stress at high levels, the heroes of our society—the police, firefighters, emergency medical personnel, physicians, and nurses. No one is immune, not even our children. As part of her sixth grade health course, my daughter was given a questionnaire identifying the levels of and sources of stress in her life!

So it's unpleasant. Isn't functioning as an adult, at least in part, facing the hand we're dealt and coping? Certainly. But stress in the extreme can ruin not only your emotional and mental health, it can also potentially destroy your physical health and lead to death. That alone should be enough justification to explore the phenomenon more deeply.

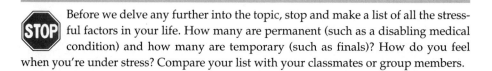

Before we delve any further into the topic, stop and make a list of all the stressful factors in your life. How many are permanent (such as a disabling medical condition) and how many are temporary (such as finals)? How do you feel when you're under stress? Compare your list with your classmates or group members.

The first to explore the association of physical health and stress was a Canadian physician named Hans Selye (1956). Selye worked with mice and exposed them to differing levels and types of *stressors:* electric shock, nonlethal doses of poison, extreme cold, and diets close to the starvation level. These he perceived to be not only physical but psychological stressors.

He found that there was a predictable series of responses to these stressors which he dubbed the **general adaptation syndrome (GAS).** In the first stage of the syndrome, the body reacts by kicking in a physiological reaction known as the **fight-or-flight response.** This response is extremely primitive in that it does not differentiate the type of stressor being encountered. The stressor could be stepping off the sidewalk to cross the street and noticing a speeding truck bearing down on you, or it could be an exam in a course on group dynamics. The body does the same things, regardless.

All of the responses are intended to prepare the body to stand and defend itself, or run away as quickly as possible. Adrenaline shoots through the body arousing nerves and hormonal reactions. The blood flow is shifted more toward the muscles that will need to be used. Because these muscles work on oxygen, the breathing and heart rate speed up to introduce more oxygen into the system. Metabolism is increased to help counteract the toxins created by muscular overuse. And the immune system is temporarily strengthened. The entire state of readiness is known as an **adrenalergic state.** Our bodies are energized and ready to "rock." We won't feel pain if we are injured in this state and individuals can do feats of strength that would be impossible otherwise—as in cases where we hear of someone lifting a damaged car off an accident victim.

This reaction in the GAS is known as the **alarm reaction.** The body has recognized and prepared to cope with the stress. If the coping mechanisms don't work, mice who are stressed for an extended period of time become ill. The body simply can't maintain this state of hyper-preparedness over any period of time. It must revert to a **cholinergic state** of physical homeostasis to rest and heal. When Selye sacrificed the mice and examined their bodies, he found evidence of

> *bleeding ulcers, diseased adrenal glands, a withered thymus, abnormally high levels of blood salts and sugars, and a high white blood count. The animals had been suffering from an excessive adrenalergic state over time of prolonged stress.*
>
> (O'Connell & O'Connell, 1997, p. 145)

Ideally, the alarm reaction allows the individual to cope successfully in a relatively short time so the body can return to normal. If the individual cannot cope successfully with stressors they enter into the **stage of resistance.** Autopsies on mice from this stage indicated healing of tissues and blood counts. However, continued application of the stressors on the mice resulted in the third stage of the GAS, the **stage of exhaustion.** Mice in this stage again became ill and died. Selye discovered that even if an animal could successfully cope with one stressor, adding additional stressors overtaxed the animals' ability to cope and sometimes they would simply drop dead of stress.

Selye generalized his work from animals to people. He believed that a number of what he called **diseases of civilization** such as arthritis, heart disease, and even some cancers were the result of stress over time on the body. This belief has been supported by other researchers. An obviously extreme source of stress would be incarceration in a concentration camp. Many of the prisoners of World War II German camps were ill when they were rescued. However, Wolff (1962) examined health records of the prisoners after they had returned to normal life. Six years after their release they reported twice the expected rate of depression and suicide. In addition, they had twice the normal death rate from various cancers. The American Cancer Society reported that emotional trauma experienced by cancer patients who were in remission was related to a tendency for the cancer to recur (Berenblum, 1967).

The **broken heart effect** (Lynch, 1977) is found in widowers and widows in the first two years after their bereavement, particularly the first six months, and particularly for men (Kaprio, Koskenvuo, & Heli, 1987). This effect consists of a dramatically increased probability of death of the surviving spouse within these two years of being widowed. This remains true for all age groups and for healthy as well as already ill individuals. The stress of losing one's life partner can be overwhelming. As we will soon see, the death of a spouse is considered to be the single most stressful life event people can experience.

Even the "common cold" has been implicated as a reaction to stress. Clinical therapists noted a pattern in their clients of coming down with a cold approximately two to three days after suffering a stressful experience at home or on the job—especially if they didn't cry at the time, but bottled up their emotions instead (Dunbar, 1992).

After fifteen years in the college classroom, I still expect to spend Christmas with a cold or the flu. My university gives final exams in the week preceding Christmas. The classrooms sound like hospital wards, with everyone sniffling, sneezing, and coughing. Students have been under stress to complete the semester and many faculty (myself included) are also under the stress of expectations from family to be in charge of all the traditional stressors of the holiday season. Many students do not regard putting up a tree, writing Christmas cards, baking cookies, decorating the house, and buying Christmas presents as stressful. However the "ladies" magazines are always full of tips on how to "de-stress" the holidays, and these are for the most part written for individuals who don't hit the most stressful part of their jobs right at the holidays. Students, teachers, retail workers, and postal workers are all suffering from depressed immune systems from stress and, particularly in colder climates, are trapped in rooms full of germs. No wonder everyone gets sick!

GROUPS DESIGNED FOR STRESSFUL TASKS: POLICE AND MILITARY

Some groups are created to deal with stressful situations. SWAT (Special Weapons and Tactics) teams, police officers on the beat, individuals in the military, and medical personnel such as ambulance crews and emergency room and surgical teams all have an extraordinarily high level of stress with which to deal as they try to accomplish their tasks—protecting the populace, engaging in combat, or saving lives. These circumstances require not only very special people, but special preparation during the membership phase and opportunities after the task is accomplished to allow themselves to recover from the stressful situation. Individuals who are unable to complete the grueling initiation into these groups are perceived as likely to either succumb to the effects of stress or be unable to work with the team to accomplish the task. Individuals who do not take the time out after the task to deal effectively with the stress face a high probability of burnout.

A key difference between other task groups and these high-stress groups is the extent to which coordination of the highest quality is necessary. It is thus necessary to emphasize and foster cohesiveness and trust among team members. Thus in the early phases of the group, training is conducted under situations imitating the actual situations that will be encountered. Boot camp, the entrance into the military, is usually approximately six weeks of extreme physical and psychological stress. Drill instructors (DIs) have only a limited time to not only teach such skills as armed and unarmed self-defense, they must also force the creation of bonds within the group. This is often accomplished by becoming so strict and abusive to the inductees that the DI becomes the enemy. By creating an outside threat to the group, the DI forges greater cohesiveness within her unit. The DI also has the task of taking individuals and forging them into a unit that will respond unquestioningly to orders.

SWAT teams have the advantage of recruiting police officers who have already been trained in basic police skills and identified as highly intelligent, able to function under stress, emotionally stable, physically fit, able to bond with the team, and eager to join the unit. SWAT teams consist of volunteers. Their training as a team is continuous and is conducted under stressful and lifelike conditions (Snow, 1996).

Other teams who must function under stressful circumstances also arrive with their training completed for their roles on the team. The primary focus for emergency room teams, surgical teams, and ambulance crews is to forge bonds that will allow for extreme levels of coordination between them. Fortunately, in these cases the group goal and the individual's goals coincide—saving or treating the patient. Prima donnas and non-team players find themselves removed from teams if they cannot show a sufficient level of cooperation.

Looking back at all of the principles we have explored together in this text, these stressful groups have a number of characteristics in common. They have highly focused goals, they require extraordinarily high levels of cohesiveness and trust, they are highly structured as to roles and norms, and the status levels are distinct, formal, and very rigid. Leadership is clearly identified and direction must be obeyed immediately and unquestioningly. If you look back to the very first chapter of this text you will see that these requirements represent the extremes of the definitional characteristics of groups. Whereas groups of other types (e.g., sororities and bridge clubs) can afford to use participative decision making, the nature of the task of these stressful groups eliminates that possibility. These groups have very clear criteria of success and failure and success attained only through an almost choreographed performance of interdependence. They represent in some ways the purest and cleanest examples of group dynamics.

MEASURING STRESS

How do we measure the amount of stress an individual is experiencing? Is it purely a subjective experience, or do we just wait until the individual becomes physically or emotionally ill before we can help? No, fortunately we have other ways to measure stress, and coincidentally the research on measurement of stress contributed to our modern definition of stress. Before the measurement research began, stressors were identified as the bad things that happen to individuals, the things that upset or hurt us physically or psychologically. That turns out to be too narrow a definition.

Psychologists Holmes and Rahe (1976) began their work with individuals who were already hospitalized for medical or psychological problems. The patients were asked to think back over the past eighteen months and identify all the important life events they had experienced during that time. From this research, Holmes and Rahe developed their **Social Readjustment Rating Scale (SRRS).** This scale consists of a list of events with a number of points associated with their impact on the lives of individuals. At the top of the list is the death of a spouse, associated with 100 *life-change units* (LCUs). One takes the scale, identifies all of the events experienced in the preceding year and a half and adds up the (LCUs) associated with each one.

Holmes and Rahe were then able to make predictions about future physical and psychological problems based on these scores. Among individuals who scored 300 points on the scale, 50 percent developed problems. Among individuals who scored 400 points, the percentage was eighty! (By the way, you've probably already figured out that we have reason to be concerned for Alex's welfare. We'll discuss more reasons later.)

One of the major contributions of this research, besides verifying that the general adaptation syndrome applied to human beings, was the fact that the important life events identified were not all unhappy. People had reported getting married, pregnancy, outstanding personal achievements, vacations, and Christmas! In fact, on the scale, getting married is associated with 50 LCUs and being fired from a job is associated with 47 LCUs! So you can have a happily eventful eighteen months that will still overstress you.

So for the first time it was recognized that desired events can be just as hard on the mind and body as undesirable events. This can be quite comforting when it helps someone understand why they feel so depressed when they've gotten married and taken a dream honeymoon/vacation, graduated from college, gotten their dream job, moved to another city, gotten pregnant, and bought a house in a year and a half.

The Holmes and Rahe scale is useful with individuals older than the average college student, but includes events that are generally irrelevant to college students such as retirement, trouble with in-laws, or son or daughter leaving home. It doesn't consider such stressful events of students such as final exams, paying tuition, scheduling work and school to give sufficient time for both and a social life, breaking up with a "steady," an unwelcome, unplanned pregnancy, failing a course, or achieving a straight "A" grade point average.

Multiple scales have been developed (e.g., see Mark and others, cited in O'Connell & O'Connell, 1997) for multiple ages, even down into the childhood years where stressors are such events as death of a grandparent or pet. So the development of these scales has helped expand the definition of a stressor into anything that requires adjustment or change on the part of the individual.

SOURCES OF EVERYDAY STRESS

Not everyone experiences a life full of major life events or works in an inherently stressful environment. But most of us have a lot of dumb little things go wrong on a daily basis. In the past two days I've had my car battery die when I was taking the family out to dinner, forgotten to buy dishwashing soap at the grocery store when that was the reason for the trip, and had my child become ill just when I'm facing the deadline for this book (just a cold, thank goodness). None of them was earthshaking but each was irritating just enough for me to feel pressured.

We've all had "one of those days" when we don't wake up to the alarm on the first day of a new job, or we put our fingernail through the toe of our last pair of pantyhose just before meeting our potential in-laws, or burned the dinner because we got involved with a TV show. Just because they aren't major in the grand scheme of things, research shows that these **hassles** on a cumulative basis can be just as damaging as an accumulation of stressful, major life events (Reich, Parrella, & Filstead, 1988).

> **STOP** How stressful is your life right now? Are you experiencing more of the major life events or just a series of hassles? Have you noticed your reactions to these stressors? Do you get sick at particularly stressful times (such as finals or the holiday season)?

A great deal of research is being conducted on the stresses unique to certain groups in the population. Certain people have personal characteristics that seem to predispose them to experience stress more intensely and to actually create situations in which they are stressed, to their physical detriment. The concept of *Type A* and *Type B personalities* was introduced in 1974 (Friedman & Rosenman). **Type A personalities** are associated with a higher risk of coronary disease and heart attack (Friedman & Booth, 1987). Type As are fiercely competitive. They are perfectionists who never feel they have enough time. If they are given enough time to complete a project, they will set their own far stricter deadline for completion. They are aggressive and impatient and they talk and walk fast. They don't like to go on vacation, and if forced will take work with them. They don't generally drink alcoholic beverages because that would take off their edge, or they drink too much because it is one of the only ways they can relax. Traffic jams make them crazy.

These people have been dubbed self-stressors. While others spend time trying to reduce the stress in our lives, they seek to maximize the stress. Being workaholics, they are often overweight from bad eating habits and lack of exercise—other predisposing characteristics for heart problems. Psychologically, they perceive themselves as without support and alone.

A more recent take on the Type A concept refers to them as **hot reactors.** In comparison to the more laid-back **Type B personality** types, hot reactors have intense physiological reactions to situations. It's as if their bodies have an exaggerated fight-or-flight response (Williams, 1989).

As we will discuss in length in the Application section, certain professions carry with them special risk factors for the phenomenon of *burnout*. But other professions carry with them stress factors that may not be immediately obvious.

Figure skaters are glamorous figures we see in their glittering costumes floating around the ice arena. Competition at the national level, however, had been associated with high levels of stress in 71 percent of the skaters interviewed (Gould, Jackson, & Finch, 1993). Skaters reported problems with relationship issues, the pressures to perform perfectly, physical and psychological demands placed on them by competition, environmental demands on resources, and concerns about their life direction.

Police work is clearly a high-stress occupation, but not always in the ways we would expect. Despite what is depicted on television, shoot-outs are almost never routine occurrences. Fatigue, problems dealing with the social service and judicial systems, the constant pressures of their jobs, the stress of dealing with the families of victims—as well as victims themselves, and frustration and anger have all been identified as sources of stress (Sewell, 1994), as well as boredom.

Military service is clearly a high-stress occupation, particularly when the servicemen and -women are stationed in dangerous locations. A study of soldiers participating in the Gulf War found that the families as well as the actual

As the cartoon demonstrates, people can serve as either a source of support or a significant source of stress.
Source: "Go away! I'm peopled out" by Guindon, March 9, 1981. Reprinted by permission of the Los Angeles Times Syndicate.

"Go away! I'm peopled out."

warriors suffered profound stress. During the time their family member was stationed in the Gulf the families reported experiencing higher levels of stress than the soldiers themselves, and that the homecoming was more stressful for both warriors and families than the departure (Figley, 1993).

Priests have also been studied for stress levels (Hoge, Shields, & Soroka, 1993). Priests surprisingly scored lower in stress on average than other occupations. However, younger priests reported higher levels of stress based on poor feedback on their job performance, inadequate rewards, over-responsibility for other people, and time pressure.

Gender and culture differences have been found in the sources of stress experienced. Men have been found to be more vulnerable to divorce itself and the aftermath than their ex-wives (McKenry & Price, 1990). This vulnerability probably stems from the same sources as the greater vulnerability of men to the broken heart effect. In traditional households, the woman is responsible for the emotional support aspects of the relationship. Her friendships with other women are also more likely to be based on emotional support. Traditional men repress emotion and their friendships with men tend to be based on sharing activities (e.g., "shooting hoops"). When a man is widowed, then, he loses most of his emotional support. And, if the marriage has been traditional in nature, he may have to take on a number of household roles that are unfamiliar to him, increasing his stress.

Women in untraditional professions such as management experience stresses from society at large because of the role-busting, from their organizations and from themselves, in trying to take on a situation in which role conflict is almost inevitable (Offerman & Armitage, 1993).

A particularly poignant study was conducted with Cambodians, Laotians, and Vietnamese refugees to the United States regarding their experiences in South Asian refugee camps (Bernier, 1992). Their unique sources of stress were reported as having to live with multicultural, multinational groups in the camps; a sense of powerlessness and physical constraint resulting in bereavement; major changes in lifestyle and living conditions; and life-threatening phenomena experienced on their way to the camps such as famine and persecution. Added to all of these stresses, of course, was the adjustment to the United States upon immigration!

The stress of crowding and uncertainty can be clearly seen in the tension on the faces of these children.

The life events described for the South Asian immigrants go well beyond what most of us would consider stress. They fall into the category of traumas. **Trauma** can also be the death of a loved one, experiencing a tornado, earthquake, war, rape, or automobile accident. Hybels-Steer (1995) defines trauma as:

1. *Something that makes you realize you could have died.*
2. *Something that makes you feel powerless, helpless, and paralyzed.*
3. *Sudden and overwhelming. It owns you, you don't own it.*
4. *A time when you experience extreme fear, even if only for a short time.*
5. *A time when you cannot think clearly.*
6. *More than stress. Stress does not have the sudden and life-threatening quality that trauma has.*
7. *A shock to the system, which is why it affects the whole system and creates a state of emergency.*
8. *An event with a predictable aftermath.*

(Hybels-Steer, 1995, p. 23)

There is a common pattern of reaction to trauma which includes three steps: (1) *immediate reaction,* (2) *middle period,* and (3) *resolution/reorganization.* The *immediate reaction* involves **shock, disorientation,** *confusion,* **unwanted thoughts,** and often a strong *emotional reaction*—which may very well be *denial.* Upon hearing of the death of a loved one or a diagnosis of a terminal medical condition, the most common reaction is "No, it couldn't be. There's been some mistake." There is almost obsessive review of the event, often including *self-blame.* "If only I had . . . I could have . . . I should have. . . ."

Someone who lives through a trauma when others do not often suffers **survivor guilt.** They feel that if they had done something else, the others would have survived. Or that they themselves do not deserve to live when the others did not. At this point, individuals need information and support as well as any tangible help such as medical and psychological attention.

The *middle period* of trauma reaction often involves *flashbacks* to the event. A year ago I hit (and killed) a large deer (8-point buck) on an interstate highway in the middle of a sunny afternoon. It smashed in the front of the van I was driving by rolling up onto the hood (and totalled the van), and I was told by the state trooper that had I been driving a car (which would have placed me closer to the ground) I would have had the deer in the car with me, antlers and all. Accidents with deer aren't uncommon in Wisconsin, but they usually don't occur in the middle of a sunny afternoon. They do, however, often involve serious injuries to the drivers involved.

I was lucky; I didn't get a physical scratch. However, for months afterwards I would dream about the accident and I had to pass that stretch of highway a number of times before I could do so without hanging onto something or someone with white knuckles. This middle period can also be a period of *questioning and self-blame.* I spent days trying to figure how I could have avoided the deer without hitting the car to my left, or rolling off the highway to my right. It took me weeks to realize I really had no other option than the one I took. Please understand—I am a hunter. I have killed deer deliberately to feed my family. But I couldn't handle the shock and unexpectedness and unnecessary character of the accident.

Other emotions that may be experienced during this period can be *depression, feelings of powerlessness, fear,* and *continued denial.* If others blame the victim it simply makes this period of adjustment that much more difficult. Individuals should not try to talk a victim in this period out of their emotions. Unless they work through them, the period of adjustment will be extended.

During this period it is extremely important to have a **support group.** People provide a sense of safety. If the victim is feeling powerless and vulnerable, others can provide a screen against the world. Others are important in a number of concrete ways. They can *do things for you*—after the accident my husband went to the junkyard and retrieved all of my personal possessions from my van. People can simply *stay with you.* People can *run interference* between you and those with whom you would rather not deal at the time. My mother called that evening and I didn't want to tell her until she could see that I was really all right (because I knew she wouldn't believe me long-distance). Since I had a business trip scheduled to Washington within days, I let my husband tell her I was in the bath. (I did tell her once I arrived at her house.) People can listen. My husband called almost everyone we knew that evening and would hand me the phone and have me tell the story yet again. (As a Vietnam veteran he was very wise in the handling of trauma.) People can give you *information*—I felt somewhat better being reassured by the trooper that there was, in fact, nothing else I could have done (and that he'd also hit a deer in the same spot under the same conditions in his police cruiser!).

The final period of *resolution/reorganization* takes time to attain. It involves final *acceptance* of the trauma. If other lives have been lost then the process of mourning and grief can begin. It is also important to understand that family members of an individual who has undergone a trauma are affected also. They, too, need support, however, not from the trauma victim.

One of the more traumatic events that can occur to a family is the death of a child or a miscarriage. While to the outside world a miscarriage may be a minor event, to the affected family, they have lost a child. "The death of a child violates every conception of meaning that we hold about the world" (Pennebaker, 1990). As with other traumas that have social components, families who miscarry need to turn to others to help them cope. However, often the friends of the parents who are themselves parents are too horrified and personally threatened by the event to be able to provide help and often avoid the family, just when they need people the most (Pennebaker, 1990). Friends who are able to provide support must be extremely careful what they say.

> *Bereaved father: "Please never say that you understand what we are going through, because you can't. Some of our friends say the same thing, and they don't know what they're talking about."*
>
> **(Pennebaker, 1990, p. 114)**

But people who have suffered a miscarriage or the death of a child need to go through the same steps as any other trauma victim. There may be a special sense of failure on the part of the woman if she defines fertility as a necessary part of being a woman. If the family is highly religious, there may be special guilt if the religion places a premium on large families. The parents may feel they've failed each other and also God (Kohn & Moffitt, 1992). Such families often find their religious convictions shaken to the core and are angry at God for allowing such a trauma to occur. This is a normal part of grieving and should not be discouraged nor be the source of any guilt. We will discuss later in the chapter self-help groups for families who have suffered this kind of tragic loss.

A final word about trauma. It's not just grieving parents who don't want to hear that you know just how they feel. Anyone who's been through a trauma— an accident, a miscarriage, the death of a spouse, a divorce, a rape—will resent that phrase. The fact is that because we are all unique in our psychological makeups and in the details of the event that has occurred, we don't know how anyone else feels. We know how we felt, and we can convey that to the trauma victims. Just remember, it's about them, not you.

In the aftermath of a trauma, an individual's entire experience of the world changes.

The world may not feel safe.
The world may not feel steady.
The world may not feel predictable.
The world may not feel fair.

(Hybels-Steer, 1995, p. 38)

POST-TRAUMATIC STRESS DISORDER

Post-traumatic stress disorder (PTSD) is a pattern of symptoms suffered by those who have been through events that are "outside the range of usual human experiences and that would be markedly distressing to almost anyone" (DSM IV, 1994). Many young people who have been engaged in combat in any war suffer this disorder as a lifelong pattern, especially those who suffered through combat and who were not supported upon their return to the "world" (as it was referred to by Vietnam vets). Rape victims also often suffer from this disorder.

It is only recently that we are recognizing the pervasiveness of this syndrome. This pattern of symptoms is long-lasting and intrusive to a normal life experience. Flashbacks to unpleasant events are common. These individuals suffer persistent symptoms of increased arousal (a **hypervigilance**)—a feeling that it's never safe to let down their guard; and a *persistent avoidance of the stimuli that are associated with the event.* Many rape victims avoid the site of the rape. If it occurred at home (as so many do), many victims move away very quickly. Other symptoms include *difficulty falling or staying asleep, irritability or outbursts of anger, difficulty concentrating, an exaggerated startle response,* and *an exaggerated physiological reactivity* to similar events (Kukla, Schlenger, Fairbank, Hough, Jordan, Marmar, & Weiss, 1990). For example, the sound of a car backfiring may send a vet diving for cover. For him, it's gunfire.

The most thorough research of this syndrome to date has been conducted on Vietnam veterans. The National Vietnam Veteran's Readjustment Study found lifetime incidence of PTSD in male veterans who had been Vietnam theater veterans to be 30.9 percent, and 26.9 percent in female theater veterans. Partial PTSD was found in an additional 22.5 percent of the men and 21.2 percent of the women. About one-half of the men and one-third of the women who ever suffered Vietnam-related PTSD still did in 1990.

Certain individuals were more likely to develop PTSD than others after Vietnam. Army and Marine veterans were more likely than Navy or Air Force veterans. The age at which they experienced the war was an important consideration—those entering between ages 17 and 19 were most vulnerable. The rate was higher for those entering as high school dropouts, unemployed, or with incomes less than $20,000. Religion and the point in the war at which they were stationed in Vietnam were found to be unrelated to the development of PTSD. PTSD rates were lower in those who entered the war married, as college graduates, employed, retired, or with an income of more than $30,000. However, the overwhelmingly most important factor in developing PTSD was *exposure to war zone stress.*

What happened to these individuals when they came home? The stress did not let up. We know they were not greeted as heroes—quite the opposite. They were called "baby killers" and "murderers." They were unlikely to find the kind of support we have already identified as necessary to overcome stress and trauma. Readjustment to American society did not come easily for these warriors. For men, the level of war stress experienced was highly positively related to the number of divorces, marital, and parenting problems. White men who experienced battle action were the most likely to have trouble with readjustment. Surprisingly, African-American theater vets showed fewer readjustment problems than Vietnam era vets who had served in the United States. However, all

It was not until well after her warriors returned home from Vietnam that America acknowledged their heroism and post-war traumas.

male theater vets suffered higher levels of current chronic physical problems than male Vietnam era vets (no war experience) as of 1990 (Kukla et al., 1990).

Of those who suffered high war stress, they were:

Five times more likely to report being unhappy or dissatisfied with life (24.7% compared to 4.8%)

Six times more likely to be highly isolated (46.5% vs. 7.6%)

Twice as likely to have been homeless or vagrant (16.8% vs. 8.8%)

Twice as likely to have committed more than 13 violent acts in the previous year (14.4% vs. 7.6%)

One and a half times more likely to have been arrested or jailed (39.1% vs. 27.7%)

Three times more likely to have been convicted of a felony (8.8% vs. 2.8%)

Specific gender differences in readjustment problems were noted. Men with PTSD were more likely to abuse alcohol or to display an antisocial personality. Women with PTSD were ten times more likely to report unhappiness than non-vets and eight times more likely to report extreme isolation.

As we continue to recognize the situations that can trigger PTSD and as we send more young men and women off to wars, we must become more sensitive to the necessities of support and possibly psychological treatment of these individuals in order to help them to live normal, happy, productive lives.

COPING WITH STRESS

Different people react to stress or trauma or PTSD in very different ways. What we do know is that there are some coping responses that are more useful and effective than others. Not too surprisingly, since we have been discussing a continuum of stress levels, the same sorts of coping skills and interventions are often appropriate in any of the types of stress we have discussed.

Ineffective Coping Skills

We're particularly clear about responses that not only don't help individuals cope with stress, but may exacerbate the problem. One ineffective coping response is to dull out the feelings with *alcohol* or some other consciousness-altering substance. Historically, men have been more likely to turn to alcohol, but the number of women who are using this response is increasing. **Alcohol abuse** may create interpersonal problems with family members and may also create employment problems.

Another common **ineffective coping skill** has been to seek **isolation.** The forests of the American Northwest and the jungles of Hawaii are full of Vietnam veterans with such severe PTSD that they cannot return to society. Others return to society physically but isolate themselves by limiting their contacts with others. This can be easily understood for those for whom the damage from the stress was inflicted by other people. Rape victims are often afraid of men for a period of time after the rape. Veterans who were spit on after their return from

Vietnam often limited their contacts with nonveterans for fear of further abuse. Occasionally we will encounter an individual who claims to always have been a loner and is quite comfortable in their own company and sees help from others as intrusive. Research has shown, however, that these individuals in fact were particularly vulnerable to stress effects (Larson & Lee, 1996). As we have seen repeatedly it is from other people we are most likely to obtain the most effective support.

Effective Coping Skills

The key to **effective coping skills** appears to involve interactions with other people. Of all the interventions examined to cope with stress, **social support** is the single most effective. Look back at the discussion of trauma. Every one of those situations that help us cope involves another person. Social support has been shown to reduce the physiological stress indicators during stressful times (Cohen & Wills, 1985) and to reduce the probability of illness and actually speed recovery (House, Landis, & Umberson, 1988). We will discuss in the next section the effects of groups on stress, but recent research would appear to indicate that one of the major contributing factors is the connection formed. Such research has found that bringing animals to nursing homes helps to foster connections between patients that were previously nonexistent and these increased connections improve the social climate of the institution (Fick, 1993).

MITIGATING EFFECTS OF GROUPS ON INDIVIDUAL STRESS

What specifically is it about contact with others that mitigates the effect of stress? Besides the points we have already considered, we can borrow from Yalom (1970) who discussed the factors in groups that facilitate individual change and personal development. Although these conditions were described in relation to therapy groups, I believe they apply to the situations we have already discussed.

Yalom stated seven **curative factors** that are the effects of groups. (And remember we have defined a group as anything from a dyad upwards in number.) First I'll list them, then go back and discuss each one. They are: (1) *receiving information about how others think, feel, and behave;* (2) *the opportunity to witness alternative reactions to situations;* (3) *hope;* (4) *universality;* (5) *the opportunity to practice altruistic behaviors;* (6) *the opportunity to enhance social skills;* and finally, (7) *the opportunity for catharsis.*

One of the reasons that people who have gone through a cataclysmic trauma tend to come out more healthy psychologically is the fact that they tend to congregate and share their thoughts, feelings, and describe their experiences and how they behaved. Southern Californians who have been through substantial earthquakes tend to speak of very little else for weeks. And no one gets bored or tired of hearing or talking about the event. Too often if we've gone through a personal trauma that those close to us have not, they are willing to listen for just so long before they tell us to get a life. And we may not be ready. (Here's the other reason to worry for Alex. Robert and his neighbors will probably talk about the mudslide for weeks; Alex may not have someone with whom to share, which is why we're going to talk about therapy and self-help groups shortly.)

Vietnam or Gulf War vets having trouble getting comfortable in society can benefit by hearing that others are having the same problems and finding out how they're coping with similar problems. Rape victims can model the behavior of someone who is coping well, or at least see the possibility of other responses and reactions to the situation. People can't cope without hope. When we feel damaged or depressed we must feel that there's a light at the end of the tunnel. Without that hope, too many turn to suicide. No matter how messed up we are when we enter a group or talk to another vet, if they're coping well it gives us the hope that we might also, someday. Everybody's got some problems.

Sometimes people who are actually doing quite well coping don't realize it because they think they should be happy and cheerful all the time. Psychologists worry about people who are happy and cheerful all the time. Everyone has bad things happen to them. Everyone has problems. Coping is taking the seemingly unmanageable problem and turning it into a normal everyday crummy little problem.

Universality allows people to develop perspective on their lives. Talking to another vet or another accident survivor or another rape victim may give us the chance to support them. Altruistic behavior can help with our self-esteem. And if our trauma or PTSD has resulted in negative, socially inappropriate behaviors, we can practice with others and get their feedback. Finally, as I've emphasized over and over, victims of stress, trauma, and PTSD need to talk. And talk. And talk. That's what catharsis is all about. It's a way of purging the bad feelings, and having people accept us even though we're talking about awful things. All of these curative factors can be obtained from other people. So the cliché that people need people is really a truism after all.

Another model of the ways in which groups help individuals is presented by Ormont (1992). Although there is some overlap with Yalom's model, there are several additional advantages mentioned by Ormont. The first is the opportunity for the group to *elicit self-destructive behavior* from the individual. These behaviors in reaction to other group members more likely are typical of their behavior in the outside world than would be their behavior with an individual therapist and so provide invaluable information to the therapist. Groups also allow individuals to elicit feedback on their thoughts, feelings, and behaviors from other group members with the expectation of an honest answer. That opportunity seldom occurs in the "real world." Finally, the group offers the individual a *safe environment* in which to practice new, unfamiliar behaviors.

GROUPS DESIGNED TO PROMOTE CHANGE

There are three basically different types of groups that have been designed specifically to promote changes in individuals. Members of groups can't avoid change as they go through the developmental and socialization processes of the group, but change is not the reason people join task groups. It IS the reason they join *training groups, therapy groups,* and *self-help groups.*

Training Groups

Training groups are designed to provide individuals with skills and information they would like to obtain—sort of like classes.

> *. . . time-limited structured groups in which one or more leaders use a repertoire of didactic and facilitative skills to help participants develop and maintain one or more specific lifeskills. Important features of training groups include: no assumption of psychological disturbance, systematic instruction, experiential learning-by-doing, and a high degree of participant involvement.*
>
> *(Nelson-Jones, 1992, p. 6)*

Training groups can teach job skills such as communication, listening, decision making, supervision skills, and conflict management. Training groups can also deal with life issues. Although most people become parents at some point in their lives, few have ever had any instruction on how to be good parents. Training groups can teach parenting skills such as discipline and understanding child development. People who recognize they are under stress might elect to join a training group that focuses on time management or relaxation techniques.

Training groups are generally established for a fixed length of time. If members feel they need more they can take another class or retake the first class. The leaders of the groups are only different from the participants in that they have expertise in the subject matter being conveyed. They are not mental health professionals (depending upon the subject matter) nor do they necessarily have any advanced degree. They simply have information to convey and at the end of the training group it is hoped that the members will have learned and will retain these new skills and this new information.

Have you ever attended a training group? Many organizations conduct training in certain aspects of employment. At my university we seem to have an endless number of computer literacy classes as we endlessly change operating systems and software complicates rather than simplifies computer use. Did you find the training useful? If you had access to any sort of training group, what skill would you most like to learn?

Therapy Groups

Therapy groups are designed with an entirely different agenda in mind than training groups. The goal of therapy groups is to remediate problems the group members are experiencing. These are people in pain who need a mental health professional to help facilitate change. Although the terms *therapy, counseling,* and *personal growth groups* are sometimes used interchangeably, they actually represent three different levels of intervention (Schaffer & Galusky, 1989).

Therapy groups are the most serious form of mental health intervention. They take place in a clinical setting, the length of time the group exists may be quite extended, and they are run by mental health professionals. (By the way, in Chapter 1 I asked you how many psychologists it takes to change a light bulb.

The answer is one, but the light bulb really has to want to change.) **Counseling** seeks to guide rather than remediate. We don't expect to see the same level of dysfunction in such groups. They may deal with issues such as retirement counseling or job search counseling. Or they may deal with relationship counseling. Thus they may appear in educational, organizational, or clinical settings. They may or may not be led by a mental health professional, again based upon the content area. **Personal growth groups** are simply groups of individuals who get together to expand their horizons. These could include reading groups. Often they have no formal leader.

Therapy groups may be led by a variety of types of mental health professionals. But they must be led by trained mental health professionals. Such individuals are equipped to deal with issues and situations that might arise in groups with which untrained individuals could not cope.

Let's list the types of group leader you might encounter then discuss the types. Therapy groups can be led by M.D.s **(psychiatrists),** Ph.D.s **(clinical psychologists),** Psy.D.s **(doctors of psychology),** Ed.D.s (doctors of education in counseling), M.A.s (masters degrees in psychology), M.S.W.s (masters degrees in social work), or (occasionally) **psychoanalysts.** Most of these people may run the same therapy groups, however two are quite different. Psychiatrists are physicians who have attended medical school and spent additional years serving a residency in psychiatry. They are the only ones of the group who are allowed to write prescriptions for medications. This may not sound like an important point, but as research in brain chemistry advances we are discovering more disorders that appear to be most capably managed not by psychological therapy but by pharmaceutical therapy or some combination of the two. Schizophrenia can be controlled in approximately 90 percent of those patients who can tolerate and will maintain their medical regimen. Depression responds more effectively to medications than to psychological therapy (although a combination is often employed).

However, we would probably not ever have a group of schizophrenics, anyway. When they are medicated they are often indistinguishable from anyone else. When they are unmedicated and having a break, they are not in contact with reality and don't interact with others appropriately. We might well have a group whose primary symptom is depression, but often other clinicians have a relationship either with a psychiatrist or with the clients' primary care physician through which medications can be prescribed.

The second different type of therapist is the *psychoanalyst*. These individuals need no other credential than having gone through training and undergoing psychoanalysis themselves. Personally I have always thought the best therapists have been through therapy for two reasons. First, you can't be a good therapist unless you are fairly well put together psychologically, and second, I feel it's a good thing for therapists to have experienced what they will be doing to others. There aren't many psychoanalysts these days, however, because this therapy is based upon Freudian theory, which generally means that the intent is to dismantle the personality to sometime before the age of six and reconstruct it. That takes a tremendous amount of time and effort and money. Often such groups meet five times a week for an hour a day for years.

How often do other groups meet, and how long do they last? That entirely depends on the **theoretical orientation** of the therapist. There are a number of different theoretical orientations, and the explanation for different problems will differ with the theory, as will the treatment. There are behavioral therapies focused on one symptom that might last six weeks; there are humanistic therapies based on emotional issues that might last (for one individual) for a year or more; then there are the psychoanalysts.

What does one gain from group therapy as opposed to individual therapy? Actually, group therapy has a number of advantages. Because a number of individuals are sharing the therapist's time they also share the cost of that time. Group therapy is less expensive than having a therapist all to yourself. But not having the therapist all to yourself means you are not always the focus of attention, which provides another benefit. You can watch and be watched. You can provide and receive feedback. You can practice new behaviors. And you can understand that you are not alone and create bonds with the group members. The therapist can also observe how you interact with others—which would be impossible in one-on-one therapy.

The $64,000 question is whether or not therapy is effective. The answer is a qualified "yes." There are good therapists and not-so-good therapists. There are therapists who are particularly good at dealing with some issues and not so good at dealing with others. And there are therapists you like, and those you instinctively don't like. There needs to be matching on a number of dimensions to determine **therapy effectiveness.**

And the client must have completed the therapy to know whether or not it was effective. As you might expect there are not really very good statistics or studies of "graduates" of psychoanalysis because so few actually spend as long as the psychoanalyst feels is necessary. Generally, however, we can say that therapy is effective in *reducing stress* and *improving self-concept* (Barrera, 1986; Cohen & Willis, 1985; Dalgard et al., 1990; and Yalom, 1985).

How can we keep clients from prematurely terminating from their therapy groups? The key appears to be in **pregroup preparation of clients** (Burlingame & Fuhrmann, 1990; Fuhrmann & Burlingame, 1990). People who have not been prepared often enter therapy expecting the therapist to do one of three things: (1) tell the client they're right, it's the rest of the world that's nuts; (2) wave their magic wand, sprinkle some pixie dust, and declare the client cured; or (3) do all the work.

Therapy is hard emotional work. It can be exhausting. Individuals entering therapy often find themselves tired all the time at first. That's actually a good sign. It means that the client is working on issues. And instead of instantly feeling better, the more common (and better therapeutic) pattern is for the client to start feeling worse and worse. They assume, in a state of panic that they're getting worse and drop out of therapy.

Nothing could be further from the truth. Often before entering therapy the only way the client is able to cope with day-to-day reality is to stuff all the problems down as deeply into the background of their consciousness as possible. Upon entering therapy, they've opened Pandora's box. All the bad feelings jump out. No wonder they feel worse! To the therapist this is a good sign. The client is actually working on their problems. And clients who are warned about this phenomenon correctly perceive it as a positive rather than a negative indicator.

Self-Help Groups

Our final type of group is the **self-help group,** formed by individuals who have a problem in common. They developed in response to the perception that the mental health profession wasn't being very helpful in a number of situations. The first self-help group was **Alcoholics Anonymous** which was started by a physician and a businessman who had run the gamut of what the physicians and the psychologists had to offer for their alcohol addiction. These groups are not usually led by mental health professionals although they often keep ties with such professionals in case of emergency. The leaders are individuals with the same problem or issue as their fellow group members.

There are a number of types of self-help groups. Some are aimed at what are perceived as lifelong problems such as alcoholism or compulsive gambling or overweight. Members of these groups such as Alcoholics Anonymous (AA), Al-Anon (for family members of alcoholics), or Gamblers Anonymous believe that their problem still exists, even though it may be under control at the moment. That's why members of AA never refer to themselves as ex-alcoholics, no matter how long it's been since their last drink. The group is seen as a bulwark against falling back into the problem behavior.

Other groups are intended to be somewhat temporary in nature. Groups like Parents Without Partners (for single parents), Bereaved Parents and Compassionate Friends (for parents who have lost a child through death or miscarriage) are intended to provide support and contact with individuals going through the same situation. Generally the grief process runs for approximately a year to a year and a half. If people are not ready to move on with their lives after that point, individual therapy may be necessary. Self-help groups exist to provide a safe place to meet with like-minded others and to find a way to cope.

Summary

In this final chapter we have examined the phenomenon of stress at various levels and identified people as the most important source of remediation. We have identified effective and ineffective coping skills and the types of groups that may be sought out to provide support and care.

Key Terms

adrenalergic state
alarm reaction
alcohol abuse
Alcoholics Anonymous
broken heart effect
cholinergic state
clinical psychologist
  (Ph.D.)

counseling
curative factors
diseases of civilization
disorientation
doctor of psychology
  (Psy.D.)
effective coping skills
fight-or-flight response

general adaptation
  syndrome (GAS)
hassles
hot reactors
hypervigilance
ineffective coping skills
isolation
personal growth groups

post-traumatic stress disorder (PTSD)	Social Readjustment Rating Scale (SRRS)	theoretical orientation
pregroup preparation of clients	social support	therapy effectiveness
psychiatrists (M.D.)	stage of exhaustion	therapy groups
psychoanalysts	stage of resistance	trauma
self-help groups	stress	training groups
shock	support group	Type A personality
	survivor guilt	Type B personality
		unwanted thoughts

APPLICATION

Stress in the Workplace: Identifying and Dealing with Burnout

The phenomenon of career burnout results in a large number of lost hours of work and individuals lost to careers. Burnout is a response to a "combination of very high expectations and chronic situational stress" (Pines & Aronson, 1988, p. 9). Unfortunately it is most likely to happen to those individuals who started out the most enthusiastic and idealistic and set high standards for themselves and the job situation and to individuals in jobs where there is a lot of contact with people (Maslach, 1982).

Over time, they develop feelings of helplessness, hopelessness, disillusionment, a negative self-concept, and negative attitudes toward work, their co-workers, and life. The symptoms look almost like those of chronic stress. The individuals complain of physical exhaustion, low energy, chronic fatigue, and weakness. They become accident prone, susceptible to illness, develop headaches, and muscular tension. They either eat too much or too little. They experience sleep problems and nightmares. They become irritable and nervous and perceive their families as just another hassle to be dealt with (Pines & Aronson, 1988).

These stress-related symptoms can be grouped into three job-related factors: (1) *emotional exhaustion*, (2) *depersonalization*, and (3) *reduced personal accomplishment*. People who report emotional exhaustion feel drained and used up. They feel they are "running on empty" with no source of replenishment in sight. They begin to feel they can't give any more. One response to this is to withdraw and detach from the job situation. This can often be seen in emergency room personnel who experience so many tragic and stressful events that their only defense may be to just stop feeling. Years ago I sprained my ankle badly about ten o'clock at night. We weren't sure if it was broken so my husband sent me off in a cab to the emergency room (it was a school night, my daughter was asleep upstairs, and I had no idea how long I'd be at the ER). As it turned out, I was there four hours. At 2:00 A.M. after two sets of X rays and no pain medication, the physician walked in to tell me there was no break, just a severe sprain. I had "hit the wall" shortly before and was laying on the gurney crying. The physician looked at me in surprise and asked me what was wrong! I was scared, I hurt, and I was exhausted. But she had become so detached from people in the ER that she was actually surprised that an injured patient might cry.

The second response to burnout, depersonalization, often results in a level of extreme cynicism about people.

> *The provider may derogate other people and put them down, refuse to be civil or courteous to them, ignore their pleas and demands, or fail to provide the appropriate help, care, or service.*
>
> *(Maslach, 1982, p. 4)*

The final step of burnout is a reduced sense of personal accomplishment that results in a reduced sense of self-esteem because the victim knows they are not doing the job as well as they should, which may lead to depression. In addition to lowered work standards we might also see decreased efficiency and increased mistakes; obsessiveness on the job; excessive reliance on rules; tardiness; clock-watching; absenteeism; or workaholism (Smith, Birch, & Marchant, 1986). Edelwich and Brodsky (1980) were able to track the stages in burnout in librarians:

> *Stage 1: Enthusiasm—occurs during graduate school and first position*
> *Stage 2: Stagnation—occurs after about one to two years of "real job"*
> *Stage 3: Frustration—occurs after about seven years (Rettig, 1986)*
> *Stage 4: Apathy—difficult to see behavioral switch from stage 3 to stage 4*
> *Stage 5: Intervention*

If no intervention is attempted it is highly possible the librarian will leave the profession.

We can trace two primary sources of burnout-related stress: (1) the characteristics of the individual and (2) work-related or organizational causes. Women are more likely to experience emotional exhaustion and to experience it more intensely than men. Men are more likely to depersonalize and to become callous.

This may be related to the different types of service jobs men and women generally occupy. Women are more often in positions requiring emotional involvement such as nursing and social work while men are more likely to be involved in traditionally masculine service occupations such as police work.

There are small ethnic differences in the propensity to develop burnout. Asian-Americans are similar to whites, but show slightly more emotional exhaustion, slightly more depersonalization, and have a somewhat lower sense of accomplishment. African-Americans are less likely to burn out than whites or Asian-Americans. Perhaps this is because of a closer sense of community (Maslach, 1982).

Older workers are less likely to express burnout, perhaps because those who burned out young have already left the profession. Maybe it's because younger workers start their careers filled with youthful optimism that doesn't match the reality they find on the job.

Level of education is positively related to burnout. Individuals without a college education are least likely to suffer burnout, individuals with a bachelor degree are more likely, and those with graduate educations are most likely to suffer burnout (Caputo, 1991).

Family status is also related to burnout. Married individuals burn out less often than divorced individuals, who burn out less often than single individuals (Maslach, 1982). The presence of children in the home is reduced to a lower level of burnout. Perhaps family serves as a buffer for the stresses experienced on the job.

Certain clusters of personality characteristics appear related to burnout. Among the characteristics identified are lack of assertiveness, impatience, intolerance, lack of self-confidence, conventional beliefs, strong need for approval, and a strong need for control (Maslach, 1982). Others have found overcommitment, excessive dedication, inability to separate from work, idealism, and perfectionism (Caputo, 1991).

Organizational characteristics associated with burnout include a lack of professional autonomy, having to deal with the public, role conflicts, role ambiguity, decreased opportunities for personal accomplishment, inadequate positive feedback, continuously heavy workload, and stressors in the physical environment such as noise and interruptions (Caputo, 1991).

Burnout can also result when co-workers become a source of stress rather than a source of support or when supervision is inadequate. Among the complaints against supervisors of burned-out workers are: poor criteria for worker evaluation; pressure to meet quantitative rather than qualitative standards; lack of feedback; and lack of trust in both directions.

Are there any solutions to burnout? Maslach (1982) suggests that those workers who feel they are on the verge of burning out should work "smarter," not harder. They should set realistic goals, change the way they do things, find opportunities to break away, take care of things less personally, take care of themselves, change jobs, or, perhaps "get a life."

Discussion Questions

Apply the concepts from the chapter to consider the following questions:

1. Compare and contrast burnout and PTSD. How are they the same? How are they different?
2. Besides the suggestions made by Maslach, what skills mentioned in the chapter might be used to head off or to treat burnout?
3. Can you think of any use of groups that might help with the problem of burnout? What would such a group look like? What would be its goals?
4. Would you consider therapy groups or self-help groups more appropriate placements for individuals who have suffered a trauma? Does it depend on the type of trauma, the type of person, or the type of group?
5. Can you design any type of training group that could be used as a prophylaxis against burnout?

Glossary

acceptance   Internalizing the message in a communication situation. Identification by other group members as belonging to the group.

acceptance/maintenance   The stage of group socialization in which the individual has moved into full membership and must work on establishing her or his niche in the group. The major activity at this stage is role maintenance.

achieved roles   Sets of behavioral expectations based upon some deliberate activity on the part of the individual (e.g., college graduate).

achievement-oriented leader   Leader whose primary focus within the group is group productivity or achievement.

acquittal   Verdict in trial indicating lack of evidence to convict. Not equivalent to "not guilty" determination. Criteria for acquittal differ between civil (preponderance of evidence) and criminal (belief in guilt beyond a reasonable doubt) trials.

active listening   Listening with the specific goal of understanding what is being said. Involves concentration and asking questions for clarification.

activity trap   The tendency for groups (and individuals) to feel the need to be constantly active, failing to recognize the sometimes appropriate alternative of inactivity.

actual equity   The situation in which the input/outcome equation is balanced between parties. In situations of inequality, restoring actual equity involves actual changes to the situation to balance the equation.

additive task   Task in which the desired outcome is based on the quantity (e.g., distributing flyers for an election or a tug of war).

adjourning stage   Final stage of group development in which the group members' individuality is again emphasized and any final business (task or emotional) is completed.

adjudication   Solution to conflict based upon resorting to the courts. Tendency to use adjudication differs between cultures.

adrenalergic state   State of physiological arousal as initial part of fight-or-flight response. Involves changes in hormone levels, heart rate, and respiration rate and efficiency.

affection   Positive emotional bonds between individuals. Level of unconscious need for affection influences tendency to join groups.

affiliation   Unconscious need or desire to be with other people. Level of need will influence tendency to join groups.

alarm reaction   First stage in the general adaptation syndrome identified by Selye. Body moves into fight-or-flight state to deal with stressor.

alcohol abuse   Excessive use of alcohol. Not necessarily equivalent to alcoholism. Tendency to alcohol abuse higher in victims of post-traumatic stress disorder, particularly male victims.

Alcoholics Anonymous   First of the twelve-step self-help programs developed by individuals not in the professional mental health community to deal with problem behaviors (in this case alcoholism).

all-channel networks   Communication networks in which all individuals are in contact with all other group members. This model tends to increase member satisfaction, but proves to be inefficient for complex problems, as many of the links are redundant.

allocation of resources norms   Method employed by group to distribute rewards. Various styles include equality and equity.

altruist   Type of social orientation in which the individual ALWAYS places the needs of others over their own needs.

altruistic decisions   Type of decision in which the needs of others are placed above the individual's own needs.

ambiguity about power   One of the three criteria found by Fiedler to result in differences in the most effective style of leadership. (See *Fiedler's contingency theory*.)

analogue research   Research in which the sample studied is not equivalent to the group to which the results are intended to be generalized (e.g., using college sophomores for research on management styles). May be used as a matter of convenience or when a more appropriate type of sample may be difficult, or impossible, to get as when studying stigmatized groups such as HIV-positive individuals.

androgyny   The behavioral flexibility to respond with either stereotypically masculine or feminine behaviors dependent upon occasion. (See *Bem Sex-Role Inventory*.)

anti-conformity   Behavior that deliberately violates norms of conformity. (See also *psychological reactance* and *counterconformity*.)

appearance norms   Implicit standards established by a group as to appropriate clothing, hairstyle, or ornamentation (e.g., business suits in the office or tattoos and piercings in a rock band). These standards emphasize group membership.

appointed leaders   Leaders who have the advantage of being chosen either from outside of the group or elected by the group. Appointment increases ability of the leader to employ legitimate power, particularly in newly formed (immature) groups.

arbitration   Method of third party conflict resolution. Two types: nonbinding (when groups agree to listen to proposed solution), and binding (where groups agree in advance to comply with proposed solution).

ascribed roles   Sets of behaviors based upon characteristics over which the individual has no control (e.g., age, sex, or race).

attention   Important component of effective communication. Involves focusing on what is currently being said and not on formulating a reply.

attribution theory   Theory that seeks to explain the reasons for behaviors—of others and our own. Attributions may be internal (based on personality or disposition) or external (based on the influence of the situation).

authority   Based on French and Raven's legitimate power, the "right" to influence the behavior of others. More easily employed by appointed leaders than emergent leaders.

autistic conflict   Perceived conflict where none exists. Problem is misunderstanding or misattributing causes of others' behaviors. Also known as "false conflict."

autocratic leadership   Style of leadership in which all decisions are made by the leader. Results may include lower satisfaction on the part of the group and lowered levels of quality of group product.

autokinetic effect   Visual illusion employed by Sherif to study conformity. Individuals make estimates of movement of stationery light (apparent movement is inherent to visual system), first individually, then as part of a group, then again individually. Individual ratings tend to conform to the group response.

autonomy   Independence. Leadership neutralizer. When group members are high in autonomy, there is need for less direction from leader.

averaging inputs   Decision criterion created with goal of reducing impact of group politics from affecting decision. Used in situations where no objective measure is available, as in sports such as gymnastics and diving in competition. To reduce tendency to rate members of one's own group based on group membership rather than ability, a panel of judges each rates the performance, then the highest and lowest scores are eliminated.

avoidant-insecure   Type of bond created between infant and primary caretaker (usually mother) in which child does not find mother to be source of safety and comfort. Usually based on caretaker's nonresponsiveness to infant.

backchannels   Behaviors of listener in conversation that indicate understanding and agreement. Cultures differ in use of backchannels in that collectivist cultures are more likely to employ them in conversation.

balance theory   Theory established by Heider that offers model of attitude creation and change. Individuals are comfortable when their attitudes agree with their friends, and uncomfortable when they agree with their enemies (e.g., an unbalanced system). Individuals will alter attitudes toward individual or object to recreate (or create) balance.

bald speech   Lowest level of politeness in conversation consisting of direct, unelaborated request.

bargaining   General label for assortment of methods seeking to resolve conflict.

behavioral approach to leadership   Leadership style in which focus is on productivity issues in the group and not on feelings and needs of group members.

behavioral assimilation   Shift in behavior in response to antisocial behavior seen in individuals with a cooperative social orientation. Individualists and competitors who defect on a cooperator will find that on second encounter, the cooperator has shifted to match the defecting behavior.

Bem Sex-Role Inventory (BSRI)   Questionnaire developed by Sandra Bem to measure an individual's identification with masculine, feminine, and androgynous gender roles.

binding arbitration   Third party intervention in conflict situation in which third party presents proposed resolution to conflict to which all parties have agreed to comply.

blue ribbon juries   Type of jury employed until early 1960s in some complex legal cases where it was considered important that jurors have some expertise or increased probability of understanding the nuances of the case.

boasting   Type of self-aggrandizement which varies across cultures and genders. In the United States (a highly individualistic culture) it is seen more frequently in masculine individuals.

body language   Colloquial term for nonverbal communication.

bolstering   Method of avoiding group discussion of alternatives in decision making. Decision is made based upon very little consideration, then the remainder of the time is employed to rationalize the decision. Based on cognitive dissonance.

boomerang effect   Demonstration of psychological reactance on the part of group members when leader attempts to employ autocratic form of leadership.

brainstorming   Commonly misunderstood method of generating ideas. Requires training and two separate meetings—the first to generate ideas in the absence of any feedback (positive or negative) followed by a meeting to evaluate the quality of the ideas. When done properly, creates higher quality and higher quantity of alternatives. As usually employed, actually results in fewer, poorer quality alternatives.

breakpoints   Point in conversation where there is change of speaker.

bridging   Method of conflict resolution which seeks to identify underlying needs of parties and to develop solution that satisfies these needs.

broken heart effect   Tendency of widows and widowers to have dramatically higher probability of dying within two years of death of spouse than the probability of dying of others of their age and sex. Particularly high for males. Colloquially, "dying of a broken heart."

carrying capacity   Number of users of resource who can effectively exploit resource without damage.

ceiling effect   Statistical effect when the frequency of a behavior stops increasing and flattens out graphically. Found in conformity studies by Asch after only three confederates created unanimously incorrect majority. Addition of confederates only slightly increased with additional numbers of confederates.

centralized networks   Communication patterns where some of the possible communication links are not employed. Information passes in to central individual(s) who filter the information and relay only relevant information to other group members.

channels   Connections between individuals in communication networks.

charismatic leadership   Type of leadership based upon characteristics of leader. Allows for expanded use of legitimate and referent power bases. Examples include Jesus and Hitler.

chicken game   Decomposed game in which payoff matrix is structured so that the best outcome for all is the cooperative choice.

chicken game structure = T > R > S > P   Temptation to defect is larger than reward for mutual cooperation which is larger than the sucker's payoff which is larger than the punishment for mutual defection.

cholinergic state   State of body after it returns to normal homeostasis from fight-or-flight response.

"choose a number" method of conflict resolution   Situation where individual who chooses number closest to that chosen by a third party to the conflict "wins." Often deficient solution because it represents a win/lose situation in which the loser has the motivation to ignore or even sabotage the "winning" solution.

clarity (of roles)   Situation where individual attaining role (e.g., bank president) in which expected behaviors are clearly delineated.

classism   Type of prejudice and/or discrimination based upon the target's socio-economic status.

clinical psychologist (Ph.D.)   Individual who has earned research doctoral degree in clinical psychology. Often practices therapy.

cliques In-groups based upon criteria chosen by group. Particularly evident in adolescence (e.g., "jocks" or "geeks").

coercive power Behavior resulting from threat of negative consequences. Creates high probability of compliance, and high probability of negative feelings on part of target.

cognitive dissonance Elaboration of balance theory proposed by Festinger. Situation in which individual's own ideals, values, thoughts, and behaviors are inconsistent. Discomfort created by this inconsistency (cognitive dissonance) will be reduced by altering inconsistent components to create balanced system.

cohesiveness Strength of the relational bonds connecting group members. Too little cohesiveness results in "nongroup" that is unlikely to succeed. Too much cohesiveness may result in group that socializes at expense of task productivity. Moderate amount of cohesiveness results in strong identification with group and high motivation for group success.

collaboration Working together to achieve jointly valued result.

collectivist cultures Cultures in which there is a high degree of emphasis on the group and not the individual. The Japanese culture tends to be highly collectivistic as compared with the American culture which is highly individualistic.

commitment Degree of allegiance to the group which is particularly high when individual is in the membership stage of group socialization. Correlated with severity of initiation.

comparison level (Cl) From Thibault and Kelley's theory of social exchange. Level of rewards to which the individual feels entitled. If the relationship or group is providing fewer rewards than this level, the individual will be unhappy. Highly individualistically idiosyncratic, rewards that would result in dissatisfaction with the group for individual A (lower than Cl) might result in a high level of satisfaction for individual B (whose Cl is lower than the level of rewards).

comparison level for alternatives (Cl$_{alt}$) Also from social exchange theory (see comparison level, above), the evaluation of relationships or groups other than those in which the individual is a member. If alternatives appear more satisfying, the theory predicts that the individual would leave to join this superior group.

compensatory task An example of a divisible, maximizing task. The group usually does better on this task than all but the best individual group members.

competitive Seeking to claim limited resources for the self while at the same time attempting to keep others from claiming the rewards. (For example, in football the team seeks to win not only by making the most points themselves, but also by preventing the opposing team from making points.)

competitor Type of social orientation in which the individual wishes not only to "win," but also to beat others. Thus the competitor will choose an outcome in which she earns fewer rewards than possible as long as she maximizes her rewards relative to her opponent. Also known as relative gains orientation.

complementary roles The enactment of individual roles elicits a complementary response from others. For example, when an individual is playing the role of "husband" another individual is enacting the behaviors expected of the role of "wife."

complex decision paths Frequently encountered approach to decision making in which the group goes through cycles of decision making in which the results of one decision create situations requiring another decision-making cycle.

complexity of roles Number and types of behaviors included in a role. To take an example from literature, the role of Juliet in Shakespeare's play is far more complex than is that of one of the nonspeaking members of Romeo's group of friends.

compliance Altering behavior in response to direct order or command.

compromise Lose/lose solution to conflict. Because neither side has attained any of their goals, this solution is highly unstable. Should be chosen only when problem solving approaches have failed.

concern for people One of the two types of focus for leadership behaviors in Blake and Mouton's managerial grid. Emphasizes feelings and relationships of group members.

concern for production The second type of focus of leadership behaviors in the managerial grid. Emphasizes goal attainment.

conflict Situation in which two or more group members are in disagreement; usually seen first in middle stages of group development. Appropriate handling of conflict is necessary for group success.

conflict aftermath The last of Pondy's stages of conflict. This is the period of time after the conflict has been stopped. The effects on the group depend upon the level of group members' satisfaction with the resolution.

conflict-prone responsibilities Some roles, in groups or in society at large, consist of roles that are likely to create or encounter conflict, such as police officers, hostage negotiators, or IRS auditors.

conformity The tendency of individuals to "go along" with the implicit pressure of a group to follow the group's norms.

confrontation The stage in group development in which conflict is encountered. If appropriately dealt with, the group will improve in both productivity and socioemotional areas. If confrontation is dealt with ineffectively, the group may self-destruct.

conjunctive task One of the types of task that influences whether a group or an individual would have a higher level of potential productivity. In this type of task the group is not "done" until every member has completed the task (e.g., a relay race). Thus the group performs at the level of the worst member.

consensus Complete agreement. In making group decisions, consensus may be desirable if it is important that all group members contribute to the implementation of the decision. If all members agree, at least publicly, there is less potential for free riding or sabotage. The disadvantage of consensus is that it often takes a very long time to reach.

Consequences The final stage of Bower and Bower's DESC model of communication. In this stage the consequences accompanying the desired changes are delineated.

consideration One of the two types of leadership identified by the Ohio State University research. In this style, the leader is concerned with the group members as individuals with feelings.

consultative-type leaders One of the types of leaders identified by the Vroom and Jago normative leadership theory. This type of leader makes the decision based upon information obtained from the group. The two other types are autocratic and group.

contending A model of response to conflict in which there is high attention paid to the individual's own needs and low attention paid to the needs of others.

contingent conflict Conflict between two or more group members that is based upon the incompatibility of behaviors. Is solved through the use of negotiation.

continuous public goods dilemma Type of social dilemma in which it is not possible to deny access to the resource to those individuals who fail to contribute to its upkeep (e.g., public television or radio stations).

contracts   A formal type of agreement used in adjudication. Cultural differences are found in the tendency to use contracts. Americans like contracts as they feel it anticipates and heads off disagreement. The Japanese, on the other hand, feel a request for a contract indicates a lack of trust.

contractual management conflict specialist   Individual whose task is to serve as a third party in the resolution of conflict.

conversion   The process through which attitudes are changed. This may involve the process of persuasion.

cooling-off period   Time taken during a conflict to separate the two parties and allow emotions to settle.

cooperative   Refers to a type of behavior in which the individual is concerned with the outcome of the group as a unit more than his or her own outcomes.

cooperator   An individual whose social orientation is to behave in a cooperative manner. If others respond with antisocial behavior, the cooperator will respond with behavioral assimilation.

coordination problems   One of the disadvantages of using a group rather than an individual to complete a task. Also known as the Ringelmann effect.

coordinators   One of the many alternative terms for leader often preferred by collectivistic cultures and by women.

costcutting   The process of bringing requests for resources into realistic terms that are less likely to invoke conflict in the group.

correspondence of outcomes   The basis of interdependence. A's outcomes depend not only on his behaviors, but also on B's behavior.

counseling   Providing advice. Is not the same as providing therapy.

counterconformity   Behavior in which the individual agrees with the group's behavior, but acts counter to its beliefs (e.g., a juror who votes to convict when all others are voting to acquit). May stem from attempt to prevent mandate phenomenon, or from trying to slow the group decision process down.

credibility of source   One of the factors affecting persuasion. A source who is perceived as credible (knowledgeable) is more likely to be believed.

critical listening   Listening closely with the attempt to understand the communication.

curative factors   Yalom's list of factors that must be present in order for group therapy to be effective.

death-qualified jury   A jury in which all members have expressed a willingness to apply the death penalty as punishment if a conviction occurs. Such juries are more likely to convict than nondeath-qualified juries.

decentralized networks   Communication networks in which many channels are employed and information does not pass through a central filter. Good for group satisfaction, sometimes ineffective for group productivity.

deception cues   Behavioral or verbal behaviors that indicate an individual is not telling the truth.

deception guilt   The societally ingrained guilt about lying which creates the deception cues picked up by polygraphs and observers.

decision criteria   The "rules" that are established to determine how a decision will be made (e.g., whether by voting or averaging inputs).

decision-making meetings   Meetings whose entire purpose is focused upon reaching a decision.

Decision Style Inventory (DSI)   Questionnaire that identifies four types of decision-making styles: directive, analytical, conceptual, and behavioral.

decoding   In the process of communication, the receiver must translate the message into his or her own ideas. This process is known as decoding.

decomposed games   A method of creating situations in which the payoff matrix is equivalent to that of a "real life" situation (e.g., prisoner's dilemma or the chicken game).

defective choices   Choices made in either a decomposed game or in an actual situation in which the individual chooses the behavior that is not best for the group.

deficient equilibrium   The result in a social dilemma where the behavioral choices result in everyone's losing.

deindividuation   The situation in which an individual seeks to escape from their own individual responsibilities and identity in order to make it easier to perform anti-social acts. Can also be used to change the person who is a target of aggression from an individual into a "thing," possibly through the use of epithets (e.g., nigger, spic, etc.) to simplify aggression.

delegating   A behavior employed by a leader in which she shifts some of her responsibilities or tasks onto another group member.

Delphi technique   Type of nominal group technique in which experts from anywhere on the planet can act as a group. Each is provided a summary of the problem and asked to respond with ideas for potential solutions. These are combined and resubmitted to the members, who react to the report with further ideas. Three rounds is usually the point at which maximum effectiveness is reached. This technique has been highly facilitated and in some cases replaced by increases in technological communication.

democratic leadership   A style of leadership in which the leader provides structure for the group, but allows the group to make decisions. When compared with autocratic and laissez-faire styles of leadership, this style provided the highest level of satisfaction and overall productivity (considering both quantity and quality).

demonstrations of self-interest   One of the potential outcomes of conflict. It brings to light individual agendas that may have been secret.

DESC model   Model of communication/assertiveness training developed by Bower and Bower. Consists of four steps: **D**escribe, **E**xpress, **S**pecify, and **C**onsequences.

Describe   The first step in the Bower and Bower model in which the individual describes the behavior they desire to have changed. The description should be objective, concrete, and based upon specific behaviors.

detecting lies   One of the purported uses of the polygraph. In reality, the actual accuracy is very low, producing an unacceptably large number of both false negatives and false positives.

devil's advocate   Role of group member in which the individual questions all group decisions and ideas in order to force the group to improve its ideas. Based on the method by which the Catholic Church chooses saints—the devil's advocate's role is to question the reasons and suggest reasons against sanctification.

diagnostic information   One of the possible outcomes of group conflict. Repeated similar conflicts can provide information about the sources of the group's problems.

difficulty concentrating   One of the symptoms of PTSD (post-traumatic stress disorder).

diffusion of responsibility   The basis of the tendency for an individual to receive help if there are only a few bystanders rather than a crowd. The more people around, the less individual responsibility each feels to become involved.

directive leader Style of leadership in which leader provides structure, makes decisions, and assigns tasks.

directive style Type of behaviors demonstrated by a directive leader.

discrete (step-level) public goods dilemma A public goods dilemma in which a certain minimum amount of contribution is necessary for the existence of the resource (e.g., Vietnam Veterans' Memorial cannot be built unless sufficient funds are collected to buy the parcel of land on which the memorial is to be built).

diseases of civilization Phrase coined by Dr. Hans Selye to refer to medical conditions based upon the stresses created from living in "civilization."

disenchantment One of the possible outcomes of group socialization leading to an individual leaving a group.

disjunctive task Type of task in which there is only one correct answer. There are two types: the "eureka" type in which the correct answer stated by one group member is immediately recognized by the rest (in which case a group ALWAYS is superior to an individual) and the "non-eureka" type task in which the correct answer is not immediately recognizable and powerful group members may incorrectly convince the group the answer is wrong.

disorientation One of the symptoms reported by individuals with PTSD.

disoriented-insecure The type of bond formed between an infant and an unresponsive primary caretaker. The caretaker does not provide any stability or comfort to the infant when distressed.

display rules Societal norms which vary across cultures regarding the appropriateness of nonverbally expressing certain emotions (e.g., Japanese express less anger nonverbally than Americans).

dispositional Based upon an individual's personality or character. One of the types of attribution (and the source of the fundamental attribution error) is the tendency to ignore the impact of the situation and make dispositional attributions for others' behavior.

divergence One of the possible stages in group socialization in which either the individual becomes disenchanted with the group and chooses to leave or the group decides to let the individual go.

divisible task Characteristic of task that allows it to be divided up into smaller, individual tasks for group members (e.g., blowing up balloons to decorate for the prom). Potential productivity for this task indicates a group is ALWAYS superior to an individual—even the best individual in the group.

doctor of psychology (Psy.D.) Terminal degree in psychology which is more oriented toward producing practitioners than researchers.

dominance Assuming control over others.

dominant behaviors The behavior that is most likely to occur in any given situation (e.g., although a hungry dog could do a lot of things, when faced with food it will probably eat).

dominating strategies Term employed by Dawes to refer to the dominant behaviors of individuals in social dilemmas.

dyad (dyadic) A group consisting of two persons.

effective coping skills Behaviors that help with handling stress and are not detrimental to the individual. The most effective appears to be social support.

ego The conscious part of the personality as defined by Freud.

egoistic decisions   Decisions made by individuals that take only their own good into consideration.

egoistic deprivation   A form of relative deprivation in which we feel that others have more of some desired resource than we possess.

egoistic incentives   An alternative explanation for cooperative behavior in which Axelrod posits that cooperators are not just altruistic "good guys," but rather cooperate because their cooperation will result in a larger pool of resources from which they will receive a share.

electronic mail   The technological method by which individuals can communicate instantly through a computer with anyone similarly equipped.

elicit feedback   One of the advantages to the individual from group therapy, the individual can ask for and react to others' perceptions of their behaviors.

elicit self-destructive behaviors   One of the other potential results of group therapy is to identify the tendency of the individual to do themselves injury.

emblems   In nonverbal communication, physical movements whose meaning is culturally shared—such as in America, nodding the head to indicate agreement.

emergent leaders   A type of leader who is not appointed from the outside nor elected from the inside, but rather must assume control of the leadership of the group through her or his own efforts.

emergent third party   An individual who acts as a third party in conflict resolution but who has allegiances to one or the other of the conflicting groups.

emphasize group differences   Another outcome of group conflict. Differences within the group are highlighted.

encoding   The process of the sender in communication to take ideas or feelings and turn them into symbols (words or gestures) to create the message to be sent.

entrapment   When individuals become so invested in "winning" in a conflict they will sacrifice anything to do so, even if the costs far exceed the rewards accrued.

equality reward distribution   One of the types of distribution of resources in a group in which each person receives an equal share. Usually preferred by those who have invested less or came into the group with fewer resources.

equity   A form of "fairness." In equity theory the individual compares the ratio of their own inputs and outcomes to the same ratio for others. If these are equal, the situation is considered equitable; if not, the situation lacks equity.

escalating conflict   The most serious threat to the group of the various types of conflict. Consists of a pattern of small, seemingly unrelated conflicts that divert the group's attention and energy from the task. Generally the conflicts are really over an underlying issue such as power or control.

ethical conflict   Situation in which there is a disagreement between the parties' perceptions of morally acceptable solutions.

"eureka" disjunctive task   Correct solution to task with only one correct solution which is immediately obvious. A group is always most appropriate for increasing potential productivity on this type of task as each member increases the probability that someone will find the correct solution.

evaluation   One of the major issues in group socialization. The individual and the group reciprocally consider the potential advantages and disadvantages to membership for the individual.

evaluation apprehension   Concern about how others are perceiving one's performance. Offered as one of the bases for the phenomenon of social facilitation.

evaluation of decision   One of the final steps in the decision-making process. Helps the group to determine whether the appropriate decision was reached and if not, where the process faltered.

exaggerated physiological reactivity   One of the symptoms of PTSD often expressed as an exaggerated startle response to an unexpected sound.

expanding the pie   Method of problem solution. Accruing more resources to meet the needs of all.

expert power   One of the six bases of power from French and Raven. Expert power is based upon our assumption that the person who is attempting to influence our behavior is possessed of superior training, experience, knowledge (e.g., we follow our physician's orders because we assume she knows more and has our best interests in mind). Perceived by employees as one of the characteristics of popular leaders.

expertise of source   One of the bases of persuasion. We are much more likely to believe a piece of information when that information comes from someone who has much knowledge in that area.

exposure   One of the steps in the persuasion process.

exposure to war stress   A primary contributor to cases of PTSD among Vietnam (and other war) veterans.

Express   The second step in the Bower and Bower model of communication (DESC). In this step the communicator expresses their feelings about the change they are requesting.

eyewitness identification   A type of courtroom evidence based upon an individual who was present at the scene of the crime. Although often perceived as compelling by juries, research has shown this type of evidence to be often very inaccurate.

factor analysis   A statistical technique used to narrow down a large number of terms or adjectives by identifying those to which individuals similarly respond.

false conflict   An apparent conflict in a group based upon a misunderstanding, not an actual conflict. Also known as autistic conflict.

false negative   A result on a test (such as a polygraph test) which inaccurately identifies the individual as not possessing a characteristic (or in the case of the polygraph a result that inaccurately identifies a person as not telling a lie—when in fact the person is lying).

false positive   A result on a test which inaccurately identifies a person as possessing a characteristic. A false positive on a tuberculosis test would indicate that the person is infected when in fact they are not. On a polygraph, a false positive calls an honest person a liar.

familiarization theory   A theory that seeks to identify the bases of group polarization. An idea is introduced which initially sounds outrageous, but as the group discusses the idea, it becomes more familiar, thus seeming a more plausible solution.

fear of sucker's payoff = P − S   Punishment for mutual defection minus the sucker's payoff.

felt conflict   The third step in Pondy's theory of conflict in which the conflict within the group has risen to the level of awareness.

Fiedler's contingency theory   Leadership theory that proposes that the best type of leadership depends upon the characteristics of the situation under which the group would be working.

fight-or-flight response   The physiological response to a stressor that puts the body into an adrenalergic state, prepared to engage in battle or to run.

FIRO-B Test developed by Schutz to identify needs satisfied by group membership: inclusion, control, and affection (fundamental relations orientation).

foreman of jury Individual chosen by the jury to represent them to the court.

formal aspects of groups The way things are "supposed to be" as opposed (sometimes) to the way things actually are.

formal group goals The goals that the group publicly identifies for attainment.

formal networks The way communications are supposed to be channeled within the group.

formative feedback Information on the appropriateness of how the task is being accomplished during the time the work is progressing. Allows the group to identify appropriate, or change inappropriate, behaviors.

forming The first stage of group development in the Tuckman and Jensen model of group development.

fraternal deprivation A type of relative deprivation based not upon our own lack, but the lack of a resource by a group with which we identify (such as a gang or an ethnic group).

free riding An individual not contributing to the work of the group because they feel their contribution would not have any impact (often used as an excuse by nonvoters).

functional approach The functional approach to group membership states that there are various types of needs that are satisfied by group membership.

fundamental attribution error The very common mistake of attributing another person's behavior upon some internal or dispositional cause and underestimating the impact of the environment.

general adaptation syndrome (GAS) Physical and psychological series of reactions to stress that begin with the recognition of the stressor and end with effective coping or even potentially, death.

goal incompatibility One of the bases for conflict within or between groups.

goals The reason for the group's existence. Having goals directs the group's behavior.

goal setting theory Locke's theory that setting specific, difficult (but attainable) goals will enhance group productivity.

grapevine The informal communications channels in organizations and groups. Often lightening fast. Often carry accurate information about the organization and often inaccurate information about group members.

greed = T − R The amount of greed is defined as the amount of temptation to defect (size of payoff) minus the reward for mutual cooperation.

GRIT Graduated Reciprocation in Tension developed by Osgood as a method of intergroup conflict resolution by mutual concessions.

group climate The group emotional state (e.g., relaxed, tense, etc.).

group development The stages through which groups progress as they travel through time and change in terms of issues such as tension, trust, and cohesiveness.

group dynamics The effects of group membership upon individuals' feelings, interactions, and productivity.

group leader The individual within the group who assumes the behaviors associated with the role of leader either through appointment (or election) or emergence.

group polarization The tendency for groups to make more extreme decisions (either riskier or more conservative) than those same individuals would make on their own.

group spatial ecology   The arrangement of the space the group occupies. Some arrangements (sociopetal) encourage group interaction, others (sociofugal) discourage interaction.

groupthink   A phenomenon observed in groups defined by Janis in which the group loses touch with the outside environment and makes extremely bad decisions.

guilty verdict   Decision reached by a judge or a jury in a trial. In a criminal case the jury is to reach this verdict when there is no reasonable doubt about the guilt of the accused. In civil cases, this verdict is to be reached when the preponderance of guilt points to the accused. Both types of trial may be held for the same act for the same individual without violating the principle of "double jeopardy."

hassles   The little, everyday things that go wrong in everyone's lives that serve as stressors.

head-of-the-table effect   The tendency for groups to grant leadership status to the person who sits at the head of the table. Works for all-male, all-female, and mixed groups with a male at the head of the table. Works considerably less frequently in mixed groups with a female at the head (found by Porter).

high-contact cultures   Refers to the cultural tendency to maintain different amounts of distance when communicating. High-contact cultures tend to maintain smaller distances.

homophobia   An exaggerated fear and hatred of homosexuals.

hope   One of Yalom's curative factors believed necessary for group therapy to be effective.

hot reactors   A more recent approach to the Type A personality which sees them as highly reactive both physiologically and psychologically to stress.

hung jury   A jury unable to meet the criteria necessary for a decision. While usually this requires unanimity, the Supreme Court has allowed in non-capital cases for the criterion for guilt to be a simple majority.

hypervigilance   A tendency to exaggerated reactions. Found in individuals with PTSD and Type A personalities.

id   The original part of the personality according to Freud, unconscious and guarded from entrance by the ego (which itself develops from the id).

identification of alternatives   An important step in the process of decision making. The more alternatives that are identified, the higher the probability that one will be optimal.

idiosyncrasy credits   Units of permission to disregard group norms the leader accrues through status and adhering to and policing adherence to norms by others.

illustrators   Movements made by individuals to accompany their speech (e.g., talking with your hands).

immediate reaction to trauma   The initial stages of the reaction to trauma usually results in a great deal of upset including eating, sleeping, working, and emotional patterns.

implementation   Putting a group decision into action.

implicit favorite model   Theory proposed by Power and Aldag that subverts the decision-making process. Rather than enter the evaluation stage with an open mind, individuals have had a favored outcome in mind from the beginning and try to shape the process in favor of their favorite.

implicit leadership theories   The theory that everyone carries a template for leadership around in their heads and that we use these templates to determine who should be a leader and to evaluate the performance of leaders.

improvisation   One of the differences found by Jones between African-American and white culture.

inclusion   One of the three needs measured by Schutz's FIRO-B.

independence   The situation when our outward behaviors are congruent with our attitudes and opinions—we disagree with the group and we enact their behaviors.

indirectness   Used in the off-the-record level of communicative directness, indirectness involves stating a request in such an oblique manner that although the request is implied, it is never actually stated (e.g., I want a drink from the kitchen so I ask my daughter if she's thirsty).

individual autonomy   One of the "neutralizers"—characteristics of the group that make the enactment of leadership behaviors less necessary.

individual conflict   Conflict that goes on within an individual (e.g., a desire to be thin and a desire to eat a quart of ice cream).

individual differentiation   The stage in group development that follows confrontation. The group improves in most measures: cohesiveness, trust, and productivity.

individualist   The social orientation that involves the person placing their own needs above the needs of others. If the individualist has a choice between two alternatives equally favorable to himself, but with one clearly more favorable to the other individual than the other alternative, the individualist will choose the alternative that best serves the other.

individualistic cultures   Cultures that value the individual over the group, such as the United States.

ineffective coping skills   Behaviors enacted by individuals in response to stress or trauma that involve escaping, not solving the issues. Examples include use of alcohol and drugs and denial.

informal aspects of groups   As opposed to the "way things are supposed to be" (formal aspects), informal aspects of the group are the "way things really are."

informal group goals   Unstated, implicit goals of the group.

informal networks   The channels through which communication actually spreads (e.g., the grapevine).

informational influence   Changing another's behavior through information.

informational needs   Individual needs for information that can only be measured subjectively that can only be obtained from other people (e.g., does this skirt make me look fat?).

informational power   The weakest of the French and Raven power bases in which an individual's behavior is influenced by a shared piece of minor information (e.g., there's a new episode of "X-Files" on tonight). If the information is irrelevant to the target, then there will be no influence.

information-seeking questions   One of the types of task-related questions.

information-sharing meetings   Meetings whose sole purpose is to communicate information to the group.

in-group   The group with whom we identify and toward whom we feel a sense of belonging.

initiating structure   One of the two types of group issues identified by the Ohio State University researchers.

initiations   Ceremonies or procedures undergone to attain membership in a group.

inoculation defense   Method to attempt to increase immunity to persuasion through introducing weaker forms of the argument.

inquisition process   A type of third party conflict intervention process in which the third party collects information from both groups (who are allowed only to answer questions—not present a case) and then makes a binding decision as to the resolution of the conflict.

insecurely-bonded infant   An infant who does not develop a closeness and sense of safety with the primary caretaker, based upon an unpredictably responsive environment.

integrative solution   A problem-solving based approach to conflict resolution in which each side feels they have won on at least some of the issues.

interaction   Situations in which individuals engage in mutual behavior.

interdependence   The situation of correspondence of outcomes in which your outcomes are affected by your behaviors AND my behaviors.

intergroup conflict   Conflict between two (or more) groups.

intermediate goals   When long-term goals involve a number of steps or changes, intermediate goals can be established to identify the appropriate direction of behavior along the way.

interorganizational conflict   When two organizations are in conflict (e.g., IBM and Apple).

interpersonal conflict   Conflict between two or more people; can arise from numerous sources.

interpersonal orientation (IO)   Behavior in social dilemmas that are concerned with the welfare of the other.

interpersonal relations   The relationships between individuals.

interpersonal role conflict   When two individuals seek to occupy the same role. A form of rivalry.

inter-rater reliability   The correlation between the measured observations of researchers. Correlations of at least +.9 should be attained.

inter-role conflict   Conflict felt within the individual when two or more roles they are expected to interact are mutually exclusive (e.g., your daughter's dance recital is at the same time as the board of directors' meeting).

interruption   Beginning to speak before another has stopped. May be an attempt to dominate, or an attempt to "overlap" and create a sense of connection.

intimate distance   The area of distance (which differs across cultures) we maintain between ourselves and those with whom we have an intimate relationship.

intragroup conflict   Conflict or disagreement which arises within the group.

intra-role conflict   Discomfort felt when a single role occupied by an individual is defined differently by two or more others (e.g., newlyweds discover that they have differing definitions of the appropriate behaviors associated with the role of husband).

intuitive model   A recent move away from the more logical and rationally based models of decision making that allows for the less easily identified methods of recognizing a correct solution (e.g., playing a hunch).

investigation   The initial stage in Moreland and Levine's group socialization model in which the individual and the group are trying to determine whether they are interested in following up on the connection.

invidious comparisons   Comparisons between our own possessions and those of others that may result in feelings of relative deprivation.

irritability   One of the symptoms of burnout.

isolation   One of the symptoms of both PTSD and burnout.

jargon   A type of language shorthand that serves to improve communication within the in-group and to identify and isolate individuals from the out-group.

job discrimination   Behavior in the employment arena which disadvantages an individual based upon a characteristic or behavior.

"jumping in"   The term employed by gang members to refer to the often brutal initiation rites individuals must endure to become a member of the gang.

jury nullification   When a jury disregards the letter of the law and makes their decision based upon other criteria.

kinesic behavior   Nonverbal communication through movement. Often referred to as "body language."

latent conflict   The first of the five stages of conflict in Pondy's model in which the conditions for conflict (such as scarcity of resources) exist, but have not reached the level of awareness.

leader   The individual in the group who assumes the behaviors identified with the role of leader.

leader effectiveness   The ability of the leader to move the group to completion of its goals while attending to socioemotional issues.

leader power   One of the three situational factors identified by Fiedler as affecting the appropriate leadership style.

leakage   Information that is inadvertently conveyed by an individual (often nonverbally) that indicates deceit.

legal action   The potential outcome from various types of conflict.

legitimacy of dependence   The ability of the powerless to influence our behavior through their own helplessness (e.g., small children and the elderly).

legitimacy of equity   Appropriateness of attempt to influence our behavior based on the societal norm of fairness.

legitimacy of reciprocity   Appropriateness of influence attempts based on the norm of reciprocity (e.g., I owe you one).

legitimate power   Also known as authority—influence based on the agreement between target and wielder of influence that such influence is appropriate based on roles (e.g., obedience to a police officer).

leniency bias   The tendency for a jury that has not started out unanimous to acquit a defendant, even when the initial majority was for conviction.

level of ambiguity   One of the characteristics of the environment that can add to the difficulty of the group's success.

level of cooperativeness   One of the intragroup characteristics that can ease or make group success more difficult.

lie detectors   Polygraphs. These machines measure not the lie, but the emotional reaction to the lie, which is why they are extremely unreliable.

life-change units (LCUs)   Units of measure on stress scales which identify the amount of stress experienced and predict the probability of emotional or physical reaction.

life cycle theory of leadership   The model of leadership, developed by Hersey and Blanchard based on the maturity of the group and its members.

light to heavy conflict resolution   The predictable increase in unsolved conflicts.

likeability of source   An important aspect of persuasion. We are unlikely to change our minds in response to an appeal from someone we dislike.

listening for the ego   Not paying attention to what our partner in conversation is saying; waiting for the next pause so we can present our own side.

listening selectively   Hearing only those parts of a communication that we want to hear or those that fit with our currently held attitudes and values.

listening to ignore   A form of nonlistening when we pretend to listen but do not pay attention to what is being said.

logrolling   An integrative conflict resolution technique in which each party is allowed to win on the issues they find most critical while conceding those less crucial. Can also be done temporally as when a legislator promises her vote to others in return for their votes on her "pet" issue.

lose face   Being forced to lose our dignity and to be proved wrong with an audience. The importance of losing face varies across cultures.

loss of trust   A potential side effect of conflict that may permanently damage the effectiveness of the group.

low-contact cultures   Cultures which maintain large zones of distance between speakers.

lying   Not communicating the truth. Can be done actively or passively (although failing to mention a fact is not perceived by all as lying).

majority wins   One of many potential decision criteria. The problem is in the lack of clarity: what kind of majority? 51%? 2/3?

managerial grid   Approach to leadership developed by Blake and Mouton based on the belief that leaders can be trained to be equal and flexible in their concern with people and their concern with productivity.

managers   Leaders in an organizational setting.

mandate phenomenon   The tendency of a leader chosen with overwhelming support to capitalize on this support to extend and cement their power.

manifest conflict   The fourth of Pondy's five stages of conflict in which the conflict has emerged and is visible to others.

maximizing tasks   Tasks for which the criterion of success is based on quality.

mediation   A form of third party intervention in a conflict that involves the least intrusion, in which the third party serves as a facilitator in helping the parties themselves solve the conflict.

mediation/arbitration   A recent addition to the types of third party intervention in a conflict which involves two steps. First the mediator writes down and seals in an envelope the solution which will be employed if the parties cannot settle through mediation (step 1). If the mediation does not work, the envelope is opened, and the arbitrator's solution is binding on both parties.

membership   The first stage in Cohen, Fink, Gadon, & Willits's model of group development in which the group has just begun and is very polite, very superficial, and very ineffective at the task.

mere presence explanation for social facilitation   The explanation for social facilitation favored by Zajonc that states that just having another of our species around increases our physiological arousal level, which accounts for the social facilitation phenomenon.

message   In communication, the encoded ideas of the sender as they are conveyed to the target of the communication.

message content   There is a tendency to use selective perception on the content of messages in terms of positivity/negativity. Individuals tend to exaggerate the severity of negative messages and fail to hear the level of positivity in complimentary messages.

metaanalysis   A statistical technique that allows for comparison over a number of research studies of a phenomenon by comparing the size and direction of their findings.

middle period of reaction to trauma   This is the period where reorganization begins. The severity of initial symptoms recedes and individuals are able to begin to move toward a normal life.

mindlessness   The tendency found by Langer for Americans to comply to requests for behavior without examining the appropriateness of the reason for the request.

mixed-motive situations   Situations where behavior is pulled in different directions (e.g., Eating the eclair now will be pleasing, but will interfere with our goal of losing weight).

mock juries   Juries created for the purpose of analogue research in which participants are asked to enact a trial. The results of such research are controversial as the level of consequences for behavior cannot be compared to a real trial jury.

nature vs. nurture   The ubiquitous controversy in psychology over whether traits and behaviors are based on biology (nature) or on learning (nurture).

need for nurturance   One of the possible needs satisfied by group membership identified with the functional theory of group formation. Individuals who receive insufficient or ineffective nurturing as infants grow up with impairments.

need for power   One of the unconscious psychological needs satisfied by membership in groups. With power identified as the ability to influence others, we must have others in order to satisfy this need.

negative politeness   Third level of Brown and Levinson's theory of politeness in communication in which the speaker attempts to conceal the level of imposition of the request (e.g., *Since you're going to the store anyway*, would you buy me some milk?).

negotiation   Attempts to solve a conflict through communication.

neotenous   Resembling the facial structure of a baby. Such faces are identified as highly physically attractive.

networks   Patterns of linkages between individuals based on communication.

neutralizers   Characteristics of the task, the group, or the situation that require less direction from the leader.

nightmares   Symptoms of PTSD and the first stage of reaction to trauma.

nominal group techniques   Techniques where groups do not actually meet and interact, but individuals pool their resources to solve a problem.

nondominant behaviors   The array of behaviors that are not chosen when a dominant behavior is chosen in a situation. For example, a hungry dog given food will probably eat (the dominant response); however, he could bark, whine, jump, sit, or any number of other (nondominant) behaviors.

"non-eureka" disjunctive task   Disjunctive task in which the only correct answer is not immediately obvious; thus an individual with high status or strong persuasive skills may talk the group out of accepting the correct answer.

nonlistening   The ultimate method of avoiding listening—refusing to allow the other to attempt communication with us.

normative influence   The effect of norms in causing individuals to conform.

normative model   Leadership theory presented by Vroom and Yetton and revised by Vroom and Jago in which leadership types are distinguished by differences in whether the leader or the group, or some combination thereof, makes the final decision.

norming   The stage after confrontation equivalent to "individual differentiation," in which the group functions at a high level of productivity and social interaction.

norm of equity   The societal implicit rule that requires that we treat others fairly.

norm of reciprocity   The societal expectation that we will return favors performed for us by others.

norms   Implicit, unwritten expectations for behaviors.

number of issues   As conflicts increase in intensity the number of issues under contention tends to increase.

obedience   The behavioral compliance with a direct order.

Ohio State (leadership) research   One of the groups identifying two basic group and leadership issues—task and social issues.

operational definition   The operation or behavior that is used to measure a construct that cannot be measured directly (such as love or hunger). An operational definition of hunger would usually be based on some concrete measure such as hours since eating or level of blood sugar.

opinion-seeking questions   Questions that are intended to elicit the positions of others on the issues facing the group.

opportunity for catharsis   One of the advantages to the individual obtained from group therapy.

opportunity to enhance social skills   Group therapy provides a safe environment to practice social behaviors and receive feedback, thus enhancing social skills.

opportunity to practice altruistic behavior   Positive result of participating in group therapy.

opportunity to witness alternative reactions   Watching how others react to situations and how those reactions differ from our own is another advantage of group therapy.

optimizing model   Harrison's elaboration of the utility model of decision making by introducing the concept that the first step should be whether, in fact, a decision needs to be made at all.

optimizing tasks   Tasks for which the success of the group is based on the quality of the product.

oral expression   Expression of information through speech.

organizers   One of the many euphemisms women tend to prefer to the term "leader" when applied to themselves.

orientation-seeking questions   Questions that are intended to determine the structure of the group.

outbursts of anger   Typical symptom of PTSD victims.

out-group   The other groups with whom we don't identify and to which we don't belong.

overbenefitted   In an equity equation the individual who is getting more benefits in proportion to their inputs than their partner. In theory they should be as unhappy as their partner, but they seldom are.

overconformity   An attempt to go well past the behavior required by the group to indicate the level of commitment to the group.

overdetermination   The fact that many conflicts are fueled by many sources defines them as overdetermined. All sources must be dealt with or the conflict will not be solved.

overlap   The type of interruption where one speaker begins to talk before another has finished in order to introduce some statement of connection or understanding. More often employed by American women than men.

P = punishment for mutual defection   The amount one suffers if both partners in a situation of interdependence make the antisocial behavioral choice.

paralinguistics   Level and type of emotion communicated by changes in the voice such as loudness or pitch.

path-goal leadership theory   Leadership theory by House that believes that the most appropriate type of leadership depends not only on situational characteristics, but also the characteristics of group members. A variation on the contingency-type theory of leadership.

payoff matrix   Numerical representation of the results of behaviors in a situation of interdependence.

perceived conflict   Second stage of Pondy's theory of conflict in which the source of conflict has been identified by one of the potential participants, but the conflict has not yet manifested itself.

performance-related norms   Unwritten rules that groups establish for themselves concerning the amount of work that should be accomplished in a certain time period. Workers violating this norm by working too hard and thereby identifying the cushion that has been built into the system are known as rate busters and are dealt with as negatively as any norm breakers.

performing   The final stage in the Cohen et al. model of group development; when the group has reached its optimal performance level.

permissible error rate   The number of mistakes that are acceptable before the group steps in.

persistent avoidance   In the early stage of reaction to trauma (such as a rape) the victim may consistently refuse to return to the site of the attack—even if it was her home. Such victims often move to another domicile.

personality clashes   Differences in values and preferences that may be a source of intragroup conflict.

person characteristics   Another term for one of the two basic issues for groups (the other being task issues).

personal distance   This is the physical distance reserved in each culture for friends and acquaintances. This differs greatly between cultures.

personal growth groups   A type of self-help group that focuses not on repairing a defect, or providing support through a crisis, but a group that helps a person acquire new skills that will improve their already effective level of functioning.

persuasion   The process of convincing an individual to change their mind.

persuasive arguments theory   One of the theories proposed to explain the group polarization phenomenon. This theory suggests that persuasive individuals in favor of extreme solutions convince the rest of the group to join them.

physical attractiveness   One of the bases for interpersonal attraction. The definition of physical attractiveness differs across cultures and across time, but is held in common in the culture at any given time.

physical danger   Protecting individuals from danger is one of the functions performed by the group in the functional model.

policy-seeking questions   Questions whose role is to clarify the procedures of the group.

politeness   An issue affecting the encoding of a message that is influenced by the relationship between the individuals, the status of the individuals, and the size of the favor being sought.

polygraphs   The actual name for the more commonly labeled "lie detectors."

position power   The ability to influence others based upon one's place in the group or organization. Leaders and supervisors possess position power.

positive politeness   The level of politeness that seeks to soften the request through the use of a "tag question."

post-traumatic stress disorder (PTSD)   A psychological disorder suffered by individuals who have undergone a potentially life-threatening experience.

potential productivity   The amount that could be produced in a given situation if all aspects were at optimal levels.

power   The power to influence the behavior of others.

power bases   The taxonomy developed by French and Raven of six categories into which all influence attempts may be placed.

power from   The ability to avoid unwanted situations.

power over   The ability and authority to influence others.

power to   The ability to control one's behavior.

pregroup preparation of clients   Familiarizing individuals before they begin either group or individual therapy as to what they can expect has a direct effect on reducing the probability that clients will leave treatment prematurely.

primary tension   The normal apprehension felt by individuals in a new group.

prisoner's dilemma   A situation structured so that the payoff matrix favors defective choices by both competitors and individualists.

prisoner's dilemma structure $= T > R > P > S$ and $2R > (T + S)$

problem diagnosis   One of the most important tasks of a problem-solving group.

problem solving   The optimal approach to conflict resolution in which an integrative solution is sought, creating a win/win stable solution to the conflict.

procedure for determining winner   Decision made in advance of the decision criteria which will be applied in the group to identify the chosen solution.

procedure-seeking questions   Questions intended to delineate the rules of functioning of the group.

process behaviors   Behaviors focusing on how things are done in the group.

procrastination   An attempt to avoid conflict in decision-making groups by putting off the decision until there is insufficient time for a conflict, or until missing a deadline makes a decision moot.

productivity   The extent to which the group is successful in completing their task.

projective techniques   A method of psychological testing for unconscious needs in which the individual is presented with an ambiguous stimulus. Lacking an obviously correct response, the ego has no alternative but to project the individual's personality on the stimulus.

proxemic behavior   The area of nonverbal communication that studies the group spatial ecology.

proximity   One of the strongest measures of physical attraction, proximity is the physical closeness to the individual.

proximity-maintaining behavior   Movement (particularly on the part of children) to maintain physical closeness to a desired individual.

psychiatrists (M.D.s)   Individuals who have attended medical school then completed a residency in treating psychological disorders. Primary difference from other types of therapist is the ability to write prescriptions for medication.

psychoanalysts   Individuals who provide psychoanalysis based on Freudian or neo-Freudian theory. Must undergo psychoanalytic training, part of which involves becoming a patient of psychoanalysis.

psychological equity   In a situation defined as inequitable, the underbenefitted individual usually wishes to restore equity by actually altering the inputs or outcomes until equity is restored.

psychological reactance   Theory developed by Brehm which states that when an individual feels their independence is threatened they will do the exact opposite of the requested action to emphasize their independence.

public distance   In kinesics, the distance we maintain between ourselves and strangers. Differs between low- and high-contact cultures.

public goods dilemma   A situation of mixed motives in which the resource is essentially inexhaustible and individuals may partake of the resource without contributing (e.g., public radio).

R = reward for mutual cooperation

rank disequilibrium   Status incongruities which invite invidious comparisons.

rapport talk   The type of communication identified by Tannen as appropriate for private talk with the goal of making connections. More commonly employed by American women in both private and public settings.

rational decision-making model   A model of decision making that assumes it is possible to identify all possible alternatives and all their possible outcomes. Impossible to actually enact, it however serves as a reminder to identify as many alternatives as possible.

reactance   Also known as psychological reactance, behavior identified by Brehm which involves proving our independence by performing the behavior that is the exact opposite of the request made to us. Also the basis for the "pop" psychology term "reverse psychology."

realistic group conflict theory   An approach that states that some conflicts are based upon the fear of one group that another will threaten their lifestyle by taking their jobs or otherwise negatively impact their lives.

receiver   The individual in the communication process to whom the message is intended.

referent power   The power to influence based on liking and identification with the individual making the request. Used in advertising in choosing a likeable spokesperson for a product (e.g., If Michael Jordan wears those shoes, I want them too!).

reinforcements   Reactions of the environment or individuals that are pleasant and increase the likelihood of the behavior being repeated.

relational questions   Questions within the group that are intended to delineate the interpersonal bonds between group members.

relationship-oriented leadership   One of the two types of identified leadership, this leader is primarily concerned with how group members interact and feel about the group.

relationships within the group   One of the three factors Fiedler identified as affecting the most appropriate style of leadership.

relative deprivation   A feeling, based on invidious comparisons, that we are under-benefitted in some way in comparison to those around us.

reliability   In measures of psychological traits, the stability of the measure over time (assuming the trait is stable).

remembrance   The final stage of group socialization in which the ex-member and the group both look back on the situation. Unless the parting was mutually desired or the individual had a "good" reason to leave, cognitive dissonance may lead to negative memories of the entire experience on the part of both the group and the individual.

report talk   The type of communication identified by Tannen as being appropriate for conveying facts in a public setting. More likely to be employed by American men in both public and private settings.

resistant-insecure   Inappropriate type of bond between infant and primary caregiver in which the infant actively avoids seeking nurturance or comfort from the caregiver. May be based on history of nonresponse of caregiver to distress of the infant.

resolution/reorganization reaction to trauma   The final stage in the reaction to traumatic events in which the individual has returned to normal life and activities after working through the trauma issues.

resocialization   Stage in Moreland and Levine's model of group socialization in which an individual who was wavering on the brink of leaving the group returns to full membership, or in which the group decides not to exclude the member.

retention of message   The penultimate step in the persuasion process. The individual must remember the message before it can be turned into a behavioral change.

"reverse psychology"   The "pop" psychology term for reactant behavior.

reward orientation   The type of reward distribution (equity or equality based or some other) of the individual.

reward power   The ability to influence another's behavior by offering a desired outcome for compliance with a request. One of the strongest of the French and Raven power bases.

rhythm   One of the differences between classic American white behavior and African-American behavior identified by Jones.

Ringelmann effect   The detrimental effect to group productivity based on coordination problems.

ringi method (of consensus)   A method employed by the Japanese to ensure group consensus.

risky shift   The earlier misconception in research that groups always make riskier decisions than individuals; in fact, one side of the group polarization phenomenon.

Robert's Rules of Order   Excruciatingly detailed set of rules by which to run meetings. Only useful in groups smaller than twenty individuals.

roles   Sets of expected behaviors that accompany a position. For example, the role of teacher involves (among other things) standing in front of a classroom and lecturing.

role conflict   The generic term which applies to the various types of difficulties which can arise from roles in individuals and in groups.

role emergence   A process in the development of a group in which individuals find their niche in terms of their behaviors in the group.

role expectation   The set of behaviors that is anticipated when an individual assumes a particular role.

role of leader   Set of behaviors covering both task and social issues that must be enacted (or delegated to another to enact) in a successful group.

role perception   An outsider's view of an individual's expected behaviors.

role strain   When the enactment of roles does not proceed smoothly; may include role ambiguity and the types of role conflict (intra-, inter-, and interpersonal).

role transitions   The changes in expected behaviors as an individual moves through the process of socialization in the group from nonmember through full membership.

runaway norms   One of the explanations for the phenomenon of groupthink identified by Janis. In losing touch with the larger social environment, the group is free to create their own inappropriate norms.

S = sucker's payoff   The amount gained by the defecting member with a cooperating partner in a prisoner's dilemma situation.

satisficing   A behavior almost always present in groups in which the group does not find the "perfect" solution (as defined by the rational decision-making model) but rather finds a solution that is "good enough."

saving face   Behaviors that allow an individual to retain their public dignity.

scarce resources   One of the common bases for conflicts.

scientific jury selection   The controversial process of using psychology to identify the ideal juror for whichever side of a court case has the resources to hire a consultant.

scope of the task   One of the situational factors identified in Fiedler's contingency theory as affecting the appropriate style of leadership.

secondary tension   The type of tension felt in a group when conflict is imminent.

securely-bonded infant   Strong, comforting infant bond with responsive primary caregiver.

selective attention   The tendency to pay attention only to those facts that are salient to us or which reinforce our beliefs.

self-aggrandizement   Also known as boasting. The use differs across cultures and genders.

self-awareness theory (of social facilitation)   The explanation for social facilitation presented by Duval and Wickland that states we compare our actual performance on a task with the optimum level of performance we expect of ourselves, and any discrepancy causes anxiety, which further interferes with performance on complex tasks.

self-effacement   The tendency in communication to play down one's strengths or accomplishments. Use differs across cultures and genders.

self-fulfilling prophecy   Setting up a situation so that the predicted behavior becomes inevitable.

self-help groups   Groups intended to help with problems (e.g., addictions or illness) established by individuals not members of the mental health profession in response to a felt lack of appropriate treatment.

separation of knowledge and authority   A source of conflict and poor productivity in a group when the person in charge is not the person with the expertise to successfully accomplish the task.

sexual harassment   Unwanted behaviors directed at an individual on the basis of their sex. Often a source of conflict in organizations.

shock   One of the probable reactions to trauma in the first stage.

short-term goals   Goals that are intended to be reached in a relatively short period of time (e.g., a month) that will lead on to attainment of long-term goals.

shuttle diplomacy   Technique for use in conflict situations where tensions are so high that it is optimal to keep the groups separate and use a third party to take messages of negotiation back and forth between the groups.

silence   A technique in conversation that may indicate submission, or (through refusal to interact) dominance.

similarity   One of the bases of interpersonal attraction. We are attracted to individuals who have the intelligence and good taste to share our values and attitudes.

size (of group)   Factor affecting group dynamics such as ability to communicate, coordinate, etc.

sleep problems   Symptomatic of PTSD victims and victims of trauma.

small group   Usually defined in the literature as a group having between 4 and 20 members.

social comparison theory   The tendency to obtain information regarding the appropriateness of behaviors based on observation of others.

social dilemmas   Situations of mixed motives in which payoffs for short-term behaviors may negatively affect the long-term welfare of the group.

social dimensions   Aspects of the group that involve interpersonal relationships and feelings.

social distance   An aspect of kinesics that determines the distance we keep between ourselves and friends and acquaintances.

social exchange theory   Theory of group formation presented by Thibault and Kelley which states that satisfaction with a group and continuance in the group are based on different criteria. Satisfaction is based on receiving at least as many rewards as we believe we deserve, and staying or leaving the group is based on whether a better alternative presents itself.

social facilitation   Phenomenon in which the presence of others sometimes increases or improves behavior and other times decreases or damages behavior.

social fence   The opposite of social traps in which short-term losses result in long-term gains.

socialization   Process through which the individual becomes a member of a group.

social loafing   The tendency for individuals to lessen their contribution to the group as the size of the group increases. Based on the belief that someone else will take up the slack.

social orientation   A long-term stable tendency to respond in a particular fashion when faced with mixed-motive situations. The three most common are cooperators, competitors, and individualists.

Social Readjustment Rating Scale (SRRS)   Measuring instrument developed by Holmes and Rahe to measure the number and severity of stressors encountered within the previous year. Measured in LCU's, these correlate with probabilities of future medical and psychological problems.

social support   The single best antidote to stress.

sociobiology   A discipline that believes that all social behavior has a biological component that has been selected through the Darwinian process of evolution.

sociofugal arrangements   Arrangements of group spatial ecology that discourage social interaction—such as placing chairs in rows.

sociopetal arrangements   Arrangements of group spatial ecology that encourage group social interaction—such as arranging chairs in circles.

source (of message)   An important aspect of the persuasion process. The source must be credible and likeable for persuasion to occur.

Specify   The third step in the Bower and Bower model of communication in which the individual requesting the change explicitly specifies the desired changes.

spiral model   Approach to decision making that states that the process is seldom linear in nature.

spirituality   One of the areas of basic differences between African-Americans and white Americans identified by Jones.

spreading false information   One of the methods to increase conflict.

stage of exhaustion   Final stage in Selye's general adaptation syndrome in which the stressor is overcome or the individual begins to suffer physically or psychologically from the stress.

stage of resistance   The second stage in Selye's GAS in which the body's resources are in place to attempt to deal with stress.

states   Temporary conditions. Emotions and dispositions such as depression can either be temporary (states) or permanent (traits).

statistical significance   The agreed-upon level of evidence required to allow us to accept the idea that the results in an experiment did not occur by chance.

status   Varying levels in the formal organization of the group. Higher status confers different levels of influence and variability in performance within the group.

status consensus   When all group members agree on the status of an individual.

status incongruities   When group members disagree upon the status of a certain individual, often leading to conflicts.

step-level public goods dilemma   See *discrete public goods dilemma.*

storming   Another name for the confrontation stage of group development.

"strange situation"   Series of situations into which infants are placed to measure the strength of their bonding to their primary caretaker.

strategic planning   The setting of long-term goals for the group and establishing policies and procedures enabling their attainment.

stress   The psychological and physiological reaction to anything (stressor) that requires us to adjust our behaviors.

structure of the task   One of Fiedler's situational factors that influences the "best" style of leadership.

structures of situations   Differences in payoff matrices that help determine the behaviors of group members.

subgrouping   The stage in early group development that is marked by the development of coalitions.

summative feedback   Information regarding the quality of the product after final completion. Allows no room during the process to alter direction.

superego   Final part of personality, as defined by Freud, to appear. Is unconscious and consists of the internalized norms of the society.

support group   Group whose purpose is to provide emotional, tangible, and advisory support for individuals.

surface talk   The relatively shallow level of communication often referred to as "small talk."

survival needs   One of the classes of needs satisfied by group membership in the functional approach to group formation.

survivor guilt   Psychological distress often felt by survivors of trauma—feelings that "I didn't deserve to be the one spared."

synergy   The combination of energies of group members that creates the potentially higher levels of group creativity.

syntality   A synonym for synergy.

talents and abilities (discovered)   Often an outcome of group conflicts.

target   The individual to whom communication or influence attempts are directed.

task dimensions   Those aspects of the group which are connected with reaching the group's goals.

task-oriented leadership   The type of leader who is more concerned with productivity than with the individuals within the group.

teleconferencing   The ability, through technological advances, to conduct an interactive meeting when members are spatially separated.

temporal change   The changes undergone by any group or relationship based on the length of time the group has been in existence.

tension   May be of two types. Primary tension is the normal anxiety felt by all in a new group. Secondary tension is connected with group conflict.

termination   The final stage in group development, which involves unraveling the group by tying up loose ends of business and placing emphasis on individuals rather than on the group.

territory   The area in group spatial ecology that has been identified as belonging to a group.

test-retest reliability   A method of measuring the reliability of a measure by testing twice with an interval in between. The results of the tests should be highly correlated.

Thematic Apperception Test (TAT)   A projective technique consisting of ambiguous drawings that are used to measure unconscious psychological needs.

theoretical orientation The school or theory accepted by a practitioner of therapy that will affect the definition of impairment, and the type of treatment deemed appropriate.

Theory X A leadership style identified by McGregor that believes that individuals only work because they are forced to and that leaders should adopt an autocratic leadership style.

Theory Y The second leadership style identified by McGregor that believes that individuals find work as normal a behavior as play, allowing leaders to adopt a democratic style of leadership.

therapy effectiveness The outcome of therapy that indicates that the individual is "cured."

therapy groups Problem-centered groups run by mental health professionals to solve psychological problems.

third party intervention When conflicts cannot be solved by the parties involved, an outsider is brought in to help bring about resolution.

time One of the differences identified by Jones as differing between African-American and white culture.

time pressure A factor that may result in a less than optimal group decision or product.

"tossing of coin" to resolve conflict One of the possible (but not very effective) decision criteria a group can establish to resolve a conflict situation.

tragedy of the commons Situations in which the payoff matrix is similar to the prisoner's dilemma in that the defective choice is favored, but which involve larger numbers of people.

trait Long-term stable personality characteristic.

trait approach to leadership An early disproven theory that leaders were individuals who possessed certain traits and lacked other traits.

training groups Groups intended to create change in knowledge. Very similar to classes.

trauma Anxiety provoking or threatening experience that causes distress and psychological disruption.

triad A group consisting of three people.

trivializing A method employed by groups to put off difficult decisions by choosing a small, unimportant aspect of the decision and focusing the group's energy on that detail.

trust The belief that an individual will behave in a manner that will not provide injury. A facet of groups that changes over time and affects the quality of the group's product.

trustworthiness of source An aspect of persuasion that posits that we will not be persuaded by a source we do not perceive as telling the truth.

truth-supported-wins rule The probability that the group will only accept the correct response in a "non-eureka" disjunctive task if a number of members independently arrive at the same conclusion.

truth-wins rule The probability that a group will accept the correct answer on a "non-eureka" disjunctive task if one individual finds the correct solution that becomes immediately obviously correct to the rest of the group.

two-thirds majority rule A decision criterion in decision making that requires that more than two-thirds of the group accepts the alternative. A problem may arise in that this means a minority of the group may control the group's decisions.

Type A personality   An individual who self-stresses and is a hot reactor. Type A's have a higher than average rate of coronary disease.

Type B personality   An individual who is more relaxed and less stressed than the Type A. Type B personalities have lower rates of coronary disease than Type A personalities.

type of task   A strong factor in the choice of an individual or a group based upon the largest potential productivity on the task type.

unanimity of majority   An incorrect majority may elicit conformity, but the rates are much lower when the incorrect majority is not unanimous in their incorrect choices.

unconscious psychological needs   Needs for affiliation, affection, and power that are unconscious and are satisfied by membership in a group in the functional approach to group formation.

underbenefitted   The individual in an inequitable situation who feels they are getting fewer rewards compared to inputs than are others. Generally these individuals prefer that actual equity be re-established.

unitary paths   The simplest form of decision-making paths.

unitary task   A task that cannot be broken down into subtasks to be assigned to individuals. Tends to favor individual rather than group solution.

universality   The recognition by a patient in a therapy group that everyone has problems, that no one has a perfect life. One of Yalom's curative factors.

unwanted thoughts   Symptomatic of victims of PTSD and trauma. Often flashbacks to the traumatic situation.

utilitarian decisions   Decisions whose goal is the good of the group or the least harm to the group.

utility models   Decision-making models that are based upon the rewards accumulated by the group.

verbal communication   Communication between individuals using words.

voir dire   The process of selecting a jury in which the judge and the attorneys ask questions of potential jurors and may eliminate those who are deemed inappropriate.

volunteer dilemma   A type of social dilemma in which everyone profits from not volunteering unless there is no volunteer.

vote   One of the methods by which a group may make a decision.

whistle-blowing   Calling attention of supervisors to unethical or problem behavior in the group. Often results in retaliation by group members.

yielding   One of the possible responses to conflict in which the individual puts the needs of other ahead of her or his own.

zero-based budgeting   A method of keeping requests for resources close to reality by requiring that each new request be justified.

zero-sum (situations)   Situations in which if I win, you lose.

References

ABANES, R. (1996). *American militias: Rebellion, racism and religion*. Downers Grove, IL: Intervarsity Press.

ABRAMSON, J. (1994). *We, the jury: The jury system and the ideal of democracy*. NY: Basic Books.

ALLPORT, F. H. (1924). *Social psychology*. Boston: Riverside Editions, Houghton Mifflin.

ANASTASI, A. (1968). *Psychological testing* (3rd ed.). NY: Macmillan.

ANDREWS, P. H. (1988). Group conformity. In R. Cathcart & L. Samova (Eds.), *Small group communication* (5th ed., pp. 225–235). Dubuque, IA: Wm. C. Brown.

ANDREWS, P. H. (1992). Sex and gender differences in group communication: Impact on the facilitation process. *Small Group Research, 23,* 74–94.

APPLEWHITE, 4/1/97, Heaven's Gate Website.

ASCH, S. (1946). Forming impressions of personality. *Journal of Abnormal and Social Psychology, 41,* 258–290.

ASCH, S. (1955). Opinion and social pressure. *Scientific American, 19,* 31–35.

AXELROD, R. (1984). *The evolution of cooperation*. NY: Basic Books.

BAILYN, L. (1987). Experiencing technical work: A comparison of male and female engineers. *Human Relations, 40,* 299–312.

BAIRD, J. E., JR., & WEINBERG, S. B. (1977). *Communication: The essence of group synergy*. Dubuque, IA: Wm. C. Brown.

BAIRD, J. E., JR., & WEINBERG, S. B. (1981). *Communications: The essence of group synergy* (2nd ed.). Dubuque, IA: Wm. C. Brown.

BAKER, H. G. (1985, July). The unwritten contract: Job perception. *Personnel Journal.*

BALES, R. (1950). *Personality and interpersonal behavior*. NY: Holt, Rinehart & Winston.

BANTZ, C. R. (1993). Cultural diversity and group cross-cultural team research. *Journal of Applied Communication Research, 21,* 1–20.

BARON, R. S., KERR, N. L., & MILLER, N. (1992). *Group processes, group decision, group action*. Pacific Grove, CA: Brooks/Cole.

BARON, R. S., MOORE, D. L., & SANDERS, G. S. (1978). Distraction as a source of drive in social facilitation research. *Journal of Personality and Social Psychology, 36,* 816–824.

BARRERA, M., JR. (1986). Distinction between social support concepts, measures, and models. *American Journal of Community Psychology, 14,* 413–422.

BASS, B. M. (1960). *A preliminary report on manifest preferences in six cultures for participative management* (Technical Report 21). Rochester, NY: University of Rochester Management Research Center.

BASS, B. M. (1990). *Bass & Stogdill's handbook of leadership: Theory, research, and managerial applications* (3rd ed.). NY: Free Press.

BAXTER, G. W., JR. (1972). Personality and attitudinal characteristics in cooperation in two-person games: A review. In L. S. Wrightsman, J. O'Connor, & N. J. Baker (Eds.), *Cooperation and competition* (pp. 97–103). Belmont, CA: Brooks/Cole.

BECHLER, C., & JOHNSON, S. D. (1995). Leadership and listening: A study of member perceptions. *Small Group Research, 26,* 77–85.

BEHLING, O., & McFILLEN, J. M. (1996). Charismatic leadership. *Group & Professional Management, 21,* 163–191.

BEND, C. F. (1982). Social facilitation: A self-presentational view. *Journal of Personality and Social Psychology, 42,* 1042–1050.

BENJAMIN, A. (1978). *Behavior in small groups.* Boston, MA: Houghton Mifflin Co.

BENNE, K., & SHEATS, P. (1948). Functional roles of group members. *Journal of Social Issues, 4,* 41–49.

BENNIS, W. (1989). *On becoming a leader.* Reading, MA: Addison-Wesley.

BERENBLUM, I. (1967). *Cancer research today.* Elmsford, NY: Pergamon.

BERMAN-ROSSI, T. (1997). Empowering groups through understanding stages of group development. *Social Work with Groups, 15,* 239–255.

BERNIER, D. (1992). The Indochinese refugees: A perspective from various stress theories. *Journal of Multicultural Social Work, 2,* 15–30.

BERNSTEIN, M., & CROSBY, F. (1980). An experimental examination of relative deprivation theory. *Journal of Experimental Social Psychology, 16,* 442–456.

BHATNAGAR, D. (1988). Professional women in organizations: New paradigms for research and action. *Sex Roles, 18,* 343–355.

BLAKE, R. R., & MOUTON, J. S. (1964). *The managerial grid.* Houston, TX: Gulf.

BLOOD, P., TUTTLE, A., & LAKEY, G. (1992). Understanding and fighting sexism: A call to men. In M. Andersen & P. H. Collins (Eds.), *Race, class, and gender.* Belmont, CA: Wadsworth.

BLUMNER, R. E. (1996). "Don't Ask, Don't Tell"? Don't Be Ridiculous! American Civil Liberty Union of Florida Website.

BOAR, R., & BLUNDELL, N. (1983). *The world's most infamous murders.* NY: Exeter Books.

BONI, M. B., LLOYD, N., & PROVENSEN, A. (1947). *The fireside book of folk songs.* NY: Simon and Schuster.

BORMANN, E. G. (1990). *Small group communication: Theory & practice* (3rd ed.). NY: Harper & Row.

BOVASSO, G. (1992). Social structure in two national political subcultures. *Social Psychology Quarterly, 55,* 292–299.

BOWER, S. A., & BOWER, G. H. (1976). *Asserting your self.* Reading, MA: Addison-Wesley.

BOWLBY, J. (1969). *Attachment and loss* (Vol. 1). NY: Basic Books.

BRAUER, M., JUDD, C. M., & GLINER, M. D. (1995). The effects of repeated expressions on attitude polarization during group discussions. *Journal of Personality and Social Psychology, 68,* 1014–1029.

BRAY, R. M., KERR, N. L., & ATKIN, R. S. (1978). Effects of group size, problem difficulty, and sex on group performance and member reaction. *Journal of Personality and Social Psychology, 36,* 1224–1240.

BREHM, J. W. (1966). *A theory of psychological reactance.* NY: Academic Press.

BREHM, S. S. (1992). *Intimate relationships* (2nd ed.). NY: McGraw-Hill.

BRENNER, S. N., & MOLANDER, E. A. (1977, January–February). Is the ethics of business changing. *Harvard Business Review,* pp. 57–71.

BRESNEN, M. J. (1995). All things to all people: Perceptions, attributions, and constructions of leadership. *Leadership Quarterly, 6*, 495–513.

BRICKMAN, P., HARKINS, S. G., & OSTROM, T. M. (1986). Effects of personal involvement: Thought-provoking implications for social loafing. *Journal of Personality and Social Psychology, 51*, 763–770.

BRILHART, J. K. (1986). *Effective group discussion* (5th ed.). Dubuque, IA: Wm. C. Brown.

BRIMELOW, P. (1995). *Alien nation: Common sense about America's immigration disaster.* NY: Random House.

BROCK, D. (1996). *The seduction of Hillary Rodham.* NY: Free Press.

BROWN, P., & LEVINSON, S. (1987). *Politeness: Some universals in language use.* Cambridge, England: Cambridge University Press.

BRUINS, J., DEN OUDEN, M., DEPRET, E., & EXTRA, J. (1993). On becoming a leader: Effects of gender and cultural differences on power distance reduction. *European Journal of Social Psychology, 23*, 411–426.

BUGENTHAL, D. B. (1993). Communications in abusive relationships: Cognitive constructions of interpersonal power. *American Behavioral Scientist, 36*, 288–308.

BUGLIOSI, V. (1974). *Helter skelter.* NY: Bantam Books.

BURGSON, J. K., OLNEY, C. A., & COKER, R. A. (1987). The effects of communication characteristics on patterns of reciprocity and compensation. *Journal of Nonverbal Behavior, 11*, 140–165.

BURKE, K., & CHIDAMBARAM, L. (1995). Developmental differences between distributed and face-to-face groups in electronically supported meeting environments: An exploratory investigation. *Group Decisions & Negotiation, 4*, 213–233.

BURLINGAME, G. M., & FUHRMANN, A. (1990). Time limited group therapy. *The Counseling Psychologist, 18*, 93–118.

BURLOW, A. K., & JOHNSON, J. L. (1992). Role conflict and career advancement among African American women in nontraditional professions. *Career Development Quarterly, 40*, 302–312.

BUSHMAN, B. A. (1988). The effects of apparel on compliance. *Personality and Social Psychology Bulletin, 14*, 459–467.

BUSS, D. M. (1989). Sex differences in human mate preferences: Evolutionary hypotheses tested in 37 cultures. *Behavioral and Brain Sciences, 12*, 1–49.

BYRNE, D. (1971). *The attraction paradigm.* NY: Academic Press.

BYRNE, D., & MURNEN, S. K. (1988). Maintaining loving relationships. In R. J. Sternberg & M. L. Barnes (Eds.), *The psychology of love.* New Haven, CT: Yale University Press.

BYRNES, H. (1986). Interactional style in German and American conversations. *Text, 6*, 189–206.

CALLANAN, J. A. (1984). *Communicating: How to organize meetings and presentations.* NY: Alexander Hamilton Institute.

CAMPBELL, J. D., TESSER, A., & FAIREY, P. J. (1986). Conformity and attention to the stimulus: Some temporal and contextual dynamics. *Journal of Personality and Social Psychology, 51*, 315–324.

CAMPBELL, J. L., & SNOW, B. M. (1992). Gender-role conflict and family environment as predictors of men's marital satisfaction. *Journal of Family Psychology, 6*, 84–87.

CAMPBELL, J. P., DUNNETTE, M. D., LAWLER, E. E. III, & WEICK, K. E. (1970). *Managerial behavior, performance, and effectiveness.* NY: McGraw-Hill.

CAMPBELL, N. C. G., GRAHAM, J. L., JOLBERT, A., & MEISSNER, H. G. (1988). Marketing negotiations in France, Germany, the United Kingdom, and the United States. *Journal of Marketing, 52*, 49–62.

CANN, A., & SIEGFRIED, W. D. (1990). Gender stereotypes and dimensions of effective leader behavior. *Sex Roles, 23*, 413–419.

CAPORAEL, L. R., DAWES, R. M., ORBELL, J. M., & VAN DE KRAGT, A. J. C. (1989). Selfishness examined: Cooperation in the absence of egoistic incentives. *Behavioral and Brain Sciences, 12,* 683–699.

CAPUTO, J. S. (1991). *Stress and burnout in library service.* Phoenix: Oryx Press.

CATTELL, R. B. (1948). Concepts and methods in the measurement of group syntality. *Psychological Review, 55,* 48–63.

CHAIKEN, A. L., GILLEN, H. B., DERLEGA, V., HANEN, J., & WILSON, M. (1978). Students' reactions to teachers' physical attractiveness and nonverbal behavior: Two exploratory studies. *Psychology in the Schools, 15,* 588–595.

CHAPMAN, J. G., ARENSON, S., CARRIGAN, M. H., & GRZCKIEWICZ, J. (1993). Motivational loss in small task groups: Free riding on a cognitive task. *Genetic and General Psychology Monographs, 119,* 57–73.

CHENG, B. S., & YANG, K. S. (1977). Supervisory behavior skill level, and interpersonal dominance as determinants of job satisfaction. *Bulletin of the Institute of Ethnology, 44,* 13–45. (In Chinese.) Cited in Hui, C. H. (1990). Work attitudes, leadership styles, and managerial behaviors in different cultures. In R. W. Brislin (Ed.), *Applied cross-cultural psychology* (Vol. 14). Cross Cultural Research & Methodology Series. Newbury Park, CA: Sage Publications.

CHILLADDINAI, P., MALLOY, D., IMAMURA, H., & YAMAGUCHI, Y. (1987). A cross-cultural study of preferred leadership in sports. *Canadian Journal of Sports Sciences, 12,* 106–110.

CHRISTENSEN, L. (1994). *Skinhead street gangs.* Boulder, CO: Paladin Press.

CHUA-EOAN, H. (1997, April 14). The faithful among us. *Time,* pp. 44–46.

CLADIS, S. D. (1985). Notes are not enough. *Training and Development Journal, 30,* 39.

CLARK, R. D. III, & SECHREST, L. B. (1976). The mandate phenomenon. *Journal of Personality and Social Psychology, 34,* 1057–1061.

CLIFFORD, M. M., & WALSTER, E. (1973). Research note: The effects of physical attractiveness on teacher expectations. *Sociology of Education, 46,* 248–258.

COHEN, A., FINK, S., GADON, H., & WILLITS, R. (1980). *Effective behavior in organizations. Revised Edition.* Homewood, IL: Richard D. Irwin, Inc.

COHEN, S. (1995). Psychological stress, immunity, and upper respiratory infections. *Current Directions in Psychological Sciences, 5,* 86–90.

COHEN, S., & WILLS, T. A. (1985). Stress, social support and the buffering hypothesis. *Psychology Bulletin, 98,* 310–357.

CORSE, S. J. (1990). Pregnant managers and their subordinates: The effects of gender expectation on hierarchical relationships. *Journal of Applied Behavioral Science, 26,* 35–47.

CORSINO, J. (1982). Malcolm X and the Black Panther movement: A social psychology of charisma. *Psychohistory Review, 10,* 165–184.

COTTRELL, N. B. (1972). Social facilitation. In C. G. McClintock (Ed.), *Experimental social psychology.* NY: Holt, Rinehart & Winston.

COTTROLL, R. J. (Ed.). (1994). *Gun control and the Constitution.* NY: Garland Publishing.

COURNOYER, R. J., & MAHALIK, J. R. (1995). Cross-sectional study of gender-role conflict examining college-aged and middle-aged men. *Journal of Counseling Psychology, 42,* 11–19.

COWLEY, G. (1997, April 14). Viruses of the mind: How odd ideas survive. *Newsweek,* p. 14.

CRITTENDEN, K. S. (1991). Asian self-effacement or feminine modesty? Attributional patterns of women university students in Taiwan. *Gender and Society, 5,* 98–117.

CROCKER, J., CORNWELL, B., & MAJOR, B. (1993). The stigma of overweight: Affective consequences of attributional ambiguity. *Journal of Personality and Social Psychology, 64,* 60–70.

CROMWELL, P. F., MARKS, A., OLSON, J. N., & AVARY, D. (1991). Group effects on decision-making by burglars. *Psychological Reports, 69,* 579–588.

CROSS, J. G., & GUYER, M. J. (1980). *Social traps*. Ann Arbor, MI: University of Michigan Press.

CUNHA, D. (1985). *Interpersonal trust as a function of social orientation*. Unpublished doctoral dissertation, University of Delaware.

CUNNINGHAM, M. R., ROBERTS, A. R., BARBEE, A. P., DRUEN, P. B., & WU, C. H. (1995). Their ideas of beauty are the same as ours: Consistency and variability in the cross-cultural perception of female physical attractiveness. *Journal of Personality and Social Psychology, 68*, 261–279.

CUSHMAN, D. P., & KING, S. S. (1985). National and organizational cultures in conflict resolution: Japan, the United States and Yugoslavia. In W. B. Gundykunst, L. P. Stewart, & S. Ting-Toomey (Eds.), *Communication culture, and organizational processes* (pp. 114–133). Beverly Hills, CA: Sage.

DALGARD, O. S., ANSTORP, T., BENUM, K., SORENSEN, T., & MOUM, T. (1990). Social psychiatric field studies in Oslo. In S. Wheelan, E. Pepitone, & V. Abt (Eds.), *Advances in field theory* (pp. 230–243). Newbury Park, CA: Sage.

DARWIN, C. (1871). *Origin of the species*. Oxford Press.

DAVIDSON, A. R., & JACCARD, J. J. (1979). Variables that moderate the attitude-behavior relation: Results of a longitudinal survey. *Journal of Personality and Social Psychology, 37*, 1364–1376.

DAVIS, J. H. (1969). *Group performance*. Reading. MA: Addison-Wesley.

DAVIS, M. S. (1969). Variation in patients' compliance with doctors' advice: An empirical analysis of patterns of communication. *American Journal of Public Health, 58*, 274–288.

DAWES, R. M. (1980). Social dilemmas. *Annual Review of Psychology, 31*, 169–193.

DAWKINS, R. (1989). *The selfish gene*. NY: Oxford Press.

DEAUX, K., & WRIGHTSMAN, L. S. (1988). *Social psychology* (5th ed.). Pacific Grove, CA: Brooks/Cole.

DELBECQ, A. L., & VAN DE VEN, A. H. (1971). A group process model for problem identification and problem planning. *Journal of Applied Behavioral Sciences, 7*, 466–492.

DELBECQ, A. L., VAN DE VEN, A. H., & GUSTAFSON, D. H. (1975). *Group techniques for program planning*. Glenview, IL: Scott, Foresman.

DEPAULO, B. M., & KIRKENDOL, S. E. (1989). The motivational impairment effect in the communication of deception. In J. Yukl (Ed.), *Credibility assessment*. Belgium: Kluiver.

DEPAULO, B. M., LEMAY, C. S., & EPSTEIN, J. A. (1991). Effects of importance of success and expectations for success on effectiveness at deceiving. *Personality and Social Psychology Bulletin, 17*, 14–24.

DEPAULO, B. M., STONE, J. I., & LASSITER, G. D. (1985). Deceiving and detecting deceit. In B. R. Schlenker (Ed.), *The self and social life*. NY: McGraw-Hill.

DEPAULO, B. M., ZUCKERMAN, M., & ROSENTHAL, R. (1980). Humans as lie-detectors. *Journal of Communication, 30*, 129–139.

DERSHOWITZ, A. M. (1996). *Reasonable doubts: The O.J. Simpson case and the criminal justice system*. NY: Simon & Schuster.

DEUTSCH, M. (1949). A theory of cooperation and competition. *Human Relations, 2*, 129–152.

DEUTSCH, M. (1960). The effect of motivational orientation upon trust and suspicion. *Human Relations, 13*, 123–140.

DEUTSCH, M. (1973). *The resolution of conflict*. New Haven, CT: Yale University Press.

DEUTSCH, M. (1985). *Distributive justice: A social psychological perspective*. New Haven, CT: Yale University Press.

Diagnostic and Statistical Manual of Mental Disorders (DSM-IV). (1994). Washington, DC: American Psychiatric Association.

DICKENS, C. (1991 reissue). *A Christmas carol*. (S. Applebaum, Ed.). NY: Dover Publications.

DIENER, E. (1980). Deindividuation: The absence of self-awareness and self-regulation in group members. In P. B. Paulus (Ed.), *Psychology of group influence*. Hillsdale, NJ: Erlbaum.

DIENER, E. (1984). Subjective well-being. *Psychological Bulletin, 95*, 542–575.

DION, K. K. (1972). Physical attractiveness and evaluations of children's transgressions. *Journal of Personality and Social Psychology, 24*, 207–213.

DION, K. K., BERSCHEID, E., & WALSTER, E. (1972). What is beautiful is good. *Journal of Personality and Social Psychology, 24*, 285–290.

DIPBOYE, R. L. (1977). Alternative approaches to deindividuation. *Psychological Bulletin, 84*, 1057–1075.

DIPBOYE, R. L., SMITH, C. S., & HOWELL, W. C. (1994). *Understanding industrial and organizational psychology: An integrated approach*. Ft. Worth, TX: Holt, Rinehart & Winston.

DOVIDIO, J. F., BROWN, C. E., HILTMAN, K., & ELLYSON, S. L. (1988). Power displays between women and men in gender-linked tasks: A multichannel study. *Journal of Personality and Social Psychology, 55*, 580–587.

DOVIDIO, J., EVANS, N., & TYLER, R. B. (1986). Racial stereotypes: The contents of their cognitive representations. *Journal of Experimental Social Psychology, 22*, 22–37.

DRUCKMAN, D., BENTON, A. A., ALI, F., & BOGEN, J. S. (1981). Cultural differences in bargaining behavior. *Journal of Conflict Resolution, 20*, 413–449.

DUBRIN, A. J. (1992). *Human relations: A job oriented approach* (5th ed.). Englewood Cliffs, NJ: Prentice Hall.

DUERST-LAHTI, G., & KELLY, R. M. (1995). On governance, leadership, and gender. In G. Duerst-Lahti & R. M. Kelly (Eds.), *Gender power, leadership, and governance*. Ann Arbor: University of Michigan Press.

DUNBAR, E. (1992). Adjustment and satisfaction of expatriate U.S. personnel. *Journal of Intercultural Relations, 16*, 1–16.

DUVAL, S., & WICKLAND, R. A. (1972). *A theory of objective self-awareness*. NY: Academic Press.

DYER, J. (1997). *Harvest of rage: Why Oklahoma City is only the beginning*. Boulder, CO: Westview Press.

EAGLY, A. H., & CARLI, L. L. (1981). Sex of researchers and sex-typed communications as determinants of sex differences in influenceability: A metanalysis of social influence studies. *Psychological Bulletin, 100*, 283–308.

EAGLY, A. H., & CHRVALA, C. (1986). Sex differences in conformity: Status and gender-role interpretations. *Psychology of Women Quarterly, 10*, 203–220.

EAGLY, A. H., & WOOD, W. (1982). Inferred sex differences in status as a determinant of gender stereotypes about social influence. *Journal of Personality and Social Psychology, 17*, 306–315.

EAKINS, B. W., & EAKINS, R. G. (1978). *Sex differences in communication*. Boston: Houghton Mifflin.

EDELWICH, J., & BRODSKY, A. (1980). *Burnout: Stages of development in the helping professions*. NY: Human Sciences Press.

EKMAN, P. (1985). *Telling lies: Clues to deceit in the marketplace, politics, and marriage*. NY: W. W. Norton.

EKMAN, P. (1992). An argument for basic emotions. *Cognition & Emotion, 6*, 169–200.

EKMAN, P., & FRIESEN, W. (1971). Constants across cultures in the face and emotion. *Journal of Personality and Social Psychology, 17*, 124–129.

ELIRAM, T., & SCHWARZWALD, J. (1987). Social orientation among Israeli youth: A cross-cultural perspective. *Journal of Cross Cultural Psychology, 18*, 31–44.

ELLIS, D. G., & FISHER, B. A. (1994). *Small group decision making: Communication and the group process* (4th ed.). NY: McGraw-Hill.

ELLISON & BARKOWSKI, (1995). National Public Radio.

EREZ, M., EARLEY, P. C., & HULIN, C. L. (1985, March). The impact of participation on goal acceptance and performance: A two-step model. *Academy of Management Journal*, pp. 50–66.

ERIKSON, E. H. (1968). *Childhood and Society*. New York: Norton.

FESTINGER, L. (1954). A theory of social comparison processes. *Human Relations, 7,* 117–140.

FESTINGER, L. (1957). *A theory of cognitive dissonance*. Evanston, IL: Row, Peterson.

FEYNMAN, R. www.Feynman.com

FICK, K. M. (1993). The influence of an animal on social interactions of nursing home residents in a group setting. *American Journal of Occupational Therapy, 47,* 523–534.

FIEDLER, F. E. (1967). *A theory of leadership effectiveness*. NY: McGraw-Hill.

FIGLEY, C. R. (1993). Weathering the storm at home: War-related family stress and coping. In F. W. Kaslow (Ed.), *The military family in peace and war*. NY: Springer.

FISCHOFF, B., & JOHNSON, S. (1990). The possibility of distributed decision making. In National Research Council (Eds.), *Distributed decision making*. Washington, DC: National Academy Press.

FISHBEIN, M., & AJZEN, I. (1975). *Belief, attitude, intention, and behavior: An introduction to theory and research*. Reading, MA: Addison-Wesley.

FISHER, B. A., & STUTMAN, R. K. (1987). An assessment of group trajectories: Analyzing developmental breakpoints. *Communication Quarterly, 35,* 105–124.

FLEISHMAN, E. A., & HARRIS, E. F. (1962). Patterns of leadership behavior related to employee grievances and turnover. *Personnel Psychology, 15,* 43–56.

FLEISHMAN, E. A., & PETERS, D. A. (1962). Interpersonal values, leadership attitudes, and managerial success. *Personnel Psychology, 24,* 127–143.

FOA, U. G., & FOA, E. B. (1974). *Societal structures of the mind*. Springfield, IL: Charles C. Thomas.

FOLKES, V. S. (1985). Mindlessness or mindfulness: A partial replication and extension of Langer, Blank, and Chanowitz. *Journal of Personality and Social Psychology, 48,* 600–604.

FORSYTH, D. R. (1990). *Group dynamics* (2nd ed.). Pacific Grove, CA: Brooks/Cole.

FOXWORTHY, J. (1996). *No shirt, no shoes . . . no problem!* NY: Hyperion.

FRANCIS, G. J., & MELBOURNE, G., JR. (1980). *Human behavior in the work environment: A managerial perspective*. Santa Monica, CA: Goodyear.

FRANK, M. O. (1989). *How to run a successful meeting—in half the time*. NY: Simon & Schuster.

FRENCH, J. P. R., & RAVEN, B. H. (1959). The bases of social power. In D. Cartwright & A. Zander (Eds.), *Group dynamics* (2nd ed., pp. 607–623). Evanston, IL: University of Chicago Press.

FRIEDMAN, H. S., & BOOTH, K. S. (1987). The disease-prone personality. *American Psychologist, 42,* 539–555.

FRIEDMAN, H. S., & ROSENMAN, R. H. (1974). *Type A behavior and your heart*. NY: Fawcett.

FUHRMANN, A., & BURLINGAME, G. M. (1990). Consistency of matter: A comparative analysis of individual and group process variables. *The Counseling Psychologist, 18,* 6–63.

FUJISHIN, R. (1997). *Discovering the leader within: Running small groups effectively*. San Francisco, CA: Acada Books.

FUKUDA, S., FUKUDA, H., & HICKS, J. (1994). Structure of leadership among preschool children. *Journal of Genetic Psychology, 155,* 389–395.

GABRENYA, W. K., JR., WANG, Y. E., & LATANE, B. (1985). Social loafing on an optimizing task: Cross-cultural differences among Chinese and Americans. *Journal of Cross-Cultural Psychology, 16,* 223–242.

GAERTNER, S. L., MANN, J., MURRELL, A., & DOVIDIO, J. F. (1989). Reducing intergroup bias: The benefit of recategorization. *Journal of Personality and Social Psychology, 57,* 239–249.

HARE, A. P., & NAVEH, D. (1984). Conformity and creativity: Camp David, 1978. *Small Group Behavior, 17,* 243–268.

HARKINS, S. G., & SZYMANSKI, K. (1987). Social loafing and social facilitation: New wine in old bottles. In C. Hendrick (Ed.), *Review of personality and social psychology* (Vol. 9). Newbury Park, CA: Sage.

HARLOW, H. F., & HARLOW, M. K. (1966). Learning to love. *American Scientist, 54,* 244–272.

HARRISON, A. A. (1977). Mere exposure. In L. Berkowitz (Ed.), *Advances in experimental social psychology, (Vol 10).* NY: Academic Press.

HARRISON, E. F., (1981). *The managerial decision-making process* (2nd ed.). Boston: Houghton Mifflin.

HASLETT, B., & OGILVIE, J. R. (1992). Feedback processes in task groups. In R. Cathcart & L. Damovar (Eds.), *Small group communication* (6th ed.). Dubuque, IA: Wm. C. Brown.

HASTIE, R. (1986). Review essay: Experimental evidence on group accuracy. In G. Owen & B. Grofman (Eds.), *Information pooling and group behavior,* 129–157. Westport, CT: JAI.

HATFIELD, E., GREENBERGER, E., TRAUPMANN, J., & LAMBERT, P. (1982). Equity and sexual satisfaction in recently married couples. *Journal of Sex Research, 18,* 18–32.

HATFIELD, E., & SPRECHER, S. (1986). *Mirror, mirror: The importance of looks in everyday life.* Albany, NY: SUNY Press.

HAWKINS, K. W. (1995). Effects of gender and communication content of leadership emergence in small task-oriented groups. *Small Group Research, 26,* 234–249.

HEIDER, F. (1958). *The psychology of interpersonal relations.* NY: Wiley.

HEIDER, J. (1985). *The Tao of leadership: Lao Tsu's "Tao Te Ching" Adapted for a new age.* Atlanta, GA: Humanics New Age Publishing.

HEILMAN, M. E., BLOCK, C. J., MARTELL, R. E., & SIMON, M. C. (1989). Has anything changed? Current characterizations of men, women, and managers. *Journal of Applied Psychology, 74,* 935–942.

HEINEMANN, S. (1996). *Timelines of American women's history.* NY: Berkley Publishing Group.

HEINLIEN, R. (1987). *Time enough for love.* NY: Ace Books.

HERMAN, E. S., & CHOMSKY, N. (1988). *Manufacturing consent: The political economy of the mass media.* NY: Pantheon Books.

HERSEY, P., & BLANCHARD, K. H. (1969). Life cycle theory of leadership. *Training and Development Journal, 23,* 25–34.

HINKIN, T. R., & SCHRIESHEIM, C. A. (1990). Relations between subordinate perceptions of supervisor influence tactics and attributed bases of supervisory power. *Human Relations, 43,* 221–237.

HOGAN, D. E. (1993). *The correlation between managers' use of power, job satisfaction, and productivity.* Unpublished manuscript, University of Wisconsin, Oshkosh.

HOGE, D. R., SHIELDS, J. J., & SOROKA, S. (1993). Sources of stress experienced by Catholic priests. *Review of Religious Research, 35,* 3–18.

HOLLANDER, E. P., & JULIAN, J. W. (1969). Contemporary trends in the analysis of the leadership process. *Psychological Bulletin, 71,* 387–397.

HOLMES, J. G., & MILLER, D. T. (1976). Interpersonal conflict. In J. W. Thibault, J. T. Spence, & R. C. Carson (Eds.), *Contemporary topics in social psychology.* Morristown, NJ: General Learning Press.

HOLMES, T. S., & RAHE, R. H. (1976). The social readjustment rating scale. *Journal of Psychosomatic Research, 14,* 121–131.

HOLTGRAVES, T., & YANG, J. (1992). The interpersonal underpinnings of request strategies: General principles and differences due to culture and gender. *Journal of Personality and Social Psychology, 62,* 246–256.

HOSTETLER, J. A. (1993). *Amish society* (4th ed.). Baltimore: Johns Hopkins University Press.

GEFFNER, R., & GROSS, M. M. (1984). Sex-role behavior and obedience to authority: A field study. *Sex Roles, 10*, 973–985.

GIFFORD, D. (1997). *Waco: The rules of engagement.* Somford Entertainment.

GILLESPIE, M. A., JACOBS, G., FRENCH, M., SHANGE, N., DWORKIN, A., AND RAMOS, N. (1995). Where do we stand on pornography? A *Ms.* Roundtable. In Stan, A. M. (Ed.), *Debating sexual correctness: Pornography, sexual harassment, date rape, and the politics of sexual equality.* NY: Delta Books.

GIRE, J. T., & CARMENT, D. W. (1993). Dealing with disputes: The influence of individualism-collectivism. *Journal of Social Psychology, 133*, 81–95.

GLASER, A. N. (1982). Drive theory and social facilitation: A critical reappraisal. *British Journal of Social Psychology, 19*, 119–136.

GLEASON, J. B., & GREIF, E. B. (1983). Men's speech to young children. In S. U. Philips, S. Steele, & C. Tanz (Eds.), *Language, gender, and sex in comparative perspective* (189–199). Cambridge: Cambridge University Press.

GLENN, E. S., WITMEYER, D., & STEVENSEN, K. A. (1977). Cultural styles of persuasion. *International Journal of Intercultural Relations, 1*, 52–66.

GOAD, J. (1997). *The redneck manifesto.* NY: Simon & Schuster.

GOAD, J., & GOAD, D. (1994). Ho Chi Minh's revenge: Vietnamese gangs invade America. In J. Goad & D. Goad, *Answer me!* San Francisco, CA: AK Press.

GOETHALS, G. R., & ZANNA, M. P. (1979). The role of social comparison in choice shifts. *Journal of Personality and Social Psychology, 37*, 1469–1476.

GOFFMAN, E. (1967). *Interactional ritual.* Garden City: Doubleday.

GOLDBERG, H. M. (1996). *The prosecution responds: An O.J. Simpson trial prosecutor reveals what really happened.* Seacaucus, NJ: Birch Lane Press Books.

GOULD, D., JACKSON, S., & FINCH, L. (1993). Sources of stress in national champion figure skaters. *Journal of Sport and Exercise Psychology, 15*, 134–159.

GOULDNER, A. W. (1960). The norm of reciprocity: A preliminary statement. *American Sociological Review, 25*, 161–171.

GRAHAM, J. L. (1981). A hidden cause of America's trade deficit with Japan. *Columbia Journal of World Business, 16*, 5–13.

GRAY, J. (1994). *Men are from Mars, women are from Venus.* NY: Harper Collins Publishers.

GREGOR, W. J. September, 8, 1991. Military should exclude homosexuals. Ann Arbor, MI. Quoted in: Servicemember's Legal Defense Fund (1995) The Reality of Gay Military Life. Washington, D.C.: Servicemember's Legal Defense Fund.

GRUBER, K. J., & GAEHELEIN, J. (1979). Sex differences in listening comprehension. *Sex Roles, 5*, 299–310.

GUTHRIE, R. V. (1976). *Even the rat was white.* NY: Allyn & Bacon.

HACKMAN, M. Z., HILLIS, M. J., PATERSON, T. J., & FURNESS, A. H. (1993). Leaders' gender role as a correlate of subordinates' perceptions of effectiveness and satisfaction. *Perceptual and Motor Skills, 77*, 671–674.

HACKMAN, R. J. (1968). Effects of task characteristics on group products. *Journal of Experimental Social Psychology, 4*, 162–187.

HALL, E. T. (1959). *The silent language.* Garden City, NY: Doubleday.

HALL, E. T. (1995). *The silent language.* Greenwich, CT: Fawcett.

HALL, J. A. (1978). Gender effects in decoding nonverbal cues. *Psychological Bulletin, 85*, 845–857.

HALL, J. A. (1987). On explaining gender differences: The case of nonverbal communication. In P. Shaver & C. Hendrick (Eds.), *Sex and gender.* Newbury Park, CA: Sage.

HANS, V. P., & VIDMAR, N. (1986). *Judging the jury.* NY: Plenum Press.

HARDIN, G. (1968). The tragedy of the commons. *Science, 162*, 1243–1248.

HARDIN, G. (1995). *The immigration dilemma: Avoiding the tragedy of the commons.* Washington, DC: Federation for American Immigration Reform.

HOUSE, J. S., LANDIS, K. R., & UMBERSON, D. (1988). Social relationships and health. *Science, 241,* 540–541.

HOUSE, R. L. (1971). A path-goal theory of leader effectiveness. *Administrative Science Quarterly, 16,* 231–238.

Houston Chronicle. (1993, October 10).

HOVLAND, C. I. (1957). *Order of presentation in persuasion.* New Haven, CT: Yale University Press.

HOVLAND, C. I., JANIS, I. L., & KELLEY, H. H. (1953). *Communication and persuasion: Psychological studies of opinion change.* New Haven, CT: Yale University Press.

HOVLAND, C. I., & WEISS, J. (1951). The influence of source credibility on communicative effectiveness. *Public Opinion Quarterly, 15,* 635–650.

HUI, C. H. (1990). Work attitudes, leadership styles, and managerial behaviors in different cultures. In R. W. Brislin (Ed.), *Applied cross-cultural psychology* (Vol. 14). Cross-Cultural Research & Methodology Series. Newbury Park, CA: Sage.

HUMPHREY, D. (1996). *Final exit: The practicalities of self-deliverance and assisted suicide for the dying* (2nd ed.). NY: Dell Publishers.

HUMPHREY, M. A. (1988). *My country, my right to serve: Experiences of gay men and women in the military, WW II to the present.* NY: Harper Collins Publishers.

HYBELS-STEER, M. (1995). *Aftermath: Survive and overcome trauma.* NY: Simon and Schuster.

INGHAM, A. G., LEVINGER, G., GRAVES, J., & PECKHAM, V. (1974). The Ringlemann effect: Studies of group size and group performance. *Journal of Personality and Social Psychology, 10,* 371–384.

Internet: www.mayhem.net/Crime/cults.html

ISIKOFF, (1997, April 14). *Newsweek.*

ITOI, R., ONBUCHI, K. I., & FUKUNO, M. (1996). A cross-cultural study of preference of accounts: Relationship closeness, harm severity, and motive of account making. *Journal of Applied Social Psychology, 26,* 913–934.

IVEY, D. C. (1995). Family history, parenting attitudes, gender roles, and clinician perceptions of family and family member functioning: Factors related to gender inequitable practice. *American Journal of Family Therapy, 23,* 213–226.

JACKSON, J. M., & HARKINS, S. G. (1985). Equity in effort: An explanation of the social loafing effect. *Journal of Personality and Social Psychology, 49,* 1199–1206.

JACKSON, J. M., & WILLIAMS, K. D. (1985). Social loafing on difficult tasks: Working collectively can improve performance. *Journal of Personality and Social Psychology, 49,* 937–942.

JANIS, I. (1967). Effects of fear arousal on attitude change: Recent developments in theory and experimental research. In L. Berkowitz (Ed.), *Experimental social psychology* (Vol. 3). San Diego, CA: Academic Press.

JANIS, I. L. (1982). *Victims of groupthink.* (2nd ed.). Boston: Hougton-Mifflin.

JANIS, I. L., & MANN, K. L. (1944). *Decision making: A psychological analysis of conflict, choice, and commitment.* NY: Free Press.

JAROFF, L. (1997, April 14). The man who spread the myth. *Time.*

JOHNSON, F. A., & MARSELLA, A. J. (1978). Differential attitudes toward verbal behavior in students of Japanese and European ancestry. *Genetic Psychology Monographs, 97,* 46–78.

JOHNSON, P. (1976). Women and interpersonal power. In I. Frieze, P. Johnson, J. E. Parsons, D. N. Ruble, & G. L. Zellman (Eds.), *Women and sex roles: A social psychological perspective.* NY: Norton.

JOHNSON, V. (1993, February). Intuition in decision making. *Successful Meetings,* pp. 148–151.

JONES, E. E. (1979). The rocky road from acts to dispositions. *American Psychologist, 34,* 107–117.

JONES, J. M. (1972). *Prejudice and racism.* Reading, MA: Addison-Wesley.

JONES, L. B. (1995). *Jesus, CEO: Using ancient wisdom for visionary leadership.* NY: Hyperion.

JOURARD, S. M. (1971). *Self-disclosure: An experimental analysis of the transparent self.* NY: Wiley.

KAGAN, S., & MADSEN, M. C. (1971). Cooperation and competition of Mexican, Mexican-American, and Anglo-American children of two ages under four instructional sets. *Developmental Psychology, 5,* 32–39.

KAGAN, S., & MADSEN, M. C. (1972). Rivalry in Anglo-American and Mexican children of two ages. *Journal of Personality and Social Psychology, 24,* 214–220.

KAGAN, S., & ZAHN, G. L. (1983). Cultural differences in individualism? Just artifact. *Hispanic Journal of Behavioral Sciences, 5,* 219–232.

KAHN, R. L., WOLFE, D. M., QUINN, R. P., SNOECK, J., & ROSENTHAL, R. A. (1978). *Organizational stress: Studies in role conflict and ambiguity.* NY: Wiley.

KALLMAN, E. A., & GRILLO, J. P. (1996). *Ethical decision making and information technology.* NY: McGraw-Hill.

KALVEN, H., & ZEISEL, H. (1966). *The American jury.* Boston: Little, Brown.

KAPRIO, J., KOSKENVUO, M., & HELI, R. (1987). Mortality after bereavement: A prospective study of 95,647 widowed persons. *American Journal of Public Health, 77,* 283–287.

KARAN, S. J., & WILLIAMS, K. D. (1993). Social loafing: A metanalytic review and theoretical integration. *Journal of Personality and Social Psychology, 65,* 681–706.

KATES, D. B., JR. (1982). *Why handgun bans can't work.* Bellevue, WA: Second Amendment Foundation.

KATES, D. B., JR., & KLECK, G. (1997). *Essays on firearms and violence.* San Francisco, CA: Pacific Research Institute for Public Policy.

KELLEY, H. H. (1983). Love and commitment. In H. H. Kelley, E. Berscheid, A. Christensen, J. H. Harvey, T. L. Huston, G. Levinger, E. McClintock, L. A. Peplau, & D. R. Peterson. *Close Relationships.* NY: Freeman.

KELLEY, H. H., & THIBAULT, J. W. (1978). *Interpersonal relations.* NY: Wiley.

KENRICK, D. T., REICH, J. W., & CIALDINI, R. B. (1978). Justifications and compensation: Rosier skies for the devalued victim. *Journal of Personality and Social Psychology, 34,* 654–657.

KEPHART, W. M. (1950). A quantitative analysis of initial group relationships. *American Journal of Sociology, 60,* 544–549.

KERR, N. L. (1983). Motivational losses in task-performing groups: A social dilemma analysis. *Journal of Personality and Social Psychology, 45,* 819–828.

KERR, N. L., & MACCOUN, R. J. (1985). The effects of jury size and polling method on the process and product of jury deliberation. *Journal of Personality and Social Psychology, 48,* 349–363.

KERR, S., & JERMEIR, J. M. (1978). Substitutes for leadership: Their meaning and measurement. *Organizational Behavior and Human Performance, 22,* 375–403.

KIDWELL, R. E., & BENNETT, N. (1993). Employee propensity to withhold effort: A conceptual model to intersect three avenues of research. *Academy of Management Review, 18,* 429–456.

KIESLER, S. (1978). *Interpersonal processes in groups and organizations.* Arlington Heights, IL: AHM Publishing.

KILDUFF, M., & JAVERS, R. (1978). *The suicide cult.* Rosamond, CA: Bantam Books.

KILHAM, W., & MANN, L. (1974). Level of destructive obedience as a function of transmitter and expectant roles in the Milgram obedience paradigm. *Journal of Personality and Social Psychology, 29,* 696–702.

KING, C. S. (1995). Sex-role identity and decision styles: How gender helps explain the paucity of women at the top. In G. Duerst-Lahti & R. M. Kelly (Eds.), *Gender power, leadership, and governance* (pp. 67–92). Ann Arbor, MI: University of Michigan Press.

KING, L. A. (1993). Emotional expression, ambivalence over expression, and marital satisfaction. *Journal of Social and Personal Relationships, 10,* 601–607.

KIRCHMEYER, C. (1995). Demographic similarity to the work group: A longitudinal study of managers at the early career stage. *Journal of Organizational Behavior, 16,* 67–83.

KLECK, G. (1997). *Targeting guns.* NY: Aldine de Gruyter.

KLEINKNECHT, W. (1996). *The new ethnic mobs: The changing face of organized crime in America.* NY: Free Press.

KNIGHT, G. P., & DUBRO, A. F. (1984). Cooperative, competitive, and individualistic social values: An individualized regression and clustering approach. *Journal of Personality and Social Psychology, 46,* 98–105.

KNIGHT, G. P., & KAGAN, S. (1977). Development of prosocial and competitive behaviors in Anglo-American and Mexican Children. *Child Development, 48,* 1385–1394.

KNIGHT, G. P., & KAGAN, S. (1977). Apparent sex differences in cooperation-competition: A function of individualism. *Developmental Psychology, 17,* 783–790.

KNIGHT, G. P., KAGAN, S., & BURUL, R. (1982). Perceived parental practices and prosocial development. *Journal of Genetic Psychology, 141,* 57–65.

KNOX, M., & WALKER, M. (1998). *The private diary of an O.J. juror: Behind the trial of the century.* Thousand Oaks, CA: Dove Books.

KOBERG, C. S., & CHYSMIR, L. H. (1989). Relationship between sex-role conflict and work-related variables: Gender and hierarchical differences. *Journal of Social Psychology, 129,* 779–791.

KOEHLER, J. W., ANATOL, K. W. E., & APPLEBAUM, R. L. (1976). *Organizational communication: Behavioral perspectives.* NY: Holt, Rinehart & Winston.

KOHN, I., & MOFFITT, P. L. (1992). *A silent sorrow: Pregnancy loss.* NY: Dell.

KOHN, M. L. (1969). *Class and conformity.* Homewood, IL: Dorsey.

KOMORITA, S. S., & PARKS, C. D. (1994). *Social dilemmas.* Dubuque: Brown & Benchmark.

KOPEL, D. B. (Ed.). (1995). *Guns: Who should have them?* NY: Prometheus Books.

KRAMER, B. J., & KIPNIS, S. (1995). Eldercare and work role conflict: Toward an understanding of gender differences in caregiver burden. *Gerontologist, 35,* 340–348.

KRESSEL, K., & PRUITT, D. G. (1989). Conclusion: A research perspective on the mediation of social conflict. In K. Kessel & D. G. Pruitt (Eds.), *Mediation research.* San Francisco: Jossey-Bass.

KROGER, R. O., & WOOD, L. A. (1992). Are the rules of address universal? Comparisons of Chinese, Korean, and German usage. *Journal of Cross-Cultural Psychology, 23,* 148–162.

KROON, M. B., VAN KREVEID, D., & RABBIE, J. M. (1992). Group versus individual decision making: Effects of accountability on gender and groupthink. *Small Group Research, 23,* 427–458.

KUHLMAN, D. M., CAMAC, C. R., & CUNHA, D. A. (1986). Individual differences in social orientation. In H. A. M. Wilke, D. M. Messick, & C. G. Rutte, (Eds.), *Experimental social dilemmas* (pp. 151–176). Frankfurt: Verlag Peter Lang.

KUHLMAN, D. M., & MARSHELLO, A. (1975). Individual differences in game motivation as moderators of preprogrammed strategic differences in prisoner's dilemma. *Journal of Personality and Social Psychology, 32,* 922–931.

KUHLMAN, D. M., & WIMBERLY, D. C. (1976). Expectations of choice behavior held by cooperators, competitors, and individualists across four classes of experimental games. *Journal of Personality and Social Psychology, 32,* 69–81.

KUKLA, R. A., SCHLENGER, W. E., FAIRBANK, J. A., HOUGH, R. L., JORDAN, B. K., MARMAR, C. R., & WEISS, D. S. (1990). *Trauma and the Vietnam War generation.* NY: Brunner/Mazel Publishers.

KULIK, J. A., & MAHLER, H. I. M. (1989). Stress and affiliation in a hospital setting: Preoperative roommate preferences. *Personality and Social Psychology Bulletin, 15,* 183–193.

KULIK, L. (1995). The impact of ethnic origin and gender on perceptions of gender roles: The Israeli experience. *Journal of Social Behavior and Personality, 10,* 199–214.

LAKOFF, R. (1973). Language and women's place. *Language in Society, 2,* 45–80.

LANDY, D., & ARONSON, E. (1969). The influence of the character of the criminal and his victim on the decisions of simulated jurors. *Journal of Experimental Social Psychology, 5*, 141–152.

LANDY, F. J., & TRUMBO, D. A. (1980). *The psychology of work behavior.* Homewood, IL: Dorsey Press.

LANGER, E. J., BLANK, A., & CHANOWITZ, B. (1978). The mindlessness of ostensibly thoughtful action. *Journal of Personality and Social Psychology, 36*, 635–642.

LANGER, E. J., CHANOWITZ, B., & BLANK, A. (1985). Mindlessness-mindfulness in perspective: A reply to Valerie Folkes. *Journal of Personality and Social Psychology, 48*, 605–607.

LANGER, E. J., & NEWMAN, H. M. (1979). The role of mindlessness in a typical social psychology experiment. *Personality and Social Psychology Bulletin, 5*, 295–298.

LAPIERE, R. T. (1934). Attitudes vs. actions. *Social Forces, 13*, 230–237.

LARSON, R., & LEE, M. (1996). The capacity to be alone as a stress buffer. *Journal of Social Psychology, 136*, 5–16.

LATANE, B., & DARLEY, J. M. (1970). *The unresponsive bystander: Why doesn't he help?* NY: Appleton-Century-Crofts.

LATANE, B., WILLIAMS, K., & HARKINS, S. (1979). Many hands make light the work: The causes and consequences of social loafing. *Journal of Personality and Social Psychology, 37*, 822–832.

LATHAM, G. P., & YUKL, G. A. (1983, Spring/Summer). A review of the research. *Journal of Management*, pp. 55–64.

LAUGHLIN, P. R. (1980). Collective induction: Group performance, social combination processes, and mutual majority and minority influence. *Journal of Personality and Social Psychology, 54*, 254–267.

LAUGHLIN, P. R., & ADAMOPOULOS, J. (1980). Social combination processes and individual learning for six-person cooperative groups on an intellective task. *Journal of Personality and Social Psychology, 38*, 941–947.

LAUGHLIN, P. R., & McGLYNN, R. P. (1986). Cooperative versus competitive concept attainment as a function of sex and stimulus display. *Journal of Personality and Social Psychology, 7*, 398–402.

LAVIGNE, Y. (1996). *Hell's Angels: Three can keep a secret if two are dead.* Secaucus, NJ: Carol Publishing Group.

LAZARUS, E. (1877). The new colossus. In: Lippincott's Magazine. Philadelphia, PA.

LAZARUS, R. S. (1966). *Psychological stress and coping process.* NY: McGraw-Hill.

LEHRER, T. (1981). "National Brotherhood Week."

LEUNG, K., & LIND, E. A. (1986). Procedure and culture: Effects of culture, gender, and investigator status on procedural preferences. *Journal of Personality and Social Psychology, 50*, 1134–1140.

LEWIN, K., LIPPITT, R., & WHITE, R. (1939). Patterns of aggressive behavior in experimentally created "social climates." *Journal of Social Psychology, 10*, 271–299.

LIBO, L. (1953). *Measuring group cohesiveness.* Ann Arbor, MI: University of Michigan Institute of Social Research.

LICHTER, S., ROTHMAN, S., & LICHTER, L. L. (1986). *The media elite: America's new power brokers.* Bethesda, MD: Adler & Adler.

LIEBRAND, W. B. G., & MESSICK, D. M. (1996). Social dilemmas: Individual, collective and dynamic perspectives. In W. B. G. Liebrand & D. M. Messick (Eds.), *Frontiers in social dilemmas research.* Heidelberg, Germany: Springer-Verlag.

LIEBRAND, W. B. G., & VON RUDEN, G. J. (1985). The effects of social motives on behavior in social dilemmas in two cultures. *Journal of Experimental Social Psychology, 21*, 86–102.

LINTON, R. (1936). *The study of man.* NY: Appleton-Century.

LIPS, H. (1991). *Women, men, and power.* Mountain View, CA: Mayfield Publishing.

LIPS, H. M. (1985). Gender and the sense of power: Where we are and where are we going? *International Journal of Women's Studies, 8*, 483–489.

LIVSEY, C. (1980). *The Manson women: A "family" portrait.* NY: Richard Marek Publishers.

LOCKE, E. A. (1968). Toward a theory of task motivation and incentives. *Organizational Behavior and Human Performance, 3*, 157–189.

LOFTUS, E. F. (1979). Eyewitness testimony. Cambridge, MA: Harvard University Press.

LOFTUS, E. F., MILLER, D. G., & BURNS, H. J. (1987). Semantic integration of verbal information into a visual memory. *Journal of Experimental Psychology: Human Learning & Memory, 4*, 19–31.

LORGE, I. D., FOX, J., DAVITZ, J., & BRENNER, M. (1958). A survey of studies contrasting the quality of group performance and individual performance. *Psychological Bulletin, 55*, 337–372.

LORD, R. G., FOTI, R. J., & PHILLIPS, J. S. (1982). A theory of leadership categorization. In J. G. Hunt, U. Sekaram, and C. A. Schriesheim (Eds.), *Leadership: Beyond establishment views.* Carbondale, IL: Southern Illinois University Press.

LOTT, A. J., & LOTT, B. E. (1974). The role of reward in the formation of positive interpersonal attitudes. In T. Huston (Ed.), *Foundations of interpersonal attraction.* NY: Academic Press.

LUBLIN, J. S. (1991,). Sexual harassment is topping agenda in many executive education programs. *The Wall Street Journal,* B1, 134.

LYKEN, D. T. (1987). The detection of deception. In L. S. Wrightsman, C. E. Willis, & S. M. Kassin (Eds.), *On the witness stand: Controversies in the courtroom.* Newbury Park, CA: Sage.

LYNCH, A. *Thought contagion,* cited in Cowley, G. *Newsweek,* April 14, 1997.

LYNCH, R. (1977). *The broken heart: The medical consequences of loneliness.* NY: Basic Books.

LYNDON, J. E., & ZANNA, M. P. (1990). Commitment in the face of adversity: A value-affirmation approach. *Journal of Personality and Social Psychology, 58*, 1040–1047.

MACCOBY, E. E., & JACKLIN, C. N. (1974). *The psychology of sex differences.* Stanford, CA: Stanford University Press.

MACCOUN, R. J., & KERR, N. L. (1988). Asymmetric influence in mock jury deliberations: Jurors' bias for leniency. *Journal of Personality and Social Psychology, 54*, 21–33.

MADSEN, M. C. (1971). Development and cross-cultural differences in the cooperative and competitive behavior of young children. *Journal of Cross Cultural Psychology, 2*, 365–371.

MADSEN, M. C., & SHAPIRA, A. (1970). Cooperative and competitive behavior of urban Afro-American, Anglo-American, Mexican-American, and Mexican village children. *Developmental Psychology, 3*, 16–20.

MADSEN, M. C., & YI, S. (1975). Cooperation and competition of urban and rural children in the Republic of South Korea. *International Journal of Psychology, 10*, 269–274.

MAJOR, B., & FORCEY, B. (1985). Social comparisons and pay evaluations: Preferences for same-sex and same-job wage comparisons. *Journal of Experimental Social Psychology, 21*, 393–405.

MAKI, J. E., & McCLINTOCK, C. G. (1983). The accuracy of social value prediction: Actor and observer influences. *Journal of Personality and Social Psychology, 45*, 829–838.

MANN, L. (1980). Cross-cultural studies of small groups. In H. C. Triandis & R. W. Breslin (Eds.), *Handbook of cross-cultural psychology* (Vol. 5). Boston: Allyn & Bacon.

MARTIN, R., & DAVIDS, K. (1995). The effects of group development techniques on a professional athletic team. *Journal of Social Psychology, 135*, 533–535.

MASLACH, C. (1982). *Burnout: The cost of caring.* NY: Prentice Hall.

MASTERS, W. H., JOHNSON, V. E., & KOLODNY, R. C. (1995). *Human sexuality* (5th ed.). NY: Harper Collins.

MATLIN, M. W. (1997). *Cognition* (4th ed.). NY: Harcourt Brace College Publishers.

McClintock, C. G. (1974). Development of social motives in Anglo-American and Mexican-American children. *Journal of Personality and Social Psychology, 29,* 348–354.

McClintock, C. G. (1977). Social motivation in settings of outcome interdependence. In D. Druckman (Ed.), *Negotiations: Social-psychological perspectives* (pp. 49–77). Beverly Hills: Sage.

McClintock, C. G., & Liebrand, W. B. G. (1988). Role of interdependence, structure, individual value orientation, and another's strategy in social decision making: A transformational analysis. *Journal of Personality and Social Psychology, 55,* 396–409.

McClintock, C. G., & McNeel, S. P. (1966). Reward and score feedback as determinants of cooperative and competitive game behavior. *Journal of Personality and Social Psychology, 4,* 606–613.

McClintock, C. G., & Van Avermaet, E. (1982). Social values and rules of fairness: A theoretical perspective. In J. Grzelak & V. Derlaga (Eds.), *Living with other people* (pp. 43–71). NY: Academic Press.

McGregor, D. (1960). *The human side of enterprise.* NY: McGraw-Hill.

McGuire, W. J. (1964). Inducing resistance to persuasion: Some contemporary approaches. In L. Berkowitz (Ed.), *Advances in experimental social psychology* (Vol. 1). NY: Academic Press.

McGuire, W. J. (1968). Personality & attitude change: An information-processing theory. In A. G. Greenwood, T. C. Brock, & T. M. Ostrom (Eds.), *Psychological foundations of attitudes.* NY: Academic Press.

McKenry, P. C., & Price, S. J. (1990). Divorce: Are men at risk? In D. Moore & F. Leafgren, (Eds.), *Problem-solving strategies and interventions for men in conflict* (pp. 95–112). Alexandria, VA: American Association for Counseling and Development.

Meade, G. H. (1934). *Mind, self, & society.* Chicago, IL: University of Chicago Press.

Megargee, E., Bogart, P., & Anderson, B. (1966). Prediction of leadership in a simulated industrial task. *Journal of Applied Psychology, 50,* 292–295.

Messick, D. M., & Brewer, M. B. (1983). Social traps and temporal traps. *Personality and Social Psychology Bulletin, 9,* 105–110.

Michael, R. T., Gagnon, J. H., Laumann, E. O., & Kolata, G. (1994). *Sex in America: A definitive survey.* NY: Warner Books.

Miles, R. H. (1980). *Macro organizational behavior.* Santa Monica, CA: Goodyear.

Milgram, S. (1963). Behavioral study of obedience. *Journal of Abnormal and Social Psychology, 67,* 371–378.

Miller, A. G., & Thomas, R. (1972). Cooperation and competition among Blackfoot Indian and urban Canadian children. *Child Development, 43,* 1104–1110.

Miller, M. (1997, April 14). Secrets of the cult. *Newsweek,* pp. 29–36.

Miller, N., & Brewer, M. (Eds.). (1984). *Groups in contact: The psychology of desegregation.* Orlando, FL: Academic Press.

Miller, R. F., & Pincus, M. (1997). *Running a meeting that works.* Hauppauge, NY: Barron's Educational Press.

Molloy, J. (1993). *Dress for success.* (Re-issue). NY: Warner Books.

Monge, P. R. (1987). Emergent Networks. In Joblin, F., Putnam, L., Roberts, K., & Porter, L. (Eds.) *Handbook of organizational communication.* Newbury Park, CA: Sage

Monge, P. R., Edwards, J. A., & Kirste, K. K. (1983). Determinants of communication network involvement: Connectedness and integration. *Group & Organization Studies, 8,* 83–111.

Moore, C. (1995). *The Davidian massacre.* Springfield, VA & Franklin, TN: Legacy Communications & Gun Owners Federation.

Moore, D., & Gobi, A. (1995). Role conflict and perceptions of gender roles: The case of Israel. *Sex Roles, 32,* 251–270.

Moran, R. T. (1985). *Getting your yen's worth: How to negotiate with Japanese.* Houston: Gulf.

MORELAND, R. L., & LEVINE, J. M. (1982). Role transitions in small groups. In V. L. Allen & E. Van de Vliert (Eds.), *Role transition: Explorations and explanations*. NY: Plenum.

MORELAND, R. L., & ZAJONC, R. B. (1982). Rejection as a consequence of perceived similarity. *Journal of Personality and Social Psychology, 9,* 147–152.

MORLEY, I. E. (1987). Negotiating and bargaining. In O. Hargie (Ed.), *A handbook of communication skills.* London: Croom Helin.

MORRISON, T. L., & STERN, D. D. (1985). Member reaction to male and female leaders in two types of group experience. *Journal of Social Psychology, 125,* 7–16.

MOSCOVICI, S. (1985). Social influence and conformity. In G. Lindzey & E. Aronson (Eds.), *The handbook of social psychology* (3rd ed.). NY: Random House.

MOSCOVICI, S., & ZAVALLONI, M. (1969). The group as a polarizer of attitudes. *Journal of Personality and Social Psychology, 12,* 125–135.

MURRAY, H. A. (1938). *Explorations in personality.* NY: Oxford Press.

MYERS, D. G. (1978). The polarizing effects of social comparison. *Journal of Experimental Social Psychology, 14,* 554–563.

NAPIER, R. W., & GERSHENFELD, M. K. (1993). *Groups: Theory & experience* (5th ed.). Boston: Houghton Mifflin.

NELSON-JONES, R. (1992). *Group leadership: A training approach.* Pacific Grove, CA: Brooks/Cole.

NEMETH, C. (1977). Interactions between jurors as a function of majority vs. unanimity decision rules. *Journal of Applied Social Psychology, 7,* 38–56.

NOVAK, D. W., & LERNER, M. J. (1968). Rejection as a consequence of perceived similarity. *Journal of Personality and Social Psychology, 9,* 147–152.

O'CONNELL, A., & O'CONNELL, V. (1997). *Choice and change* (5th ed.). Upper Saddle River, NJ: Prentice Hall.

OFFERMAN, L. R., & ARMITAGE, M. A. (1993). Stress and the woman manager: Stresses, health outcomes, and interventions. In E. A. Fagenson (Ed.), *Women in management: Trends, issues and challenges in managerial diversity* (pp. 131–161). Newbury Park, CA: Sage.

OLSEN, M. (1965). *The logic of collective action: Public goods and the theory of groups.* Cambridge, MA: Harvard University Press.

ONYX, J., LEONARD, R., & VIVEKANANDA, K. (1995). Social perception of power: A gender analysis. *Perceptual & Motor Skills, 80,* 291–296.

ORBELL, J. M., & DAWES, R. M. (1981). Social dilemmas. In G. Stephenson & J. H. Davis (Eds.), *Progress in applied social psychology* (Vol. 1). Chichester, England: Wiley.

ORMONT, L. R. (1992). *The group therapy experience: From theory to practice.* NY: St. Martin's Press.

OSBORN, A. F. (1957). *Applied imagination.* NY: Scribner.

OSGOOD, C. E. (1962). *An alternative to war or surrender.* Urbana: University of Illinois Press.

OYSTER, C. K. (1982). *Communication of affect & status in sexually heterogeneous and homogeneous dyads.* Unpublished doctoral dissertation, University of Delaware.

OYSTER, C. K. (1992). Perceptions of power: Female executives' descriptions of power usage by "best" and "worst" bosses. *Psychology of Women Quarterly, 16,* 527–533.

OYSTER-NELSON, C. K., WOODS, D. J., FONEY, J., FRANKLIN, D., & GRIFFIN, A. (1982, August). *Physical attractiveness of rapist and victim: An interaction effect on assignment of blame.* Presented at American Psychological Association Annual Meeting, Washington, DC.

PADAKI, R. (1989). Job attitudes. In J. Pandey (Ed.), *Psychology in India: The state-of-the-art organizational behavior and mental health.* (Vol. 3), New Delhi: Sage.

PARKS, Y. Y. (1987). Organizational development and culture contact: A case study of Sokagakkai in America. *Journal of Ethnic Studies, 10,* 1–16.

PARSONS, T., & BALES, R. F. (1954). *Family socialization & interaction process.* Glencoe, IL: Free Press.

Pavitt, C. (1994). Another view of group polarization: The reasons for one-sided oral argumentation. *Communication Research, 21,* 625–642.

Pennebaker, J. W. (1990). *Opening up: The healing power of confiding in others.* NY: Wm. Morrow.

Perrett, D. I., May, K. A., Yoshikawa, S. (1994). Facial shape and judgments of female attractiveness. *Nature, 368,* 239–242.

Peters, D. K., & Cantrell, P. J. (1993). Gender roles and role conflict in feminist lesbian and heterosexual women. *Sex Roles, 28,* 379–392.

Pines, A., & Aronson, E. (1988). *Career burnout: Causes and cures.* NY: Free Press.

Platt, J. (1973). Social traps. *American Psychologist, 28,* 641–651.

Podsakoff, P. M., & Schriesheim, C. A. (1985). Field studies of French & Raven's bases of power: Critique, reanalysis, and suggestions for future research. *Psychological Bulletin, 97,* 387–411.

Pondy, L. R. (1967). Organizational conflict: Concepts and models. *Administrative Science Quarterly, 12,* 300–305.

Poole, M. S., & Doelger, J. A. (1986). Developmental processes in group decision making. In R. Huokawa & M. S. Poole (Eds.), *Communication and group decision making.* Beverly Hills, CA: Sage.

Poole, M. S., & Roth, J. (1989). Decision development in small groups IV: A typology of group decision paths. *Human Communication Research, 15,* 323–356.

Porter, N., & Geis, F. L. (1981). Women and nonverbal leadership cues: When seeing is not believing. In C. Mayo and N. Henley (Eds.), *Gender and nonverbal behavior* (pp. 39–59). NY: Springer Verlag.

Power, D. J., & Aldag, R. J. (1985, January). Soelberg's job search and choice model: A clarification, review, and critique. *Academy of Management Review,* pp. 48–58.

Pruitt, D. G., & Carnevale, P. J. (1993). *Negotiation in social conflict.* Pacific Grove, CA: Brooks/Cole.

Pruitt, D. G., McGillicuddy, N. B., Welton, G. L., & Fry, W. R. (1989). Process of mediation in dispute settlement centers. In K. Kressel & D. G. Pruitt (Eds.), *Mediation research* (pp. 368–393). San Francisco, CA: Jossey-Bass.

Raspail, J. (1987). *The camp of the saints.* Petoskey, MI: The Social Contract Press.

Raven, B. H. (1965). Social influence and power. In I. D. Steiner & M. Fishbein (Eds.), *Current studies in social psychology.* NY: Holt, Rinehart & Winston.

Raven, B. H. (1992). A power/interaction model of interpersonal influence: French & Raven thirty years later. *Journal of Social Behavior and Personality, 7,* 217–244.

Ray, R. D., Col. (1993). *Military necessity and homosexuality.* NY: Brassey's.

Reich, W. P., Parrella, D. P., & Filstead, W. J. (1988). Unconfounding the hassles scale: External sources versus internal responses to stress. *Journal of Behavioral Medicine, 11,* 239–250.

Reiken, H. W., & Homans, G. C. (1954). Psychological aspects of social structure. In G. Lindzey (Ed.), *Handbook of Social Psychology, 11,* 786–832. Reading, MA: Addison-Wesley.

Renwick, G. (1985). *Malays and Americans: Definite differences, unique opportunities.* Yarmouth, ME: Intercultural Press.

Reskin, B. F., & Padavic, I. (1994). *Women and men at work.* Thousand Oaks, CA: Pine Forge Press.

Reusch, J., & Bateson, G. (1951). *Communication: The social matrix of psychiatry.* NY: Norton.

Rice, R. W. (1984). Leadership ratings for male and female military cadets. *Sex Roles, 10,* 885–901.

Robbins, S. P. (1989). *Organizational behavior: Concepts, controversies, and applications* (4th ed.). Englewood Cliffs, NJ: Prentice Hall.

ROBBINS, S. P. (1996). *Organizational behavior: Concepts, controversies, applications.* (7th ed.). Englewood Cliffs, NJ: Prentice Hall.

ROBERT (1868). *Robert's Rules of Order.*

ROBINSON-STAVELEY, K., & COOPER, J. (1990). Mere presence, gender, and reactions to computers: Studying human-computer interaction in the social context. *Journal of Experimental Social Psychology, 26,* 168–83.

ROGERS, R. (1993). Cognitive and physiological processes in fear appeals and attitude change: A revised theory of protection motivation. In J. T. Cacioppo & R. E. Petty (Eds.), *Social psychology: A sourcebook.* NY: Guilford Press.

ROJAHN, K., & WILLEMSEN, T. M. (1994). The evaluation of effectiveness and likability of gender-role congruent and gender-role incongruent leaders. *Sex Roles, 30,* 109–119.

ROOK, K. S. (1987). Reciprocity of social exchange and social satisfaction among older women. *Journal of Personality and Social Psychology, 52,* 145–154.

ROSS, L. (1977). The intuitive psychologist and his shortcomings: Distortions in the attribution process. In L. Berkowitz (Ed.), *Advances in experimental social psychology* (Vol. 10). NY: Academic Press.

RUBIN, J. Z., & BROWN, B. R. (1975). *The social psychology of bargaining and negotiation.* NY: Academic Press.

RUBIN, J. Z., PRUITT, D. G., & KIM, S. H. (1994). *Social conflict: Escalation, stalemate, and settlement* (2nd ed.). NY: McGraw-Hill.

RUBLE, T. L., & THOMAS, K. W. (1976). Support for a 2-dimensional model of conflict behavior. *Organizational Behavior and Human Performance, 16,* 143–155.

RUNCIMAN, W. G. (1966). *Relative deprivation and social justice.* Berkeley: University of California Press.

SACKOFF & WEINSTEIN (1988).

SAGRESTINO, L. M. (1992). Power strategies in interpersonal relationships: The effects of expertise and gender. *Psychology of Women Quarterly, 16,* 481–495.

SAKS, M. J. (1977). *Jury verdicts: The role of group size and social decision rule.* Lexington, MA: Heath.

SCHACTER, S. (1959). *The psychology of affiliation: Experimental studies of the sources of gregariousness.* Stanford, CA: Stanford University Press.

SCHACTER, S. (1964). The interaction of cognitive and physiological determinants of emotional state. In L. Berkowitz (Ed.), *Advances in experimental social psychology* (Vol. 1). NY: Academic Press.

SCHACTER, S., & SINGER, J. E. (1962). Cognitive, social, and physiological determinants of emotional state. *Psychology Review, 69,* 379–399.

SCHAFER, R. B., & KEITH, P. M. (1980). Equity and depression among married couples. *Social Psychology Quarterly, 43,* 430–435.

SCHAFFER, J., & GALUSKY, M. D. (1989). *Models of group therapy* (2nd ed.). Englewood Cliffs, NJ: Prentice Hall.

SCHEIDEL, T. M., & CROWELL, L. (1964). Idea development in small discussion groups. *Quarterly Journal of Speech, 50,* 140–145.

SCHEIN, E. H. (1980). *Organizational behavior* (3rd ed.). Englewood Cliffs, NJ: Prentice Hall.

SCHEIN, V. E. (1973). The relationship between sex-role stereotypes and requisite management characteristics. *Journal of Applied Psychology, 57,* 95–100.

SCHELLING, T. C. (1960). *The strategy of conflict.* Cambridge, MA: Harvard University Press.

SCHELLING, T. C. (1978). *Micromotives and macrobehavior.* NY: Norton.

SCHILLER, L., & WILLWERTH, J. (1997). *American tragedy: The uncensored story of the Simpson defense (now with the untold story of the civil trial).* NY: Avon Books.

SCHLENKER, B. R. (1975). Liking for a group following an initiation: Impression management or dissonance reduction? *Sociometry, 38,* 99–118.

SCHMIDT, K. D. (1979). *Doing business in France, Germany, and the United Kingdom* (pamphlets). Menlo Park, CA: SRI International Business Intelligence Programs.

SCHMIDT, K. D., & KOCHMAN, T. A. (1972). Conflict: Toward conceptual clarity. *Administrative Science Quarterly, 17,* 359–370.

SCHRIESHEIM, C. A., HINKIN, T. R., & PODSAKOFF, P. M. (1991). Can ipsative and single-item measures produce erroneous results in field studies of French and Raven's (1959) five bases of power? *Journal of Applied Psychology, 76,* 106–114.

SCHUTZ, W. C. (1966). *FIRO: A three dimensional theory of interpersonal behavior.* NY: Rinehart.

SCHWARTZ, S. H. (1992). Universals in the content and structure of values: Theoretical advances and empirical tests in 20 countries. In M. Zanna (Ed.), *Advances in experimental social psychology* (Vol. 25). NY: Academic Press.

SCHWARTZ-SHEA, P., & BURRINGTON, D. D. (1990). Free riding: Alternative organization and cultural feminism: The case of Seneca Woman's Peace Camp. *Women and Politics, 10,* 1–37.

SEARS, D. O., PEPLAU, L. A., & TAYLOR, S. E. (1991). *Social psychology* (7th ed.). Englewood Cliffs, NJ: Prentice Hall.

SELYE, H. (1956). *The Stress of life.* NY: McGraw-Hill.

SERVICEMEMBER'S LEGAL DEFENSE FUND. (1995). *The reality of gay military life.* Washington, DC: Servicemember's Legal Defense Fund.

SEWELL, J. G. (1994). The stress of homicide investigations. *Death Studies, 16,* 565–582.

SHAW, M. E. (1981). *Group dynamics: The psychology of small group behavior* (3rd ed.). NY: McGraw-Hill.

SHEPPERD, J. A. (1993). Productivity loss in performance groups: A motivational analysis. *Psychological Bulletin, 113,* 67–81.

SHERIF, M. (1935). A study of some social factors in perception. *Archives in Psychology, 27,* 187.

SHERMAN, J. J., JUDD, C. M., & PARK, B. (1989). Social cognition. *Annual Review of Psychology, 40,* 281–336.

SHILTS, R. (1994). *Conduct unbecoming: Gays and lesbians in the U.S. military.* NY: Fawcett Columbine.

SIAU, K. L. (1995). Group creativity and technology. *Journal of Creative Behavior, 29,* 201–216.

SIKES, G. (1997). *8 ball chicks: A year in the violent world of girl gangsters.* NY: Anchor Books.

SINGH, D. (1995). Female health, attractiveness, and desirability for relationships: Role of breast asymmetry and waist-to-hip ratio. *Ethology and Sociology, 16,* 465–481.

SINHA, J. B. P. (1980). *The nurturant task leader: A model of the effective executive.* New Delhi: Concept.

SMITH, N. M., BIRCH, N. E., & MARCHANT, J. (1986, Fall). Stress, distress, and burnout: A survey of public reference librarians. *Public Libraries,* pp. 83–85.

SMITH, E. R. (1993). Social identity and social emotions: Toward a new concept realization of prejudice. In D. Mackie & D. Hamilton (Eds.), *Affect, cognition, and stereotyping.* San Diego, CA: Academic Press.

SMITH, P. B., & BOND, M. H. (1994). *Social psychology across cultures.* Needham Heights, MA: Allyn & Bacon Publishers.

SNOW, R. L. (1996). *SWAT teams: Explosive face-offs with America's deadliest criminals.* NY: Plenum Publishers.

STEINER, I. D. (1972). *Group process and productivity.* NY: Academic Press.

STERN, K. S. (1997). *A force upon the plain: The American militia movement and the politics of hate.* NY: Simon & Schuster.

STOCKARD, J., VAN DE KRAGT, A. J., & DODGE, P. J. (1988). Gender roles and behavior in social dilemmas: Are there sex differences in cooperation and in its justification? *Social Psychology Quarterly, 51,* 154–163.

STRASSER, G., KERR, N. L., & DAVIS, J. H. (1980). Influence processes and consensus models in decision-making groups. In P. B. Paulus (Ed.), *Psychology of group influence* (2nd ed.). Hillsdale, NJ: Erlbaum.

STREMLOW, M. V. (1990). *Coping with sexism in the military.* NY: Rosen Publishing.

STRODTBECK, F. L., JAMES, R. M., & HAWKINS, C. (1957). Social status in jury deliberations. *American Sociological Review, 22,* 713–719.

STRODTBECK, F. L., & LIPINSKI, R. M. (1985). Becoming first among equals: Moral considerations in jury foreman selection. *Journal of Personality and Social Psychology, 49,* 927–936.

SULLIVAN, J., PETERSON, R. B., KAMEDA, N., & SHIMADA, J. (1981). The relationship between conflict resolution approaches and trust: A cross-cultural study. *Academy of Management Journal, 24,* 803–815.

SWAP, W. C., & RUBIN, J. Z. (1983). Measurement of interpersonal orientation. *Journal of Personality and Social Psychology, 44,* 208–219.

SWIERCZEK, F. W. (1991). Leadership and culture. *Comparing Asian Managers, 12,* 3–10.

SZASZ, T. (1970). *The manufacture of madness: A comparative study of the Inquisition and the mental health movement.* NY: Harper & Row.

TABOR, J. D. (1995). Religious discourse and failed negotiation. In S. A. Wright (Ed.), *Armageddon in Waco.* Chicago: University of Chicago Press.

TAJFEL, H., BILLIG, M., BUNDY, R., & FLAMENT, C. (1971). Social categorization and intergroup behavior. *European Journal of Social Psychology, 1,* 149–178.

TANAKA, Y. (1972). A study of national stereotypes. In H. C. Triandis (Ed.), *The analysis of subjective culture.* NY: Wiley.

TANNEN, D. (1990). *You just don't understand: Women and men in conversation.* NY: Ballentine Books.

TANNEN, D. (1994). *Gender and discourse.* NY: Oxford University Press.

TANNEN, D. (1995). *Talking from 9 to 5: Women and men in the workplace: Language, sex and power.* NY: Avon Books.

TANNENBAUM, R., WESCHLER, I. R., & MASSARIK, F. (1961). *Leadership & organizations: A behavioral science approach.* NY: McGraw-Hill.

TEMPLE, L. E., & LOEWEN, K. R. (1993). Perceptions of power: First impressions of a woman wearing a jacket. *Perceptual & Motor Skills, 76(1),* 339–348.

TETLOCK, P. E., JERVIS, R., STERN, P. C., TILLY, C., & HUSBANDS, J. L. (Eds.). (1990). *Behavior, society, & nuclear war. Volume 1.* Cambridge, England: Oxford University Press.

THIBAULT, J. W., & KELLEY, H. H. (1959). *The social psychology of groups.* NY: Wiley.

THOMAS, K. W. (1976). Conflict and conflict management. In M. Dunnette (Ed.), *Handbook of industrial organizational psychology.* Chicago, IL: Rand McNally.

TICHY, N. M. (1981). Networks in organizations. In Nystrom, P., & Starbuck, W. (Eds.), *Handbook of organizational design, Vol. 2.* New York: Oxford University Press.

TJOSVOLD, D. (1984). Effects of leader warmth and directiveness on subordinate performance on a subsequent task. *Journal of Applied Psychology, 69,* 422–427.

TODA, M., SHINOTSUKA, H., McCLINTOCK, C. G., & STICH, F. (1978). Development of competitive behavior as a function of culture, age, and social comparison. *Journal of Personality and Social Psychology, 36,* 835–839.

TRAUPMANN, J., HATFIELD, E., & WALSTER, P. (1983). Equity and sexual satisfaction in dating couples. *British Journal of Social Psychology, 22,* 33–40.

TRIANDIS, H. C. (1994). *Culture and social behavior.* NY: McGraw-Hill.

TRIPLETT, N. (1898). The dynamogenic factors in pacemaking and competition. *American Journal of Psychology, 9,* 507–533.

TUCKMAN, B. W., & JENSEN, M. A. (1977). Stages of small group development revisited. *Group and Organizational Studies, 2,* 419–427.

TURNER, J. C., BROWN, R. J., & TAJFEL, H. (1979). Social comparison and group interest in in-group favoritism. *European Journal of Social Psychology, 9,* 187–204.

UNGER, R. (1990). Conflict management in group psychotherapy. *Small Group Research,* *21,* 349–359.

UNIFORM CODE OF MILITARY JUSTICE

UNITED STATES GOVERNMENT ACCOUNTING OFFICE. (1993). *Department of Defense's on homo-* *sexuality: Report to Congressional requesters on defense force management.* NY: Brassey's.

URY, W. L., BRETT, J. M., & GOLDBERG, S. (1988). *Getting disputes resolved.* San Francisco: Jossey-Bass.

VAN DE VLIERT, E., & PREIN, H. C. M. (1989). The difference in the meaning of forcing in the conflict management of actors and observers. In M. A. Rahim (Ed.), *Managing* *conflict: An interdisciplinary approach.* NY: Praeger.

VAN IJSENDOORN, M. H., & KROONENBERG, P. M. (1988). Cross-cultural patterns of attach-ment: A metanalysis of the strange situation. *Child Development,* 59, 147–156.

VINOKUR, A., & BURNSTEIN, E. (1978). Depolarization of attitudes in groups. *Journal of* *Personality and Social Psychology,* 36, 872–885.

VROOM, V. H., & JAGO, A. G. (1978). On the validity of the Vroom-Yetton model. *Journal of* *Applied Psychology,* 63, 151–162.

VROOM, V. H., & YETTON, P. W. (1973). *Leadership & decision making.* Pittsburgh, PA: Uni-versity of Pittsburgh Press.

WALLACH, M. A., KOGAN, N., & BEM, D. J. (1962). Group influences on individual risk taking. *Journal of Abnormal and Social Psychology,* 65, 75–86.

WALSTER (HATFIELD), E., WALSTER, G. W., & BERSCHEID, E. (1978). *Equity: Theory and re-search.* Boston: Allyn & Bacon.

WATZLAWICK, P., WEAKLAND, J. H., & FISCH, R. (1974). *Change: Principles of problem forma-tion and problem resolution.* NY: W. W. Norton.

WEST, C., & ZIMMERMAN, D. H. (1983). Small insults: A study of interruptions in cross-sex conversations between unacquainted persons. In B. Thorne, C. Kramaral, & N. Henley (Eds.), *Language, gender, and society* (pp. 103–117). Rowley, MA: Newbury House.

WEST, C., & ZIMMERMAN, D. H. (1985). Gender, language and discourse. In T. A. Van Dijk (Ed.), *Handbook of discourse analysis: Discourse analysis in society* (Vol. 4, pp. 103–124). London: Academic Press.

WHEELAN, S. A. (1994). *Group processes: A developmental perspective.* Boston: Allyn & Bacon.

WHEELAN, S. A., & VERDI, A. F. (1992). Differences in male and female patterns of com-munication in groups: A methodological artifact? *Sex Roles,* 27, 1–15.

WHITE, S. (1989). Backchannels across cultures: A study of American and Japanese. *Lan-guage in Society,* 18, 59–76.

WIERSMA, U. J., & VAN DEN BERG, P. (1991). Work-home role conflict, family climate, and domestic responsibilities among men and women in dual-career families. *Journal of* *Applied Social Psychology,* 21, 1207–1217.

WILLIAMS, K. B., HARKINS, S., & LATANE, B. (1981). Identifiability as a deterrent to social loafing: Two cheering experiments. *Journal of Personality and Social Psychology,* 40, 303–311.

WILLIAMS, R. H. (1995). Breaching the "wall of separation": The balance between reli-gious freedom and social order. In S. A. Wright (Ed.), *Armageddon at Waco.* Chicago: University of Chicago Press.

WILLIS, E. (1995). Feminism, moralism and pornography. (sic). In Stan, A. M. (Ed.), *De-bating sexual correctness: Pornography, sexual harassment, date rape, and the politics of sex-ual equality.* NY: Delta Books.

WILSON, E. O. (1980). *Sociobiology: The abridged version.* Cambridge, MA: Harvard Univer-sity Press.

WILSON, G. L. (1996). *Groups in context: Leadership and participation in small groups* (4th ed.). Boston: McGraw-Hill.

WILSON, W. J. (1987). *The truly disadvantaged: The inner city, the underclass, and public policy.* Chicago: University of Chicago Press.

WOOD, W. (1982). Retrieval of attitude-relevant information from memory: Effects of susceptibility to persuasion and on intrinsic motivation. *Journal of Personality and Social Psychology, 42,* 798–810.

WOOD, W. (1987). A metanalytic review of sex differences in group performance. *Journal of Personality and Social Psychology, 49,* 1169–1183.

WOOD, W., POLEK, D., & ARKEN, C. (1985). Sex differences in group task performance. *Journal of Personality and Social Psychology, 48,* 63–71.

WORCHEL, S. (1986). The role of cooperation in reducing intergroup conflict. In S. Worchel & W. G. Austin (Eds.), *The psychology of intergroup relations* (pp. 153–176). Chicago: Nelson-Hall.

WRIGHT, S. A. (1995). Construction and escalation of a cult threat: Dissecting moral panic and official reaction to the Branch Davidians. In S. A. Wright, (Ed.), *Armageddon in Waco: critical perspectives on the Branch Davidian Conflict* (pp. 75–94). Chicago: University of Chicago Press.

WRIGHTSMAN, L. S., WILLIS, C. E., & KASSIN, S. M. (EDS.). (1987). *On the witness stand: Controversies in the courtroom.* Newbury Park, CA: Sage.

YALOM, I. D. (1970). *The theory and practice of group psychotherapy.* NY: Basic Books.

YALOM, I. D. (1985). *The theory and practice of group psychotherapy* (3rd ed.). NY: Basic Books.

YAMAGISHI, T. (1986). The structural goal/expectation theory of cooperation in social dilemmas. *Advances in Group Process, 3,* 51–87.

YUKL, G., & BRUCE, T. J. (1992). Consequences of influence tactics used with subordinates, peers, and the boss. *Journal of Applied Psychology, 77,* 525–535.

ZACCARO, S. J. (1984). Social loafing: The role of task attractiveness. *Personality and social psychology bulletin, 10,* 99–106.

ZAJONC, R. B. (1965). Social facilitation. *Science, 149,* 269–274.

ZAJONC, R. B. (1980). Compresence. In P. Paulus (Ed.), *Psychology of Group Influence* (pp. 35–60). Hillsdale, NJ: Erlbaum.

ZEISEL, H., & DIAMOND, S. (1978). The effect of peremptory challenges on jury and verdict: An experiment in a federal district court. *Stanford Law Review, 30,* 491–531.

ZIMBARDO, P. G., & LEIPPE, M. R. (1991). *The social psychology of attitude change.* NY: McGraw-Hill.

Photo Credits

Index